In the Shadow of the Giant

JÜRGEN BUCHENAU

In the Shadow
of the Giant

The Making of Mexico's

Central America Policy,

1876–1930

THE UNIVERSITY OF ALABAMA PRESS

Tuscaloosa and London

Library of Congress Cataloging-in-Publication Data

Buchenau, Jürgen, 1964–
    In the shadow of the giant : the making of Mexico's Central
America policy, 1876–1930 / Jürgen Buchenau.
        p.   cm.
    Includes bibliographical references and index.
    ISBN 0-8173-0829-6 (pbk. : alk. paper)
    1. Central America—Foreign relations—Mexico.   2. Mexico—Foreign
relations—Central America.   3. Mexico—Foreign
relations—1867-1910.   4. Mexico—Foreign relations—1910-1946.
    5. Central America—Foreign relations.   6. United States—Relations—
Foreign countries.   I. Title.
F1436.8.M6B83   1996
327.720728—dc20   95-49581

British Library Cataloguing-in-Publication Data available

To Anabel

Contents

Preface

Why hasn't Mexico backed the United States . . . [in] Central America?

Assistant U.S. Secretary of State Elliot Abrams, 1986

In 1979, Mexican President José López Portillo stunned many observers when he became the first head of state to sever diplomatic relations with the faltering Nicaraguan dictatorship of Anastasio Somoza Debayle. In the next three years, the world's amazement grew as Mexico became a key ally of the revolutionary Sandinista regime. During that period, the López Portillo administration provided the Sandinistas with loans, food, medical supplies, and diplomatic support. Much of this happened right before the eyes of U.S. president Ronald Reagan—a president committed to stopping "the spread of Communism to Central America," a goal that included the elimination of the Sandinistas. At least superficially, Mexico's daring diplomacy appeared surprising, for the country had precious little to gain from antagonizing Reagan over Central American matters.

No one should have been surprised at López Portillo's audacious policies, however. A look at the history of Mexico's foreign policy toward Central America reveals that the initiatives of the 1979–82 period followed a historical pattern dating back to the nineteenth century.[1] An analysis of the historical development of Mexico's Central America policy is crucial for a better understanding of recent Mexican initiatives, and, indeed, for the country's foreign policy in general.

Even though the López Portillo initiatives have triggered intense scholarly interest in the subject of Mexico's Central America policy, however, such interest has been limited almost exclusively to the recent past.[2] Apart from Daniel Cosío Villegas' dated study of Porfirio Díaz's foreign policy in the 1876–1910 period,[3] no in-depth historical analysis of Mexican foreign policy toward Central America has yet appeared. Indeed, most historians have ignored Central America (and the rest of Latin America) as an important area for Mexican policy makers. This omission has occurred primarily because most scholars have studied

Latin American foreign relations from U.S. viewpoints, or with primary recourse to U.S. archives.[4]

This study attempts a corrective to this U.S. centrism in the literature on Latin American foreign relations. It examines Mexico's difficult but persistent challenge to U.S. influence in Central America during the 1876–1930 period—a period during which the Mexican government was particularly active in its rejection of U.S. intervention in Central America. I will also discuss other goals pursued by Mexican policy, including the containment of Guatemalan hostility, the extension of its own influence, and the showcasing of nationalist and anti-Yankee sentiments for the benefit of the negotiation of government rule.[5]

Made aware of the dangers of U.S. expansion by the conflict over Texas during the 1830s and 1840s, the Mexican government attempted to mitigate U.S. influence in several ways. Most importantly, it provided diplomatic support to Central American leaders who were critical of the growing U.S. influence in the region. Afraid that such influence might engulf the country from both the north and the south, the Mexican leadership also countered U.S. initiatives in the region with proposals of its own. In these efforts, Mexico met with at least temporary success: from 1903 to 1910, Mexican mediation delayed and softened U.S. intervention in Central America. Occasionally, the Mexican government even went a step further than these cautious diplomatic moves. On two separate occasions, in 1910 and 1926, the Mexican government gave military assistance to Nicaraguan leaders friendly to Mexico. Last but not least, Central America figured in a number of bilateral negotiations between the United States and Mexico, often with favorable results for Mexico. Therefore, Mexican policy must be understood in terms of the country's existence "in the shadow of the giant."

But limiting U.S. influence has never been Mexico's only goal in Central America. Throughout the nineteenth century, Mexican diplomats fought with Guatemalan representatives over their countries' common boundary. In the twentieth century, the Mexican government often attempted to extend its own influence into Central America, viewing the region's five states as backward but culturally similar neighbors that could benefit from Mexican tutelage. Finally, the country's Central American policy has mattered to the domestic agenda of several Mexican regimes.

This domestic dimension of Mexican foreign policy calls for a new analysis of the *process* of Mexican policy formulation. Such an analysis entails probing the nature of foreign-policy making, a subject many historians have mistakenly dismissed as arcane and virtually irrelevant to an understanding of Mexican society. But indeed, foreign relations cannot be understood merely within the context of power rivalries with their incessant diplomatic lunge-and-parry or within a dependency framework stressing the economic power of the industrial-creditor nations. As both instrument and object of political discourse, foreign policy also helps a country's governing elite negotiate its share of power.[6] Intimately linked to a country's political culture, the formulation and rhetoric of foreign policy are thus informed by the dialectic between the rulers and the governed—one of the most important concerns of the historical profession.[7] For example, Mexico's support for the Sandinistas owed much to internal political factors: a widespread notion among elites and the middle class that their country had "arrived" as a great power, and a need to co-opt the ruling party's increasingly disenchanted left wing. To sum up, the formulation of foreign policy, even in countries adjacent to great powers, is governed in large part—even if by no means exclusively—by domestic concerns. The concept of the interdependence of domestic and foreign policy (widely accepted in the case of powerful countries but not in the less powerful ones) is central to an understanding of Mexican foreign relations.[8]

Following this conceptualization, foreign policy has played an important role in the development of modern Mexican nationalism. Since the reign of Porfirio Díaz (r. 1876–80 and 1884–1910), Mexico's foreign relations have been one of the main theaters of an "official" projection of nationalism.[9] In other words, Mexican governments since Díaz have used international initiatives to define the country over which they ruled. Thus, when the Mexican government participated in Central American peace negotiations—as it did in the 1900s and again in the 1980s—it projected an image of Mexico as Central America's big Latin American brother. This image, in turn, defined Mexico as a country committed not only to protecting its own identity and independence but also to defending the rights of other, similar countries. When López Portillo exhorted the virtues of the Sandinista revolution in his speeches, he laid claim to Mexico's own revolutionary heritage and demonstrated its vitality in the Mexican national idea.

This approach requires a new understanding of Mexico's position between the much larger United States and the much smaller Central American countries. In particular, Mexico's status as a "middle power"—a state "weaker than the great powers . . . but significantly stronger than the weaker powers" of the neighboring states system—will receive analysis.[10] As described above, three interrelated forces drive the foreign policies of middle powers toward small powers: the relationship with the great power, bilateral goals, and domestic and ideological concerns. "Great power–driven" policies make the weaker area a theater of opposition to the great power. Bilateral policies are motivated by the middle power's own goals in a weaker area, including boundary issues and the assertion of its own political, economic, or cultural influence. Domestically driven initiatives, finally, are rooted in the internal politics of a middle power. As a middle power responding to the presence of a great power, Mexico has dealt with Central America, a "small power" area, as a locus of its general opposition to U.S. "great power" influence. Mexico's co-mediation of regional disputes with the United States is a good example of such behavior. Mexico has also followed a set of bilateral concerns in Central America: the settlement of a border controversy with Guatemala is a good example. As an example of the assertion of domestic concerns, one might cite López Portillo's withdrawal of recognition of Somoza: the Mexican president knew that his action would reflect favorably on his own rule. Mexico's Central American policy since 1876 has incorporated all three concerns but in different ways at different times.

This study thus questions the familiar picture of a "defensive, xenophobic [Mexican] foreign policy" upholding "principles . . . of self-determination and non-intervention"—a vision that corresponds to a widely held view of the Mexican government as a sporadic and meek opponent of U.S. hegemony.[11] Mexico has often assumed an assertive position in Central America and has sometimes pursued an interventionist strategy of its own, independent of its concern with U.S. power.

This conceptualization follows the tradition of the "new international history," an approach that integrates external and internal dimensions of foreign policy and that calls for a multiarchival and multinational research strategy.[12] The study relies primarily on little-used Mexican documentary sources, especially the holdings of the Foreign Ministry Archive. In addition, I have drawn on private collections, such as the Colección General Porfirio Díaz and the Fideicomiso Archivos

Plutarco Elías Calles y Fernando Torreblanca. These archives contain valuable official and private correspondence of Mexico's presidents and other policy makers. The study also reviews the extensive documentation of the U.S. Department of State, public and private manuscript collections in the United States, three European diplomatic archives, and the Foreign Ministry files of the Archivo General de Centroamérica in Guatemala City.

Acknowledgments

This project would have been impossible without the help of many individuals who gave generously of their time to aid me in my efforts. My friend and graduate adviser at the University of North Carolina, Gil Joseph, taught me Mexican history, helped me become a historian, read interminable drafts of the dissertation on which this book is based, provided invaluable advice, and always found a word of encouragement during rough times. Michael Hunt has helped me with this study from its beginnings, and he introduced me to the study of U.S. foreign policy. John Chasteen and Tom Schoonover read earlier versions of this manuscript and gave a number of valuable suggestions. I am grateful to William Leuchtenburg and Lars Schoultz for serving on my dissertation committee. I would also like to thank Joseph Tulchin for his help in the beginning stages of this project. My appreciation goes also to two anonymous reviewers with The University of Alabama Press, as well as to Sally Antrobus, Malcolm MacDonald, and Elizabeth May, who all provided important suggestions and editorial advice. My student, Mandy Stacks, helped me with proofreading the notes and bibliography. Among my colleagues and friends from whose advice I have benefited, I would like to mention Alma Guerrero, Tim Henderson, Martín Medina, Doug Murphy, María-Teresa Pita Moreda, Bill Schell, Daniela Spenser, Gavin Sundwall, Alejandra Reyes, and Arne Westad. I also wish to thank my colleagues at Wingate University, and especially Bob Billinger, for their support.

Small parts of this study have been previously published in different form. I appreciate the permission to use the following two articles: "Counter-Intervention against Uncle Sam: Mexico's Support for Nicaraguan Nationalism, 1903–1910," *The Americas* 50:2 (Oct. 1993), 207–32, in chapters 3 and 4; and "Mexico and the Sandino Rebellion in Nicaragua, 1927–1930," *South Eastern Latin Americanist* 38:1 (Summer 1994), 1–10, in chapter 7.

In Mexico City, Roberto Marín introduced me to the secrets of the Archivo Histórico de la Secretaría de Relaciones Exteriores, Norma

Mereles de Ogarrio did the same for the Fideicomiso Archivos Plutarco Elías Calles y Fernando Torreblanca, María Teresa de Matabuena assisted me in the maze of the Colección General Porfirio Díaz, and Rodolfo Beristáin helped me through the Archivo General de la Nación. Dennis Brehme provided valuable help with the illustrations; I am also grateful to the Archivo General de la Nación and to the Fideicomiso Archivos Plutarco Elías Calles y Fernando Torreblanca for allowing me to use photographs from their collections. In Paris, I am grateful to Monique Constant; in Bonn, to Dr. Maria Keipert. In Davis Library at UNC-Chapel Hill, I appreciated the help of the folks at the Interlibrary Loan Office, who ordered countless reels of microfilm for me.

I truly appreciate the financial assistance of the German Academic Exchange Service, the Konrad-Adenauer-Stiftung, the UNC Department of History, the Institute for International Education, the Tinker Foundation, and Wingate University. I would also like to thank my parents, Sabine Prange and Helmut Buchenau, the Böker family in Mexico, and especially my late grandmother, Gabriele Buchenau, who first acquainted me with Mexico.

Thank you, finally, to Anabel, for everything.

Abbreviations

Politisches Archiv, Auswärtiges Amt, Bonn, Germany.	AAB
Archivo de la Embajada de México en Guatemala, AHSRE.	AEMG
Archivo de la Embajada de México en Washington, AHSRE.	AEMW
Archivo General de Centroamérica, Guatemala City.	AGCA
Archivo General de la Nación, Mexico City.	AGN
Archivo Histórico de la Secretaría de Relaciones Exteriores, Mexico City.	AHSRE
Archive du Ministère des Affaires Étrangères, Paris.	AMAE
Fideicomiso Archivos Plutarco Elías Calles y Fernando Torreblanca, Mexico City. Fondo Fernando Torreblanca.	APEC-FT
Fideicomiso Archivos Plutarco Elías Calles y Fernando Torreblanca, Mexico City. Fondo Plutarco Elías Calles.	APEC-PEC
Centro de Estudios de la Historia de México, Archivo CONDUMEX, Mexico City. Archivo Venustiano Carranza.	AVC
Centro de Estudios sobre la Universidad. Universidad Nacional Autónoma de México, Mexico City.	CESU
Cambridge History of Latin America, ed. Leslie Bethell (9 vols.).	CHLA
Acervos Históricos, Universidad Ibero-Americana, Mexico City. Colección General Porfirio Díaz.	CPD
Diplomatic Despatches, Central America: Costa Rica, El Salvador, and Nicaragua, NADS.	DDCACR
Diplomatic Despatches, Central America: Guatemala and Honduras, NADS.	DDCAG
Diplomatic Despatches, Mexico, NADS.	DDM
Decimal File, NADS.	DF
Diplomatic Instructions, Central America, NADS.	DICA
Diplomatic Instructions, Mexico, NADS.	DIM
Fondos Incorporados, Fondo Emilio Portes Gil, AGN.	FI-EPG
Foreign Relations of the United States.	FRUS
Hispanic American Historical Review.	HAHR
Historia moderna de México, ed. Daniel Cosío Villegas (9 vols.).	HMM
Journal of Inter-American Studies and World Affairs.	JIAS
Journal of Latin American Studies.	JLAS
Latin American Research Review.	LARR

Library of Congress, Washington D.C. Manuscript Division.   LCMSS
National Archives, Washington, D.C. Department of State,   NADS
   Record Group 59.
Numerical File, NADS.   NF
Nouvelle Série, AMAE.   NS
Presidentes, Fondo Obregón-Calles, AGN.   P-OC
Public Records Office, London. Foreign Office.   PRO FO

In the Shadow of the Giant

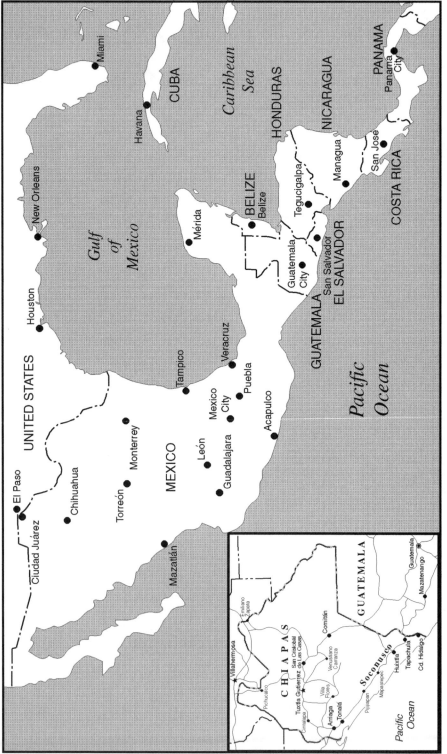

Mexico and Central America (Prepared by The University of Alabama Cartographic Research Laboratory)

1 Prologue

Mexico between the United States and Central America, 1823–1876

Picture a world of unbridled ambitions, of immense and mutual distrust, general economic crisis, unlimited tyranny, and a fear-inspiring disregard for human life.

Mexican diplomat Federico Gamboa, 1900

The peoples inhabiting Mexico have left their mark on Central America for almost a millennium. The name Nicaragua, for instance, has its origins in the Nahuatl term *nic anáhuac,* or "end of the Anáhuac," the name of the central valley of Mexico. Both the Toltec and Aztec empires ruled from there and extended their dominion at times to the isthmus. The Spanish empire followed these pre-Columbian antecedents and added Central America to the Viceroyalty of New Spain, even if its remoteness warranted its elevation to a Captaincy General with a virtually autonomous government. After Mexico broke free from Spain, the region was incorporated into Agustín Iturbide's Imperio Mexicano.

Yet if a similar geography, history, and culture might have suggested a common future for Mexico and the isthmus, the aftermath of independence told a different story. In 1823, Iturbide's downfall brought the end of the Mexican domination of Central America. Soon thereafter, a junta in Guatemala City proclaimed the independence of the United Provinces of the Center of America, a federated republic that comprised present-day Guatemala, El Salvador, Honduras, Nicaragua, and Costa Rica. Central America had terminally severed its ties with Mexico, only to fall apart into its constituent provinces sixteen years later.

Central America's secession and subsequent disintegration placed Mexico in a unique international position. To the north, the country faced a "colossus": the vigorous, expansionist United States, a future great power that Mexicans at once admire, hate, and fear. To the south, it confronted five "dwarfs": the feeble Central American countries whose political instability invited foreign intervention.

Defending the National Territory, North and South, 1823–1848

In the years after the achievement of independence in 1821, however, Mexican leaders could hardly have boasted to Central Americans about their own country. Mexico paid for its separation from Spain with a prolonged state of chaos. During the Wars of Independence, rival caudillos had carved out spheres of power. After 1821, their armies upheld their bosses' claims to both regional and national influence, defying the authority of the central government. The only one of these caudillos to remain a national force throughout the 1821–47 period, General Antonio López de Santa Anna, occupied the presidential chair many times but usually returned to his hacienda after a few months in Mexico City. Not surprisingly, the state of the Mexican economy resembled that of the country's political order. The wars had devastated the Bajío, Mexico's granary and the most prosperous region of the country. The mining industry lay in ruins, the national treasury was empty, and commerce had declined precipitously. "Mexico," as two experts on the period have stated, "was . . . just plain unwieldy."[1]

Furthermore, the country's northern frontier remained unsettled and undefended. This region was Mexico's "Wild North," a vast expanse of mostly barren terrain inhabited by some two hundred thousand people, most of whom belonged to nomadic Indian tribes. To be sure, small towns such as San Antonio and Santa Fe dotted the landscape as tiny islands of Hispanic presence. But on the whole, this region's ties to Mexico were little more than juridical in character—and they were threatened by dynamic U.S. expansion. Much like the fellow Spanish American republic of Gran Colombia,[2] Mexico faced imminent disintegration. Central America's secession in 1823 appeared to prove the point.

As a consequence, Mexican foreign policy after independence, inasmuch as the government could pursue one, sought the defense of the country's territory as its paramount goal. To remain master of the vast expanses that it had inherited from the viceroyalty, the Mexican government needed to tackle two difficult tasks: extending central government control into the entire country (and thus preventing secessions) and forestalling encroachment by U.S. settlers.

In 1823, only two years after independence, Mexico seemed to fall woefully short in achieving the first of these goals, as the new government of Guadalupe Victoria had stood idly by while Central America seceded.[3] That year, however, a problem surfaced—the Chiapas question—which demonstrated that in spite of its weakness, Mexico could act to prevent a further loss of territory in the south.

Chiapas, a part of the old Captaincy of Guatemala, had not followed suit in Central America's secession from Mexico. While the other provinces had joined Guatemala in forming the new federation, the creoles[4] and *ladinos*[5] in the Chiapanecan highlands had expressed different ideas. The urban elites in this westernmost part of Central America had always felt a stronger bond with Mexico. The main trade routes of the provincial capital, Ciudad Real, ran west, not east, and nearby Guatemala City appeared a more direct threat to regional autonomy than did remote Mexico City. Therefore, as early as February 1821, Ciudad Real (now San Cristóbal de Las Casas) and a few other towns had subscribed to Agustín Iturbide's Plan de Iguala, which proclaimed Mexico's independence. On September 26, 1821, the Ciudad Real–dominated provincial assembly had formally requested annexation by Mexico.[6] With this step, Chiapas came to form a part of Mexico proper.

However, Iturbide's fall in early 1823 called Chiapas' union with Mexico into question. Opinion in the twelve-man provisional regional junta was divided: while Ciudad Real's highland representatives favored continued association with Mexico, those of lowland Tuxtla Gutiérrez advocated either autonomy or annexation to Central America. When no decision could be reached, the junta formed a provisional government of Chiapas pending a plebiscite.[7]

Eager to retain Chiapas, the Mexican government assisted Ciudad Real in its attempt to remain with Mexico. In September 1823, President Victoria ordered one of his army units stationed in Chiapas to break up the region's provisional administration and to impose a new, pro-Mexican junta. This move, however, angered many previously pro-Mexican residents. In October, a majority of the towns of the region (but not Ciudad Real) subscribed to the Plan de Chiapa Libre, which declared that Chiapas could belong neither to Mexico nor to Central America until its own inhabitants had decided its destiny. A counterorder from

Mexico to withdraw the army unit from Chiapas came too late to reverse this resolution.[8] Nevertheless, the Mexican government had the upper hand in military terms, and it consistently pressed its advantage. In 1824, it hastily prepared a plebiscite that gave the pro–Central American factions little time to mobilize their supporters.[9] Not surprisingly, Mexico won the referendum: 62 percent of the population voting elected to remain with Mexico.[10] The pro-Mexican vote predominated particularly in the highlands, where Ciudad Real served as the principal market for both the local landowners and numerous Indian villages. Still, the vote had been closer and more divisive than expected. In Tuxtla Gutiérrez and in the lowlands of Soconusco, the results of the plebiscite had favored Central America. In those areas, the itinerant population carried on most of its trade with adjacent Guatemala and believed that annexation to Mexico threatened this commerce.[11]

In the end, Mexico prevailed. Insisting that the plebiscite had been held on the political future of all of Chiapas, the Mexican government incorporated the entire province. Initially, Soconusco was awarded special status as a demilitarized territory and was even allowed to declare itself a free state. It soon became clear, however, that this situation could not continue. The Central Americans and, after 1837, Guatemala viewed Soconusco as an entity independent of Chiapas. Guatemalan troops frequently wreaked havoc in the region. At the same time, Mexico encroached upon adjacent Guatemalan territory and incorporated it into Soconusco. Finally, in 1842, one of Santa Anna's armies invaded Soconusco and subordinated it definitively to Mexican rule. After a flurry of nationalist rhetoric lambasting the Mexican invaders, the Guatemalan government backed down.[12]

Thus, a recent Mexican president exaggerated when he labeled Chiapas "el que quiso ser de México"—the one that wanted to be Mexican.[13] Both sides had reason to claim Chiapas or parts of it for themselves, even though the breakup of the Central American federation weakened Guatemala's case.[14] Most important, the Chiapas controversy would fester, projecting Guatemala as one of the greatest sources of trouble for Mexico's future leadership. The Soconusco question in particular would linger on long after Mexico's superior political and military force had settled the issue.

With the retention of Chiapas assured, the Mexican government paid no further heed to Central America. In its precarious position, it could not affect events such as British–U.S. haggling over transisthmian canal rights or William Walker's 1855–57 Nicaragua expedition. Even though Great Power presence in Central America brought potential dangers, mid-nineteenth-century Mexico could not respond in any way to these events.

Instead, for the time being, foreign intervention and continued instability repeatedly threatened Mexico's own sovereignty. Spain's attempt at reconquest in 1827 led to the exodus of more than twenty-five thousand Spaniards, which resulted in the loss of many of the leading merchants and intellectuals of the former colony. In 1837, Britain and France used military force to obtain payment of overdue debts in the "Pastry War." A few years later, the planter elites in the Mexican state of Yucatán attempted to secede and applied to enter the United States.[15] Even though the U.S. government rejected the overture, notice had been served that further secessions in the Mexican southeast remained a possibility.

The greatest problem, however, was the proximity of the United States—a country whose settlers pushed ever westward in search of their "manifest destiny." From the beginning, the Mexican leadership expressed concern about U.S. expansion, a concern that grew in proportion to the U.S. territorial acquisitions of the first half of the nineteenth century.[16] In particular, the Mexican government feared the de facto annexation of the region of Texas via an unbridled migration of Anglo-Saxon farmers and fortune seekers. To prevent this scenario, President Victoria in 1823 invited U.S. farmers of Catholic faith to settle permanently in Texas. As a condition, Victoria made these settlers promise to respect the sovereignty of Mexican law.

This scheme ultimately proved futile. In 1836, the settlers rebelled and succeeded in wresting Texas from Mexico; nine years later, the "Lone Star Republic" joined the United States. But Texas only whetted U.S. appetite for more Mexican territory. In 1846, complications resulting from a dispute about Texas's southwestern boundary led both countries into a war that ended with the U.S. army in Mexico City and the loss of half of Mexico's territory.[17] A deeply traumatic experience, the war with the United States drove home one important point to the warring factions: unless political stability and economic growth could be achieved, the country faced either complete disintegration or further U.S. landgrabbing. Central America, the unity of which had been shattered by Rafael Carrera's peasant revolts in the late 1830s, served as a lurid example of what could happen to Mexico if further attempts at political centralization were not successful.

In fact, Central America and neighboring Panama held potential problems in store for Mexico—and not the least because of foreign interest in that region. In particular, the possibility of constructing a transisthmian canal, either across southern Nicaragua or across the Colombian province of Panama, drew U.S., Dutch, British, and French attention to the area. By the late 1840s, the United States and Great Britain found themselves in a bitter rivalry for the canal project. In 1850, the two powers signed the Clayton-Bulwer Treaty, which stipulated that neither party could begin the construction of a canal without consulting the other. This treaty put the canal issue on temporary hold, but it showed that Central America had become a geopolitical prize of enormous proportions. The existence of two British colonial enclaves on the Atlantic coast and Walker's 1855 seizure of power in Nicaragua demonstrated the area's vulnerability to foreign intervention. A transisthmian canal under U.S. military protection, a Nicaraguan government under the boot of a filibuster from Tennessee, and, finally, U.S. President Abraham Lincoln's plans to populate Central America with black freedmen—all of these prospects conjured up the threat of Mexico being virtually "encircled" by U.S. expansion.

U.S. activity in Central America could also trouble Mexico in less direct fashion if it linked up with the country's adversaries in the region, which was a distinct possibility. As early as 1822, with the rest of the isthmus in imperial Mexican hands, the city of San Salvador had requested annexation by the United States to avoid incorporation into Mexico. As subsequent events showed, this profession of pro-U.S. sentiments was not an isolated incident. Central American elites often sought U.S. help against a feared Mexican scheme to reconquer the isthmus. For that reason, the Central Americans had invited the United States to attend the 1826 Panama Conference, a meeting the original purpose of which had been the attainment of Latin American solidarity. Moreover, many Central Americans, and particularly the Liberal factions, viewed the United States as a model for the region's progress.[18] Finally, Guatemala occasionally looked to the United States for help for its various irredentist goals: to recover British Honduras, to annex Chiapas, and to reunify Central America under its leadership. Alone,

Guatemala could not attain these objectives. But an alliance with the United States—to be obtained possibly with the promise of a canal concession—could put them within reach and threaten Mexico's possession of Chiapas.

These developments helped define Mexico's approach to Central America: confront both Guatemalan ambitions and the growth of U.S. power, north as well as south of Mexico. The war with the United States gave rise to thoughts about such a strategy, applied first in bilateral relations with the United States and then extended to Central America. The war had fanned a deeply felt fear of U.S. expansion, articulated in different ways by different Mexican factions. After 1855, the victory of the more "pro-American" of these factions set in motion a new attempt at modernization and state building. This process would ultimately require an assertive policy in Central America for the twin goals of limiting further U.S. expansion and staking Mexico's claim as a "modern" nation capable of defending its interest beyond its own borders. Before Central America could once again enter the picture, however, Mexican elites had to strengthen central government control and redefine their relationship with the outside world.

Post-War Mexico Views the United States: Threat or Model?

The traumatic experience of foreign occupation finally helped form genuine political parties with national programs. Earlier, so-called Conservatives and Liberals had gathered in the York and Scotch Masonic lodges in Mexico City, respectively. As Santa Anna's own vacillations between factions illustrate, these labels were often meaningless covers for personal ambitions until the late 1840s. In the wake of the U.S. occupation of Mexico City, however, the influential historian and statesman Lucas Alamán formed a true Conservative party. At the same time, a genuine Liberal party coalesced around idealists such as Miguel Lerdo and Ignacio Comonfort. At the heart of the political contest between Conservatives and Liberals was an issue intimately connected to Mexican foreign policy: how to make sure Mexico would not again fall prey to secession, annexation, and foreign intervention.

Nostalgic for the days of the Spanish colony, the Conservatives preferred European influence to that of the United States. In Alamán's view, Mexico (mainly creole Mexico, of course) represented the best of Catholic Europe: a fear of God and a stable society based on hereditary privilege. The Protestant United States, he thought, threatened this idealized Hispanic Mexico, both by its push for land and by its espousal of liberty and juridical equality. Not only did Alamán deem such ideas inapplicable to Mexico; he also realized that they attacked the existing social order in his home country.[19] To minimize both U.S. political influence and the threat of future annexations, the Conservatives urged the Mexican elites to preserve the country's Hispanic heritage rather than inviting a greater foreign (U.S. or British) economic and cultural presence. They also sought to restore Iturbide's short-lived monarchy by offering the Mexican throne to a Catholic scion of a European dynasty. In addition, Alamán favored the retention of the *fueros,* special immunities enjoyed by the nobility, the Church, and the army, and he called for the veneration of the Jesuits and *conquistador* Hernán Cortés as heroes of an Ibero-Mexican tradition.[20]

For their part, Liberals admired the rapid industrial development of Great Britain, Mexico's main trading partner, and opposed protectionist trade barriers and the paternalistic fueros. They regarded the United States as a society to be admired, not just to be feared. Mexico, the Liberals maintained, needed to emulate the Anglo-Saxon nations to avoid being swallowed up by the United States. Had the U.S. success in the war, they asked, not been brought about by a superior political and economic system? In the view of the Liberals, Mexico's captivity in tradition and privilege had been its major weakness in the war with the United States.[21] In contrast to the Conservatives, the Liberals feared Spain: as early as the early 1850s, Benito Juárez, soon to be Mexico's foremost Liberal reformer, favored Cuba's independence as a means of removing the principal Spanish "springboard" in the western hemisphere.[22]

Liberalism, however, lacked the cohesiveness of Alamán's Conservatives: the Liberals soon separated into two camps: the *puros,* or radicals, and the *moderados,* or moderates. While puros like Miguel Lerdo were more anticlerical than moderados such as Ignacio Comonfort, the puros also distinguished themselves from their rivals by favoring a radical capitalist transformation as a prerequisite for political reform.[23] Seeking (at least in theory) the complete juridical equality of all Mexicans, the puros, whose members came mostly from the nascent middle sectors, advocated the primacy of private over corporately held property and favored unfettered individualism as the engine of economic growth.[24]

Thus, the Mexican elites, apart from a few radical Liberals who flirted with the idea of annexation,[25] shared a deeply rooted fear of U.S. territorial and political expansion, but they disagreed profoundly on how to prevent further annexations. In short, the Conservatives wanted Mexico to survive by turning to Spain and isolating itself from influences from the north. The Liberals dreamed of borrowing from Anglo-Saxon models to beat the United States at its own game.

At first, Alamán prevailed, and Mexican foreign policy during the late 1840s and early 1850s attained a noticeably Conservative touch. Naturally, protection of the country's sovereignty remained the primary goal. Many Mexicans still worried that the United States might ultimately annex more or all of their country,[26] and Alamán feared U.S. expansionism into Central America[27]—a scenario that Mexico could not prevent. This fear was justified: many politicians from the U.S. South, desirous of obtaining slave territories, openly advocated further annexations.

Therefore, the foreign policy of the immediate postwar era was cautious and legalistic in nature. Having once again failed to procure a European prince to occupy the Mexican throne, Alamán sought to enhance relations with the European powers and to increase diplomatic contact with the other Latin American republics. Alamán's ultimate Bolivarian dream—to situate Mexico in an international web of Hispanic culture to safeguard against both the real external threat posed by the United States and the potential internal threat of an uprising against the creole elites[28]—remained elusive.

Paradoxically, the very anti-Yankee feelings espoused by Alamán contributed to the downfall of the Conservatives. In 1853, Santa Anna's sale of a strip of Sonora to the United States resulted in widespread outcry over this further loss of territory. Subsequent plans to sell off even more of the Mexican north helped end Santa Anna's reign. Shortly after that, the Conservatives, who had looked to him as a symbol of national cohesion, fell from power. The era of chaos had invited U.S. annexation of half of Mexico, and further U.S. territorial gains appeared likely. The task in which Conservatives had thus far failed so dismally—the political centralization of the country—had, in the minds of many Mexicans, become a matter inextricably intertwined with the survival of national sovereignty.

In 1855, puro Liberals, among them Lerdo and Juárez, assumed the reins of power. Thus began a wave of political reform known as La Reforma. The Reforma was backed by a large and diverse coalition that included landowners; merchants and other members of the petite bourgeoisie; officers of the Mexican army; and, in some cases, peasants.[29] These groups advocated a wide range of often conflicting reforms. But they agreed on one fundamental issue: to achieve political stability, Mexico required economic modernization through the promotion of private capital accumulation. In the view of the puros, the attraction of foreign immigrants and investment as well as the disentailment of the Church were necessary steps to that end. The seizure of Church wealth in particular served as an important binding agent for the coalition, offering Liberal supporters a chance to profit personally from the Reforma. Ideally, the Reforma would have created a capitalist yeoman class; the fact that large commercial estates ultimately benefited most from the redistribution mattered little to the program's original appeal.

The puros' signature impact on the Reforma, especially that of Miguel Lerdo (on economics) and Juárez (on politics) became apparent in the reform legislation of the years 1855–58. During these years, the puros passed a variety of radical measures, aimed for the most part at economic modernization. The "Ley Juárez" ended the juridical privileges of both the Church and the army. The "Ley Lerdo" annulled most ecclesiastical ownership of land. The Constitution of 1857, finally, was an effort to establish permanent constitutional, civil government: the new document created a strong presidency and a unicameral congress; it abolished all fueros; it invalidated corporate land titles; and it broke the Church's hold on education.

In matters of foreign policy, the puro Liberals were friendly to the United States, suspicious of the European powers, and—as the following section will discuss—hostile to Guatemala. They did not fail to recognize the expansionist nature of the "northern colossus"; nor did Juárez, provisional Liberal president after 1858, want to sell more Mexican territory. But they did believe that a "special economic relationship" could help Mexico build up its infrastructure and attract immigrants, and thus make the country strong enough to prevent further foreign invasions and annexations.[30] The exact nature of this relationship became the subject of debates within the Liberal leadership during the years 1855–61. The basics carried a broad consensus: the puros, as they proposed in the abortive 1857 Montes-Forsyth treaties, desired to accord U.S. investors a dominant position in exchange for a buyout of Mexico's debt with the European powers. Whether the goal was a U.S. economic protectorate, as one scholar has called the scheme,[31] or a milder form of economic hegemony,[32] the Liberals pursued a difficult double strategy. They intended to give U.S. business interests free rein to develop Mexico "from without" in order to blunt both U.S. territorial expansion and European debt collection à la the Pastry War.

This Liberal plan had the backing of U.S. minister John Forsyth, but not of his superiors. The administration of President James Buchanan did not demonstrate a great interest in intimate economic ties with Mexico. To the contrary, its goals were primarily strategic and territorial. Pressed by southern expansionists, Buchanan sought territorial concessions from Juárez in exchange for diplomatic recognition and assistance. In particular, he desired the cession of the northwestern states of Baja California and Sonora, as well as U.S. transit rights across the Isthmus of Tehuantepec.

In matters of political sovereignty, however, the Liberals were no pushovers: against tremendous U.S. pressure, they refused to sell territory. In the question of transit rights, they proved more flexible, albeit only under duress. The 1859 McLane-Ocampo treaty, negotiated at the nadir of Liberal fortunes during the War of the Reforma (1858–61), illustrates this point. While Mexican Conservatives had Juárez on the ropes near Veracruz, the puros promised the U.S. government free transit rights across Sonora and Tehuantepec in exchange for assistance, a step they later regretted.[33] Fortunately for Mexico, the U.S. Senate, which earlier had rejected the Montes-Forsyth treaties, demurred on this agreement as well. Had the treaty been approved, Juárez would doubtless have joined Santa Anna as one of the greatest *vendepatrias* (sellers of the fatherland) of all time.

Briefly after his victory in the War of the Reforma, Juárez got a second chance to demonstrate his patriotism. In 1862, the French Emperor Napoleon III, backed by Britain and Spain, sent an invasion force into Mexico, ostensibly to collect overdue debts. Two years later, Napoleon installed Maximilian of Habsburg on the throne of a re-created Mexican empire. Aided by the Conservatives, Maximilian's forces brought Juárez once again to the brink of disaster. But Maximilian's waffling on key political issues, and the departure of the French army in March 1867, gave Juárez an opportunity to seize the momentum. Deserted by its erstwhile allies, Maximilian's regime collapsed and the Liberals rode triumphantly into Mexico City. The French Intervention, a "tragicomedy of errors,"[34] bestowed nationalist credentials upon the Liberals and thus strengthened their rule. Aside from Juárez, the victorious heroes of the First Battle of Puebla on May 5, 1862, Ignacio Zaragoza and Brigadier General Porfirio Díaz, received popular adulation for defending the national dignity. The Conservatives, on the other hand, had suffered from their association with Maximilian. Whereas the Conservatives had criticized the Liberals for the McLane-Ocampo treaty, they now found themselves discredited as Maximilian's collaborators.

The futile French takeover also helped the Liberal cause in a different way; it further heightened awareness about Mexico's vulnerability to foreign intervention. If distant France had been able to impose and sustain a monarch in Mexico for three years, how could Mexicans hope to resist another U.S. invasion that might signal the end of their country as an independent nation? To be sure, by 1865 the United States did not pose such a threat, with the southern expansionists defeated and the country emerging from its own destructive civil war. But in Mexico, the memories of 1846 and 1862 were too vivid even to ponder the possibility of another war with a foreign power. Thus, the specter of foreign aggression strengthened Juárez's case for creating a strong presidency in Mexico. A surge in banditry and a series of violent social revolts during the 1860s, inspired in part by the disentailment of Indian village land, further buttressed this case. If Mexico's regional barons did not concede to the government some real power, they might well be torn asunder without a single bullet fired by a foreign aggressor.

Therefore, in the late 1860s and early 1870s, the period of the "Restored Republic," the Liberal government began to establish its authority in much of Mexico. The Juárez government created a rural police force, the *rurales;* it smoothed out differences with the Church; it strengthened a burgeoning executive apparatus at the expense of the legislature; and it began to negotiate with regional caudillos to obtain their allegiance. The final result, which Porfirio Díaz would consummate in the 1880s, was the construction of a political "machine" capable of brokering power at the local, regional, and national levels.[35] Frightened by the new wave of social unrest and influenced increasingly by positivist ideas, many Liberals had given up on their earlier dreams of democracy to embrace elitist authoritarian rule, long deemed indispensable by the Conservatives.

The construction of the post-Reforma state entailed, then, a co-optation of the Conservatives through compromise. Embracing both modernization and authoritarianism, "Conservative Liberalism," also known as the doctrine of "scientific politics," became a dominant doctrine in post-1867 Mexico and formed the ideological bedrock for the subsequent Díaz regime.[36] With this synthesis of Conservative, Liberal, and positivist ideas, Mexico followed a general trend within Spanish- and Portuguese-speaking nations, and, especially, Spain.

This growing approximation, however, encouraged rather than ended further political debate in Mexico. By the end of the Restored Republic, three different major factions had emerged within the governing elite: the militarists, the puros, and the *científicos*.[37] These groups not only represented different perspectives within a larger "Conservative-Liberal" consensus; they also expressed different ideas about Mexican foreign policy.

The militarists were in essence "reform Conservatives." Many of them had fought against the Liberals until the end of the French Intervention and had only recently reconciled themselves with the Reforma. Free from Alamán's infatuation with Spain, the militarists cast an admiring glance at newly unified Germany and Italy as models for national integration. Both Germany and Italy had been unified by "blood and iron":[38] while the militarists conceded the significance of economic development, they thought that true national integration could only be achieved by military means. Concentrated within the army, and characterized by strong anti-Yankee sentiments, the militarists advocated the building of a strong military to counter threats from abroad, whether from the United States or from an irredentist Guatemala. Future President Manuel González, who had fought for the Conservatives in the beginning of the war against the French, was among the most influential militarists in the Restored Republic.

The puros,[39] by contrast, continued to advocate the adoption of Anglo-Saxon political and economic models. Tempered by political realism and sobered by Buchanan's aggressive diplomacy, puros like Juárez had given up on the more radical versions of a "special relationship" with the United States. But despite their declining enthusiasm for the United States, the puros were easily the least anti-American of the three factions, and also the only one that still entertained the notion that republican democracy was feasible in Mexico.[40]

The "científico" group, finally, dominated by Comtean and Spenserian positivists within the Mexico City elites, emphasized the need for a strong, authoritarian state at the expense of individual liberties.[41] The científicos, some of whom had numbered among the moderados in the Reforma period, argued that a type of "democratic Caesarism" was a necessary step in the country's evolution from a backward to a progressive nation—thus their motto "order and progress." More impressed with European than with U.S. models, many científicos denigrated the United States and displayed a predilection for European immigration in order to "whiten" the Mexican genetic stock.[42] Examples of prominent científicos, whose influence grew rapidly in the 1870s, included Justice Secretary Gabino Barreda.

Led by the puro Juárez, the Restored Republic enjoyed a blossoming friendship with the United States, but not with the Triple Alliance (the interventionist alliance of Britain, France, and Spain).[43] The intervention had disrupted Mexico's relations with these three powers. Diplomatic relations existed only with the United States and a few smaller European countries. The U.S. government had given diplomatic and financial help to Juárez and now posed as the major international supporter of the Mexican republic. Moreover, U.S. Secretary of State William H. Seward cultivated a friendly relationship with the Mexican minister, Matías Romero, and reassured him that the era of U.S. territorial acquisitions in Mexico was over. Therefore, relations with the United States soon became cordial.[44]

Assured of U.S. goodwill, Juárez did not budge on the question of restoring relations with the Triple Alliance, which still insisted on collecting debts arising from the War of the Reforma. The clearest manifestation of this "negative and passive"[45] stance came during the inauguration of the Mexican congress in December 1867. On this occasion, Juárez spoke at length on the subject of the Triple Alliance. Rather than proposing an active agenda for reestablishing diplomatic ties, he cast his remarks in distinctly negative tones. He claimed the Europeans had "voluntarily" broken diplomatic relations. Mexico would reestablish relations with these countries only if these powers assumed the initiative. Juárez also demanded that the Triple Alliance forfeit all treaties signed prior to 1862 and that new accords be negotiated on "just and fair" premises. With this principled stance, he gained many admirers in Mexico,[46] and he established a precedent for a nationalist discourse on matters of foreign policy. Inevitably, however, he thrust his country into the embrace of the United States: Spain, France, and Britain refused to renew diplomatic relations. Juárez's position toward the independence struggle in Spanish-held Cuba manifested this anti-European position. From 1868 to 1870, the Mexican government awarded the Cuban rebels moral and political (but not material) support.[47]

From the Mexican standpoint, much was to be gained by deepening the entente with its former enemy. The onset of large-scale industrialization in the United States offered a chance to revive the Liberals' old quest for a "special economic relationship" that would bring "all the fruits of annexation without any of the dangers."[48] Indeed, with the victory of northern industrial over southern agricultural interests, the goals of U.S. diplomacy had shifted. While plans for further territorial growth remained immobilized, access to Latin American raw materials and an end of the European military presence in the hemisphere attained a crucial importance.[49] Mexico, with its proximity to the United States, its hostility to the European powers, and its great diversity in agricultural and mining products, seemed the best Latin American candidate for a close partnership, both in economic and in security terms. Even though U.S. capitalists initially had little money to spare, Juárez hoped that the lure of the rich mines in northern and central Mexico would induce them to fund the construction of a railroad system.[50] Thus, Juárez instructed Romero to promote Mexico as a target for U.S. investments. In particular, he sought the assistance of bankers and railroad magnates to promote the development of Mexico's desert north. Juárez envisioned the construction of railroads linking Mexican mining centers with North American markets. This project represented the old puro strategy of using economic development as a shield against U.S. invasions.

This strategy, however, entailed a pronounced Mexican dependence on its relationship with the United States, accentuated by the scarcity of contacts to the rest of Latin America and the absence of diplomatic relations with the Triple Alliance. In the end, such a unilateral dependence could only bring harm to Mexico. For this reason—and because the Juárez regime incorporated a growing number of anti-Yankee militarists and científicos—the Mexican government slowly moved away from its exclusive reliance on U.S. goodwill. Juárez's successor, the científico Sebastián Lerdo de Tejada, was less enthusiastic about the railroad project, as his famous line "between strength and weakness, [let there be] the desert" indicates.

By 1876 Liberal rule in Mexico was solidified, and European and Yankee aggression appeared a thing of the past. The leaders of postwar Mexico had realized that the United States would henceforth play a dominant role in their country. They had disagreed on how to confront that role: whether to reject it through alliances with European powers or whether to embrace it in the hope of leading U.S. influence into constructive channels. The faction that had advocated the latter course had won out against the determined resistance of the Conservatives, the Church, and the Triple Alliance, even if much of its program had fallen victim to expediency and compromise.

Mexico's position toward the great powers was well defined. The country would seek the economic benefits of its proximity to the northern colossus, but it would not give up its sovereignty. As long as the United States sought economic gain, its influence was welcome. But if U.S. expansionism should once again threaten Mexico, the U.S. government could count on determined opposition. European political influence, on the other hand, was on the wane, a casualty of the last intervention.

Mexico and Central America, 1854–1876: Threat or Opportunity?

These events helped reshape Mexican policies toward Central America. Mexico's internal problems had long stunted the country's role in the area. The only Mexican legation in Central America, technically accredited to all five of the isthmian countries, stood in Guatemala City. During much of the period before 1867, this legation was left under the direction of a chargé d'affaires, who had little leverage to negotiate with the Guatemalan government. Moreover, the Mexican representative almost never ventured outside Guatemala to visit the other

Central American republics. With Mexico torn by civil war, there was little that a Mexican diplomat could have accomplished there.

But this lone representative pursued one important goal: a permanent boundary treaty with Guatemala. Settlement of this nagging issue lay primarily in Mexico's and not in Guatemala's interest. The War of the Reforma disrupted the ongoing efforts of the central government to establish effective control over Chiapas. In Chiapas, as in other regions, localist and regionalist sentiments reasserted themselves, and the Liberal army could not pacify these remote reaches of the country. All of a sudden, the specter of Chiapas seceding had reappeared, and a concerned Juárez petitioned the Guatemalan government to negotiate a conclusive border agreement.

But Guatemala's caudillo Rafael Carrera, who had not given up hope of recovering at least part of Chiapas, could afford to wait patiently. His ruling Conservative party, like its Mexican namesake, opposed the development of dynamic export economies and promoted "state nationalism"[51] in association with the clergy. Just as the Mexican Conservatives had drawn much of their appeal from their unflinching opposition to U.S. encroachment, Carrera painted Mexico (and Great Britain because of its possession of Belize) as the villainous thieves of half of Guatemala's territory. With the isthmus in Conservative hands after the 1857 defeat of William Walker, Carrera faced no external threats. Demanding that Mexico agree to discuss the Soconusco issue, Carrera refused to enter into bilateral negotiations limited to a discussion of the border demarcation,[52] a posture that rallied Central American elites around him. Carrera detested the Mexican Liberals; he gave military aid to the Conservatives during both the War of the Reforma and the French Intervention.[53]

As a consequence, the 1860s saw no progress on the subject of the border controversy. The Mexican Secretaría de Relaciones Exteriores (hereafter referred to as the Mexican Foreign Ministry) waged a bitter exchange of notes with its Guatemalan counterpart regarding Soconusco and the precise location of the common border. Nevertheless, as long as Central America was governed by Conservative, pro-Carrera leaders, this exchange had not been productive. The brief tenure of Gerardo Barrios, the anti-Carrera, Liberal president of El Salvador, had not made a dent in this pattern, as a Carrera invasion in 1863 put an end to this challenge to Guatemalan dominance in Central America.[54]

But the Carrera-Barrios feud had once again revealed a Central American weakness that Mexico would often exploit in the future: incessant infighting among the isthmian elites. Since the end of Spanish rule, the leadership of each of the five countries has been guilty at one time or another of intervening in the affairs of a neighboring republic, imposing a president of their choice there, or even setting off a larger war, which often engulfed three or more of the Central American countries.[55] Some of the wars, paradoxically, occurred in the name of restoring Central American unity, usually under the aegis of Guatemala, the country endowed with the largest population. Such unification attempts, while generally popular, always met with opposition, especially among the leadership of Costa Rica, Nicaragua, and El Salvador. It was, in the words of one popular saying, "better to be the head of a mouse than the tail of a lion." Other wars were fought to weaken or consolidate Guatemala's leadership in Central America. Quite often, Guatemalan, Nicaraguan, or Salvadoran efforts to control Honduras touched off these conflicts; but direct confrontations between Guatemala and its greatest rival, El Salvador, were no less common. Yet other skirmishes were fought in the name of Conservatism or Liberalism, labels similar in content to their Mexican counterparts.

The origin of these repeated clashes lay deep in the past. Like Mexico, Central America was ethnically diverse, even in pre-Columbian times. But in the isthmus, the Spanish conquest had furthered these regional divisions. Three sets of *conquistadores* had conquered Central America: one from Mexico, one from Panama, and one from Santo Domingo. During the colonial period, the descendants of these conquerors had coalesced into rivaling family networks based in different cities. Central America's geographical vulnerability had compounded the problem of disunity: throughout the years of the colony, British, Dutch, and French filibusters had made a mockery out of the titular Spanish sovereignty over Central America, and they had frequently allied themselves with local *caciques* against the central government. After independence, Great Power rivalry in Central America, and especially British meddling, had further worked to encourage factionalism.[56]

It was thus not surprising that the end of Spanish rule had unleashed centrifugal processes that led first to Central America's separation from Mexico, then to the destruction of the federation, and finally to the interlocking factional rivalries within each of the five republics. By the days of Iturbide's short-lived Mexican Empire, Guatemala City was locked into a fierce struggle with San Salvador for isthmian supremacy. The towns of Comayagua and Tegucigalpa wrestled for dominance in Honduras. In Nicaragua, the Conservative inhabitants of Granada battled Liberals from León, and a total of four towns fought for the control of Costa Rica. For a while, Carrera's tenuous coalition of the army, peasants, and the Church appeared to transcend these divisions. With only brief interruptions during the 1837–65 period, the Guatemalan caudillo remained the strongest leader in Central America, thwarting all challengers. But his constant wars sapped much energy and ultimately only cemented his own rule: after his death in 1865, his successor, Vicente Cerna, could not prolong this era of Guatemalan dominance.[57]

After Carrera's death, the rise of "new Liberal" caudillos, so named by one scholar because of their positivist synthesis of Liberal-style modernization and Conservative-style authoritarianism, ushered in a new peak of internecine wars in Central America that lasted until after World War One.[58] These new conflicts were partially due to the absence of Carrera's strong hand and the relative decline of Guatemalan supremacy over Central America. Equally important, however, was that the surge in fighting originated in Liberal modernization efforts. Some of the struggles in the 1865–1923 period were fought to contest prizes of modernization: Nicaragua and Costa Rica went to war several times to revise a border close to a potential site for the transisthmian canal, Guatemala and Honduras fought over land slated for banana production, and Nicaragua and Honduras bickered over key Atlantic ports. The borders in general emerged as a source of controversy, as the attraction of foreign capital into border regions required a definitive settlement of existing territorial disputes, usually undertaken by armed force. Thus, the growth of export economies in Central America (especially coffee in Guatemala, El Salvador, and Costa Rica, and, later, bananas in Guatemala and Honduras) made competitors out of the five nations and further increased tensions among them. Finally, the political and social structure of the Central American countries contributed to the political instability: the new Liberal caudillos relied on old-fashioned family networks, coffee planters, and the national armies as their main bases of power. They could not create a political "machine" like that of the Restored Republic to countervail the armed forces. With the army's role as the "creator and destroyer" of governments in the isthmian countries,[59] intra–Central American politics assumed the look of pre-Reforma Mexico—witness Federico Gamboa's remarks in the epigraph to this chapter. This unstable political system invited wars, coups d'état, and new foreign intervention.

But for Mexico, the ascendancy of the new Liberals and the resultant renewed strife could bring benefits. During the late 1860s, tensions between Guatemala and El Salvador mounted, which forced Cerna to pay attention to his country's eastern border. A weakened Guatemala would more likely negotiate an agreement with Mexico; at the very least, the days of Guatemalan obduracy on this matter seemed past. Moreover, as an ideologically congenial group that resembled the Mexican científicos, the new Liberals could be potential allies for the Juárez regime. At the very least, they could not be worse than Carrera's Conservatives, who had admired and supported Maximilian.

Not surprisingly, Mexico played a decisive role in the Liberal revolution in Guatemala. In early 1871, a Liberal revolt began close to the Mexican border, in the region of Los Altos, under the direction of Miguel García Granados and Justo Rufino Barrios. Juárez lent material assistance to the Liberal forces, and he allowed them to use Chiapas as a base for their operations.[60] In late June, bolstered by help from both Mexico and El Salvador, García Granados and Barrios rode triumphantly into Guatemala City.

For the first time since the days of the Empire, Mexico had helped effect a change of government in Central America. Juárez's meddling in Guatemala had shown that the Mexican government had begun to assume effective control over Chiapas. It could now assume an active and not just a primarily reactive role in isthmian affairs. Of course, Mexico still played only a marginal part in Central America. Fighting a protracted "caste war" in Chiapas, the Mexican government did not figure in the Liberal seizures of power in El Salvador, Honduras, and Costa Rica.[61] Still, Juárez's intervention in Guatemala served as a first step in a long-term Mexican involvement in Central America.

Juárez's sponsorship of the Liberal rebellion, however, did not yield an immediate payoff in the border controversy. Quite to the contrary— both García Granados, who ruled Guatemala from 1871 to 1873, and his successor Barrios proved as nationalist as Carrera. Juárez had miscalculated if he had hoped that the Guatemalan Liberals would prove more amenable to a border settlement. The powerful caudillo Barrios, in particular, dreamt a variety of irredentist dreams, which included the annexation of Chiapas and Belize as well as the reunification of Central America under his direction. He soon made it clear that he intended to pursue these dreams by military force: in 1876, Barrios provoked a war with El Salvador under the banner of Central American union. But at least, as this skirmish demonstrated, Guatemala no longer controlled El Salvador nor its other neighbors. Some day, either Barrios or another Guatemalan ruler might find it profitable to strike a deal with Mexico in order to pursue other objectives further east.

By 1876, as we have seen, Mexico's Central America policy still pursued a border agreement with Guatemala as its only goal. With the breakup of Carrera's hegemony on the isthmus and the resumption of intermittent warfare, Mexico appeared closer than ever to this objective. While Juárez's support of the Guatemalan Liberals had not yet yielded the desired result, the Guatemalan-Salvadoran rift promised to give Mexico some leverage.

Mexico's Central America policy until 1876, then, was bilateral in character, and focused on the resolution of a narrow but significant political issue. This policy was not strongly motivated by considerations of domestic political benefit, as Juárez never made an attempt to exploit publicly the border controversy as an issue of nationalist pride. Nor did Mexico's policy correspond to the behavior of a middle power: in its weak position, Mexico could not respond to U.S. policies toward the isthmus, such as the Walker expedition, canal projects, or Lincoln's black colonization schemes. Until 1876, Mexico's Central America policy was directed exclusively toward Guatemala, and the role of the United States in the isthmus did not yet figure in it. Central America, conversely, had not played a part in the turbulent U.S.–Mexican relations of the period. But with the coming of the Porfiriato and greater U.S. interest in Central America, the day had drawn near when the Mexican government would find itself in a "fatal triangle": called upon to oppose U.S. influence from two different directions.

2   The Beginnings of the Fatal Triangle, 1876–1898

There are no other two neighboring countries as completely ignorant of
one another as Mexico and Guatemala.

> French diplomat Boulard Pouqueville, Mexico, 1898

During the 1876–98 period, Mexico began to play a more assertive role
in Central America, for reasons both domestic and international. After
1876, the regime of Porfirio Díaz consummated the Liberal state-building project, and it fomented an "official nationalism" to help achieve
this goal. Foreign policy, which promised more successes now that Mexico had become politically stable, became an instrument for the promotion of this official nationalism. The growing influence of the United
States in both Mexico and Central America—which placed Mexico at
one corner of a "fatal triangle"—reinforced this need to play an active
role in the isthmus.

Therefore, Mexican foreign policy assumed a function much broader
than the defense of the country's territorial integrity that had marked
Mexico's diplomacy in the first fifty years since independence. An assertive policy toward the United States, the source of the lion's share of
new foreign investment, could demonstrate Mexico's independence vis-
à-vis the colossus of the north. On the other hand, a paternalistic posture toward weaker, poorer Central American nations like Guatemala
could show off alleged and real benefits of Porfirian modernization. By
1898, a Mexican presence in the isthmus had become a matter of both
expediency and necessity.

The Porfirian National Project and Mexican Foreign Policy

In January 1876, Porfirio Díaz called for the overthrow of President Sebastián Lerdo de Tejada in the Plan de Tuxtepec. Even though

this program lacked specifics, it articulated legitimate grievances felt by the regional elites: the abuse of presidential power, especially at the state and municipal level, and government corruption.[1] Rallying around the popular slogan "effective suffrage, no reelection," the Porfiristas ousted the cerebral and arrogant Lerdo. In April 1877, Díaz, who had felt defrauded of victory on two earlier occasions, formally assumed the presidency.

At that point, no one would have guessed that this coup would usher in a long and decisive period in Mexican history—one that would come to be known by Díaz's own first name. To be sure, Díaz, the son of a modest mestizo family from the southern Mexican state of Oaxaca, was one of the last great caudillos of the war against the French still active in public life.[2] But don Porfirio's first government was weak internally. During his first term in office, Díaz confronted several rebellions by disaffected Lerdistas and the "legalists" around Lerdo's constitutionally designated successor, as well as being faced with social unrest. Further discontent appeared inevitable: despite his popularity, Díaz was not considered a capable leader in the científico-dominated Mexico City establishment. A puro sympathizer during La Reforma, surrounded by "militarists" like his comrade-in-arms Manuel González, Díaz had few friends in the capital.[3] While many regional caudillos applauded Díaz's seizure of power, most Mexico City politicians regarded the new president as a rogue country bumpkin who had destroyed Mexico's fledgling democracy.

In spite of these enormous obstacles, Díaz emerged as the leader who brought the Liberal national project to fruition. During his long reign, which was interrupted only by a tactical retreat during the González interregnum, Díaz managed to assert control over the regional elites. Massive foreign investments built up Mexico's infrastructure and created a large, diversified export sector: mining and agriculture in the center and north, monocrop enclave economies in the southeast. A growing middle class emerged both in the capital and in the provincial towns. At the same time, Díaz himself cultivated a more cosmopolitan image: his marriage to Carmen Romero Rubio, the daughter of a prominent científico, symbolized his conversion from caudillo to president. By the end of the nineteenth century, the trials of earlier years seemed but a distant memory: Mexico's borders had been secured and its caudillos co-opted, exiled, or beaten into submission. The national treasury ran a steady surplus, and the country's export economy burgeoned. Mexico's old enemies, be they Spain, France, Britain, Guatemala, or the United States, no longer posed a threat to the country's territorial integrity.

Part of Díaz's success, of course, he owed to larger historical circumstance. The "second wave" of the Industrial Revolution brought large-scale industrialization to continental Europe and the United States and made Mexican raw materials attractive for exploitation. Concomitantly, new technologies made the transportation of these resources (and also the assertion of central government control) easier than ever before. As a result, the United States of the Gilded Age finally lived up to the hopes that Juárez had placed in it ten years earlier: its citizens poured into Mexico capital that soon amounted to over 60 percent of total foreign investment there. It might therefore be said that Díaz simply was able to connect Mexico to a larger trend of Liberal modernization evident throughout the hemisphere.[4]

But as our glimpse of Central America in the previous chapter has revealed, political stability did not always accompany modernization. To understand why the Porfirian state, despite Mexico's previous political difficulties, came to rival that of Brazil and Argentina in terms of its capacities by the end of the century, we need to consider the dynamics of Mexican politics, and especially Díaz's own strategy. In that strategy, his foreign policy played an important role.

In particular, Díaz's practice of "divide and rule" paid benefits. Immediately after his seizure of power, Díaz wooed regional strongmen by placing many of them on the payroll as generals in an enlarged army. He also pursued a dual strategy with his enemies: prominent Lerdistas lost their posts but not their property. Díaz offered the rewards of his project—whether former peasant land declared "public" or a lucrative post as *jefe político* or governor, posts that offered contacts with foreign investors—to all those members of the rural elites willing to accept such overtures.[5] On the other hand, he did not forgive those who refused his deals, and he ruthlessly crushed rebels who took up arms against him.

To attract further allies, Díaz promised to prohibit immediate reelection for the presidency and all state governorships. This promise brought Díaz the support of the "out-candidates": those leaders kept from power by the continuous reelection practiced by the incumbents. He subsequently made the Mexican congress amend the constitution to this effect, and in 1880, he stepped down in favor of his friend, Manuel González. Then Díaz fashioned an ingenious plot to ensure the success of his agenda and his future return to the presidency. It fell to González to pursue a number of unpopular means of the Porfirian strategy: legislation to facilitate foreign ownership of agriculture and the subsoil, reciprocity arrangements with foreign powers, and a crackdown on urban dissenters.[6] In 1884, Díaz used González's unpopularity to promote his own candidacy. Once elected, he did not yield the presidential chair again.

Díaz's approach to international relations—and in particular his handling of a crisis with the United States—contributed a crucial building block of the Porfirian state. Snubbing traditional diplomatic practice, U.S. President Ulysses S. Grant did not award recognition to the new regime, even though the Porfirista forces had established effective control over the national territory. This crisis had been long in coming. Grant hoped to delay recognition as long as possible in order to obtain diplomatic leverage in the numerous disputes left over from the Lerdo regime. Among other issues, he sought the abolition of the Mexican duty-free zone, and he demanded payment for damages inflicted by indigenous tribal bands who had used the Mexican border as a sanctuary. In 1877, the new U.S. president, Rutherford B. Hayes, assumed an even more belligerent attitude, even though the Díaz regime had made the desired payment. Hayes wanted "a piece of Mexico" in exchange for recognition and dispatched U.S. troops to the frontier, instructed to pursue marauders into Mexico without obtaining Díaz's consent.[7]

Other Mexican presidents of the nineteenth century might grudgingly have sought to placate Hayes. Strapped for credit and unsuccessful in its attempts to reestablish ties with Europe, the Mexican government could ill afford not to play his game. But Díaz refused to budge and sent troops to the border; meanwhile, his agents in the United States helped influence the U.S. press in favor of recognition.[8] Prodded by South Texas investors, some of whom had bankrolled Díaz's insurrection,[9] Hayes finally gave in, seeing that only an unpopular war could bring about the surrender of the Mexican government. In 1878, Díaz obtained

U.S. recognition and two years later, the U.S. army withdrew from its positions.[10]

This abortive U.S. intervention once again pointed up the need for greater political stability in Mexico and thus facilitated Díaz's effort to rally regional and local power brokers behind him. But the episode also had important consequences for Porfirian policy itself. The difficulties with Grant and Hayes made Díaz believe that the U.S. government constituted a much more immediate threat to Mexican sovereignty than did Yankee investors. Moreover, the incident illustrated anew the aggressive nature of U.S. diplomacy. If Díaz had harbored any notions that the Civil War had ended the era of U.S. interventionism, Hayes' actions disabused him of such ideas. As a result, beneath an often cordial demeanor toward the U.S. government, Díaz would retain a fundamental mistrust of its intentions in the political and diplomatic spheres. Finally, the episode impressed upon the Mexican strongman the necessity of patching up relations with the Old World. Breaking with Juárez's position, Díaz paved the way for recognition of his government by France, Spain, Germany, and Great Britain. Thus, a reversal of alliances had occurred: while Juárez had used the United States to counter the threat posed by the European powers, Díaz and González improved relations with the Old World to lessen Mexico's ever greater economic dependence on the United States.[11]

The U.S. intervention offered Díaz a chance to employ foreign policy as a nationalist cement for his regime. Mid-nineteenth-century Mexican nationalism had centered around a fear of foreign invasion, which gave rise to popular notions of *patria*.[12] Mexico's social and regional divisions made the meaning of the term contested: in some instances, it referred to the *patria chica,* or region; in others, it denoted the *patria grande,* or country. Díaz now launched an effort to promote the *patria grande* in order to strengthen central control and thus crush the *patrias chicas.*

In this effort to foment an official nationalism as an aid in the larger project of state building, Díaz often pointed to his foreign policy. Long after the crisis had passed, he used the conflict with Hayes to show himself off as a patriotic leader, an image that built on his earlier heroics facing the French Intervention.[13] The significance of Díaz's principled position vis-à-vis the United States thus had transcended the strictly diplomatic realm. A foreign policy attuned to questions of "national honor," duly applauded by the loyal press, had allowed Díaz to tap into an important well of Mexican nationalism: the fear of foreign invasion.

Díaz made sure that Mexicans would not forget his newfound nationalist credentials: his supporters began to propagate a Liberal patriotic cult that insinuated strong continuities from Juárez's nationalist posture to that of Díaz. With his tribute to Juárez, Díaz not only portrayed himself in Juárez's footsteps; he also extended an olive branch to the old Juaristas, some of whom still resented don Porfirio's seizure of power by force. This effort at constructing an official nationalism became ever more important as Porfirian modernization created a "national ruling class" in Mexico.[14]

How did the Porfirians propagate this official nationalism? They lacked modern means of propaganda, like radio, television, or even the dissemination of printed information to a large literate public. But the Porfirians did employ important media to spread their agenda outside their small ruling circle: newspapers, anniversary commemorations, schools, and public works projects. History textbooks, street names, plaques, and statues soon reminded Mexicans of the Liberals' nationalist deeds.[15]

It is difficult to measure the actual effect of this official nationalism for the political cohesion of Porfirian Mexico. The radical Liberal opposition venerated its own version of the nationalist Juárez, and many Conservatives still viewed Díaz as a pro-Yankee iconoclast.[16] But despite the Porfirians' predictable failure to monopolize the nationalist discourse in Mexico, they had provided a set of readily identifiable symbols that promoted the "imagining" of a national community[17] and thus strengthened their rule. The revolutionary governments—and to a greater extent, those of the Partido Revolucionario Institucional—would only refine this strategy.

With their power solidified, the Porfirians formulated a new approach to foreign policy. They pursued conflicting goals: to ensure the flow of foreign investments, to ward off threats to Mexico's sovereignty, and to show off Díaz as a nationalist ruler. Abroad, Porfirian diplomacy projected the image of Mexico as a stable country of unlimited economic potential, a nation that rewarded foreign investment.

It also addressed dangers to the country's sovereignty—dangers conjured up by U.S., Guatemalan, or European policies. At home, Porfirian foreign policy attempted to show Mexicans that their country had "arrived" in world affairs, and that no nation, including the United States, would dare to violate Mexican sovereignty. These goals required a difficult double strategy: in investment negotiations, the Porfirians agreed to relinquish national control over key resources, but on political matters, they often stridently asserted Mexican national interests.

Such a foreign policy required attention by a diplomatic staff unsuited for such a task. Consequently, in 1883, President González restructured Mexico's Foreign Ministry. Through this reorganization, the government greatly strengthened its diplomatic representation. After 1883, Mexico operated sixteen consulates and a legation in the United States,[18] and it maintained a permanent legation in Guatemala City in charge of all of Central America. The minister dispatched to the isthmus undertook frequent trips to the other Central American republics, particularly El Salvador.[19] Mexican policy attained further dynamism with the appointment of the nationalist Ignacio Mariscal as head of the Foreign Ministry and Matías Romero's return to his post as minister in Washington.

Like the Porfirian government as a whole, this foreign-policy apparatus represented different factions within the Mexican governing elite. The Foreign Ministry worked as a hierarchically structured agency that fine-tuned all decisions of the Díaz cabinet and launched many initiatives on its own. Even though the Porfiriato might be cited as a prime example of "presidentialism," diplomacy was not one of the president's exclusive domains. Rather, the militarist-leaning Mariscal himself made many of the crucial decisions and, as we shall see, frequently elevated his opposition to Guatemala above other foreign-policy concerns. Much to the chagrin of the puros and científicos, who desired to avoid international trouble, Díaz often deferred to the opinions of his fellow Oaxacan during cabinet meetings.

The more "pro-American" forces, however, also obtained their niche in the Mexican diplomatic staff. As the country's representative in Washington, Mariscal usually chose a senior official who could accommodate the State Department as well as national and state authorities.[20] Most of them, including Romero, sometimes exercised more deference to U.S. wishes than the Foreign Secretary might have desired. In this fashion, these officials successfully projected the Díaz regime as pro–United States. At the same time, they relayed data about the risks that Díaz's policy could take without antagonizing Mexico's powerful neighbor.[21]

In the manner in which he chose his diplomats elsewhere, Mariscal followed the French example. Many of the Porfirian emissaries in Europe and Latin America were noted men of letters who had studied in the Old World and who ranked among the most influential poets and novelists of Porfirian Mexico. Most of them belonged to a different generation than Mariscal's; as relative youngsters, they often identified themselves only to a limited extent with the Porfirian inner circle. These diplomats formed an often obstreperous, anti-Yankee element within the foreign-policy apparatus—a pattern Mexico's revolutionary governments would follow in the 1920s.[22]

By the late 1880s, the Porfirians had created the conditions for utilizing foreign policy to further their overall economic and political goals. Díaz's foreign policy had clear objectives, namely to aid the project of centralization and modernization, and to defend Mexican political sovereignty. To achieve these sometimes contradictory ends, the Porfirians had created a diplomatic apparatus that could speak in different voices as the situation required. Partially as a result, their foreign policy was not always entirely predictable or consistent.

How did Mexican diplomats view Central America? Many members of Díaz's diplomatic service found Central America a horrendous assignment. In their view, none of the isthmian countries had matched Mexico's success. Diplomatic reports of the Díaz era describe Central America's capitals as squalid snake pits, its countryside as untamed wilderness, its rulers as despotic barbarians or *porfiritos* (little Porfirios), and its people as backward, uneducated "Indians."[23] The Mexican upper classes, and particularly the científicos, considered Central America inferior to Mexico. The official press rarely discussed isthmian affairs beyond reprinting the dispatches of international news agencies, but its commentary invariably attempted to drive home an important point: the Porfirians had helped make Mexico a better place than the "backward" Central American countries.[24]

Yet throughout the Porfiriato, important diplomatic work was to be done in Central America. Díaz had inherited a difficult problem: the border controversy with Guatemala.

The Mexican-Guatemalan Boundary Agreement, 1876–1882

By the early 1870s, the development of export economies in the border region had added a new twist to the boundary issue. Guatemala had found a lucrative export crop in coffee, a product that could be farmed on small, mountainous plots, but which required an abundance of cheap wage labor. Heavily Indian southwestern Guatemala met both of these conditions: the climate and the terrain proved ideal, and a labor draft did not constitute a major problem in a region where numerous pueblos were overpopulated. Therefore, the southern portion of the Guatemalan borderland and the Alta Verapaz region north of the capital became dotted with coffee plantations. European farmers invested heavily in the coffee industry, even though the national oligarchy also obtained an important share of the plots.

The growth of the Guatemalan coffee economy soon found imitators in Mexico. To be sure, by 1870 Soconusco counted a bare twenty thousand souls, and the economy of the region remained geared toward subsistence production. But the Juárez regime recognized the potential of Soconusco, blessed with almost ideal conditions for the production of coffee (near the coast) and corn (in the mountains), and it promoted economic development in Mexico's southeasternmost corner. Under Romero's prodding, Juárez made Soconusco a trial balloon for the development of export agriculture, and Romero himself bought a small coffee *finca* near the Guatemalan border.[25] The first attempts to produce coffee, maize, and other staples failed, but the government's interest in the economic future of the area had become manifest.[26]

By the time of Díaz's rise to power, Mexico needed a solution to the border problem. Throughout the 1870s, a caste war wracked much of Chiapas. In addition, Mexico's political fortunes in Soconusco were inextricably tied to the region's economic development. Unless the Díaz regime could induce a coffee boom in the area, the nearby Guatemalans might do it themselves; Guatemalan President Justo Rufino Barrios, in fact, already owned a finca in Soconusco. Economic development, however, depended in large part on an agreement with Guatemala on the exact boundary between the two countries. As long as the border remained defined by oral tradition and interpretation of contradictory colonial documents, the Mexican government could not expect to lure prospective landowners into this remote corner of the country or to ensure the availability of Indian labor.

Fortunately for Mexico, the Guatemalan government faced the same problem. To be sure, only a small part of Guatemala's coffee-producing areas lay close to the Mexican border. Nevertheless, Guatemala also had much to gain from a conclusive settlement of the boundary question, as investors hesitated to purchase land close to an internationally disputed area. Thus, when Guatemala's great "Renovator"[27] emerged in the person of Barrios, a strongman who shared the economic philosophies of the Porfirians but not their apprehension about the United States, the two governments set to work on a definitive agreement.

The first step appeared easy: in December 1877, Díaz and Barrios agreed to create a joint commission to survey the entire boundary. The commission, however, could not finish the work in the time allotted to it, even with an extension.[28] It was at this point, in 1878, that the larger problem came into full view. In Barrios's opinion, the Díaz regime used the existence of the survey commission to affirm Mexico's title to its present territorial possessions, including Soconusco. Díaz, on the other hand, expressed increasing irritation with a series of raids across the border that were allegedly abetted by Barrios, and he threatened to defend Chiapas by military force if necessary. Thus, Barrios saw the surveying commission as a vehicle to renegotiate the border, while Díaz viewed it as an instrument to determine the precise border demarcation; in the words of Romero, the "possession of Chiapas was not a negotiable item."[29] These adamant positions temporarily derailed any further discussion of the boundary issue.

In June 1881, Barrios took a step that fundamentally changed the dynamics of Mexican-Guatemalan relations. Citing Mexico's alleged desire to expand into Central America, he instructed his minister in Washington to ask for U.S. mediation of the border dispute.[30] Barrios obviously hoped that the U.S. government would aid him in his conflict with Mexico.

There was reason to believe that the U.S. State Department would side with Guatemala in an arbitration with Mexico. U.S. Secretary of State James G. Blaine regarded Guatemala as the linchpin to the achievement of key U.S. objectives in Central America: the construction of a U.S.-controlled interoceanic canal, the promotion of U.S. investments, and the elimination of British influence. If Porfirian Mexico was any indication, all of these goals could best be achieved by the unification of the five Central American republics under one strong hand. A unified Central American state could put an end to the perennial conflicts among the isthmian strongmen. It could guarantee political stability, both in and around a canal zone and in the areas slated for coffee and banana production. Ideally, a strong unified state backed by the United States might even put an end to the two British enclaves in Central America: Belize and the Nicaraguan Mosquito Coast. Blaine viewed Barrios, the ruler of the region's most populous country, as the ideal leader at the ideal time to realize a Central American union under U.S. tutelage.[31] Barrios was an unabashed admirer of U.S. institutions, and a fervent adherent to the unionist cause. Moreover, events in Italy and Germany had just shown the world the great success of campaigns of national unification.[32]

By 1880, Nicaragua's refusal to negotiate a canal treaty with the United States and French plans to construct a waterway in Panama had convinced Blaine that he needed to act quickly and decisively in Central America.[33] Therefore, Barrios' plea did not fall on deaf ears. Having identified the Guatemalan as the strong hand the isthmus needed, Blaine decided to help him in any manner possible in his dispute with the Mexican government. In 1881, he offered to help Barrios with "some directly practicable method by which the United States could aid in the establishment of a strong and settled union between the independent Republics of Central America."[34] He also instructed his representative in Mexico to express the dissatisfaction of the United States with the protracted border controversy and to cooperate with the Guatemalan minister in finding a solution.[35]

From the Mexican perspective, Blaine's partisanship for Barrios gave the border controversy a new and sinister aspect. Mexico's position between two neighbors with whom it had sustained territorial disputes had been bad enough. With the Blaine-Barrios alliance, however, the country seemed ensnared in a trap. Needless to say, Blaine's offer of arbitration greatly alarmed the Porfirians. Like Díaz in 1876, however, his protégé González did not yield to U.S. pressure. Instead, Foreign Secretary Ignacio Mariscal denied Mexican intentions to grow territorially at the expense of Guatemala and informed the U.S. minister that "there was nothing . . . to arbitrate."[36] Mexico was not to be cowed into submission to Blaine's wishes.

Blaine's intervention worsened relations between Mexico and Guatemala. In November 1881, tensions between the two countries reached a fever pitch when Mariscal fervidly denounced Barrios as a ruthless dictator. In response, Blaine bluntly warned González that Mexico's posture was "injurious to the best interests of all the republics of this continent."[37] This standoff even brought both sides close to war in early 1882.[38]

At this juncture, however, reason prevailed, and Blaine left his post as secretary of state. His successor, Frederick Frelinghuysen, did not share his enthusiasm for a Guatemalan-led union. Barrios realized that he could not force the Chiapas issue onto the negotiating table under these circumstances. Deeming his union project more significant than the border issue, he traveled to Washington to offer Romero a significant concession: Mexico could keep all of Chiapas in exchange for small strips of the states of Tabasco and Campeche.[39] On the Mexican side, González and Mariscal knew that their country could not subdue Guatemala by military force. They also understood that only a diplomatic settlement could calm the waters and permit their government to commence the economic development of Soconusco. Therefore, González agreed to the Guatemalan proposal.[40] On September 27, 1882, Mexican and Guatemalan representatives signed a treaty affirming Mexico's possession of all of Chiapas.

The González regime had emerged victorious from the border dispute. Not only had Mexico retained Chiapas, but the new boundary actually amounted to a net territorial gain over the country's previous possessions.[41] Of equal importance, González had taken a principled stand against U.S. intervention in bilateral problems between Mexico and Guatemala; and what was most significant, a conclusive settlement had come peacefully, not by the force of arms.

Nevertheless, those around González and Díaz did not delude themselves that Mexico and Guatemala had permanently settled their differences. The border was yet to be surveyed by another joint commission, and there was no guarantee that later Guatemalan governments would respect the treaty. Moreover, the equanimity with which Barrios had accepted the boundary award—later bemoaned by Guatemalan politicians and historians[42]—raised worries about his true intentions.

The Beginnings of the Fatal Triangle 33

As events soon showed, Barrios had only assured himself of peace with Mexico to pursue his old dream of a Central American union, and this time without U.S. help.

Díaz versus the Central American Union

As soon as Barrios's envoys had completed the border negotiations, the Guatemalan president set about trying to achieve the reunification of Central America under his leadership. Reunification would have made him the leader of all of Central America and would have enshrined Guatemalan dominance over the rest of the region. But Barrios had yet another motive: the existence of a politically stable Central American union would entice the U.S. government to go ahead with the construction of a canal on the San Juan River on the border of Nicaragua and Costa Rica. Such a canal, Barrios reasoned, could bring to the Central American elites enormous benefits, such as infrastructure, government revenues, and foreign investment. A canal could do for the entire isthmus what railroads were doing for the Porfirians.

Of course, failed attempts at union had been legion on the isthmus.[43] Yet this one held particular promise. The Guatemalan caudillo had imposed puppet governments in Honduras and El Salvador, and distant Nicaragua and Costa Rica appeared to offer no opposition to his plan. Moreover, isthmian Liberals everywhere in Central America favored the idea.[44] It came as no surprise, then, when Barrios followed up the settlement with Mexico with a vigorous campaign to persuade the other Central American leaders to agree to some form of confederation. At first he encountered considerable success. By 1883, El Salvador and Honduras had signed on to his plan,[45] and only Nicaragua and Costa Rica had voiced reservations. Even if those two countries could not be won over to the project, Barrios believed they would ultimately gravitate toward the new federation, which comprised 80 percent of the population of Central America.

If persuasion had worked to bring Central America's leaders closer to union, however, haste scuttled these achievements. Buoyed by the enthusiastic reception of his ideas in Guatemala, Barrios moved too swiftly to become the undisputed ruler of the isthmus. On February 28, 1885, he declared Central America unified and named himself supreme military commander of the new state. The Guatemalan congress unanimously approved the unification decree,[46] and Barrios sent notes to the United States, Mexico, and the principal European powers communicating the consummation of the Central American Union.[47] When Salvadoran leader Rafael Zaldívar proved reluctant to sign on to the union, Barrios drew up his armies on Guatemala's eastern border.

These militant actions forged an anti-Barrios alliance. Alarmed about the imminent use of force, three of the Central American countries immediately registered their opposition to the Barrios plan. Zaldívar protested against Barrios's preparations for war with El Salvador and asked Mexico for "moral support." Nicaragua and Costa Rica, where popular sentiment opposed union,[48] also appealed to Mexico for help against the pretensions of their more powerful neighbor.[49] Even the U.S. State Department, now under the leadership of Thomas Bayard, refused to support Barrios's moves. Only the weak Honduran government, its political survival dependent on Guatemalan goodwill, stood by Barrios.

Díaz, who had just begun his second term in office, did not hesitate to help the anti-Barrios alliance. Fear of the United States played only a minor role in his decision to combat the consummation of the Central American union. Díaz worried far more about the power of a greater Guatemala than about U.S. support for Barrios's plan. If Barrios had succeeded in unifying the isthmus by force, little could have stopped him from attacking Chiapas as well; the fact that some U.S. officials liked the idea of union was a secondary consideration.

Mariscal instructed Romero to investigate the attitude of the State Department. He worried that Barrios had bought the support of the United States in exchange for a promise of a U.S.-controlled isthmian canal route.[50] Mariscal also assured Zaldívar and the Nicaraguan government of Mexican solidarity with their stand. Díaz himself wrote to Barrios that both Central American and Mexican public opinion rejected the plan; this fact, Díaz contended, would "influence" the attitude of his government.[51] The same day, Mariscal cabled his counterpart in Guatemala City a message which further explained Mexico's position:

> Mexico will always view with pleasure the political unification of
> . . . Central America, as long as it emanates from the freely and
> clearly expressed will of the people . . . but it cannot fail to re-

prove any resort to force for [achieving] this goal, before the desires of the majority in each one of the nations . . . have been unquestionably ascertained. The decree [establishes a] . . . dangerous precedent . . . for the weak countries in their relations with the powerful.[52]

The argument appeared logical enough; Mexico's own experiences with foreign invasions led it to oppose all unilateral and arbitrary steps toward territorial aggrandizement. But Mariscal's reference to popular sovereignty in this quote was slightly ironic: the Mexican government had never "unquestionably ascertained" the wish of the Soconuscan population to remain Mexican.

This rhetoric masked an unalterable Mexican opposition to Central American unification under Guatemalan leadership. Mariscal proceeded to warn Barrios that Mexico had no alternative but to provide for its own defense, just "like any prudent nation [would] in the event of war among its neighbors."[53] Even as Guatemala protested against what it labeled interference in the internal affairs of Central America, the other isthmian countries except Honduras thanked Mexico for its intercession.[54]

Díaz found limited backing for his position in Washington. Romero vainly attempted to persuade Bayard to exert "moral influence" in order to avoid bloodshed.[55] Bayard explained that his country remained entirely neutral in the affair and enjoined Mexico to adopt the same position. In a telegram to his minister in Guatemala, however, the U.S. secretary of state appeared less unbiased: He stated that the United States could not countenance any "display of force on the part of any one or more States to coerce the others," even while he looked favorably upon "a voluntary combination of interests in Central America."[56]

Given its ambivalence on the issue, it was not surprising that the U.S. government acquiesced in a Mexican military maneuver. Immediately after the official promulgation of the Central American Union, Díaz had sent an army into Chiapas, which diverted a large fraction of the Guatemalan forces poised to invade El Salvador. When Barrios's foreign minister complained to a U.S. diplomatic representative in Guatemala about what he labeled Mexican interference,[57] the State Department refused to intervene. Bayard apparently believed Romero's assurances that the Díaz regime would not risk the loss of Chiapas by invading a country that boasted a mobilized army of twenty thousand—a much greater number than Díaz had at his disposal in the area.[58] Romero had discussed Central American issues on a daily basis with Bayard, and he had impressed the secretary of state with his well-argued reasoning. The puro strategy espoused by Romero had paid off: Mexican interests could be protected best by negotiation with the United States.

While Barrios prepared the Guatemalan army to march east, his government came under increasing international pressure. Mariscal ordered the Mexican legation to move temporarily to San Salvador.[59] With this step, the Mexican government effectively interrupted relations with the Barrios regime. At the same time, the U.S. government gave up its initially ambivalent position. The U.S. Senate condemned the unification plan, and Bayard told Romero that his government opposed Central American unification if it were by force.[60]

When Guatemalan forces invaded El Salvador in late March, the Mexican government decided that Barrios was to remain Guatemala's president no longer. In Mariscal's words, Mexico "could not have a head of state as a neighbor who does not respect the most fundamental principles of international law."[61] In a telegram to Romero, Mariscal stressed the futility of any attempt at communication with Barrios. In his view, Barrios would only understand a declaration of war.[62] Mexican diplomacy then once again attempted to pry the U.S. State Department away from its passive attitude. Now that Barrios had invaded El Salvador, Romero told Bayard, a war between Mexico and Guatemala appeared inevitable. Bayard, however, knew that Romero was merely bluffing. He underscored his advocacy of "moral suasion" and cautioned against any unprovoked military action, even though he implied that the State Department would not impede Mexican military moves.[63]

In early April, the governments of Nicaragua, El Salvador, and Costa Rica asked Díaz to join in a military alliance against Barrios. Unsure of the U.S. position, however, the Mexican did not dare to strike militarily at Guatemala and decided to remain in his merely menacing posture. Citing a "lack of instructions" as a pretext for avoiding such a commitment, the Mexican minister to Central America did not seize this opportunity to enter the coalition formally.[64] Soon thereafter, happenstance rendered moot all these deliberations. On April 15, while his forces were being routed by Salvadoran troops, Barrios died in battle. His death ended his bold attempt at a Central American union: his army quickly retreated, and the Guatemalan congress declared the unification decree null and void.

The Díaz regime had proven an active outside force in the battle against Barrios. Throughout the affair, it was Mexico, more so than the United States, that had taken the initiative to resolve the conflict. The U.S. offer of good offices had hardly changed the course of events; by contrast, the Mexican dispatch of troops to the Guatemalan border had diverted part of Barrios's invasion army toward the west and thus helped the alliance forces defeat the Guatemalan army.

Díaz's strategy during the controversy proved to be successful. With a policy of a "saber-rattling moral suasion," he had struck a middle ground that satisfied nationalist Mexicans eager for a military campaign as well as foreign investors nervous about a militant posture. Mexican foreign policy had yielded two important results: Mexican influence, if applied judiciously, could play a decisive role in containing Guatemala, and Díaz could use U.S. influence to neutralize Guatemalan ambitions. Díaz's retreat in the face of U.S. pressure, however, had also pointed up the limits of Mexican activity in Central America.

After Barrios's death, the Díaz regime tried with limited success to capitalize on its increased stature in the region. By threatening Guatemala with war, Mariscal attempted to impose his own candidate to succeed Barrios.[65] Anti-Mexican sentiments among the Guatemalan elites and the opposition of the U.S. State Department, however, soon ended this heavy-handed experiment at intervention. Continued cooperation with Costa Rica and El Salvador, on the other hand, yielded the desired result of promoting sympathetic governments in the rest of Central America.

After 1885, the Central American dynamic itself rarely challenged Díaz to act. The new, weaker rulers of Guatemala, Lisandro Barillas and José María Reyna Barrios, failed in enlisting U.S. support for a revision of the disputed Mexican boundary. A new surveying commission failed to make much headway in the demarcation of the border, but that mattered little. After the fall of Barrios, Guatemala's various irredentias— except the Belize question, which did not concern Mexico at this point—appeared irrevocably consigned to the history books.

Only the surveying of the Mexican-Guatemalan border continued to claim Díaz's attention. Barrios's successors proved more intractable on the subject of the border controversy than had the great "Renovator" himself. While Barrios had ensured the swift ratification of the 1882 border treaty, his successors dragged their feet on the process of surveying the boundary. The treaty had revitalized the joint commission of 1876, and both governments named an equal number of representatives for the task. But once in the field, the Guatemalans filibustered on every occasion. Therefore, the process took more than thirteen years to complete.[66] In good measure, Guatemala's delay strategy arose from an ominous trend that would soon require a Mexican response: a greater U.S. economic and political presence in Central America. For that reason, the 1890–98 period would prove an important turning point in Mexican policies toward Central America.

Mexico and the Beginnings of U.S. Primacy in Central America

In 1889, James Blaine, having returned to his old post as U.S. Secretary of State, summoned delegates from all American republics to the First Inter-American Conference in Washington. He then presented the delegates with a blueprint for fostering inter-American commerce and political understanding. At the heart of the agenda were two proposals that illustrated the U.S. desire to expand its influence in Latin America at the expense of the region's ties with Europe: a hemispheric customs union and a treaty of mandatory arbitration. The Mexican and Central American delegations reacted quite differently to these ideas. The Mexicans, mindful of their country's ties to Europe and the dangers involved in U.S. arbitration, opposed both initiatives; the Central American governments, interested in ending British territorial encroachments, supported both. But in the end, these differences between Mexico and Central America amounted to little. Another proposal— that U.S. businesses in legal difficulties in a Latin American country be allowed to appeal to the U.S. State Department before submitting to national courts—offended the Latin Americans sufficiently that the meeting ended in Blaine's failure.[67]

While this inter-American conference had few practical results, it did illustrate the newly assertive nature of U.S. policy toward Latin America. Labeled alternately the new empire, the age of U.S. imperialism, or the Open Door era, the new diplomacy had many faces. The United States had emerged from the Reconstruction period a stronger, more self-confident polity. The U.S. government had long tested its diplomatic muscle. It had meddled on behalf of the Cuban independence fighters in the Ten Years War; it had come close to annexing the Dominican Republic; and during his first term in office, Blaine had attempted to mediate the War of the Pacific among Chile, Peru, and Bolivia. In a sense, the United States simply joined the imperialist Great Power politics in vogue at that time: the 1878 Berlin Conference had carved up Africa, European powers had established colonial beachheads in China, and French and British colonial expansion clashed at various points of the globe. Moreover, industrialization had begun to transform the meaning of U.S. foreign policy. With industrialization, new economic interest groups demanded attention. These interest groups sought a closer economic relationship with Latin America for two reasons: to find markets for the new industrial products, and to ensure access to raw materials. As a consequence, railroad and mining interests, among others, had begun to lobby for the attention of the State Department.

The 1890s, a period of political and economic crisis, witnessed the first culmination of the quest for U.S. primacy in Latin America. The U.S. government stepped up its efforts to secure a canal route; it meddled in the independence struggle of Cuba; it promoted U.S. investments; and it sought to assert the long-forgotten Monroe Doctrine against European gunboat diplomacy. These policies led to a shift in Mexico's position between the United States and Central America. Despite the Porfirians' continuing concerns about Mexico's bilateral relations with Guatemala, U.S. influence in the Caribbean gradually became an important source of Mexican preoccupation as well.[68]

In particular, Blaine's return prompted Díaz to take a renewed interest in isthmian conflicts. In 1890, he initially refused to respond to a Salvadoran request to intervene in a border skirmish between Guatemala and El Salvador because he feared a spreading of the conflict. Then, however, when Blaine offered arbitration to both contending parties, Díaz made himself available as a co-mediator. The Mexican president not only wanted to ensure that Blaine did not brush aside Salvadoran interests; he also feared that U.S. mediation might invite the State Department to take even more assertive steps in future Central American disputes.[69] With this action, Díaz set an important precedent for his future isthmian policies: co-mediation was the best strategy to blunt Guatemalan and U.S. policies in Central America.

After Blaine's departure in 1893, Central America became even more important in U.S. policies. The second Grover Cleveland administration (1893–97) intensified efforts to procure a transoceanic canal under U.S. control. In 1894, Cleveland showed that this quest for the canal overrode other policy concerns. Despite the clamor of U.S. residents of La Mosquitia, a British-held Indian preserve on Nicaragua's Atlantic coast, he backed President José S. Zelaya's successful efforts to incorporate the preserve into Nicaraguan jurisdiction.[70] For the U.S. government, the removal of the British from an area close to a projected canal route had taken precedence over the protection of U.S. citizens. U.S. interest in the canal also accounted for a last-ditch U.S. effort to involve itself in arbitration of Mexican-Guatemalan disputes: in 1895, however, Díaz and Mariscal stated definitively that Mexico would not permit U.S. intervention in Mexican "internal affairs."[71]

The new U.S. policies alarmed the Díaz government. Even after Blaine's second tenure as Secretary of State ended, the Mexican government remained on guard and actively considered alternate strategies for dealing with this new threat from the north. Díaz, for one, was not afraid to envision radical solutions to the problem. In 1894, he confided to Romero that Mexico or Colombia might one day have to annex Central America if the small countries did not put their houses in order.[72] Díaz never attempted to implement this idea, but his expressing it underscores the Porfirians' fear that political instability on the isthmus could one day invite U.S. military intervention.

Then, beginning in 1894, Díaz saw his regime facing a formal U.S. attempt to assume a paramount position in the Americas—an attempt that resulted in the formulation of one of the cornerstone declarations of Porfirian foreign policy. The U.S. initiative took the form of a response to the British-Venezuelan border crisis of 1894. During this conflict, the British attempted to revise the boundary of their South American mainland colony, British Guyana, at Venezuela's expense. Terming the British encroachments a violation of the Monroe Doctrine, which opposed European colonization in the Americas, the U.S. State Department joined the fray in favor of Venezuela. When the British retreated, the U.S. government had won a major diplomatic victory:

it could boast that its main rival in Latin America had at last accepted the Monroe Doctrine. In 1895, U.S. Secretary of State Richard Olney even bragged that his country was "practically sovereign" in the hemisphere and that its "fiat" was law.[73] This declaration encapsulated the Olney corollary: the notion that the Monroe Doctrine constituted a declaration of paramount status.

Later that same year, Olney launched a vigorous campaign throughout the Americas to gain universal endorsement of the Monroe Doctrine in an attempt to *codify* it as international law. His optimism for winning such support stemmed from his reasoning that the doctrine protected the hemisphere against outside attacks. The British claims against Venezuela had revealed a danger to all Latin American governments, many of which had experienced European intervention in the past. Several Latin American governments did endorse the Monroe Doctrine.[74]

While the Porfirians sympathized with the main principle embodied in James Monroe's 1823 Doctrine—the idea that the Americas were no longer open to colonization and European intervention—they could not accept the notion that the United States alone was responsible for upholding this principle. Playing for time, Díaz waited for months before, pressed for a reply, he gave a definite answer.[75] Finally, on April 1, 1896, he declared in an address to the Mexican Congress:

> [I am a] partisan of Monroe's principles, if well understood. . . .
> But we do not think . . . that the responsibility for helping the
> other republics of the hemisphere against the attacks of Europe
> . . . should be solely incumbent on the United States. . . . Each
> one of those republics ought to . . . proclaim . . . that every attack
> . . . of a foreign power . . . would be considered an attack upon it-
> self.[76]

In a private letter, Díaz further explained his suspicions about any assumption of an "officious protectorate" on the part of the United States: "The Monroe Doctrine neither has the reach that the North American statesmen want to give it, nor can it be accepted . . . by the Hispano-American republics; unless it . . . prescribes mutual rights and obligations within the spirit of unharmed sovereignty for all."[77]

The Díaz Doctrine—the belief that the Monroe Doctrine should be multilaterally enforced by all countries in the Americas—has since formed an important cornerstone of Mexican foreign policy. On the surface, the doctrine appeared evenhanded in its rejection of both European and U.S. intervention. But the wording and timing of Díaz's address suggest that it was primarily directed against U.S. interventionism. The Díaz Doctrine, in fact, marked the coming of a new era in the history of Mexican foreign policy. With European intervention and problems on Mexico's southern border remote threats, U.S. expansion took center stage.[78]

Díaz's stance on the Olney corollary was one of his finest moments. Since the Mexican president had affirmed the general principles of the Monroe Doctrine, Olney could not help but proclaim himself satisfied.[79] Díaz's remarks received favorable comments in both the Mexican and the U.S. press, and many Central and South American newspapers concurred.[80]

The Porfirians' mettle, however, had yet to be tested, as the late 1890s witnessed another shift toward an aggressive U.S. posture in Latin America.[81] While President Cleveland had not committed U.S. military resources to extend U.S. power in the Caribbean, the administration of William McKinley (1897–1901) ushered in a new era. Backed by popular support for bringing the "blessings" of the United States to distant lands, and encouraged by large corporations, hawkish government officials, and William R. Hearst's yellow press, his government decided to put an end to European influence in the Caribbean.

The target of McKinley's diplomacy was Cuba, the largest of Spain's remaining American colonies, where an independence movement had launched attacks on Spanish control since 1868. The U.S. government had long favored independence for the island, seeing in it both an abominable enclave of Old World colonialism and a future U.S. pathway to the Caribbean. The precise motives for U.S. policy regarding Cuba have been the subject of a long and varied debate.[82] What matters to this analysis is that the Díaz regime feared that U.S. meddling in Cuba, which culminated in the 1898 war with Spain, might lead to subsequent imperialist actions in Mexico and Central America. Therefore, Díaz attempted to mediate between Spain and the United States.[83] When this effort failed—a failure cautiously criticized in Mexico's opposition papers—Díaz realized that diplomatic skill alone would not prevent U.S. unilateral action in the Caribbean.

The events of 1898 can best be characterized as Mexico's "Cuba

Shock": a sudden awareness of the danger of U.S. intervention in Latin America. This awareness made Díaz's job as president much more difficult. Even though the U.S. actions did not threaten Mexican sovereignty, the Conservative and radical Liberal opposition now united in their demands for a nationalist, anti-Yankee foreign policy. Thus, the Cuba Shock linked up with significant political changes within Mexico to help focus Díaz's Central America policy on the prevention of U.S. intervention.

Mexican Politics and Foreign Policy in the Age of the Cuba Shock

By 1898, the clique of dynamic young Liberals who had led the 1876 Tuxtepec coup had become gerontocrats. Díaz and Mariscal were approaching their seventieth birthdays and other cabinet members were not much younger. Díaz had already served five terms in office, and he no longer respected the norms of the 1857 Constitution. In 1880, he had stepped down in order to satisfy his own amendment that forbade immediate reelection. In 1887, however, Díaz had made the Mexican Congress allow him to win another term, and in 1892, the legislature had scrapped the old amendment altogether. By the turn of the century, Díaz's long tenure as president had made a change of leadership seem inconceivable. The Porfiriato had become El Necesariato,[84] the rule of "the necessary," or the indispensable one. No opposition party existed, Congress had no real power, and political promotion could only be obtained with Díaz's blessing.

This process of political ossification weakened Díaz's own erstwhile allies, the puros. Much tempered in their idealistic views in the age of "Conservative Liberalism," the puros—with Romero as their most visible protagonist—had dominated the Porfirian inner circle until the late 1880s. While they had reconciled themselves with the Catholic Church, they still advocated unfettered capitalism and the establishment of democratic institutions. In the early days of the Porfiriato, this platform had served the puros well: Díaz's apparent commitment to the Constitution had won him widespread support. But when Díaz undermined Mexico's republican institutions, he repudiated key tenets of the puros' political philosophy. Until 1892, many upper-class Mexicans had sincerely believed that political democracy was feasible for their country. By 1900, however, this optimism had given way to skepticism: Mexico, many believed, needed a strong hand. As a consequence, the puros faced a serious problem: their platform called for representative democracy, yet they had abetted the tyranny they professed to abhor. After 1892, the puros split into two factions: those who agreed with the científico justification of the Necesariato (the argument that the popular will approved of a Porfirian "democratic Caesarism"); and those who refused to compromise their principles. Labeled "Jacobins" by their opponents, these dissenters had no place within the Porfirian political firmament and soon went underground.[85]

The effects of U.S. economic penetration, which the puros had advertised as bringing "all of the fruits of annexation without any of the dangers,"[86] further made Mexicans question classical Liberal notions. By the turn of the century, the Díaz regime had itself become aware that the laws which had encouraged this penetration entailed disadvantages. U.S. economic cycles wreaked havoc with the Mexican economy, and many middle-class Mexicans found their options limited by a large influx of U.S. white-collar workers. With every economic downturn, the faint stirrings of a new anti-Yanquismo could be heard, prevalent especially among the Mexican elite and middle classes. As a result, Díaz himself pondered policies that sought to balance U.S. investments with European ones.[87] He also allowed the Conservative newspaper *El Tiempo* and the Liberal press, led by *El Diario del Hogar,* to print editorials warning against the consequences of the "Pacific conquest." Thus, the few remaining puros lost influence within Díaz's coalition because their infatuation with Anglo-Saxon economic ideas had failed as conspicuously as had their belief in U.S. political institutions.

In 1898, the death of Mexico's ambassador to the United States, Matías Romero, deprived the puros—and in general, those who advocated cooperation with the United States—of their main voice within the foreign-policy making process. Romero, one of Mexico's most prominent puros, had been instrumental in promoting Mexico as an investment target. As a diplomat who had spent more than thirty years north of the Rio Grande, he had also contributed greatly to making Díaz understand the viewpoints of the U.S. government. With Romero dead, the less pro-Yankee Mariscal became Díaz's only experienced adviser on matters of foreign policy.

As a result, factions within the Mexican governing elite opposing the

Pacific conquest gained importance. The científicos, and Finance Minister José Y. Limantour in particular, argued in favor of balancing U.S. influence in Mexico with European investment.[88] In fact, the French-born Limantour viewed the United States with about as much distrust as had Lucas Alamán, sharing with Mexico's foremost Conservative a cultural and philosophical disdain for Anglo-Saxon ways. With his influence in the ascendancy after Romero's death, Limantour—backed up by Secretary of Education Justo Sierra, who had urged Díaz to intervene in the Cuban conflict[89]—steered the Díaz government away from its great reliance on U.S.-driven development. Thus, he induced Díaz to award important concessions to European rather than U.S. contractors.[90] But Limantour's own views revealed a dilemma of the Porfirian strategy: he knew that U.S. capital remained essential for Mexican development.[91]

The Reyistas—an openly nationalist faction around General Bernardo Reyes—were more hawkish than the científicos in their approach to the United States. Reyes was widely regarded as the most able candidate to succeed Díaz. Entrenched within the army and northern elites, his faction followed in the tradition of the militarists around Manuel González. Reyes called for a military reform to make the Mexican army a capable force in the event of war. He soon became one of Díaz's most important retainers, and he had the support of Mariscal and a number of other cabinet members. By the early 1900s, the "militarist" Reyistas significantly influenced policy.[92]

These processes set in motion a transformation of Mexican nationalism. As we have seen, Díaz sought to utilize nationalism in an effort to strengthen central government power. By the 1890s, the inculcation of official nationalism had begun to bear fruit. Mirroring trends in Europe and the United States, Mexican nationalists came to favor "imperial" ideas: they desired to see their country play an active role in world affairs, and especially in "weaker areas" such as Central America.[93]

Because the Cuba Shock had shown that the United States had become strong enough to limit any such "external" manifestations of Mexican greatness, Mexican anti-Yanquismo waxed following a half-century of decline after the U.S.–Mexican War. Many members of Mexico's cultural elite were swept up along with the rest of Latin America in an anti-Yankee wave which rapidly gained force. Many Mexicans read the writings of the Cuban José Martí, the Nicaraguan Rubén Darío, and the Uruguayan José Enrique Rodó, who attacked what they viewed as the materialist and self-centered "American way of life." Authors such as Federico Gamboa (who would play a prominent role as Mexican minister to Central America) shared these opinions and expressed nationalist sentiments in their own writings.[94] Along with this growing criticism of Yankee imperialism, critique of Díaz's inability to confront U.S. influence also mounted.

As a result, the Díaz regime increasingly followed policies independent of those of the United States, and it desired to showcase to the country's public this commitment to preserving Mexican independence. Mexican sovereignty could be defended more easily in the political than in the economic arena; therefore, foreign policy once again served as a venue for demonstrations of nationalism. After 1898, Central America became the key target in this endeavor.

Between 1876 and the early 1890s, concerns about Guatemala had remained the prime determinant of Mexico's Central America policy. To be sure, U.S. influence increasingly figured in the formulation of Díaz's Central America policy. But as their policies toward Barrios' unification effort showed, the Porfirians worried about the U.S. presence in Central America primarily inasmuch as it affected Mexico's relationship with Guatemala. The pattern of Mexican policies in the 1870s and 1880s therefore chiefly reflected bilateral concerns: Díaz pursued goals in Central America geared toward the security of the Mexican border and the weakening of Guatemala.

After 1890, however, strategies for confronting the U.S. presence in Latin America had become a growing source of Mexican worries. Even though it still lacked the desire to intervene in the isthmus, the U.S. government paid increasing attention to the area as its strategic significance grew with each step taken toward the construction of a transoceanic canal. The Mexican government would soon face a delicate balancing act: how to limit U.S. political influence in Central America at a time when a new, ambitious Guatemalan strongman once again attempted to dominate the region. To achieve the goal of reining in both U.S. and Guatemalan ambitions, Mexico would do its best to maintain the isthmus in a tenuous political equilibrium. "Great power–driven" policies therefore had become more important.

The Beginnings of the Fatal Triangle 47

Close to his death, Matías Romero, the Porfirian official who knew most about the United States, had foreseen a difficult future for his country. In an article for the *Bulletin of the American Geographical Society,* he wrote that Mexico was a Central American—and not a North American—country.[95] Romero's musings illustrated growing doubts about the Porfirian project. Mexicans sought to emulate the U.S. success, but could they ever expect their country to be more than a poor, weak appendage of North America—more than the "backwardness" that Mexican diplomats had seen in the Central American countries? Coming from a leading advocate of U.S. investment, these views indicated growing fears of the United States. As Mexico glided ever more deeply into the shadow of the giant, these fears were bound to change the direction of the country's foreign policy.

3 Don Porfirio and Uncle Sam Bring the "Porfiritos" into Line, 1898–1907

Since independence, Mexico has seen all of Central America with paternal eyes. Being larger and stronger, incomparably stronger, it has desired for [the area] the well-being that we have achieved . . . as a result of all of our traumatic experience.

Federico Gamboa, 1900

At the dawn of the new century, Díaz turned his attention to the prevention of interstate war in Central America. This effort was crucial for several reasons: a peacekeeping role could enhance Díaz's stature as an international leader; Mexican mediation could thwart a new Guatemalan bid for supremacy in the region; and the U.S. government displayed a growing willingness to show that its fiat was law in Central America as well as in the Caribbean. To Díaz, the specter of U.S. military intervention coupled with Guatemalan gains was troubling indeed.

As a response, Díaz attempted to find diplomatic solutions to Central American disputes in order to stave off both Guatemalan dominance and U.S. intervention. Realizing the futility of his early, unilateral efforts, he then co-mediated a number of crises with the U.S. government. Díaz played a risky game with his co-mediation. His assistance in the peacekeeping effort lent a measure of legitimacy to U.S. meddling in the area[1]—and Díaz had little to gain with the Mexican public by appearing as Uncle Sam's handmaiden. But the Díaz regime undertook the co-mediation with its own goals in mind and was at least partially successful in attaining them.[2]

Porfirio Díaz, Mexico's "Eternal" President, 1900
(Courtesy of the Archivo General de la Nación, Mexico City)

The Failure of Unilateral Mediation, 1898–1902

Justo R. Barrios's death in 1885 had left a void in dominating political personalities in Central America. The Salvadoran Rafael Zaldívar, the Guatemalans Lisandro Barillas and José María Reyna Barrios, the Nicaraguan Adán Cárdenas—none of these leaders matched Barrios's power, vigor, or political vision. Honduras remained the weakest isthmian state, and Costa Rican politicians stood ever more aloof from the rest of Central America.

But by 1898, three strong leaders had emerged who would do much to define the character of Central American politics over the next two decades. In 1893, José Santos Zelaya had finally put the Liberal party in power in Nicaragua; only a year later, he had shown his political acumen by edging the British out of the Mosquito Coast. In 1895, Zelaya founded the República Mayor de Centroamérica, a fusion of Nicaragua, El Salvador, and Honduras; in 1898, however, the union collapsed in the wake of the uprising of Tomás Regalado in El Salvador.[3] That same year in Guatemala, General Manuel Estrada Cabrera overthrew Reyna Barrios in a bloody coup.

Zelaya, Regalado, and Estrada Cabrera: these three bitter rivals all sought to emulate the Porfirian project in their respective countries. Each one of these Porfiritos, or little Porfirios, viewed himself as the redeemer of Barrios's quest for a unified Central America. As the nineteenth century ended, the spoils of isthmian leadership had become enormous indeed, and especially for Zelaya. The U.S. victory over Spain made the construction of a transisthmian canal much more likely, and one of the two prominent routes ran along the San Juan River along the Nicaraguan–Costa Rican border.

The emergence of the three Porfiritos led to another flareup of Central American warfare. Estrada Cabrera, Regalado, and Zelaya all sought to alleviate domestic political problems by meddling in the affairs of neighboring Central American countries—an easy thing to do since extensive ties of family and friendship among the Liberal elites still crossed national boundaries. Their base of power was slim indeed: the army remained their main source of authority. Unlike Díaz, none of these dictators could construct a strong enough consensus to rule without the approval of army leaders. But if any one of the three Porfiritos had been able to control the rest of Central America and use the revenue from the canal route for the consolidation of his rule, he would have managed to break this stranglehold. Thus, each of the three leaders had ample reason to try and become the undisputed boss on the isthmus. As a consequence, Díaz paid close attention to events in Central America.

In particular, the start of Estrada Cabrera's "sinister dictatorship"[4] rekindled Díaz's apprehension about Guatemala. Estrada Cabrera courted U.S. friendship with two goals in mind: achieving isthmian leadership, and gaining an ally in his country's troubles with Great Britain. Guatemala had repeatedly defaulted on its large outstanding debt with British banks. Estrada Cabrera hoped that the U.S. government would help him oppose a gunboat expedition to enforce debt collection. Moreover, he was shameless in his dealings with the United Fruit Company (UFCO), the new U.S. concern that spearheaded banana cultivation in Central America. He gave UFCO virtually complete control over Guatemala's railroads and ports in return for payoffs and secretly held shares in the company.[5] The fact that his rule was despotic and cruel—more so than that of Díaz himself—did nothing to endear him to Mexicans.[6]

Estrada Cabrera and Díaz never got along well. Trying to offset his failure to address Guatemala's economic woes, Estrada Cabrera frequently appealed to vintage anti-Mexican sentiments. Attempting to copy Díaz's strategy of using nationalist symbols as a cement of his rule, he often expressed a desire to recover parts or all of Chiapas. On the Mexican side, Mariscal and his minister to all of Central America, Federico Gamboa, harbored a vituperative (and duly reciprocated) hatred of the Guatemalan president. Gamboa, who resided in Guatemala City, disliked Central Americans in general and Estrada Cabrera in particular: he viewed him as a quasi-Oriental tyrant in a land of "a fear-inspiring disregard for human life."[7] These largely personal misgivings inaugurated a new period of strained relations between the two countries.[8]

Moreover, U.S. diplomats in Guatemala loomed as potential adversaries for Mexico. During the 1898–1907 period, U.S. representatives in Guatemala often pursued Estrada Cabrera's interests; in their dispatches to the State Department, many of them uncritically praised the policies of the Guatemalan government. Diplomats such as Leslie Combs, a business partner of Estrada Cabrera's,[9] served as virtual ministers without portfolio in the Guatemalan cabinet and frequently warned their superiors of the perceived "Mexican threat" to Guatemala.[10] As the example of Blaine had shown, such dispatches could cause trouble if they fell into the hands of a receptive Secretary of State.

Díaz, however, could count on Regalado and Zelaya to help offset any potential combination of U.S. and Guatemalan interests. Unlike Estrada Cabrera, neither of his rivals had an acute debt problem on his hands. Since Regalado did not need to court the United States for protection against gunboat diplomacy (like Estrada Cabrera) or for the purpose of obtaining the canal concession (like Zelaya) he became Díaz's favorite Central American leader. This became apparent in the crisis of 1899–1900—a conflict Díaz attempted to mediate on behalf of Regalado.

Late in 1899, Regalado's rule appeared in jeopardy, as Estrada Cabrera and Zelaya had come to an agreement to remove their common rival. Estrada Cabrera feared El Salvador's army, modernized with the help of German military advisers, and Zelaya still resented Regalado for ending his attempt at isthmian union. Regalado immediately appealed for Mexican help. In November 1899, his minister in Mexico requested that Díaz sponsor a "pacifist mission" through all of the Central American capitals. Peace in Central America, the minister stated, could be ensured only if each government issued a statement forswearing interference in the affairs of its neighbors.[11] Informed of a mobilization of troops in Guatemala, Mariscal instructed Gamboa to proceed as the Salvadorans desired. He also used this opportunity to play up the Mexican role: he asked Gamboa to invite the five Central American presidents to attend a peace conference aboard a Mexican warship.[12]

Gamboa had no difficulty obtaining the desired pledges from Estrada Cabrera and Regalado. Estrada Cabrera was unenthusiastic, but agreed to cooperate. Regalado, predictably, was a different story: "the only thing hostile to us in El Salvador," Gamboa wrote, "is its climate."[13] His next stop, San José, also proved successful; the Costa Rican government wholeheartedly backed the Mexican-Salvadoran effort.[14]

In Managua, however, Gamboa encountered an entirely different atmosphere. His first meeting with Zelaya did not leave him impressed with the Nicaraguan caudillo: "he . . . governs his country *a la militar* [italics mine] . . . he is distrustful, circumspect and cruel." The interview also confirmed Gamboa's prior suspicions about

Zelaya's dealings with Estrada Cabrera. Therefore, it did not come as a surprise to him that Zelaya had no intention of supporting his plans for disarmament and peace. The mission, Zelaya stated, aimed to drag all of Central America to Regalado's feet so that Guatemala would cease to be a threat to Mexico. Three days later, the Nicaraguan told Gamboa that he would not participate in the Mexican-sponsored peace conference, either. By his own admission, he desired the unification of Central America by military means—a project to which Mexico remained opposed. Disillusioned, Gamboa skipped his visit to Honduras (a country governed by a Zelaya ally) and returned to Guatemala with contempt for Estrada Cabrera. He concluded that Estrada Cabrera and Zelaya had toyed with him.[15]

Gamboa's efforts had resulted in failure. Even though war never came, as relations between Estrada Cabrera and Zelaya soon turned sour, Mexican prestige had suffered. Moreover, Gamboa had failed to get the required support for the peace conference; a conference which would have enhanced Mexico's prestige in the area greatly. Being the sole Mexican representative in Central America, Gamboa had been woefully misinformed about Zelaya. Moreover, as his remarks in the epigraph to this chapter show all too well, he had displayed a patronizing attitude toward Central America. With this disappointment, Mexico's freelance diplomacy in Central America had been dealt a serious blow. From now on, the Díaz regime carefully monitored the opinions of all of the parties involved before committing itself to action.[16] In addition, Díaz secretly aided Regalado.[17]

Two years later, Zelaya himself assumed the role of peacemaker. Buoyed by U.S. assurances that the canal would be built through Nicaragua, Zelaya had grown confident about his own future.[18] When tensions between Guatemala and El Salvador again loomed in late 1901, the Nicaraguan invited delegates from all of the isthmian countries to the port of Corinto. He had chosen a good moment: Venezuelan President Cipriano Castro was in arrears in his debt payments to British and German banks, and a joint gunboat expedition to collect payment loomed as a real possibility. The Central American presidents realized that the Venezuelan crisis might easily recur in the isthmus. Therefore, Regalado and his counterparts from Honduras and Costa Rica agreed to cooperate with Zelaya in order to produce a framework that might discourage such intervention. Only Estrada Cabrera, who was profoundly jealous of the Nicaraguan initiative, did not participate.[19]

Even without Guatemala, Zelaya would not be denied in his attempt to create a permanent peace framework for Central America. In early January 1902, the four delegations present signed a promise of peace and noninterference, and they agreed to submit all future questions arising among them to a court of arbitration staffed by their own nationals. They also took steps toward the establishment of an isthmian free-trade zone.[20] Better yet, both the U.S. and the Mexican governments recognized the validity of the Corinto accords and the court of arbitration established in it—Estrada Cabrera was thus internationally isolated.[21] Zelaya had achieved an impressive goal: he had created a workable Central American arbitration apparatus. Zelaya now stood poised to increase his power vastly: his country was the frontrunner for the canal, and he had sponsored a Central American peace agreement that might serve as a framework for an eventual union.

Even though the Díaz regime had not participated in the proceedings at Corinto, the agreements—and especially the establishment of the court of arbitration—vindicated its foreign-policy positions. At the Second Inter-American Conference held in Mexico City in 1901-2, Mexico's delegates had unsuccessfully proposed the creation of a hemispheric court in which each country would be accorded one vote. By such a mechanism, Díaz hoped to create the institutional framework for the application of his views on the Monroe Doctrine.[22] Now, the Central American countries, under the leadership of Zelaya, had created a blueprint for a truly Pan-American treaty among equal and sovereign states. If this framework functioned in Central America, Díaz had reason to be optimistic about bringing his idea up again at the next conference in Rio de Janeiro.

In the 1898–1902 period, Central America had come to resemble a powder keg, which held formidable dangers for Mexico. While the bickering among the isthmian leaders did not threaten Mexico directly, either the victory of the anti-Mexican Estrada Cabrera or U.S. intervention could cause trouble. The Corinto agreement might prevent interstate war for a while. But with Estrada Cabrera not a signatory to the treaty, further trouble seemed inevitable.

Mexican unilateral efforts had failed to achieve a more permanent and comprehensive peace accord. But as events soon showed, the U.S. government had a virtually identical desire for political stability—albeit for very different reasons. The challenge for Díaz was to cooperate with the United States in the common goal of a peaceful Central America without appearing to help with the consolidation of U.S. influence. With the isthmus in a tenuous state of political stability after 1902, Díaz needed to come to terms with the U.S. presence in the region itself.

Confronting U.S. Policies, 1902–1906

U.S. policy in this era must be understood foremost in terms of the quest for a U.S.-controlled transisthmian canal. Under President McKinley, the U.S. government further stepped up its efforts on this matter. The issue had attained urgency with the settlement of the western United States and trade expansion into the Pacific. During the war with Spain, the three-month trip of the U.S.S. *Oregon* from Puget Sound to the Caribbean via Cape Horn had graphically pointed up the strategic problems of a nation that bordered two oceans. Therefore, McKinley proclaimed in 1898 that the canal issue had become a national priority.[23]

The timing soon became propitious. Both Britain and France—the main rivals to the United States in this endeavor—were busy with foreign crises: the British with the Boer War in South Africa, and both countries with a surging Germany and colonial rivalries in Asia and Africa. Britain in particular was eager to assure itself of U.S. friendship at a time that a European war became ever more likely. As a consequence, in 1900–1, the British government agreed to abrogate the old Clayton-Bulwer compromise by means of the two Hay-Pauncefote treaties. The road was clear for a U.S.-controlled waterway, to be constructed either in Nicaragua or in the Colombian province of Panama. At first, the Nicaraguan route seemed the favorite—hence Zelaya's bullish enthusiasm about his own political future. But following years of intense lobbying by both sides, the U.S. Senate chose the Panama route in June 1902.

With this decision, the U.S. government assured Nicaragua of a "dwarfed economic future"[24] and alienated a leader who had so far been supportive of U.S. policies. Having long courted U.S. friendship in order to receive the nod for the canal, Zelaya soon became the only Central American leader to oppose actively the extension of U.S. influence on the isthmus. In appropriating a wave of anti-Yankee sentiment following the Senate vote, he acted to deflect widespread criticism that he had failed to procure a concession that had appeared firmly in his hand.[25] The U.S. Senate's rejection of the Nicaragua Canal route channeled Zelaya's energy toward the domination of the rest of Central America. One half of his strategy (the canal) had failed, but the Nicaraguan wasted no time pursuing his other goal: unification of Central America under his leadership.

These developments made Zelaya an invaluable asset to Díaz. Zelaya, who only three years earlier had rebuffed Gamboa, now spoke in admiring terms about the Díaz regime, stating that Mexico was "the nation of this continent which best conserves the character traits of its race and history."[26] Of all the Central American leaders, his political philosophy resembled most closely that of Porfirian Mexico. No longer perceiving a need to coddle the U.S. government, he aggressively countered the U.S. economic presence in Nicaragua with political and commercial agreements with European powers.[27] More than Díaz, Zelaya resisted unilateral dependence on the United States.[28] Thus, he even negotiated with French and British companies interested in building a second canal.[29]

As for the new U.S. president, Theodore Roosevelt, Zelaya at first remained the least of his worries. The U.S. and Colombian governments quickly came to an agreement on the canal issue; but in August 1903, the Colombian senate rejected the resultant treaty in hopes of extracting greater financial compensation from the Roosevelt administration. Roosevelt, however, would not hear of it—instead, he aided a band of rebels who proclaimed the secession of Panama. On November 18, 1903, representatives of the United States and the new republic of Panama signed a hastily revised canal treaty: one that gave the U.S. government greater privileges than the one the Colombian senate had rejected.[30]

In Mexico, the mutilation of Colombia evoked disgust, as well as an acute sense of impotence.[31] Since he knew from his experience with Cuba that he could not oppose the U.S. government on matters of vital strategic concern, Díaz refused the Colombian minister's call for help.[32] But he did try the avenue of collective action: he vainly attempted to gain the support of other Latin American governments for a common policy of nonrecognition toward the new Panamanian regime. Not until a year later, when the major South American countries had awarded recognition to the new state, did he recognize Panama as a sovereign state.[33] The events in Panama reinforced the Cuba Shock: they made Mexicans fear that the U.S. government would not hesitate to use military force in Latin America.

With canal construction under way, U.S. attention shifted to protecting the prospective route, a policy goal that might entail future U.S. military intervention. To the measure of its ability, the U.S. government would step in to prevent any unrest that might impede the smooth construction and operation of the canal—and not only in Panama itself but also in the adjoining Central American countries.[34] Rapid growth in the U.S. economic stake in Central America reinforced this trend toward intervention. A dynamic, U.S.-financed banana sector spearheaded by the United Fruit Company experienced exponential growth between 1900 and 1914, and U.S. investments also poured into railroads, port construction, mining, timber, and coffee. As a consequence of the turbulent isthmian politics, many U.S. investors found cause to lodge complaints with the State Department for diplomatic intervention on their behalf. Even though the U.S. government had thus far not intervened militarily on behalf of "big business" in Central America, these complaints could increase U.S. meddling in the future. Finally, the issue of European debt collection by military force invited a U.S. response.[35]

That Roosevelt would not hesitate to intervene became clear with the formulation of the "Roosevelt corollary to the Monroe Doctrine." Once again, trouble with Venezuela had provided the case for a reinterpretation of the hemispheric policy of the United States. In 1902, President Castro had stopped payment on his country's obligations with European banks. As expected, Britain and Germany had sent warships to force Castro to resume debt service. Originally, Roosevelt had acquiesced in the maneuver. But following a storm of protest in the U.S. press, he had sent sharp notes to London and Berlin, claiming that the naval expedition violated the spirit of the Monroe Doctrine. Desiring U.S. goodwill at a time of mounting international tensions, the Europeans had backed off in early 1903.[36]

In 1904, Roosevelt formulated his administration's Latin America policy by reinterpreting the Monroe Doctrine. The venerable declaration, the president asserted, implied the right of the United States to act as a hemispheric police force to prevent conditions in Latin America that could provoke European intervention.[37] When the United States fought "wars with barbarous or semi-barbarous peoples," Roosevelt argued, it was exercising "a most regrettable but necessary . . . duty which must be performed for the sake of the welfare of mankind."[38] This corollary served two purposes: it assured the U.S. public that Roosevelt would not permit European military excursions into the American hemisphere, and it warned Latin Americans to assume political and fiscal "responsibility."

The Roosevelt corollary threw the Díaz regime into a quandary. In refuting the European right to enforce debt payment, Roosevelt had in effect backed the Drago doctrine, a principle universally acclaimed in Latin America as a protective measure against gunboat diplomacy.[39] But Díaz had to oppose any assumption of a U.S. protectorate that would prevent European intervention; the corollary could be applied at any time to the Central American countries, whose public finances were in a perpetual state of disaster.[40] In the end, he refused to give official comment and limited himself to inducing *El Imparcial* and other loyal Mexico City newspapers to print editorials applauding the Drago and Díaz doctrines.

Privately, however, Díaz worked to unite Latin American governments so that they would have a better chance of standing up to U.S. intervention. When war in Central America threatened, Díaz favored negotiation among isthmian leaders as laid down in the Corinto protocol. Briefly after Roosevelt's speech, he encouraged Zelaya to prod Regalado toward the peaceful unification of Central America (not under Guatemalan leadership, of course!) so that the new corollary might not be applied to the area. The resultant federation, Díaz and Zelaya agreed, could assist Mexico in the formation of a Latin American league. But piqued by Díaz's rebuke of his plans for a campaign against Guatemala, Regalado did not cooperate. Zelaya and Díaz had to shelve their initiative.[41]

Díaz and Mariscal then resolved to find out more about the potential threat posed by this reinterpretation of the Monroe Doctrine. They instructed Ambassador Manuel Azpíroz to sound out Roosevelt on the import of his statement as regarding Mexico and the Caribbean. On the occasion of a visit to congratulate the U.S. president on his reelection in 1904, Azpíroz carefully broached the matter, hoping to learn that Roosevelt did not plan a practical application of his corollary.

What the Mexican ambassador had to hear, however, were hardly courteous words of reassurance but the blueprint for a new political order in Latin America. If all Latin American nations behaved like Mexico, Roosevelt began, the Monroe Doctrine would become superfluous. In his view, it was disorder in the small Latin American countries that required U.S. intervention, an arduous task he desired to avoid. To remove the causes of instability, Roosevelt proposed a simple and radical measure: Mexico, he said, should extend its border to Panama, gobbling up all five Central American countries in the process. To achieve this "Great Mexico," he affirmed, Díaz could count on the support of the United States.[42] Evidently, the U.S. president thought Mexico could become watchman on the isthmus by Uncle Sam's grace. Roosevelt repeated his high-handed offer of territorial aggrandizement on various occasions over the next year. He favored "natural growth" for Mexico, the "best-governed country in Latin America." Mexico should, he stated, incorporate Puerto Rico, Cuba, and the Dominican Republic. Roosevelt made similar offers of regional leadership to Brazil and Argentina, hoping to enlist the larger Latin American countries as "policemen" to enforce his corollary.[43]

But while Brazil welcomed its new role as a South American great-but-subordinated power, Azpíroz's successor, Joaquín Casasús, reacted to these schemes in a lukewarm fashion. The Brazilian government was eager to find U.S. support against German plans to convert Rio Grande do Sul (a province with a large German population) into a "New Germany."[44] Casasús, on the other hand, saw the offer of territorial acquisitions as nothing but a bait to prod Díaz to aid U.S. gunboat diplomacy; he characterized Roosevelt's approach as an attempt "to laud, in the American way, our national vanity." Casasús had a good point: Roosevelt would never have offered any other power Cuba or Puerto Rico, two islands that the U.S. government considered of prime strategic and economic importance. Therefore, the Mexican ambassador courteously rejected all of Roosevelt's proposals. Even if "Mexico might not refuse growth," he replied to the U.S. president, "history revealed that Mexico had never shown any inclination whatsoever to grow . . . at the expense of other countries."[45]

Mexican resistance forced Roosevelt to shift gears. A year later, he attempted to sell at least a U.S.–guaranteed role of a middle power to the Díaz regime. On February 13, 1906, the U.S. president told Casasús that "it would be convenient to let Mexico, Brazil, Argentina and Chile participate whenever the American government might judge it necessary to protect the other nations of the continent from [European] attacks."[46]

But again, Díaz would not agree to help enforce Roosevelt's corollary. As the Mexican government saw it, Roosevelt desired to lend a veil of legitimacy to U.S. intervention by joint action with major Latin American countries. Even though the plan promised to increase Mexico's prestige, Casasús, in contrast to his Chilean and Brazilian colleagues, rejected the idea, terming it vague and injurious to the interests of the smaller nations. As he commented to Mariscal, "it was not decorous to offer our share to [U.S.] foreign policy."[47] The creation of virtual spheres of secondary imperialism could give Mexico only the vacuous privilege of acting as Roosevelt's enforcer in the Caribbean. Mindful not to provoke unnecessary discord, however, Casasús declined to reiterate the Díaz Doctrine—a step that would otherwise have been appropriate at this point.[48]

But a compromise was on its way. Even if he would not be tied to the "big stick," Díaz had long realized the significance of cooperating with Roosevelt in some way. In 1905, the U.S. government, invoking the new corollary, had seized the customs house of the Dominican Republic. U.S. forces had begun to administer a protectorate over the island state. The heavily indebted Central American states might easily meet the same fate, unless such action could be circumscribed by international law. Roosevelt, for his part, had realized that while Díaz would not serve as his lackey in the Caribbean, Mexican policy goals in Central America were at least partially compatible with his own. The prevention of interstate war in Central America had become a key objective for both the Mexican and the U.S. governments, but for different reasons. Díaz desired peace because he was afraid of Guatemalan dominance and U.S. intervention; Roosevelt wanted peace because of the canal and the security of U.S. property.

The two leaders therefore became strange bedfellows in a quest for a common goal: keep the Porfiritos at peace. When the U.S. and Mexican governments mediated conflicts in Central America, they did so with the common goal of peace, and with the common assumption that the "backward" Porfiritos needed straightening out. Since Díaz opposed the establishment of a formal framework, the two leaders at first attempted to use personal diplomacy to that end.

The Beginnings of Co-Mediation

The Corinto agreements had not brought lasting peace to Central America. In early 1903, Zelaya and Regalado, under the cover of the Corinto agreement, had ganged up on Estrada Cabrera. As mentioned above, Díaz had restrained the two leaders when the U.S. government threatened to intervene. Later that same year, Regalado left the Salvadoran presidency; his successor, Pedro José Escalón, never stepped out of his shadow and was regarded as a weak leader by neighboring presidents. As a result, Estrada Cabrera, sensing opportunity, schemed to overthrow Escalón, while Regalado privately gathered up funds and supporters for a revolt against the Guatemalan executive. In 1904, the anti-Zelaya Manuel Bonilla became president of Honduras, which spawned a long period of tensions between Honduras and Nicaragua. War did not break out, but the failure of subsequent peace negotiations showed that no agreement among Central American leaders could contain the ambitions of Porfiritos, who saw the states over which they ruled as personal fiefs.[49]

The powder keg finally erupted in the spring of 1906. In May, Guatemalan exiles equipped and organized by Regalado threatened Guatemala from both Mexico and El Salvador. Right from the start, Estrada Cabrera implicated the Díaz regime. While Díaz claimed that he knew nothing about the exiles' activities in Chiapas, Estrada Cabrera used the opportunity to denounce what he saw as Mexican support for an invasion of Guatemala. In the words of Leslie Combs, the U.S. minister in Guatemala, "Mexico [desires] to . . . put in power an administration dependant [sic] upon her, and under her influence . . . instead of ours."[50] Also in May, a number of insurgents indeed entered Guatemala from Mexico, while the bulk of the revolutionaries prepared for battle in western El Salvador.[51]

Even though this was a glorious opportunity for Mexico to rid itself of Estrada Cabrera, Díaz decided to show that his "respect for international law" (read: his fears that the United States might come to Estrada Cabrera's assistance) exceeded his contempt for the Guatemalan executive.[52] Moreover, Díaz feared that the U.S. government would present the Monroe Doctrine as a subject of discussion at the forthcoming Third Inter-American Conference to be held at Rio de Janeiro.[53] Therefore, he approached the U.S. ambassador, David E. Thompson, and proposed his good offices. In particular, he offered to restrain Escalón, with whom he maintained cordial relations.[54] At last, Díaz and the State Department agreed on a concurrent course of action. While the governor of Chiapas concentrated the Guatemalan rebels in Soconusco, Díaz and U.S. Secretary of State Elihu Root cabled messages to Escalón and Estrada Cabrera urging both to remove their troops from the common border. Díaz also authorized the printing of articles in the loyal press deploring the unrest, and he rejected El Salvador's request for guns and "moral support" for a direct invasion of Guatemala.[55]

Díaz's stance was well chosen, as Estrada Cabrera's forces soon gained the upper hand.[56] Significantly for a long-term evaluation of Mexican policies, his actions also demonstrated that the Porfirians—at least in this instance—worried more about U.S. intercession and the effects of a potential general Central American war than about the rivalry with Guatemala.

These measures temporarily defused the crisis, although lasting peace could not result from a few friendly diplomatic notes. Escalón did not control the situation in his own country, and Estrada Cabrera and Bonilla massed troops at the Guatemalan-Honduran border. In July 1906, Salvadoran forces under the direction of a completely intoxicated Regalado invaded Guatemala. Even though Estrada Cabrera's forces repelled the incursion within a few days, killing Regalado in the process, the Guatemalan executive used the pretext to mobilize his army against Honduras and El Salvador. A full-scale war appeared imminent.

For the U.S. government, this crisis conjured up the nightmare of military conflicts close to the canal route—a problem that could be particularly serious if Great Britain chose to protect its Belize enclave at Guatemala's Caribbean coast. Yet Root did not want to act alone if the avenue of collective U.S.–Latin American action was available.[57] Therefore, he called upon Díaz's help in resolving the new crisis.

Aware of Estrada Cabrera's superior military capabilities, Díaz quickly acceded to the request.[58] A few days later, both governments had sent telegrams similar in content to Estrada Cabrera and Escalón, inviting the belligerents to a peace conference.[59] Díaz then arranged for an armistice. With a truce obtained, Mexico and the United States proceeded to lead the contestants to the negotiating table. On July 18, representatives of all Central American governments met with Gamboa, Combs, and William L. Merry, the U.S. minister to El Salvador, Costa Rica, and Nicaragua, aboard the cruiser *Marblehead* off the coast of El Salvador. Merry served in a dual capacity as U.S. mediator and delegate from Costa Rica.[60]

Gamboa soon showed that in contrast to the intentions of the State Department,[61] he did not intend to show merely a token representation at the conference. From beginning to end, as Combs later conceded, it was Gamboa, not he and the Guatemalan representatives, who set the agenda of the conference.[62] When Combs pressed for a settlement of past disputes, including compensations for the current one, Gamboa—who chaired the meeting due to his command of both Spanish and English—refused to allow any discussion of responsibility or fault for the present war. Gamboa also valiantly fought another clause in Combs's draft treaty: the delivery of all political refugees.[63] The Mexican delegate simply would not allow the joint peacekeeping effort to turn into a punitive action against El Salvador.[64] Gamboa also objected to Combs's and Merry's evident intention to negotiate a future role for the United States in keeping peace in Central America. In his view, "the people of El Salvador . . . would never consent to the interference of outsiders in their miseries."[65]

Gamboa did not find it easy to assert Mexican policy goals at the meeting, as Combs soon became irate about his apparent partiality in favor of El Salvador. At one point, Combs shouted "Mr. Gamboa, I am [sic] a short temper." Shortly thereafter, the Mexican minister walked out of the meeting and threatened to leave the conference.[66]

When morning came, however, Combs and the Guatemalan envoys had backed down from their position; Merry had sided with Mexico. Taking advantage of discord between the two U.S. representatives, Gamboa had successfully played the U.S. representatives off against each other.[67] As he later wrote in his report, Combs and Merry had once almost had a "serious altercation"[68] during the meeting. Therefore, Gamboa prevailed, and Combs finally deferred to his two colleagues. In the end, the delegates adopted a protocol calling for disarmament, peaceful resolution of conflicts, and withdrawal of troops from all borders. Guatemala, El Salvador, Honduras, and Costa Rica then signed a formal treaty in San José on September 24, 1906.[69] Only Zelaya demurred: the San José treaty allowed for (but did not prescribe) outside arbitration of disputes and thus demolished his Corinto framework.[70]

While both the U.S. government and the Díaz regime had attained most of their goals with the ambiguous resolution of the conflict, Estrada Cabrera had emerged the loser. El Salvador, Mexico's ally, emerged from the arbitration unscathed. Whereas the Mexican government received favorable reviews in the U.S. press,[71] Estrada Cabrera had not been able to extract advantage from a situation that might potentially have placed him—as the one who had been unjustly attacked—in a strong position vis-à-vis El Salvador. Even more importantly, the *Marblehead* mediation had not established a U.S. police function, and Gamboa had successfully opposed Roosevelt's efforts to make Mexico his handmaiden in Central America. The skill in Mexican diplomacy lay in finding compromises that furthered both Mexican and U.S. objectives.

In this effort, Gamboa had exploited one of the weaknesses of Roosevelt's "big stick" diplomacy. Hay's and Root's practice of sending to Latin America diplomatic representatives who had business connections to their host countries had revealed its drawbacks during the *Marblehead* conference. Both Combs and Merry were deeply involved in the economic affairs of the elites of the countries where they were accredited: naturally, they opposed each other over many matters discussed aboard the U.S. warship.[72]

The Central American crisis of 1906 is a good example of the significance of the international system in Mexican foreign policy. Rather than attempting to help bring down the Estrada Cabrera regime, which would have been a natural course of action given Mexican attitudes about the Guatemalan dictator, the Díaz government played the part of an honest broker in restoring peace in Central America. On the whole, Mexican policies had been motivated primarily by the desire to forestall through multilateral negotiation direct U.S. intervention in Central America.

Predictably, the San José treaty did not end the trouble in Central America. Zelaya refused to abide by the *Marblehead* protocol and the San José treaty, which he labeled as unwarranted U.S. interference.[73] This refusal to support the accords antagonized the other Central American leaders and especially Fernando Figueroa, the new Salvadoran president, and Honduran leader Manuel Bonilla.[74] Zelaya's ominous words indicated that his government might be the next one to stir up trouble.

Indeed, with Regalado's death, Central America had become a chessboard for a struggle between the region's foremost leaders and the powers behind them: Estrada Cabrera, a president despised by Mexico, and Zelaya, an anti-U.S. caudillo. This scenario made the motivations behind Roosevelt's and Díaz's policies even more different than before. Roosevelt wished to prevent interstate war because of the canal, European influence, and Zelaya's dominance. Díaz desired to forestall it with a view to his domestic political situation, potential U.S. intervention, and Estrada Cabrera's aims.

Díaz, Roosevelt, and the Guatemalan-Nicaraguan Rivalry

This setting played an integral role in the mediation of the next conflict. In January 1907, Zelaya sponsored a revolt against the anti-Zelaya Honduran president, Manuel Bonilla. With his troops victorious, Bonilla asked Zelaya for permission to pursue the rebels into Nicaragua, where they had sought refuge from his advancing armies. Zelaya refused, stating that he had a sufficient number of troops in the border region to take care of the insurgents.[75] As Bonilla knew that Zelaya had instigated the revolt, he ordered Honduran forces to cross the border, and he allowed Nicaraguan exile forces to train in Honduras. When Root pressured Zelaya to adjudicate the matter peacefully, the Nicaraguan refused to submit to arbitration unless a compensation for his country's losses during the conflict were fixed as the sole object of discussion.[76]

Frustrated with the ongoing warfare, the State Department called upon Mexico's help, this time to constrain Zelaya. Díaz at first hesitated, expressing his preference to have the conflict adjudicated by the Corinto tribunal.[77] Mexico, Díaz told Thompson, could never go beyond a policy of moral suasion, much less tolerate an armed intervention in Central America. In Mariscal's words, both countries ought "to let [the Central American countries] fight for a short while until they exhaust their energies so we can guide them later toward a conclusion."[78] When Root insisted on further steps, Mariscal asked the governments of Guatemala, El Salvador, and Costa Rica to mediate.[79]

Only when this effort failed did Díaz agree to join Roosevelt in sending telegrams urging peace to the two competing parties.[80] He had long dragged his feet on co-mediation; as Thompson had reported to Roosevelt, "any joint action with you would have to be politically advantageous for [him]."[81] Fearing that the State Department sought to punish Zelaya, Díaz had delayed joining the fray until the U.S. desire to intervene had become manifest.

Irrespective of the notes, peace was not to be had. Sensing an opportunity to remove Bonilla, Zelaya claimed that Nicaragua, "wronged and insulted" by the Honduran government, would accept nothing less than reparations.[82] On February 18, Nicaraguan forces invaded Honduras. The conflict soon spread beyond these two countries: both Estrada Cabrera and Salvadoran president Figueroa, whom the Guatemalan had helped into office after Regalado's death, aided Bonilla.[83]

With this scenario, real trouble loomed ahead for Mexico. At best, Mexico could hope that Zelaya would enthrone a faction friendly to him in Tegucigalpa. In that case, a greater U.S. role in Central America seemed assured, as the State Department was determined to prevent Zelaya from assuming isthmian leadership. At worst, Estrada Cabrera, Figueroa, and Bonilla might emerge victorious and topple Zelaya. Such a turn of events, while disposing of the immediate danger of U.S. intervention, made Guatemalan dominance in the area more likely. Díaz was thus forced to play a double game. Vis-à-vis the State Department, he acted in defense of Zelaya; in a private letter to the Nicaraguan, however, he counseled caution. While Díaz suggested to Thompson's chargé that Honduras withdraw its troops first, he intimated to Zelaya that only a removal of his armies from Honduras would bring about the end of hostilities.[84]

As the crisis progressed, the U.S. and Mexican governments found it hard to agree to a joint response to the widening conflict. When Assistant Secretary of State Alvey A. Adee called for U.S. and Mexican measures to prevent warfare rather than reacting to it, Mariscal disagreed.[85] At this time, the different opinions about Zelaya also manifested themselves: in Gamboa's view, Zelaya had become an important Mexican ally in Central America,[86] while Root viewed Zelaya as the chief cause of trouble. But at last, Roosevelt and Díaz agreed to send joint resolutions to all Central American presidents urging the cessation of hostilities. For a change, the Mexican government received the accolades of the clerical opposition newspaper, *El Tiempo,* which editorialized that its action had prevented U.S. intervention.[87]

This U.S.–Mexican intercession did not stop Zelaya. In mid-March, his army defeated Bonilla's forces, and on April 23, 1907, Honduran vice president Miguel Dávila proclaimed his own accession to the presidency. While the State Department at first refused to deal with the new Honduran government, Díaz implicitly recognized Dávila only one day later by cable.[88] The Honduran soon consolidated his power and threw his support behind Zelaya. Soon thereafter, the foreign ministers of El Salvador and Nicaragua signed a peace protocol.[89] Zelaya's victory dealt U.S. goals in Central America at least a minor blow and led to growing demands in Washington for a more assertive posture. But for the moment, there was little the U.S. government could do. Following Zelaya's victory, a tenuous stability prevailed on the isthmus until the summer.

In the meantime, Díaz had realized the importance of day-to-day negotiations with the U.S. State Department on the subject of Central America and other matters.[90] Enrique C. Creel, the new Mexican ambassador in Washington, was perfectly suited to arrange the U.S.–Mexican dialogue on Central America. The choice of Creel highlighted Díaz's continued practice of sending the most pro-Yankee diplomats as ambassadors to the United States during diplomatically delicate times. Born in the northern Mexican state of Chihuahua to a U.S. father and a Mexican mother, Creel was a bilingual *científico* with a cosmopolitan aura. He did poorly as governor of Chihuahua, a post to which he was elected with Díaz's help in the fall of 1907, but he certainly did well in working in accord with the U.S. government. Creel, in fact, proved too pro-American for Díaz; often, Mariscal discarded his dovish suggestions in favor of a less accommodating approach. Thus, while Creel never achieved Romero's stature within the Díaz regime, he offered the same advantages of working cordially with Root, understanding the U.S. government's point of view, and selling Mexican positions effectively in a difficult environment.

The Díaz regime so far had taken great care in mapping out with the U.S. government a joint Central American policy that would protect Mexican interests and not play into the hands of either Estrada Cabrera or Roosevelt. Díaz had not needed to commit his country legally to keeping the peace in Central America, yet Mexico's unofficial role had proven most effective. In particular, Zelaya's war against Honduras had proven a blessing in disguise, as Estrada Cabrera had lost a valuable ally in former president Bonilla. In part due to Mexican mediation, Zelaya had emerged unharmed from the affair, as peace had been restored before Estrada Cabrera could march his troops toward Nicaragua.

Nevertheless, several pitfalls threatened to unravel this favorable situation. Zelaya increasingly found himself under scrutiny by the State Department as one of the main troublemakers in the isthmus. In addition, Estrada Cabrera had gained control of the Salvadoran leadership. Most important, however, Díaz had allowed himself to be lured ever deeper into the Central American quagmire. One day, Root might demand more than just "moral suasion" from Mexico. Equally likely, any serious conflict between Mexico and Guatemala could upset the delicate balance between Mexican and U.S. interests in Central America. In April 1907, such a bilateral problem put Díaz's Central American strategy in serious jeopardy.

The Barillas Controversy: An Embarrassing Intermezzo

On April 7, 1907, two young Guatemalans stabbed former Guatemalan president Lisandro Barillas to death on a Mexico City street. Both the Mexican press and Mariscal were quick to blame the Estrada Cabrera regime.[91] The police soon apprehended the assassins, who testified that José María Lima and Onofre Bone, two military officers close to Estrada Cabrera, had commissioned and paid them to kill Barillas.

The murder of Barillas contained troubling political overtones. He had been one of the most prominent exiles in Mexico, an outspoken adversary of Estrada Cabrera and one of the leaders of the May 1906 revolt. Only a few days before his death, Barillas had talked to Thompson, expressing his allegiance to the idea of a Central American union led by Zelaya. Speaking in the name of a group of political exiles living in Mexico City, he had assured the Nicaraguan executive of his "unconditional support" for the plan.[92] Estrada Cabrera, who operated an extensive network of spies, no doubt was apprised of his rival's support for Zelaya and decided to remove him.

The case immediately turned into a major diplomatic crisis, as well as a conflict within the Díaz cabinet. Mariscal and Gamboa appeared

Ignacio Mariscal, Secretary of Foreign Relations, 1906
(Courtesy of the Archivo General de la Nación, Mexico City)

determined to obtain vengeance from Estrada Cabrera. The hawkish followers of Bernardo Reyes, desiring to see their man head an invasion army into Guatemala, advocated war.[93] But concerned about the impact of a meaningless showdown with Guatemala on Mexico's image abroad, the doves around Limantour argued for the use of the normal legal channels to expose the complicity of the Guatemalan government.[94] Against the advice of the doves, Mariscal asked for Lima's extradition to Mexico and Bone's presence at his trial as a witness.[95] The Foreign Secretary clearly hoped that the outcry over the affair would remove Estrada Cabrera from office, or at least provoke his complete diplomatic isolation. But the Guatemalan president quickly rejected Mariscal's ridiculous request. He pointed out that the extradition treaty protected each country's own nationals from delivery to another country; indeed, Estrada Cabrera would have placed himself in an untenable situation by agreeing to extradite one of his own generals. Prodded by a German diplomatic démarche, he did offer to try Lima in Guatemala. Mariscal refused and threatened to break relations unless Estrada Cabrera delivered both suspects.[96]

At this point in the controversy, it seemed that the hawks had gained the upper hand, as Díaz's cabinet came close to deciding on an invasion of Guatemala.[97] Mexico could count on the help of Zelaya, who apparently offered to attack Estrada Cabrera's forces if Mexico should go to war.[98] When the circle of ministers met again a few weeks later, however, the president threw his weight behind the doves. Díaz, who usually supported his Foreign Secretary on matters of foreign policy, deserted Mariscal on the advice of the General Staff, which deemed a military operation against Guatemala too costly and potentially counterproductive. Disappointed, Mariscal came close to resigning his post.[99] The Díaz regime then blew off some steam by authorizing the publication of a host of articles hostile to Estrada Cabrera in the Mexico City press and by lifting its supervision over Guatemalan exiles in Chiapas.[100] These public tirades against Estrada Cabrera constituted a last-ditch effort to salvage some measure of respectability from a "disastrous diplomatic defeat," which in the words of a prominent científico, Justo Sierra, had been due to Mariscal's and Díaz's combined 155 years of age.[101] Unable to get what it really wanted, the Mexican government had maneuvered Estrada Cabrera into a position in which he appeared the villain before the Mexican public.[102] This action, however, hardly controlled the damage.

Meanwhile, a near assassination further worsened Mexican-Guatemalan relations. After there had been an unsuccessful attempt on Estrada Cabrera's life, Guatemalan Foreign Minister Juan Barrios told Gamboa he had information that the Mexican legation housed some of the participants in the ambush.[103] Gamboa's response was vitriolic, inviting Barrios in unusually harsh language to search the legation in person.[104] Even though Barrios turned down Gamboa's not-so-kind invitation, relations between Mexico and Guatemala had sunk to a new low. Mariscal ordered Gamboa whisked off to El Salvador, whence he was soon recalled to Mexico City, which constituted an effective interruption of diplomatic ties.[105] Estrada Cabrera and Díaz moved troops to the border, and Díaz belatedly heeded Gamboa's advice, ordering his troops to remain in Chiapas even after the passing of the controversy. As Díaz told U.S. Ambassador David E. Thompson, he was still prepared for war if the Guatemalans fired the first shot.[106]

During the entire conflict, the State Department attempted to calm the waters. Root repeatedly addressed the Mexican ambassador, Enrique C. Creel, offering U.S. mediation of the controversy. Mariscal refused, asserting that Mexico would neither break relations nor engage in any other hostile demonstration against Guatemala.[107] But it was obvious that Washington had weighed in with the doves in the Díaz cabinet and had aided in the about-face of the Mexican government. The softer tones emanating from the Porfirians pleased the State Department and paved the way for negotiations on the subject of posting a unit of the U.S. National Guard at Eagle Pass, Texas, to help control anti-Díaz rebels in the border region.[108] When the smoke of the Barillas controversy had cleared, Root expressed his willingness "to contain Guatemala within the limits of justice."[109]

In general, though, U.S.–Mexican relations had cooled considerably, and much to Díaz's disadvantage. Mexican diplomacy, which had appeared so adroit in the *Marblehead* negotiations, suddenly looked impetuous and ill considered. Díaz had squandered much leverage in Central American affairs: his unduly menacing attitude toward Guatemala had called into question the rationality and reliability of Mexican diplomacy. The Barillas controversy helped set in motion a trend that progressively brought the United States and Mexico into conflicting postures over Central America, a development which could only harm the much weaker Mexican position.

At home, the incident damaged the Díaz regime as well. In the beginning, the government-subsidized press as well as the opposition papers had unanimously backed Díaz's position, even if some of them had advocated a rupture of diplomatic relations.[110] After Díaz's conversion from hawk to dove, however, *El Tiempo* and other opposition papers—in mild tones, of course—accused him of giving in to Uncle Sam and failing to defend Mexico's national honor.[111] The initial hard-line position had pleased many Mexican nationalists, and success would certainly have brought applause for Díaz. When he backed down in failure, however, all too apparently prodded by the United States, Díaz became the target of criticism from all quarters.

The Mexican government had indeed suffered a "disastrous diplomatic defeat." It remained to be seen whether the Díaz regime could regroup to play an effective role in the upcoming effort to create institutions which would allow the Central American countries to adjudicate the conflicts among themselves. But regardless of the outcome, the sting of the embarrassment over the Barillas affair was not likely to fade soon.

The Barillas controversy represented a momentary assertion of domestic and ideological considerations in Mexican foreign-policy formulation. Mariscal's jingoistic posture disregarded both Mexico's inability to force Estrada Cabrera to deliver the suspects and the rest of his country's foreign-policy agenda. Imperiling important negotiations with the U.S. State Department as well as Mexico's position in the Central American peace talks, Mariscal pretended to flog the wayward Porfirito who had shown the audacity to violate Mexican sovereignty in order to kill an adversary. In so doing, the Mexican government acted on its own instincts rather than in light of the international scene. Even though U.S. pressure ultimately helped soften its stance, the Díaz regime had demonstrated that U.S. influence was not always its chief concern in Central America.

Mexico and the 1907 Washington Conference

The cessation of hostilities in April 1907 proved to be merely the lull before the storm. Estrada Cabrera and Figueroa were awaiting an opportunity to topple the Dávila regime in Honduras. Meanwhile, Zelaya still was not satisfied with his own improved position. Whereas he had gained an ally in President Dávila, Figueroa and Estrada Cabrera, heads of the two most powerful and populous states in Central America, still remained his implacable enemies and would surely threaten his rule if the possibility arose.

But Zelaya soon gathered new hope. In May 1907, Washington S. Valentine, the president of the largest mining company in Honduras, told him that both Roosevelt and Díaz favored the "national reconstruction" of Central America under Zelaya's direction. Purporting to be Root's official representative, he claimed that neither the United States nor Mexico would oppose a Nicaraguan domination of El Salvador and Honduras.[112] Zelaya believed this rumor and decided to push his perceived advantage. In June, Nicaragua's only gunboat seized the Salvadoran port of Acajutla and unloaded one hundred supporters of Prudencio Alfaro, Zelaya's candidate for Figueroa's position.[113] This move, based on wholly false information about U.S. foreign policy, once again plunged Central America into war. While Salvadoran forces defeated the Alfaristas, Guatemalan troops and Honduran exiles marched up to threaten Dávila, and war preparations resumed all over Central America.[114]

Neither the U.S. State Department nor Díaz had an easy answer to the new turmoil, but it had become apparent that the two larger powers needed either to stay out of the trouble or assume a greater and more direct role in ensuring peace. In Root's own words: "The trouble is that there is no real controversy to be settled there. Zelaya is bent on conquest . . . Cabrera seems to be a cruel tyrant under whom the political activity of Guatemala is confined to assassination. . . . Nothing would be of real use except a long period of armed intervention that we cannot undertake. Failing that these half-civilized people will have to work out their own salvation."[115] Root's remarks pointed up the dilemma of U.S. foreign policy in Central America: the U.S. government needed peace in the area but would not yet proceed unilaterally to ensure it. The memorandum of a State Department aide best summed up the only possible solution to this conundrum: a peace conference that would make Mexico and the United States the mandatory arbiters of Central American disputes.[116]

But Díaz still adroitly refused to become a lackey of Yankee interests, as he would not sanction any legal obligation of the United States and Mexico to uphold peace. His ideal solution consisted in renewing the Corinto accords to comprise all five countries and to adjudicate disputes by majority vote among the Central American countries, except for matters affecting the "national honor." By July, both sides had managed to find an acceptable compromise: the two governments decided to sponsor a peace conference with the purpose of establishing a mandatory, all-isthmian arbitration apparatus similar to the board set up at Corinto. To initiate the peace process, Roosevelt and Díaz sent telegrams to stop the ongoing hostilities and procure the general assent of the Central American presidents to their mediation effort. The two presidents then sent out invitations to a peace conference to be held in the fall of 1907.[117] Root had prevailed with his advocacy of compulsory measures, but it would be the Central Americans themselves (and not the United States or Mexico) that would keep the Porfiritos in line.

The selection of the conference site resulted in a disappointment for Díaz, who had hoped to invite the five delegations to Mexico City.[118] It was known in Washington that Dávila and Zelaya had come to favor Mexico City as the location of the meeting. Roosevelt and Root concurred, but decided to ask the Central American presidents before making their views public.[119] This step doomed the Mexican hopes to host the conference. Predictably, Figueroa and Estrada Cabrera picked Washington; Costa Rica, for fear of offending the United States, tipped the balance in favor of the U.S. capital.[120] This vote for Washington indicated a pattern that presaged a potential problem for Mexico: since the Costa Rican government despised Zelaya, Estrada Cabrera and Figueroa could easily assemble a majority against the Zelaya-Dávila coalition.

From the U.S. point of view, though, not everything went smoothly, either. Fearing Zelaya's power, Root attempted to pre-empt negotiations among the isthmian countries prior to the conference by obtaining the signatures of Creel and the Central American representatives on a preliminary armistice protocol. But in October, Zelaya upped the ante: to Root's displeasure, he met with Dávila and Figueroa for secret talks at the Honduran port of Amapala. After an apparently harmonious meeting, the three leaders promised to "forget all past differences."[121] While the Díaz government welcomed any steps on the part of the Central American leaders to sort out their problems prior to the conference, a

Root aide expressed deep concern, seeing the anti-Zelaya majority of three versus two slip away. Now, he mused, Zelaya could obtain a plurality for his motions; even the passage of a proposal to unify the isthmus under nationalist Nicaraguan auspices appeared possible.[122]

That same month, Root's visit to Mexico provided an opportunity for the two cosponsoring governments to finetune their policies to the upcoming conference. But even as lavish celebrations were held in the secretary's honor as a show of U.S.–Mexican friendship and Root's support for the Díaz regime, his trip yielded little of substance. When Root suggested a future "pacifying" role for Mexico in Central America, Díaz maintained that Mexico had to look after its own interests first. Knowing that he would obtain no more support from either the president or Mariscal, Root approached Limantour, only to be rebuffed in equally certain terms.[123] No one close to Díaz—not even Ambassador Thompson—saw any virtue in the Mexican president exposing himself to great risks in both Mexican public opinion and Central America just to enforce "big stick" policies.

The volatile Central American scene created further difficulties. The Amapala pact notwithstanding, Estrada Cabrera and Figueroa continued to plot a coup in Honduras, and Zelaya still trained Salvadoran exile forces. In the estimation of one of the members of Mariscal's staff, Estrada Cabrera and Zelaya intended to use the Washington Conference solely as a respite to prepare future attacks on El Salvador and Honduras.[124]

But finally, the opening day of the conference had arrived. Mexico was obviously the weaker partner in the negotiations, and Mariscal had assumed a realistic position toward the conference. As one of his aides instructed Creel prior to the first session: "The United States has imposed upon itself a heavy load of responsibility. . . . But [it] has elements . . . that Mexico cannot count on; it exerts unconditional influence over Guatemala, which is something Mexico will never accomplish. It thus seems inevitable that [the U.S. government] will assume the more important . . . role in the conference."[125] As a result, Creel allowed U.S. envoy William I. Buchanan to play the role of the principal public host of the conference and limited his own role to behind-the-scenes maneuvering.

Given the difficulties in assuring peace in a state system characterized by feuding personal ambitions, the participants in the Washington Conference accomplished the task they had set for themselves. After long deliberations in which Mexico and the United States took a seemingly passive part,[126] the conference produced a viable attempt to submit Central American disputes to arbitration. In resemblance to the postulates of the Díaz Doctrine, the delegates created the Court of Central American Justice, to which all pending questions had to be submitted. Mexico and the United States agreed to act merely as guarantors of the agreement itself, declining to enforce alone or jointly the decisions of the court. The treaties also committed their countries to a general amnesty, disarmament, the concentration of militant exiles, and a policy of nonrecognition toward any isthmian government assuming power by force.[127]

Neither the U.S. nor the Mexican delegation left the conference with empty hands. The U.S. government succeeded in its larger goals, but had to settle for a framework that did not allow for its own interference. The conference had established a binding arbitration apparatus for Central American conflicts—an apparatus that might work in keeping the peace while obviating U.S. intervention. The delegates had also defeated a motion that would have furthered Nicaraguan ambitions: Zelaya had authored a proposal to declare the unification of the isthmus. After Buchanan had discreetly discouraged the delegates from approving the idea, the majority had rejected the plan.[128] Creel, never a great fan of Zelaya's, had made no attempt to save the motion.

But Creel had also attained Mexico's major policy objectives. Even though a framework of mandatory arbitration was in place, the United States and Mexico had not committed themselves to enforcing any of its verdicts. The amnesty provision promised to free hundreds of Mexican prisoners held in Guatemalan jails. Moreover, Creel, Buchanan, and Zelaya's delegates had foiled a Guatemalan attempt to establish a Central American defensive alliance. As Creel perceived it, Estrada Cabrera could have used such an agreement in the case of conflict with Mexico to gain the support of the other four countries.[129] In addition, Creel had helped water down a plan that would have guaranteed Honduras a special neutrality status enforceable by U.S. and Mexican military intervention. Upon the insistence of Creel and several other delegates, a motion to strike the enforcement clause had passed. This action had left only an empty resolution to guarantee the inviolability of Honduran territory.

At the close of the conference, Creel had reason to express thorough satisfaction with the results. The newly created Court of Central American Justice finally constituted the arbitration apparatus long sought by Porfirian diplomacy. Equally significant, the Washington Conventions theoretically diminished the likelihood of future trouble, since all Central American states had signed the treaties. Thus, the treaties promised to reduce the probability of U.S. intervention in Central America. Finally, Díaz had acquired prestige in the area without committing himself to wielding the big stick jointly with the United States. He had not tied his hands to a venture that might drag him into military intervention in Central America. As Creel reported, "none of the agreements contain any obligation for Mexico, and there is nothing in the treaties that might bring us complications in the future."[130]

The Washington Conference was a watershed event in Mexican policy toward Central America. The conference greatly enhanced Díaz's prestige as an important international figure, even at a time when Díaz faced increasing difficulties at home. But as long as Estrada Cabrera and Zelaya slugged it out in El Salvador and Honduras, nagging problems remained. The Porfirians would go no further than this conference in the matter of co-mediation. They could not accommodate the U.S. government further without violating their own policy goals or giving the impression that they were abetting U.S. aggression in Central America. Thus, the Conference was at once the high-water mark and the beginning of the end of U.S.–Mexican cooperation in Central American matters.

In Washington, Mexico and the United States had reached a compromise congruent with increasingly divergent goals. The Díaz regime, wary of commitments that might entangle it further in the web of Yankee diplomacy, had helped end a war potentially harmful to U.S. economic and strategic interests. In return, the State Department, ever more eager to enforce Mexico's and its own role as peacekeepers, had acquiesced in a formal, all-isthmian framework that held few guarantees for success.

Until 1907, Díaz had successfully balanced his goals in the isthmus against the differing opinions within the Mexican governing elite and against U.S. policies. He had taken a prudent stance against making Mexico a regional policeman by Roosevelt's grace. Aboard the *Marble-*

head, Gamboa had been successful in halting both Guatemalan ambitions and a U.S. scheme to bind Mexico to mandatory mediation. During the wars of 1907, Mexican policies had contributed to strengthening Zelaya at the expense of Díaz's enemy, Estrada Cabrera. At the Washington Conference, Creel's diplomacy had contributed to the creation of an arbitration apparatus that would help prevent the landing of U.S. ground forces for at least five more years. In the lone setback, the Barillas affair had weakened Díaz's status as a fair arbiter in Central America.

There was little reason, however, to rest on these modest accomplishments. The co-mediation had pointed up the narrow limits within which Díaz could assert Mexican interests in the shadow of the United States. As a result, the Porfirians could not expect their efforts to elicit a supportive response in increasingly nationalist Mexico. To make matters worse, the workability of the Washington accords had yet to be tested. The peace framework had not definitively resolved the rivalry between Estrada Cabrera and Zelaya; nor had it tied Uncle Sam's hands in Central America. What would Díaz do if a U.S. president called for more assertive steps in case of its failure? And what would he do if Mexicans, wary of U.S. commercial and political expansion, clamored for a more assertive policy in Central America?

4 Díaz Confronts U.S. Intervention in Nicaragua, 1908–1910

The United Mexican States are the advance sentinels of Latin America and guard their northern frontier, the plow in one hand and the rifle in the other.

Mexican diplomat José M. Gutiérrez Zamora, Honduras, 1910

While the United States and Mexico had successfully worked together to resolve the Central American conflicts of 1906 and 1907, the following years saw this cooperation wrecked. Conscious of its ever growing power in the Caribbean, the U.S. government increasingly ignored Mexican advice on its isthmian policy. It embraced aggressive initiatives toward the Nicaraguan government of José Santos Zelaya, and ultimately, it helped force the Zelayistas out of power. Díaz, on the other hand, had his own reasons for tearing down the façade of cooperation: faced with growing discontent at home, he could no longer countenance in any way U.S. interference in Central America. Therefore, he openly challenged the United States on the Nicaragua issue and even gave asylum to Zelaya and his handpicked successor.

Why would the Díaz regime oppose U.S. foreign policy at the time that the Porfirian system started to crumble? After all, the Porfiriato needed U.S. support to rein in the activities of Mexican *revoltosos* north of the border. Conceivably, Díaz might well have decided to give the U.S. government a free hand in Central America in order to secure its cooperation in this vital matter.

Díaz had good reasons for terminating his cooperation with the United States in Central America. Facing a growing groundswell of xenophobia, the Porfirian regime could no longer walk the tightrope between the United States and Mexican public opinion. Within the Díaz cabinet, hawkish elements demanded an assertive foreign policy, especially at a time that U.S. policy toward Central America took on an ever more menacing hue. In short, Díaz could no longer co-mediate regional disputes without abetting aggressive U.S. policies and further alienating his domestic supporters.

The Crisis of the Porfiriato

The crisis of the Díaz regime was important in accounting for this shift in Mexican policies. As the previous instances of co-mediation had demonstrated, Díaz's ambivalent position between cultivating U.S. goodwill and responding to Mexican nationalist sentiments had always been a risky one in terms of domestic political benefit. But as a closer look at the crisis of the Porfiriato reveals, Díaz's increasing difficulties at home made a Mexican position independent from that of the U.S. government ever more important.

The 1906 miners' strike at Cananea, Sonora, and the 1907 massacre of protesting textile workers at Río Blanco, Veracruz, had been ominous portents. After more than thirty years, the Díaz coalition was coming apart at the seams. Political blunders and broken promises mobilized local, regional, and ultimately even metropolitan elites against the septuagenarian dictator. Meanwhile, a worsening crisis created new adversaries and further angered old ones. By May 1911, Díaz found himself alienated from his erstwhile supporters and facing a gathering social upheaval.

Díaz himself was responsible for losing some of his closest political allies. Through the now famous interview with U.S. journalist James Creelman published in *Pearson's Magazine* in March 1908, Díaz had turned Mexico's relatively tranquil political scene into a bustling beehive of activity.[1] Intending his remarks for consumption of a U.S.—not a Mexican—audience, Díaz had said: "I retire when my present term of office ends, and I shall not serve again. . . . I welcome an opposition party in the Mexican Republic. . . . This nation is ready for her ultimate life of freedom."[2]

While Díaz's statements were greeted with applause in the U.S. press, they backfired at home. Foreign investors, many of whom knew that Díaz had not groomed a successor, suddenly hesitated to pour additional funds into Mexico. What was more important, Díaz encouraged the aspirations of several presidential hopefuls, individuals who had long awaited a sign that the aging dictator was loosening his grip. Brimming with hope, these younger politicians wasted no time organizing presidential campaigns. It was no surprise that these leaders opposed Díaz's decision to break his word and run for one more term in 1910.

Díaz made an additional mistake that probably cost him as dearly as his broken promise: he alienated Bernardo Reyes. When Díaz announced that he would seek another presidential term, the Reyistas focused their attention on the post of vice president, held by the hated científico Ramón Corral. Slighted by Díaz in the 1904 elections, Reyes had pinned his hopes on the 1910 ballot. Yet, fearful that the popular Reyes would become too strong as vice president, Díaz opted to continue with the lackluster Corral. This decision alienated many influential northerners, who felt marginalized politically by the científico/metropolitan clique in Mexico City. To add insult to injury, Díaz installed científico governors in the states of Chihuahua and Coahuila—governors who did not cooperate with the established elites.[3] In the process, the president made enemies out of dissidents such as Coahuilan landowners Francisco I. Madero and Venustiano Carranza, who demanded a clean political process to gain entry into the country's political elite. In his favoring of the científicos, Díaz brushed aside one of the strategic groups that had previously provided him with loyal support.

From outside the Porfirian circle, other enemies loomed on the horizon. The Partido Liberal Mexicano of the Flores Magón brothers had formulated a new brand of liberalism, an ideology that sought guarantees for the victims of modernization and better conditions for Mexican workers. The unprecedented brutality with which the Porfirians confronted the PLM and other opposition movements signaled that Díaz was no longer able to use co-optation skillfully in order to defuse a crisis.

A serious economic crisis confounded this precarious political situation. By depressing the price of Mexico's principal exports, the global economic slump of 1907–8 led to a precipitous decline in real wages and to widespread unemployment, particularly among the middle sectors. It also accelerated the displacement of Mexican white-collar employees by European immigrants. Meanwhile, Mexican capitalists found themselves strapped for credit.

Coming on the heels of growing labor unrest, the crisis increased economic nationalism, particularly among Mexican entrepreneurs and white-collar employees, who saw their livelihood threatened by U.S. economic activity. These economic nationalists were not going to be satisfied with gestures of political independence and diplomatic gallantry. Focused on a lack of economic opportunity for Mexicans, economic nationalism linked up with the lack of political opportunity to bring much of the country's upper and middle classes into irreconcilable opposition to the Díaz regime.[4]

Economic nationalism, the determination to gain a measure of national control over a country's key economic sectors, was not new on the Mexican ideological scene. Lucas Alamán had warned against the dangers of U.S. commercial expansion, and Sebastián Lerdo de Tejada had refused to seek U.S. investments actively. Porfirian diplomacy had always embraced limits on the political power accorded to foreign investors: at three Inter-American meetings, Mexico had emerged as one of the principal supporters of the Drago and Calvo doctrines.[5] When unemployed members of the middle class and nearly bankrupt entrepreneurs shouted "México para los mexicanos," then, they drew upon well-established precedents. Angry at a system in which their country seemed subject to the world economy, many economic nationalists demanded a government that would intervene actively to protect their interests. In the wake of crisis, the notion of the state as a "night watchman" of the economy lost favor with the Mexican business community. As a consequence, twentieth-century economic nationalists sought a state agenda to protect Mexican jobs at the possible cost of alienating foreign investors.

Needless to say, Díaz could not count on the popular sectors to save him from the wrath of those members of the upper and middle classes whom he had alienated over the last few years. To the contrary, as the PLM's activities showed, the most important opposition to the Díaz regime came from marginalized Mexicans. In Cananea and in Río Blanco, workers had struck to protest miserable wages and living conditions—a situation that only got worse following the 1907 recession. The suppression of both strikes had demonstrated that Díaz would respond ruthlessly to lower-class challenges to Mexico's social order. By 1910, peasants in the state of Morelos were beginning to gather around the figure of Emiliano Zapata to demand the return of village lands taken by the growing sugar economy of that region. Thus, by 1910, aside from the científicos and the army, few Mexicans would stand up for a regime widely perceived as tyrannical and unjust.

As a final difficulty, Díaz found that his regime had all but lost its luster in the U.S. press. While he had long been able to rely on an intricate web of Mexican consuls, confidential agents, and U.S. businessmen to nurture a positive image among the public north of the border, the crisis in Mexico made all three of these support groups less effective. Mexico's consular representatives had their hands full monitoring the numerous anti-Porfirian groups north of the border. Many of Díaz's confidential agents now deserted the regime, becoming involved with these opposition groups and feeding to the press information critical of the Porfiriato. U.S. entrepreneurs, jittery about Mexico's future, expressed mixed feelings about what once had been a safe and sound investment target. Finally, the international press was itself forced to come to terms with the deepening crisis of the Porfiriato. When John Kenneth Turner published his controversial exposé, *Barbarous Mexico,* in 1910, this stinging indictment of the Porfiriato fell on a well-laid ground of U.S. popular opposition to the Díaz government. While the administration of Theodore Roosevelt's successor, William H. Taft, could ponder no alternative to the continuation of the Porfiriato, this outcry considerably weakened its resolve to prop up the Díaz regime.

All of these issues spelled serious trouble for the Díaz government. In 1876, Díaz himself had led his coup against Lerdo with the words "effective suffrage, no reelection." In 1878, he had satisfied Mexican nationalists by procuring U.S. recognition of his regime without giving up a square inch of territory. In 1896, Díaz had repudiated U.S. interventionism to the acclaim of many members of his domestic coalition. By 1908, however, his oligarchy that had ruled Mexico for thirty-two years was crumbling. When nationalist sentiments linked up with economic failure and social injustice, Díaz's dilemma of choosing between friendship with the United States and assuaging his domestic opposition narrowed his radius of action to such an extent that don Porfirio alienated his remaining supporters.

It is, then, hardly astonishing that Díaz, besieged from all sides, made one last attempt to shore up his prestige. As a first step, the old dictator moved to dissociate himself from the policies of the U.S. State Department.

The End of Co-Mediation

In early 1908, Mexican and U.S. consuls on Guatemala's Atlantic coast reported the fitting out of a filibustering expedition. Led by the U.S. "General" Lee Christmas and aided by Estrada Cabrera, it sought to install former president Manuel Bonilla as Honduran president.[6] Roosevelt and Díaz immediately responded to the threat: both leaders dispatched gunboats to Central American waters, and a U.S. consul warned Christmas that the State Department would not tolerate a coup in Honduras. In addition, Díaz exhorted Figueroa to respect the Washington treaties, which forbade giving support to Central American rebel movements.[7] It had become clear that the agreements signed in Washington had failed to alleviate the fundamental discord among Central American leaders.

The biggest flaw of the new treaty system was the partisan nature of the Court of Central American Justice, called into existence to adjudicate interstate disputes. Each of the five isthmian leaders had named a supposedly independent delegate: but as the court's future decisions would reveal, the delegates uncritically defended the interests of their home governments.[8] Even before the court's inauguration in May 1908, both Estrada Cabrera and Zelaya did some simple math: each leader could count on two votes, with the Salvadoran delegate voting with his Guatemalan colleague, and the Honduran representative joining Zelaya's appointee. The Costa Rican justice was somewhat of a wild card; but previous difficulties between the Nicaraguan and Costa Rican governments suggested that he would usually vote against Zelaya. That fact would be borne out in the court's very first decision: despite significant evidence to the contrary, the justices, by a three-to-two vote, acquitted the governments of El Salvador and Guatemala from the charge of plotting to overthrow Dávila.[9]

Ironically, then, the arbitration mechanism increased the likelihood of future conflicts. Estrada Cabrera knew his government probably would not lose before the court, a fact that made him more reckless in his attempts to overthrow the Dávila regime in Honduras. Zelaya knew he had to change the court to win; therefore, he supported rebels in El Salvador and Costa Rica.[10]

These stirrings promised to bring no great harm as long as Díaz and Roosevelt cooperated; and it seemed that both governments still desired to cooperate even after the Washington Conference. Very soon, however, Mexican diplomacy changed in tone, and not just in response to provocation on the part of the U.S. government. By mid-1908, it had become obvious that the crisis of the Porfirian regime compelled Díaz to distance himself from any semblance of cooperation with the United States.

The Díaz regime's new, more contrarian attitude first became manifest in its March 1908 response to Root's careless remarks before the Foreign Relations Committee of the U.S. House of Representatives. In this speech, Root had stated that the Central American countries were "stepping into the position that Cuba has traditionally been regarded as occupying toward the United States." Mexico, he had hoped, would help him enforce the treaties, if necessary, by military intervention.[11] Needless to say, these comments did not play well south of the border: in Mexico, the press greeted Root's statement with condemnation.[12]

Reading the public mood correctly, Mariscal rebutted Root in a statement to the Mexico City press. While emphasizing Mexico's support for "pacific measures," he offered his own interpretation of the Secretary's remarks, stating that nothing in them indicated "an attitude which would . . . threaten the sovereignty or the independence of the Central American republics." Root's words, he said, had referred to the growing commerce between the U.S. and the isthmus rather than to any political involvement. Mariscal added that the United States could not expect help from Mexico in the protection of its "material interests": "In this Mexico is wholly disinterested except insofar as it affects Guatemala. . . . We are not materially interested in four of these nations . . . but of course we shall always retain a moral interest in the situation. . . . In Guatemala, however, . . . we are interested both materially and morally, owing to the large number of our citizens resident there and the considerable interests which are held by some of them."[13] With these superficially cordial words, Mariscal distanced himself from Root's announcement of a more interventionist policy. Just as Díaz had criticized the Monroe Doctrine in 1896 by re-interpretation, Mariscal's paraphrase issued a subtle warning not to count on Mexican support for a military intervention in Central America.

Moreover, what looked like a retreat from the four eastern Central American republics actually amounted to an assertion of the country's parity with the United States: the Mexican chancellery claimed to be entitled to intervention wherever *its* citizens lived. The import of this statement was enormous indeed. While Mariscal recognized a U.S. right to interfere on behalf of its citizens, he implicitly demanded the same right regarding Mexican nationals living in the United States. His response to Root thus served as a platform to demand the strict application of U.S. neutrality laws toward Mexican dissidents—a critical issue at a time when opponents of the Díaz regime used the United States as a sanctuary.[14]

Mariscal's remarks achieved the desired effect. The Mexican official press freely exploited them to show off Díaz's independence in foreign-policy matters. The Porfirian regime once again had been successful in appropriating a U.S. initiative to its own benefit. Coming on the heels of the publication of the Creelman interview, the incident proved a timely windfall for the Díaz regime.

Root, however, well aware that Mariscal had managed to take advantage of his declaration, had not given up hope of involving Mexico in intervention in Central America. He proceeded with an attempt to bind Díaz informally to a commitment to prevent new conflicts in Central America. Confident of Díaz's traditional support for symbolic moves, he planned a friendly but definite reminder of the joint presence of the United States and Mexico in Central American affairs. In March 1908, Root asked Ambassador Creel to accompany U.S. envoy William Buchanan on a goodwill tour through the isthmus. The purpose of the trip, Root stated, was to thank the Central American governments for their support of the treaties and for their appreciation of the role of the Mexican and U.S. delegations in the peacekeeping process.[15]

Creel immediately grasped the larger ramifications of this idea. Root intended to confer upon Mexico and the United States the de facto role of peacekeepers in the region. The more the Díaz regime lent itself to symbolic gestures of support for the treaties, the more it seemed to help uphold them with the United States. Creel gambled for time, citing a lack of instructions, in order to confer with Mariscal about the best way of dealing with Root's initiative.[16] Word from Mexico came three days later, when Díaz told U.S. Ambassador David E. Thompson that his regime would only send a representative if all of the Central American states requested such a mission.[17] Mexico's newspapers agreed: what was the purpose, one of Mexico City's puro newspapers asked sarcastically, in sending a delegation to thank the Central American governments for their thanking Mexico and the United States for their peace-keeping efforts?[18]

When Root persisted, Díaz thought up a plethora of excuses. As he explained to Thompson, the mission would imperil the life of the Mexican emissary, as they "believed Guatemala capable of everything wrong." When the U.S. ambassador reported to Díaz that four of the Central American ministers in Washington had given oral assurances that the mission would be most welcome, the Mexican leader insisted on a written invitation from all five presidents. In addition, Creel, who served concurrently as governor of Chihuahua, claimed that he could not afford to leave his native state without risking "serious upheavals in public administration." As a final reason for rejecting the initiative, Díaz asserted that he saw little value in a mission to Central America at a time when both countries were establishing new legations in the region.[19]

None of these pretexts reflected the true motive of the Mexican government: amidst the controversy surrounding the Creelman interview, the Porfirians feared criticism at home for being a partner of Uncle Sam. Díaz realized that Root would be offended if he refused to honor his request; but for the moment at least, he feared his domestic enemies more than the disappointment of the U.S. Secretary of State. Therefore, he chose rather flimsy excuses to conceal his real concerns about the goodwill trip. The negative reception of Root's initiative in the Mexico City press had only stiffened the Porfirians' resolve.[20]

Finally, however, Mariscal and Root found a mutually acceptable compromise. Rather than sending Creel on a tour through all of the five Central American countries, Díaz agreed to send a representative to the opening day of the court. Thus, the Díaz government could posture as one of the founders of the Central American peace agreement, not as a marionette dragged along by Uncle Sam on his "big stick" demonstration tour through the isthmus.[21] It had also averted more serious ill will between the United States and Mexico. Two months later, Díaz went one step further toward meeting Root halfway. In response to Salvadoran and Guatemalan preparations to aid another coup against Dávila, he sent two Mexican gunboats to Central American waters as a demonstration of his country's presence in the isthmus.[22] But if it seemed that Díaz had lost his resolve not to cooperate with aggressive U.S. policies in the isthmus, such was hardly the case. The gunboat expedition was directed against Díaz's enemies in Central America rather than his friends, and thus furthered Mexican aims.

Nevertheless, the growing antagonism between Mexico and the United States had merely been ignored. For the first time, the Mexican government had refused to join in a policy of moral suasion and to make a symbolic gesture of U.S.–Mexican unity. Díaz's stance on the Creel-Buchanan trip had underscored his opposition to the State Department's course of action in Central America and his nervousness about Mexican public opinion.

Meanwhile, Mexican diplomats were thinking about a course of action that would reflect an independent posture in Central America. Many officials stationed in the isthmus recommended using the numerous Central American exiles in Mexico as a point of leverage against Figueroa and Estrada Cabrera. For the first time, some of them even advocated establishing social and cultural ties with the Central American peoples rather than with their governments. In the words of the Mexican minister to El Salvador: "Whenever there exist ample bonds among peoples, as those between Mexicans and Central Americans, racial instincts and mutual sympathy often assert themselves over the precepts of international law. . . . When a [diplomatic] representative cannot achieve at the same time the goodwill of a people and that of an arbitrary and unpopular government, he has to give preference to the former, since all governments pass, while the peoples remain."[23]

U.S.–Mexican cooperation in Central America, which had proven successful in meeting both countries' policy goals, had gone sour in the last year of the Roosevelt presidency. In previous years, the State Department had shown itself amenable to suggestions from Mexico, and Root had often volunteered to exert pressure on Estrada Cabrera, who had fathered so many schemes to stir up trouble in the isthmus. In 1908, however, the U.S.–Mexican dialogue had begun to unravel: Díaz grew ever more conscious of domestic criticism of his foreign policies, and therefore ever less willing to accommodate Root's goals. The Roosevelt administration, on the other hand, while it still upheld a cordial tone in dealing with Mexico, had realized Díaz's unwillingness to cooperate further. While U.S. power in Central America had increased over the past years, the teetering Porfiriato, which only yesterday had looked like a valuable partner in the region, was turning into a cranky ally and a potential rival.

But Root, at least, had deemed Mexican participation indispensable for his Central American policy. As he told Roosevelt's successor, William H. Taft: "Mexico is worth more than twenty Central Americas, and we should not forget it is the golden chain that links us to Latin America."[24] The fact that Taft never heeded Root's advice contributed in no small part to a further deterioration in relations between the United States and Mexico.

Confronting Dollar Diplomacy in Nicaragua

With the advent of the Taft administration in March 1909, cooperation became even less likely. The new U.S. government never found the cordial tone that had marked U.S.–Mexican relations under Roosevelt. In addition, Taft soon launched an effort to rein in Mexico's only ally in Central America, the anti-Yankee Zelaya. While the crisis of the Porfiriato had prompted Díaz to edge away from the co-mediation effort, Taft's aggressive policies brought the cooperation to a definitive end.

Apart from differences in style, the new, less friendly U.S. attitude toward both Zelaya and Díaz must be understood in terms of "dollar diplomacy," an effort to merge strategic goals and foreign economic policy. Following the Open Door initiatives in China, the Roosevelt administration had actively begun to encourage and protect U.S. investment in Latin America. This trend accentuated itself during Roosevelt's final years in office. As U.S. capitalists doubled their holdings in the area during the 1900–8 period, the State Department placed more emphasis on acting as a promotional and protective agency for U.S. investors.

The growth of U.S. investment and the intensification of Great Power rivalry on a global scale soon required a reassessment of the function of U.S. diplomacy in economic expansion—a reassessment that the new U.S. president translated into a new approach toward Latin America. While Roosevelt and Root had frequently cautioned entrepreneurs not to count on U.S. protection in case of disputes with the host countries, Taft considered U.S. capital a strategic asset in the American hemisphere. "Substituting dollars for bullets," Taft stated emphatically, "appeals alike to idealistic humanitarian sentiments, to the dictates of sound policy and strategy, and to legitimate commercial aims."[25] With this rhetoric, Taft had changed Roosevelt's corollary: rather than bluntly warning the Latin Americans to prevent conditions that would invite European intervention, the new president advocated using economic means to reach political aims.

Thus, dollar diplomacy pursued strategic and commercial goals at the same time. It sought to discourage European military expeditions to enforce debt collection; it attempted to establish U.S. supervision of the troubled finances of some of the Latin American countries; and it was designed to help U.S. investors abroad. Whereas the United States had sought an open door in East Asia, it attempted to close the door in its own hemisphere.

The shift to this new diplomacy, prepared by Root and consummated by his successor, the brash corporation lawyer Philander C. Knox, profoundly affected U.S. policies toward both Mexico and Central America. By inserting itself as a player in agreements concluded between Latin American governments and U.S. businesses, the State Department committed itself to safeguarding the resulting contracts. As a consequence, it frequently intervened in disputes between the parties and often used various degrees of diplomatic pressure to act on behalf of its clients. Ranging from personal efforts of U.S. consular officers to military intervention, dollar diplomacy required a continuous interference with the internal affairs of Mexico and Central America. This effort created potential problems for the Porfirians: as we have seen, Díaz attempted to counterbalance U.S. investments with European funds.[26]

In four of the five isthmian countries, dollar diplomacy initially did not confront significant opposition. The venal Estrada Cabrera continued to welcome U.S. foreign investments, but he balked at U.S. attempts to assume responsibility over his country's finances in the pattern of the protectorate over the Dominican Republic.[27] Honduras's Dávila had the same problem: as a consequence of his regime's disastrous financial management, his country found itself the target of another U.S. push to impose a Dominican solution on a Central American country. In the words of a German diplomat, U.S. investors "swallowed up" Costa Rica; with its finances sound, however, the country (like El Salvador) managed to steer clear of U.S. efforts to intervene.[28]

Zelaya's Nicaragua was a different story. As early as 1908, U.S. officials had portrayed Zelaya as the source of trouble in Central America, finding cause for alarm in his most trifling moves. When Zelaya met with Costa Rican president Cleto González Víquez in January 1908, a U.S. consul in Nicaragua speculated on the prospect of his assembling a regional coalition against Guatemala.[29] By late 1908, the U.S. minister to Nicaragua had resigned from his post after a stay of only three months, citing the "wholly false" treatment he claimed the Zelaya government had accorded him.[30] His successor inundated Knox with an avalanche of dispatches reporting exaggerated as well as imagined "abuses" of U.S. citizens and the Conservative opposition. Moreover, both Root and Knox, as we have seen, resented Zelaya's meddling in the internal affairs of El Salvador and Costa Rica.[31]

Zelaya's response to the global economic crisis of 1907–8 also accounted for much of this shift in U.S. attitudes. The recession hit Nicaragua hard, worsening its balance-of-payments deficit and bringing its central bank to the brink of default. Zelaya now had to choose between imploring the United States for help and seeking loans from European creditors. To his own eventual detriment, he negotiated a loan of over a million pounds sterling with the British Ethelburga syndicate. With the Ethelburga loan, Zelaya showed that he opposed one of the cornerstones of dollar diplomacy: the U.S. desire to replace European credit with U.S. funds. In Knox's view, Zelaya strove too aggressively for a balance of investments in Nicaragua.[32]

More bothersome yet to U.S. business lobbyists close to the U.S. legation in Managua and the State Department, Zelaya also abandoned his laissez-faire approach toward concessions granted to foreign investors. He insisted that all foreign companies fulfill their obligations with his government rather than exploit the concessions to their own benefit. Knox particularly resented Zelaya's dragging his heels on the claims of the George D. Emery Company, a U.S. lumber company whose concession the Nicaraguan government had canceled in 1906.[33] Zelaya had opposed another goal of dollar diplomacy—his attitude toward the Emery claim revealed that he would not budge in defending Nicaraguan national sovereignty against U.S. intervention. Knox's personal business connections help explain why the Emery matter was particularly upsetting to him: the law firm in which he had been a partner prior to his appointment as Secretary of State represented a mining company with claims against the Nicaraguan government.[34]

If this trouble with the U.S. government was bad enough for Zelaya, the fact that he faced increasing opposition in Nicaragua was worse.

Zelaya's rule had become tyrannical: by early 1909, not only the opposition Conservatives desired to unseat him but also the more pro-U.S. elements of his ruling Liberal party. Therefore, Zelaya felt increasingly pressured: the triad of U.S. diplomacy, domestic opposition, and Estrada Cabrera was too much for his government.

But initially, even the hawkish Knox was reluctant to exploit this advantage alone. Hoping for help from other quarters, and unaware of Mexico's strong opposition to U.S. intervention in Central America, he resolved to find out whether he could count on Mexican support for weakening Zelaya. Only one week into office, Knox told Mexican ambassador Francisco León de la Barra that the Nicaraguan was planning "warlike activities" against El Salvador and Costa Rica. He also reminded León de la Barra of the "moral right" of the United States and Mexico to enforce the Washington Conventions.[35] In response, León de la Barra made a serious mistake: without having been thusly instructed, he told a Knox aide that only the "virtual elimination" of Zelaya would help the U.S. government reach its goals in Nicaragua.[36]

Unfortunately for Mexican diplomacy, Knox misunderstood this statement as denoting Díaz's acquiescence in U.S. aggression against Zelaya. He inquired if Mexico would support him in his plan to establish a financial supervisory board for Honduras, which once again had defaulted on its foreign debt. Then he suggested something completely unpalatable to Díaz: a new Central American peace conference to be held without Nicaragua.[37]

As might be expected, the Díaz regime responded coolly to Knox's initiatives. Mariscal refused to use the "moral right," which could in no way be inferred from the text of the Washington Conventions, for anything other than moral suasion.[38] It also became clear that he did not take Knox's charges against Zelaya seriously: on repeated occasions, Mariscal denied the existence of a Nicaraguan expedition against El Salvador. To placate Knox, Díaz merely agreed to send the gunboat *General Guerrero* to Central American waters as an "observer" of the situation.[39] During his next congressional address, he pointed out that his government opposed the use of force.[40] León de la Barra's reply to the Knox initiative spelled out this opposition to the U.S. course of action. He notified the Secretary of State that Mexico could not participate in a peace conference that did not include Zelaya's representative.[41] The ambassador then set forth a counterproposal to invite Zelaya to the planned conference and to interfere in isthmian affairs only if asked to do so by all of the Central American countries.[42]

While Díaz had thus far reluctantly participated in joint moral suasion with the United States, in late April 1909 a misunderstanding between Manuel Azueta, commander of the *General Guerrero,* and a U.S. gunboat captain doomed even this semblance of cooperation. After Azueta had reported the arrival of his vessel to the commander of the U.S.S. *Colorado,* he found out that the U.S. warships had received instructions to interdict any movement against El Salvador. The *Colorado* soon moved toward the Nicaraguan shore and on one occasion harassed a merchant boat thought to carry arms to Salvadoran rebels. Upon the request of the U.S. commander, C. B. J. Moore, Azueta joined him on a courtesy call to La Unión. There, he stated, Moore instructed him to stop any filibustering expedition. Vigorously denied by Moore, these orders deeply offended the Díaz government.[43] Whatever the truth in the affair, the incident proved to be the straw that broke the camel's back in U.S.–Mexican cooperation in Central America.

Mariscal, via U.S. Ambassador Thompson, made sure Knox understood Mexico's indignation. He told Thompson that Azueta had been "prompted into violent action" and "bossed around" by the U.S. naval commander. The United States, Mariscal said, had embarked on a course toward the use of armed force in Nicaragua in which Mexico could not join.[44] He then instructed the Mexican chargé d'affaires in Washington to tell Knox that the widely divergent interests of the two countries precluded Mexico from tailoring its policy closely to that of the United States. While the United States pursued economic interests in all five isthmian countries, Mexico, the note read, entertained no "practical interest" south of Guatemala.[45]

With the stroke of a pen, Mariscal had decoupled Mexico from U.S. hostility toward Zelaya, but seemingly only at the cost of abdicating a role in most of Central America. On the surface, U.S. diplomacy had won a tremendous victory. As Knox saw it, the State Department was now free to pursue its own interests in four of the isthmian republics. In short, it could move ahead with its plans for "disciplining" Zelaya. Knox also filed the note away for use in case Mariscal should later second-guess U.S. policies in Central America.[46]

Analyzed closely, however, Mariscal's gambit appears an appropriate response to Knox's hawkish policies. The Mexican government renounced its role in joint peacemaking at a propitious time, as any further cooperation with the United States would have had the effect of aiding a move against Zelaya. Thus, the declaration amounted to a tactical, if clumsy, retreat from adversity. The Mexican government would no longer second U.S. initiatives; instead, it would pursue its own policies and criticize U.S. intervention.

The change of U.S. policies under Knox constituted the primary motivation for Mariscal's move. Root had avoided direct and unilateral involvement in isthmian affairs; therefore, the Díaz government had been able to mitigate intervention through negotiation. Even though Root's later attempts to impose rigid norms of conduct on the Central American countries had not met with Mexican approval, he had proven at least amenable to listening to Díaz's and Mariscal's views. But when Knox and his irascible aide, Francis M. Huntington Wilson, who "had an almost limitless capacity for antagonizing people,"[47] steered the State Department into overt opposition to Zelaya, any Mexican participation would have consisted in backing up initiatives that contradicted Porfirian policy goals—unless, of course, Díaz wished to confront the U.S. government directly. The time had come to state explicitly that the Porfirians would not, as a matter of principle, aid Knox in his interventionist course; the freedom of action gained compensated for the influence lost in Central America.

Knox brought the Mexican and Nicaraguan governments closer together. Zelaya proclaimed himself an "enthusiastic admirer" of the Porfirian regime.[48] His "greater approximation" to Mexico, he stated, originated in "political events of continental consequences," an obvious allusion to U.S. policies.[49] For his part, Díaz advised the Nicaraguan to cease his war preparations against El Salvador to avoid giving the United States a pretext for intervention. As a result, Zelaya toned down his posture in the isthmus and resolved the pending U.S. claims against him.[50]

Knox's blunt diplomacy finally brought the end of U.S.–Mexican cooperation; the daily exchange of ideas with the Mexican ambassador on Central American matters had ceased. Knox went ahead with his plans for the "financial consolidation" of Honduras and the elimination of Zelaya, for which he favored a joint Guatemalan-Salvadoran expedition.[51] When Díaz and Taft met at the U.S.–Mexican border in October 1909, the summit had the appearance of a carefully choreographed stage play: nothing of substance was discussed at the meeting, and the two presidents avoided the subject of foreign policy.[52]

Subsequent Mexican governments learned from the lessons of the late Díaz regime. Cooperation with the United States in isthmian affairs had become a risky exercise with scant domestic payoff. As long as interventionist hawks prevailed in Washington, Mexican diplomacy best served the country's interests by acting independently of the United States. Officially, Mexico would not "be drawn into any form of active intervention in Central American affairs,"[53] at least as far as co-intervention with the United States was concerned.

Mexico and the Fall of Zelaya

For the Díaz government, supporting Zelaya had become a vital matter. Since 1903, he had been a bitter opponent of Mexico's nemesis Estrada Cabrera. Moreover, among the rulers of the Central American countries, no one epitomized resistance to U.S. dominance more than did Zelaya. The crisis showed what might happen to a Mexican government if—on some not-too-distant day—it failed to meet the exacting standards of U.S. business interests and Knox's ambitious diplomacy.

In October 1909, a rebellion broke out on Nicaragua's Atlantic coast. Led by the Liberal Juan Estrada, whom Zelaya just had deposed as governor of one of the coastal departments, the insurgency quickly seized the undefended towns on Nicaragua's eastern littoral. Occurring far away from the centers of population, the uprising appeared to offer no serious threat to the Zelaya regime. At least some of the U.S. entrepreneurs in the area opposed the "band of malcontents . . . who have seriously interfered with business and commerce."[54] But this rebellion was not just some innocuous, homegrown revolt: Estrada Cabrera had helped equip the Nicaraguan rebels. In addition, the U.S. consul in Bluefields, Thomas P. Moffat, had maintained close contacts with the future rebel leaders for months. And although no conclusive proof exists of the active involvement of U.S. diplomats in preparing the revolt, Moffat's intimate prior knowledge of its timing and strategy suggests at least his own acquiescence.[55]

Initially, however, there was little the U.S. State Department could do to help depose Zelaya. Persistently though Moffat twisted the facts in his reporting of the progress of the revolt, the government forces soon threatened to put an end to it. As a consequence, Knox—even though favorably inclined toward the insurrection—never gave serious thought to recognizing the Estrada regime at this early date.[56]

But in November 1909, Zelaya delivered Knox a pretext for supporting Juan Estrada. While his divisions were closing in on the enemy lines around Bluefields, government forces captured two U.S. filibusters laying mines on the San Juan River. In accordance with Nicaraguan law, the two adventurers were court-martialed and executed.[57] As flimsy as it was to act on behalf of two soldiers of fortune who had taken sides in a foreign military conflict, Knox had an excuse for intervention: the Zelaya regime constituted a threat to U.S. "lives and property."[58]

Knox then acted the part of the insulted U.S. statesman: he angrily demanded an explanation for the executions and stated that the U.S. government "will not for one moment tolerate such treatment of American citizens."[59] When such an explanation was not forthcoming, U.S. warships allowed the rebels to maintain a blockade of the town of San Juan del Norte, which the Zelayistas had recaptured only days earlier. Assistant Secretary of State Huntington Wilson then tried to rally the other Central American states to a joint stance against Nicaragua. This time, however, not even Guatemala agreed to help the State Department. A U.S. invasion was a real possibility: Huntington Wilson suggested the seizure of Managua and Corinto.[60]

Beleaguered, Zelaya surrendered himself to Mexican protection. The U.S. government, Zelaya stated to the Mexican consul in Managua, wanted him out of office; to forestall a military intervention, he was prepared to resign. In return, Zelaya asked for support for the designation of a Liberal of his choice as his successor. He also asked Díaz to try to prevent the landing of U.S. troops in Nicaragua.[61]

The advantages of this plan to the Díaz regime were obvious. Zelaya's resignation, sooner or later inevitable, was a small enough price to pay to prevent a military occupation of Nicaragua. In addition, sponsorship of a graceful exit for Zelaya could only enhance Díaz's prestige, portraying him as an honorable statesman with a humanitarian interest in ousted nationalist leaders. Thus, Díaz accepted and offered Zelaya asylum in Mexico.[62] However, Mariscal instructed the Mexican minister in Managua, Bartolomé Carbajal y Rosas, to urge Zelaya to hold on to power until talks with rebels could be held to determine a successor.[63]

Carbajal actively participated in the selection process for a new president. The two possible candidates, Julián Irías and José Madriz, both promised to continue Zelaya's policies. Irías's nationalism was even more fervent than Zelaya's; as the president's "General Minister," he had been instrumental in steering Nicaragua into its confrontation with the State Department. He personally hated Estrada Cabrera and had frequently eulogized Díaz for his leadership of the Latin American world against U.S. hegemony. If nominated, Irías was a sure bet to meet with the stiff opposition of the State Department. For precisely that reason, Madriz, once a delegate to the Court of Central American Justice, appeared the smarter choice. Facing Estrada Cabrera's majority on the court, he had illustrated the responsibility of Guatemala for the revolutionary upheavals in Honduras of the preceding year. Since Madriz had long lived in Salvadoran exile, from where he had criticized many of Zelaya's policies, it seemed Knox would find little reason to object to his candidacy. Therefore, Carbajal persuaded Zelaya to nominate Madriz, who took office four weeks later.[64]

At this juncture, Díaz could present Zelaya's resignation as a prize to the State Department, one which could only be obtained without bloodshed if the United States accepted Mexico's terms. The decision for Madriz seemed to sweeten this bait considerably, and Díaz approached Taft fully confident of success. If Taft could not countenance a continuation of Zelaya's rule, Madriz, from the Mexican point of view, looked like an acceptable compromise to both parties.[65] Díaz then sent Creel to Washington to explain his plan further.[66]

This time, however, Díaz had miscalculated, as Taft answered in a noncommittal fashion.[67] In Huntington Wilson's view, Mexico's offer sought to distract U.S. diplomacy from its stated goal of eliminating Zelaya. In April 1909, he contended, the Díaz government had toyed with the United States. Now that Mexico tried to "butt in," it had become obvious that the country pursued interests in Central America driven "by the most contemptible motives." Consequently, one of his aides drafted a memorandum reminding the Mexican embassy of its earlier disclaimer, a reminder which insinuated that the U.S. would continue to act unilaterally in the Nicaraguan question.[68]

Things got even more difficult for the Díaz regime when Knox took such a unilateral step in the form of a harsh note to chargé Felipe Rodríguez. Calling the Zelaya government "a blot on the history of Nicaragua," and citing a litany of alleged abuses against U.S. citizens and violations of the Washington Conventions, Knox announced the rupture of diplomatic relations. At this point, Knox claimed, the opposition represented the Nicaraguan people more faithfully than did the Zelaya government.[69]

Received with alarm throughout Mexico, the Knox note dramatically altered the scenario.[70] By making plain that the State Department wanted Zelaya removed from power, the document emboldened the Estradistas. Just as Díaz and the Nicaraguan president were preparing a graceful exit that would have allowed nationalist Liberals to retain power, the note favored a faction pliant to U.S. hegemony. Moreover, since Estrada Cabrera had originally been one of the principal supporters of the Juan Estrada revolt, Díaz faced the nightmare of an unsympathetic administration in Washington coupled with three hostile regimes in Central America. The Knox note also raised the possibility of the landing of U.S. troops in Nicaragua.[71]

Appreciating that the United States was in the driver's seat, Mariscal proceeded with caution. While Creel and Díaz worked out strategy for Creel's trip, the Foreign Minister attempted to placate the State Department, stating that he did not "resent the action of the United States." Mariscal desired to avoid ill will in advance of his emissary's reception in the U.S. capital. Yet, he did not hide his indignation about the fact that Knox had not notified him in advance of his intention to break relations with Nicaragua.[72]

Mariscal's ostensibly passive posture cloaked a strategy to ensure the continuation of Zelayismo in Nicaragua. To that end, Mariscal instructed Carbajal to assist Zelaya in the transfer of power to Madriz and in any other necessary capacity.[73] The Mexican government also launched a press campaign in favor of the Nicaraguan Liberals. While the official press printed meek defenses of Zelaya, the opposition papers of all stripes were given free rein to condemn the actions of the United States. Many articles emphasized that Estrada Cabrera enjoyed clear supremacy in Central America thanks to the help of the United States, and Madriz was portrayed as the possible redeemer of Nicaraguan sovereignty.[74]

Creel arrived in Washington well prepared. Upon arrival, he handed Knox a long written list of questions, the answers to which he hoped would reveal more precisely the position of the State Department. The questions implied the idea of a joint U.S.-Mexican protectorate with

Mexico as the leader. Creel also asked whether the United States would allow Zelaya to leave the country.

But Creel blundered in his very first interview with Knox. He made himself immediately unwelcome with his statement that the Díaz government had a "superior understanding of Latin American views and feelings." The purpose of his mission, Creel stated, was to clear up some misconceptions which had arisen in Latin America regarding Knox's policies. As Knox saw it, the envoy presented Díaz in the leading role seeking support for a Mexican initiative.[75]

Creel probably was a poor choice for this important mission. He did not possess the State Department's confidence as Díaz thought, and his haughtiness, often displayed during his earlier tenure as ambassador, ill became Mexico's position vis-à-vis the United States. Worse still, Creel did not always represent Mariscal's viewpoints. Always amenable to the views of U.S. diplomats, the *medio gringo* ("half-American") Creel thought Zelaya guilty of most of the crimes alleged by the State Department, and unworthy of Mexican help.[76] In his view, which was also that of Finance Minister José Limantour, the mission served principally to dissociate Mexico publicly from U.S. actions. Therefore, Creel had personally held out little hope that his trip could prevent U.S. military intervention in Nicaragua.[77] The choice of Creel pointed up the tragic irony of the whole affair: while Díaz opposed U.S. policies, his regime desperately needed to maintain good relations with the State Department in a period of growing crisis.

Knox and his aides soon made up their minds that this Mexican mission was not to be trusted. In several internal memoranda, they reacted negatively to Creel's suggestions. Huntington Wilson, for one, seemed completely disinclined to consider any Zelayista as the future president of Nicaragua, insisting—in a new twist—on clean and fair elections for the office.[78]

Creel soon found out that Madriz was no more acceptable to the U.S. government than was Zelaya. Knox and Huntington Wilson regarded Madriz as a stooge who would merely continue the Zelaya nationalist policies they had so severely condemned. When Taft received the Mexican emissary, he made clear that the U.S. government could not accept "any creature of Zelaya's." Creel's assurances that Madriz had always disapproved of Zelaya's methods failed to change Taft's mind.[79] As a consequence, the envoy vainly advised Mariscal to postpone the transfer of power to Madriz.[80]

A few days later, Creel returned to the State Department to discuss his memorandum. Madriz, Creel claimed, was well liked throughout Central America—except perhaps in Guatemala—and enjoyed the complete confidence of the Mexican government.[81] But Huntington Wilson disagreed, contending that only the Estrada faction represented the will of the people of Nicaragua. He warned that unless Mexico and the United States agreed to recognize the rebel general as provisional president, the war would continue.[82] Creel then suggested other members of Zelaya's inner circle as possible presidents, only to find Huntington Wilson determined to appoint someone from the opposition.[83]

Seeing his efforts on behalf of Madriz frustrated, Creel moved on to the minimal goal of his mission: to obtain U.S. acquiescence for Zelaya's exile. He soon found the U.S. press hostile to the idea[84] and Knox "personally offended" that Mexico would "prefer" Zelaya over the U.S. government. In Creel's view, the press "tried to bring [our government] into disrepute, presenting Mexico as a barbarian country and its government as on the level of that of Nicaragua."[85] Taft also seemed reluctant to consent to asylum for the Nicaraguan, even though he was equally loath to use military force in the isthmus. Given his earlier failures, the envoy tried to scuttle his mission, cabling Díaz that the offer of asylum would do "serious damage" to Mexico because of Knox's hatred of Zelaya. As a true científico, Creel desired to advance Mexican interests, but not at the cost of openly antagonizing the United States.[86]

This time, however, the hawks in Mexico won, and so did Mexican diplomacy. Díaz replied that he regarded the issue of asylum as one involving his personal honor.[87] That same day, Creel approached Taft and reluctantly broached the subject. At first he blundered again, telling the U.S. president that Díaz had offered the asylum, rather than stating that Zelaya had requested it of the Mexican government. But then Creel added that Díaz would not honor his promise if Taft objected.[88] After consulting with Knox, Taft told the Mexican emissary that he would not prevent Díaz from carrying out his pledge. Taft added that his words implied neither an acquiescence nor an objection on the part of the U.S. government.[89] Then he issued a stern reminder of his government's hard-line stance toward the isthmian leaders: he said "someone ought to have the right to knock their heads together until they should maintain peace between them."[90]

On December 24, 1909, Zelaya went into exile aboard the *General Guerrero*. Visibly appreciative, upon arriving in Mexico, he praised that "noble and hospitable country."[91] The Díaz government gave him a warm reception in the capital. Yet soon after his arrival, Creel urged him to leave the country to avoid an extradition request:[92] Knox had announced that the State Department would file civil suit against the Nicaraguan for the execution of the two mercenaries. A month later, Zelaya traveled to the port of Veracruz, whence he left for Europe to join his family.[93]

Although Díaz ordered the Creel mission downplayed in the official press, the successful offer of asylum earned him some much-needed political mileage. Even while assailing the *agringado* Creel as Díaz's choice, the liberal *El Diario del Hogar* conceded that the Mexican government had attained a victory over the Taft administration. The clerical *El País* also rejoiced in the snub of Knox and Taft.[94] The asylum issue had ended in a victory for Díaz; he had prevailed over a U.S. Secretary of State who appeared unreasonable and unprofessional in his antagonism toward Zelaya.[95]

The granting of asylum to Zelaya once again points up the significance of ideological and domestic political considerations in Mexican foreign-policy formulation. Nothing of substance was to be gained from the asylum in terms of U.S. influence in Central America. Therefore, unlike in the previous instances of co-mediation, the Mexican action cannot be understood in the context of the traditional policy goal of lessening U.S. political influence in Central America. More than anything, asylum for Zelaya was an act of friendship and a symbolic step—one that showed that the Díaz regime defended Latin American sovereignty against Yankee encroachments.

This fact manifested itself during Zelaya's stay in Mexico: shouts of "Death to the Yankees" punctuated the Nicaraguan's public appearances, and many attendees extolled Díaz as a courageous opponent of U.S. imperialism.[96] In Nicaragua and El Salvador, demonstrations were held to denounce U.S. policy and to praise Zelaya and Díaz. Even Estrada Cabrera stated that Mexico's offer of asylum "deserved Central America's gratitude," while members of the Guatemalan opposition lauded the "opportune and efficacious" intervention.[97]

Not all had gone according to plan, however. Creel had failed in some of the most crucial objectives of his trip. He had obtained only a vague commitment that the United States would not use force in Nicaragua, and he had not received support for Madriz.[98] In dealing with Taft directly, Creel had also unwittingly intruded into the State Department's primacy in foreign policy, which Knox had reasserted after Roosevelt's personal handling of these affairs. As Huntington Wilson mused: "Diplomatic discussion is the province of the Secretary of State. Creel . . . was almost offensive in his effort to go straight to the President with his business and we should show that however much . . . Diaz may personally . . . carry on his foreign relations such is not the habit of the President of the United States."[99]

Thus, Creel had fallen short of his goals. Framed in the Roosevelt-Root era, the mindset of the Mexican envoy had proven too inflexible to deal with changed situations in Washington and Central America. This became obvious in the conclusions that he drew from his mission. Mexico, Creel wrote, needed the support of the United States more than anything else and could not risk pursuing an independent policy in the isthmus.[100] Creel simply did not understand the significance of the balancing act Díaz had attempted over the previous few years. To be sure, don Porfirio could not have the U.S. government as his enemy, but he also needed to appease at least the elite segments of the mounting opposition he faced at home. Many of these elite leaders—such as Francisco I. Madero and Venustiano Carranza—shared Díaz's fear of Yankee aggression anywhere in Latin America.

Ironically, some opponents of the Díaz regime turned its nationalist overtures against it. A leading opposition figure and ally of Madero, for example, warned Knox about what he regarded as the "duplicity" of the Mexican government. Far from assisting the United States, the informant assessed, Díaz pursued an independent policy in Nicaragua to project himself as a "saviour [sic] of the independence and integrity of the Latin American republics."[101]

Not surprisingly, Huntington Wilson would write only a few months later: "The Mexican Government, while outwardly professing sympathy with [our] aims . . . in Central America, actually holds independent views on this subject which are not in harmony with those of the American Government. . . . In fact, it does not appear that any real community of ideas or of action . . . has existed for many years."[102]

Díaz Confronts the U.S. in Nicaragua 103

Even though Creel declared in a communiqué that Mexico would resume its cooperation with the United States,[103] the two governments had emerged as antagonistic players in Central America. In its support for Madriz, the Díaz government would find out whether it could work at cross-purposes with the State Department.

Mexico's Support for Madriz

Madriz, installed as president on December 20, 1909, initially appeared in good shape in spite of U.S. opposition.[104] He inherited a full treasury because of the British loan contracted by the Zelaya government. To add to this war chest, Mexican consular agents in the United States procured several loans for Madriz, who had declared from the outset that Mexico would support and maintain him.[105] Carbajal then sponsored peace talks between the factions. He even got Estrada to agree to Madriz's recognition as provisional president in exchange for Madriz's withdrawal from the political scene after serving a six-month term. This mediation failed only because Estrada's delegate drowned en route to the meeting at which the agreement was to be finalized.[106]

To add to Madriz's apparent advantage, the rebels fared poorly on the battlefield even though they received substantial aid from Guatemala.[107] Through early 1910, loyalist forces pushed back the Estradistas, who finally found themselves cornered in Bluefields. Even Root and the commander of the U.S.S. *Albany* stationed in the area showed themselves to be Madriz partisans. Many countries, including Britain, Germany, Honduras, and Costa Rica, followed Mexico's lead in recognizing the provisional government. By May, the rebellion seemed politically isolated and militarily defeated.[108]

In June, however, just as Madriz's forces stood poised to take Bluefields and thus wipe out the rebels, the U.S. government took the step that doomed him. Citing a risk to U.S. lives and property, a U.S. gunboat commander refused to permit Madriz's only warship to blockade the port. The declaration allowed the Estradistas to regroup.[109] Demoralized, the government forces lost the initiative and retreated toward the interior; a Díaz telegram urging Taft to consider a peaceable solution achieved nothing.[110] The U.S. government had performed its first overtly interventionist acts and had taken itself one giant step closer to the military occupation of Nicaragua.

Despite the setback, the Madriz army was far from finished. Criticized in the U.S. Congress for his actions in Central America, Knox had not yet recognized Estrada as the president of Nicaragua; therefore, U.S. neutrality laws still permitted the export of weapons to both factions. Even though massive infusions of financial aid from Guatemala and U.S. entrepreneurs allowed the rebels to purchase a large share of these arms, the Madricistas persisted, receiving several shiploads of weaponry and ammunition through New Orleans. Until July 1910, the military campaigns remained inconclusive. Therefore, León de la Barra launched one last futile effort to persuade the State Department to recognize Madriz as president.[111]

If time and materiel favored the Estradistas, Mariscal's death in March 1910 perhaps proved equally significant in dooming the Madriz government. In the three decades that he had headed the Foreign Ministry, Mariscal had consistently sought out leaders in Central America who opposed both Guatemalan hegemonic aspirations and U.S. pretensions of hegemony. These leaders included Rafael Zaldívar, Tomás Regalado, Zelaya, and Madriz; and Mariscal had provided appropriate support. As a *sureño* (southern Mexican) from Oaxaca, Mariscal had always understood the significance of Central America for Mexico. Once the northern científico Creel ascended to the highest post in the agency, Mariscal's policy of balance lay abandoned. Creel proved little more than a caretaker Foreign Secretary, who needed to shore up relations with the United States and Guatemala as the Porfirian regime slipped toward its demise.[112]

In August 1910, the Zelaya faction finally fell from power. Upon the advice of Díaz, Madriz stepped down to prevent a further spreading of the war. A Mexican gunboat whisked the head of state off on his way into European exile, and Estrada became provisional president.[113] He proved a weak leader and stepped aside in 1911 in favor of Vice President Adolfo Díaz, a member of the Conservative party and an open supporter of U.S. intervention. With this turn of events, Nicaragua had definitively fallen under Uncle Sam's thumb.

By then, the Mexican government could no longer affect events in Central America. With criticism of his regime reaching crisis proportions surrounding the lavish September 1910 celebration of the centennial of Mexican independence, Díaz tried to shore up support from the Taft administration. He suppressed a number of anti-U.S. demonstrations in the capital and ordered the suspension of a pro-Madriz publication. Creel also declined to receive Madriz's envoy at the centennial celebrations.[114] In addition, Mexico's delegation kept a low profile at the Fourth Inter-American Conference in Buenos Aires. The Díaz government was afraid to offend U.S. sensibilities by raising its voice at a meeting that was widely regarded as a convention to rubberstamp Knox's unilateral interpretation of Pan-Americanism. As a sole sign of protest against U.S. policies, Díaz refused to recognize the Estrada regime.

The U.S. government, on the other hand, could no longer extricate itself from the current drawing it into full-blown military intervention in Nicaragua. In 1912, the Liberals revolted under the direction of Julián Irías and José Mena. As the majority party, the Liberals soon seemed destined to succeed. But as prominent Zelayistas headed this rebellion, Knox could not stomach a potential change of government. Therefore, he ordered two thousand Marines into Nicaragua to protect the Adolfo Díaz regime. During the next thirteen years, the United States always kept at least a small legation guard in Nicaragua in order to keep the Conservatives in power. Mired ever more deeply in the morass of intervention, Knox, in the opinion of a Mexican historian, at last handed a small victory to Mexico: through unilateral action, he had only aggravated the problems of the United States in Central America.[115]

With the end of nationalist Liberal rule, the Nicaraguan elites had lost a chance to help steer the country's modernization. As Salvador Castrillo (who as Estrada's agent in Washington contributed to the defeat of the Liberals) admitted twenty years after Zelaya's overthrow: "The fall of Zelaya brought the disgrace of Nicaragua. . . . The evils to be remedied were relative, and we could have washed that dirty laundry in the family. . . . It was paradise then compared with today."[116]

The Díaz government had done everything possible to keep the Liberals in power and prevent U.S. intervention. In the end, the State Department had used its superior resources to impose a U.S. solution to the Nicaraguan problem. But the Díaz government had shown itself to be a consistent anti-interventionist force in the isthmus. If the State Department had ultimately prevailed, it had been forced to accept periodic setbacks and detours, many of which were the consequence of Mexican diplomacy. It had also assumed a responsibility that would cause more

problems than the State Department could ever hope to solve, alone or
through joint action with Mexico.

Retrospect: Porfirian Foreign Policy in Central America

A growing anti-U.S. orientation formed the most consistent fea-
ture of Porfirian foreign policy. Antagonism toward Guatemala marked
the first twenty years of Díaz's Central America policy. Until 1898,
Mexico's concern about the United States resulted primarily from the
State Department's support of Guatemala in the boundary dispute and
schemes for the domination of Central America. During this period,
anti-U.S. rhetoric served mainly as one of the glues of the Porfirian coalition and rarely determined the actual decision-making process. Apprehension of U.S. goals in the isthmus, however, grew exponentially
after 1898 and increasingly affected the style and substance of Mexican
policy. Beginning in 1906, Mexican diplomacy became wary of Root's
efforts to force the country into an obligatory peacekeeping role. At the
same time, a growing segment of the public demanded a posture in
Central America entirely independent of that of the United States, and
the Díaz government responded with a more assertive policy. Even so,
Mexican foreign policy remained concerned about Estrada Cabrera, as
the Barillas controversy illustrated.

In the last years of the Porfiriato, however, fear of U.S. hegemony
took center stage. When Knox steered the State Department into open
confrontation with Zelaya, the Díaz government decoupled itself from
U.S. policy and tried to impose its own candidate for the presidency of
Nicaragua. U.S. military intervention and the fall of the Porfiriato
finally spelled an end of active Mexican involvement in the isthmus—
at least for the moment.

It is hard to say to what extent the growing U.S.–Mexican confrontation influenced the State Department's attitude toward the Mexican
Revolution. Knox evidently reacted in a lukewarm fashion to the outbreak of hostilities on November 20, 1910; one historian has even
claimed that the Madero revolt enjoyed his sympathy.[117] But in any
event, the Central American controversy—ahead of Díaz's growing
preference for European investments, the Chamizal dispute,[118] and
Díaz's cancelation of a U.S. lease of the coaling station of Bahía de la

Magdalena—was the most contentious issue between the United States and Mexico before the Revolution. Whereas Taft himself appreciated the political stability that had prevailed for most of Díaz's tenure, Knox viewed Mexico as an adversary in Central America. The isthmian problem certainly added to the negative tenor of the U.S. press in bringing about an increasingly narrow application of U.S. neutrality laws, which augmented Madero's radius of action.

On the whole, Porfirian policy in Central America had helped limit unilateral U.S. action there.[119] While the Dominican Republic, Haiti, and Cuba had fallen under direct U.S. control by 1905, Mexico's presence in Central America helped delay this process. If it was the single greatest failing of Porfirian foreign policy that it never effectively mobilized popular support for nationalist initiatives, no one could blame Díaz for the fact that the United States finally used military means to impose its notions of isthmian order.

The irony of Díaz's efforts in his last years in power is that they failed to meet either of two increasingly divergent goals. Díaz's stand in the Zelaya issue cost him crucial support in Washington at a moment when his regime needed help. But to many Mexicans, don Porfirio's anti-Yankee efforts seemed halfhearted and futile. Thus, as more aggressive U.S. policies further accentuated growing nationalist feelings in Mexico, the aging Díaz could no longer bridge the gap between U.S. goodwill and domestic support.

Late Porfirian diplomacy toward Central America was a good example of policies driven by fear of the great power. By 1909, bilateral goals in Central America had become subordinated to the prevention of U.S. intervention. But as the largely symbolic character of the Zelaya asylum indicates, Díaz pursued bilateral and domestically driven policies as well. In a feeble attempt to use diplomacy for propagandistic benefit, he had shown that he was concerned about the image of his foreign policy. Thus, Díaz affirmed that Mexican foreign policy responds to powerful internal motivations as well as external threats and possibilities.

5 The Mexican Revolution and Central America, 1911–1920

> For its similarity and vicinity, Central America is the natural ground for
> Mexican intellectual and moral influence and expansion.
>
> Mexican minister to Guatemala José Bermúdez de Castro, 1918

The Mexican Revolution forced an abrupt break in Mexican initiatives
in Central America. By 1920, following a decade of campaigns that cost
almost a million lives, Mexico lay in ruins. The revolutionary turmoil
had swept aside the Porfirian governing elite. A number of factions contended for power in the ensuing vacuum, and no single one was able to
attain lasting supremacy. Foreign meddling in the Revolution further
complicated matters. Both President Taft and his successor, Woodrow
Wilson, intervened in the Mexican Revolution. The European powers,
and especially Germany, Great Britain, and France, attempted to use
the factions to enhance their own presence in Mexico. With the advent
of World War One, this rivalry intensified.[1]

All these difficulties aside, even a stable Mexican government would
have had trouble accomplishing much in Central America. With the
1912 deployment of a legation guard in Nicaragua and the subsequent
negotiation of the Bryan-Chamorro Treaty, the U.S. government made
it clear that it would no longer tolerate outside interference in the isthmus other than its own. To make matters worse, Mexico's old friends
in Central America had fallen on hard times. By 1911, two anti-Mexican
governments dominated Central America: Estrada Cabrera's in Guatemala and the Conservative government in Nicaragua. Only the leaders
of El Salvador remained friendly to Mexico.[2] In addition, many Central
American leaders, fearful that their own power might one day be ques-
tioned by rebels, viewed the Mexican Revolution with suspicion. Thus,
U.S. diplomats in the region, not nearly as willing to share the spotlight
with Mexico as in Díaz's age, did not need to worry about Mexican influence.

Not surprisingly, Mexico's Central American policy in the 1911–20 period was much less assertive than in previous days. As a result of the greater external and internal limitations on policies, Mexican national leaders adopted a defensive approach to the isthmus. An analysis of Mexico's Central America policy in the 1910s shows that the country's leaders could never ignore the isthmus, not even at such difficult moments. But it also highlights the advent of an era in which any growth in Mexican influence in Central America met with the strong opposition of the U.S. government.

Madero, Huerta, and Central America, 1911–1914

When Francisco I. Madero's uprising set Mexicans on a course to overthrow the Díaz regime in November 1910, the revolt initially seemed of limited consequence. After all, the rebels merely called for don Porfirio's resignation and for strict adherence to the Constitution of 1857. "Effective suffrage, no reelection"—Díaz's own rallying cry of the 1876 Tuxtepec Rebellion now served as the theme of Madero and other disaffected Porfiristas who led the charge. To most observers, the rebellion, which quickly defeated Díaz's troops, amounted to little more than a palace revolt.

But the uprising unleashed social movements of unexpected force. In the state of Morelos, the peasant followers of Emiliano Zapata demanded land reform instead of hollow institutional changes at the top of the social pyramid. In the north, Pancho Villa led an army of peasants, sharecroppers, and bandits; individuals aggrieved by their economic and social displacement during the process of modernization. To the east of Villa's divisions, Venustiano Carranza's faction, which represented the "most flexible elements of the Porfirian political and economic hierarchy,"[3] aspired to gain the power that Díaz had awarded to his own cronies. In the northwest, middle-class rebels abounded, insurgents such as Alvaro Obregón, who struggled to reverse their slide into the lower classes.[4]

Madero had opened a Pandora's box that he could not control. An idealist who believed Mexico's salvation to lie in the adoption of western models of parliamentary democracy rather than a caudillo who could reconcile divergent goals through charismatic appeal, Madero could never please all of the factions that had initially supported him.

Trying to placate all of these groups, he only ended up alienating most of them. In the face of this unrest, Madero lost the support of U.S. President William H. Taft, who desired a strong hand at the helm of Mexico. As a consequence, elements of the army, which was still commanded by Porfirian officers, disposed of Madero in a bloody coup. Led by the former president's nephew, Félix Díaz, and aided by U.S. ambassador Henry L. Wilson, this faction installed General Victoriano Huerta as Mexico's new ruler in February 1913. But Huerta hardly did better than Madero in taming, to use Porfirio Díaz's words, "the wild beasts."[5] Led by Villa, Zapata, and Carranza, the anti-Díaz coalition once again rose up in arms. In response, Huerta attempted to address some of the social and economic grievances of the revolutionaries.[6] His piecemeal measures, however, failed to assuage the rebels.

During this uprising, Carranza, a member of the old northern oligarchy, gained national stature. Carranza and his associates had numbered among the losers in the factional jockeying that marked the last years of the Porfiriato. A wealthy landowner, Carranza belonged to the Reyista clique which had dominated politics in Coahuila for decades. In the final years of his rule, when he feared that Bernardo Reyes would challenge him, Díaz had forced this camarilla out of power in favor of its científico rivals. First, don Porfirio had made the sitting governor resign; then, he had prevented Carranza's election as governor.[7] Carranza thus had joined the Revolution as a disaffected Reyista who harbored a political—and indeed, a rather personal—grievance against Díaz. A close ally of Madero's, Carranza assumed the mantle of the defender of lawful government in Mexico.

He found an ally for his fight in U.S. President Wilson, who shared his disdain for unconstitutional rule. Seeking to promote "good government" everywhere, Wilson, whose approach to Latin America one researcher has dubbed the "Wilson Corollary to the Monroe Doctrine,"[8] stressed western democracy as the ideal form of government. Good government, he believed, reduced the threat of revolutions, coups d'état, and European gunboat diplomacy. In Wilson's view, expressed most succinctly in his famous address in Mobile, Alabama, working democracies in Latin America could better safeguard U.S. lives and property than could old-fashioned intervention. The new U.S. president therefore advocated political democracy in part out of a true—even messianic—devotion to the virtues of democracy, but also in order to find a more efficient way to push European influence out of Latin America.[9]

Ironically, Wilson's approach entailed the very intervention he professed to abhor. The U.S. president soon made it clear that he wanted Huerta removed from power. After all, the dictator not only had come to power in a coup; he also—like Porfirio Díaz—favored European economic interests.[10] Therefore, while Wilson officially assumed a position of "watchful waiting" toward the Revolution, he took advantage of the first opportunity to weaken Huerta. This opportunity came in the spring of 1914, when a commander loyal to Huerta refused to salute the U.S. flag as an apology for the erroneous arrest of a group of U.S. sailors at Tampico. Citing reports that a German gunboat was approaching Mexico's Gulf Coast with weapons for Huerta, Wilson ordered Marines into Veracruz. At the cost of hundreds of Mexican lives, his troops soon controlled the situation.

Wilson's intervention proved a crucial turning point in the Revolution: it showed Huerta's supporters that the United States would take further action unless the usurper left power. Moreover, the troops left several caches of weapons for the nearby Carrancistas; the intervention therefore decisively strengthened the Carranza faction.[11] By August 1914, Huerta had fled aboard a German warship, and central authority in Mexico had disintegrated completely.

The winter of 1914–15 proved to be the decisive stage of the military phase of the Revolution, as a bloody struggle ultimately determined the winner. After defeating Huerta, the victorious coalition split into two groups: the "Conventionists" under Villa's and Zapata's direction, and the "Constitutionalists" under the command of Carranza and Obregón. The Conventionists pursued primarily social and regional goals. They promoted Zapata's Plan de Ayala, which demanded restoration of communal peasant lands; by contrast, Zapata and Villa spent little time pondering the future political organization of Mexico. The Constitutionalist leadership, on the other hand, envisioned political and economic rather than social change. "Men who have slept on soft pillows,"[12] in Villa's words, they thought in terms of improving the Constitution, creating equal opportunities for Mexican capitalists, and reasserting an independent foreign policy.[13] When Carranza and Obregón defeated Villa and Zapata in early 1915, a city-oriented, middle-class alliance with national objectives had prevailed over a rural-based, lower-class coalition with regional goals.[14]

How did these turbulent events affect Mexico's Central America policy? The onset of hostilities between the Porfirians and the revolutionaries terminated all Mexican efforts to forestall U.S. intervention. In fact, neither Madero nor Huerta developed a Central America policy. Not only were both governments too beleaguered; U.S. policies and the Central American internal dynamic provided little leeway for action.

No matter whether Taft or Wilson lived in the White House, U.S. diplomacy in Central America remained aggressive after the fall of the Zelaya faction in Nicaragua. The U.S. government still feared unrest close to the canal, and that old problem did not seem to have abated in Zelaya's absence. A 1911 rebellion overthrew Honduran President Miguel Dávila; El Salvador witnessed several attempts at coups d'état, and in 1912, the Nicaraguan Conservatives faced defeat at the hands of Liberal rebels. Worse yet, the Taft administration had failed in one of its key initiatives in Central America: a financial reform that would have allowed U.S. experts to handle the enormous European debt of Guatemala, Honduras, and Nicaragua. As Taft and Knox had hoped, such measures would have ended the threat of European gunboat expeditions to collect overdue debts. But Central American leaders, and especially the normally pro-Yankee Estrada Cabrera, resisted this effort.[15] In the end, the U.S. State Department had to acquiesce in British saber rattling toward Guatemala, and its efforts in Honduras also were thwarted.[16]

Only in Nicaragua did Taft's diplomacy meet with success—and then at the cost of a long-term military enterprise. The new Nicaraguan government, freshly installed by U.S. intervention and increasingly dominated by the Conservative party, gladly negotiated the 1910 Dawson agreement, which gave the U.S. government a free hand to restructure the country's finances. But the new regime could not defend itself alone against revolts authored by the much stronger Liberal party. In July 1912, the Liberal commander of the Nicaraguan army, Luis Mena, rose up against President Adolfo Díaz. But when Mena's forces were on the verge of taking Managua, U.S. forces stepped in to save Conservative rule. With this step, the U.S. government effectively made itself the guarantor of the political order in Nicaragua.

Meanwhile, another issue favored the extension of U.S. control over Nicaragua: the possibility of the construction of a second transisthmian canal on the San Juan River with German, British, or Japanese money. But even though its survival depended on U.S. goodwill, the Nicaraguan government drove a hard bargain. In return for the rights to the canal, Díaz and his foreign minister, Diego Chamorro, demanded and received U.S. guarantees for Conservative rule in Nicaragua. Finally, in 1913, the two governments negotiated the Bryan-Chamorro Treaty. The agreement granted the United States perpetual rights to the Nicaragua canal route, as well as a lease on two Caribbean islands and the right to construct a naval station in the Gulf of Fonseca in return for a cash payment and U.S. support for continued Conservative rule. The U.S. Senate did not immediately approve this agreement, but one thing had become clear: rather than abandoning Taft's interventionist policies, Wilson continued to weave a U.S. military presence into the fabric of Central American politics.[17] Needless to say, all of these events went a long way toward discouraging Mexican action.

It was not surprising, then, that Madero displayed little diplomatic activity in Central America. Unwilling to be associated with Knox's interventionist policies, his government publicly disavowed its obligation to help uphold the 1907 Washington Conventions. Madero knew that the United States no longer desired Mexico's participation in Central American matters, and his government did not possess the means to pursue an independent policy. Therefore, during his brief tenure as president, Madero did not seek dialogue with Taft regarding the isthmus.[18] He also made no attempt to aid the Mena revolt in Nicaragua, and he did not back a Salvadoran initiative to keep Yankee soldiers off the Central American soil. Quite the contrary, Madero avoided antagonizing the State Department at all costs. In 1912, the Mexican minister to Nicaragua even joined in a resolution by the Diplomatic Corps to condemn Mena's siege of the capital.[19]

For its part, the Huerta regime—which had failed in its attempt to gain universal diplomatic recognition—was equally unable to pay much attention to Central America. It left vacant most of the consular appointments to the four eastern Central American countries. Both Madero and Huerta had their hands full with domestic opposition and U.S. meddling; they could ill afford to become embroiled in a Central American conflict.

Old nagging problems with Estrada Cabrera, however, persisted throughout the 1911–14 period. Haunted by bouts of diabetes and slipping into varying states of dementia, the veteran Guatemalan president still saw himself as the potential redeemer of his dreams of a united Central America including Chiapas. With the debt crisis coming to a head, Estrada Cabrera had use for foreign adversaries upon whom he could deflect mounting elite frustration. Thus, the unrest in Mexico was welcome news to him.[20] When the Madero regime faltered, Estrada Cabrera dispatched troops to the Mexican border, and he sought Taft's assistance to stave off a purported invasion of exiles from Chiapas. Yet to Mexico's good fortune, Nicaragua, whose government Estrada Cabrera detested, had replaced Guatemala as the favorite client state of the U.S. government. No longer needing the Guatemalan to hold in check nationalist strongmen in Nicaragua, the State Department gave no credit to his claims.[21]

In early 1913, Huerta's coup and Wilson's accession to the presidency ended this flurry of tensions. In fact, relations between Huerta and Estrada Cabrera were surprisingly cordial.[22] Most likely, the Wilson administration's moralistic posture was the primary reason for this détente between Mexico and Guatemala: having branded the Huerta regime the pariah of the western hemisphere, Wilson could hardly look much more kindly upon Estrada Cabrera. Both dictators had ordered the assassination of their respective predecessors, both leaders' unpopularity within their own countries was virtually universal, and both refused to step in to diminish European economic influence.[23] Therefore, facing U.S. opposition, the two dictators cooperated with each other until Huerta's fall.

Mexican influence in Central America greatly diminished in the 1911–14 period. The fighting in Mexico and U.S. intervention in both Mexico and Nicaragua discouraged Madero and Huerta from pursuing an assertive policy toward the region. Instead, their Central America policy was by necessity negative and passive in nature. With the breakdown of central authority in Mexico, the future hardly appeared brighter. Very soon, however, the faction of Venustiano Carranza would emerge on top in the ongoing military struggle. Carranza's victory established a government that, to a large extent, defined itself through its conduct of foreign relations.

Portrayed either as fervent nationalist or as conservative aristocrat,

Carranza mirrored the contradictions within his faction. Under adverse circumstances, he threw out the Porfirian bureaucracy, purged the army, and began work on a new constitution. He proved sensitive to some of the demands of urban labor, advocating unionization and restrictions on work hours. In his speeches, Carranza often boldly challenged the United States, railing particularly against the protection U.S. diplomats awarded the economic interests of their nationals. His agenda appealed to those disaffected elite and middle-class sectors that had lost opportunities during the last decade of the Porfiriato.[24] By the same token, Carranza lacked understanding of the goals of the Zapatistas and Villistas. He refused to support the Plan de Ayala, relying instead on the nineteenth-century Liberal tonic of rugged individualism.

Carranza's foreign policy between 1915 and 1918 shows a devotion to political patriotism in the Juárez-Díaz tradition, accentuated by outrage over violations of Mexican sovereignty and mixed with a dose of economic nationalism. Formulated amidst the chaos of the Revolution, it served Mexico well by successfully resisting U.S. intervention. But this allegedly "revolutionary" foreign policy marked an evolutionary rather than revolutionary departure from Porfirian precedents.[25] The fact that Carranza, like Díaz, cared primarily about the defense of Mexican sovereignty, and only secondarily about larger ideological issues, goes a long way toward explaining his approach as regards Central America. Mexican policy toward the isthmian nations in the 1915–20 period cannot be properly discussed without an understanding of Carranza's "policy of pragmatic nationalism."

Carranza's Foreign Policy of Pragmatic Nationalism

Like most Mexicans, Carranza resented foreign violations of Mexican sovereignty. It mattered little whether instances of foreign intervention helped or hurt his cause—both Ambassador Wilson's helping hand in Huerta's coup and the U.S. occupation of Veracruz wounded his patriotic pride. But Carranza also realized the political potential of manifestations of patriotic (and in this case anti-Yankee) sentiments: he knew that the occupation of Veracruz had strengthened existing anti-U.S. feelings.[26] Therefore, like Porfirio Díaz, Carranza cultivated his image as a patriot: even though he had extracted advantage from Wilson's actions, he denounced the intervention. He would

Venustiano Carranza, President in the Revolution, 1917
(Courtesy of the Archivo General de la Nación, Mexico City)

not let outside political pressures dictate the direction of the Mexican Revolution. To popular acclaim, Carranza successfully negotiated an end to the U.S. occupation of Veracruz, and he rejected the initiative of Argentina, Brazil, and Chile (the ABC countries) to mediate between him and Huerta. In late 1915, Carranza—who had not yet formally been elected president of Mexico—even procured U.S. de facto diplomatic recognition.

Once Constitutionalist forces had overwhelmed the Villa-Zapata coalition, Carranza appropriated another instance of foreign intervention to project himself as the defender of Mexican national pride. In April 1916, U.S. troops under John Pershing's direction invaded Mexico to punish Villa for his raid on a U.S. border town. This so-called "punitive expedition" greatly benefited Carranza. The presence of U.S. forces weakened Villa's position in Chihuahua, and the Constitutionalist leadership once again was able to issue calls for a patriotic *ralliement* in the face of a foreign threat.[27]

In this instance, however, Carranza played a double game with the Mexican public. While he publicly called for an immediate end to the intervention, his secret diplomacy with the Wilson government sought an orderly retreat of Pershing's forces. Without impugning Carranza's genuinely nationalist sentiments, we can conclude that he was acutely aware of the opportunistic benefits of a well-publicized, nationalist foreign policy.

Carranza's views on economic nationalism (the quest for Mexican control of national economic resources) illustrate this point well. During his campaign against Huerta, he had stated more than once that his government would guarantee the security of foreign investments in Mexico. As a consequence, foreign investors soon became convinced that Carranza would not rock the boat; indeed, the Constitutionalist victory did not affect the flow of capital into Mexico.[28] But after the defeat of the Conventionists, Carranza began to show concern with the issue of foreign control of the Mexican economy. In a series of decrees, he imposed a silver export tax, ordered all oil drilling shut down, and required full operation of the country's mines under penalty of nationalization.[29] Responding to a chorus of anti-Yankee voices, which grew louder with each instance of U.S. intervention in the Revolution, Carranza proclaimed that Mexico's resources should be controlled by native capitalists and native laws. With this posture, he exceeded Porfirio

Díaz's nationalist policies in the last years of his rule.[30] This rhetoric aside, however, Carranza's foreign economic policy was hardly "revolutionary": the Mexican leader seldom attempted to enforce his nationalist decrees, choosing instead to use them as negotiating points with the United States. Nevertheless, he had correctly read the sign of the times—economic nationalism had become an important motive for elite and middle-class involvement in the Revolution. To ignore it meant to cut into the core of Carranza's constituency.[31]

Carranza's role at the Constitutional Convention of Querétaro in late 1916 and early 1917 demonstrated this reluctance to embrace a more radical economic nationalism. Carranza desired only minor changes in the existing constitution: Mexico, he thought, needed basic law modeled after that of the United States, with a strong executive and a bicameral congress. Carranza also favored changes in Mexican law that would end the extralegal privileges and political activities of aliens.[32] Much like Madero, he and his *renovador* faction believed that such narrow political reform would open up opportunities for all Mexicans and thus cure more fundamental maladies.[33]

But at the convention, a "Jacobin" majority around General Obregón scoffed at these gradualist, elite notions. While approving Carranza's suggestions, the Jacobins added three articles that sought far-reaching social and economic change. Article 3 mandated secularized, compulsory education. Article 27 made the Mexican territory and subsoil the inalienable patrimony of the nation; from now on, foreigners could only farm, dig or drill by applying for a government concession. This article also stipulated a return of misappropriated peasant lands. Article 123, finally, guaranteed basic rights of urban labor, such as unionization and collective bargaining.[34] With these provisions, the new document became Latin America's first constitution incorporating principles of economic nationalism. Freshly elected President Carranza left Querétaro worried that foreign opposition to this new legislation might derail his efforts to obtain de jure U.S. and European recognition.

Amongst the push and pull of expectations at home, pressures from without, and his own views in the middle of these extremes, Carranza adopted an ambivalent posture toward the new constitution: he did not implement it, but he defended it against international criticism. Carranza remained a bitter opponent of the social and economic reforms embodied in the document, but he was steadfast in resisting U.S. pres-

Alvaro Obregón as Secretary of War, 1917 (Courtesy of the Fideicomiso
Archivos Plutarco Elías Calles y Fernando Torreblanca, Mexico City)

sure to amend it.[35] Knowing that the implementation of Article 27 would jeopardize his own economic interests and worsen his relationship with the U.S. government (which was bad enough at a time when U.S. Ambassador Henry P. Fletcher blamed German meddling for the nationalist provisions), the Mexican president neglected it. But conscious of criticism in the press and in his ruling circle, he adroitly defended against Fletcher's criticism his country's right to formulate its own laws.[36]

This principled stance on behalf of Mexican sovereignty carried over into Carranza's approach to Latin America in general and to Central America in particular. Like the Porfirians, Carranza assumed that the rest of Latin America could learn from Mexico's experience. In fact, he viewed his own struggle as exemplary for other Latin American nations. As Carranza told a throng in the town of Matamoros: "Mexico is the soul of all other nations that suffer the same ills. . . . It is time for Latin America to realize that [our] struggle will serve as an example for those peoples to affirm their own sovereignty and institutions, and the liberty of their citizens."[37] And, as he elaborated a little later in San Luis Potosí: "Now we are the revolutionaries not only of the Mexican nation, but those of Latin America, the revolutionaries of the Universe. . . . Mexico is the only country in Latin America which has come to constitute a nation after three centuries of domination and colonialism, and one century of internal struggle; a nation that should be a model in Spanish America."[38]

Carranza, however, remained vague on the principles he desired the rest of Latin America to emulate. Beyond a vow to establish a Pan-Hispanic union and oblique references to the need for greater cultural exchange, he rarely addressed the subject of his Latin America policy.[39] In fact, it seems the only thing the Mexican president wished to recommend to other Latin American countries was the example of the Revolution. He espoused the "right of rebellion";[40] the right of any people to choose and change its own institutions without intervention from without. Like Díaz, Carranza affirmed political nationalism mixed with a dose of anti-Yanquismo.[41]

In September 1918, Carranza finally issued a comprehensive statement on foreign policy, which encapsulated a variety of somewhat contradictory concerns. The president sought to reaffirm Mexico's existing foreign-policy models; he felt a need to address conclusively the subject of economic nationalism; he needed to allay growing U.S. fears about the safety of foreign investments in Mexico; and he desired to assume leadership in a growing Latin American movement to oppose U.S. intervention in the hemisphere. Consequently, on the occasion of the annual state-of-the-nation address, Carranza read to the Mexican Congress what has come to be regarded as the most succinct formulation of his foreign policy: "All countries are equal. . . . No country may interfere . . . in the internal affairs of others. . . . Nationals and foreigners are equal before the sovereignty of the country in which they live. . . . Diplomacy . . . must not be used for the protection of private interests."[42]

The Carranza Doctrine articulated several positions at once. Most importantly, it demanded an absolute guarantee of nonintervention by asserting, in truly Wilsonian fashion, a universal right to national self-determination. Reinforcing this concern with sovereignty, Carranza's statement denied the legality of diplomatic coercion to influence Mexican legislation. Finally, it invited the other Latin American countries to follow Mexico's example in repudiating foreign intervention.[43]

With this compromise, the Mexican president gave something to everyone. He satisfied his own penchant for gradual reforms, he placated the radicals in his government, and he eased at least somewhat U.S. Ambassador Fletcher's jitters. In this fashion, Carranza reconciled the contradictory goals of defending the Constitution and Mexico's "national dignity" and of assuring the United States that this revolution, unlike the Bolshevik one in Russia, was one that respected private property and the spirit of free enterprise. Instead of explicitly supporting the right to expropriate foreign property, Carranza railed against the political clout that such property wielded in Mexico. Rather than trumpeting the advances of the new constitution, the Mexican president defended the country's equality vis-à-vis other, more powerful nations.[44] The Carranza Doctrine, then, hardly marked a revolutionary turning point in Mexican foreign policy, but rather an elaboration of Porfirian ideas.[45]

The Carranza Doctrine deserves a prominent place in any study of Mexican–Latin American relations because it was often *perceived*, if not intended, as a call for a Latin American league to offset U.S. influence. In this way, the Carranza Doctrine registered a significant impact on Mexican foreign relations. U.S. diplomats would lambast the Carranza Doctrine whenever they saw Mexican influence at work in

Latin America. Nationalist Central American leaders, encouraged by Carranza's remarks, would often hope for Mexican support of their cause, while their foes would appeal to the United States for help against Mexican influence. Mexican diplomats, eager to seize upon a revolutionary rather than a Porfirian precedent, would point to the pronouncements as the righteous declarations of a statesman who had sought to defend Mexico's honor against U.S. intervention. Hence, the Carranza Doctrine has attained a place in the international history of Mexico that has transcended its original context.

Carranza's nationalism, in whatever way understood, did not resonate in Mexico's approach to Central America. In fact, advocates of a revolutionary, nationalist diplomacy in Latin America never found any more than rhetorical support for their goals.[46] In the midst of internal turmoil and turbulent relations with the United States, Carranza would probably have liked to ignore events in Central America. But as early as 1915, he found out that he could not afford to turn his back on the isthmus.

Securing the Border and Reestablishing Relations, 1915–1917

Once again, Estrada Cabrera proved the nuisance that would not go away. As if to parry criticism of his own ruthless rule, Estrada Cabrera paid homage to the vintage anti-Mexicanism of the Guatemalan elites, denouncing the Carranza regime in harsh terms and depicting Mexico as a chaotic society in need of law and order. He also decried Carranza's economic nationalism and repeatedly blamed Mexico for subversive stirrings within his own Liberal party.[47]

Carranza, for his part, was livid about what he regarded as Guatemalan intervention in Mexican internal affairs. In mid-1915, Estrada Cabrera joined the ABC countries, Bolivia, and Uruguay in a mediation initiative that aimed to have someone other than Carranza become the leader of Mexico.[48] Understandably, Carranza reacted with consternation and anger to Estrada Cabrera's participation. Like Porfirio Díaz, Carranza saw only ulterior motives in Guatemalan initiatives—Estrada Cabrera desired either to ingratiate himself with Wilson's diplomats or to take advantage of a rare occasion to weaken Mexico. In any case, this initiative greatly fueled the existing antagonism. In August 1915, Carranza even expelled the resident Guatemalan minister from Mexico.[49]

The crisis in relations soon escalated. As a reprisal, Estrada Cabrera gave shelter to a variety of military bands operating against the Carrancistas in Chiapas.[50] To be sure, he faced the same problem: on several occasions, Guatemalan exile troops and Mexican marauders invaded Guatemala—apparently without Carranza's knowledge.[51] But by December 1915, Estrada Cabrera had succeeded in preventing further illegal crossings, while the Mexican side of the border remained porous. As Mexican Minister of War Obregón was busy trying to control the situation in Chiapas, the Guatemalan president massed eighteen thousand troops on the border.[52]

Estrada Cabrera's treatment of Mexican residents further exacerbated tensions. Over the past four years, Guatemalan authorities had jailed a large number of Mexicans on trumped-up charges. These detainees often languished without trial in sordid prison cells for years. When Carranza attempted to repatriate these prisoners and prevent further offenses, he ran into rock-solid resistance. Backing up his local and regional authorities, especially Jorge Ubico, the *jefe político* of the department of Retalhuleu, Estrada Cabrera insisted on full punishment for all Mexicans engaged in smuggling, "conspiracy" and "subversive activities."[53]

Most galling to Carranza, however, was the matter of Guatemalan support for the counterrevolutionary movement of Félix Díaz. Don Porfirio's nephew maintained considerable support in the Mexican southeast, where the economy had remained strong through the 1907 slump. In the southeast, the regional elites, with the exception of those in Yucatán, largely desired a return of the Porfirians.[54] But Félix Díaz's success in the region was not merely the result of favorable political geography. Beginning in 1915, the Carranza government found evidence linking Estrada Cabrera to the continued vigor of the Felicistas in Chiapas. In fact, the Guatemalan government, for all its denials,[55] gave shelter to Felicista groups, bought arms for the rebels in New York, had them shipped to Guatemala on boats owned by the United Fruit Company, and possibly handed out financial assistance as well.[56]

In aiding Félix Díaz, the Guatemalan president hardly acted out of a newly discovered love for Porfirismo. As long as the military struggle continued, it was in his interest to weaken Mexican central authority in

Chiapas. Possibly, Estrada Cabrera, in his increasing state of dementia, still entertained faint hope for the secession of Chiapas. Even more importantly, at several junctures during the Díaz regime, Mexico had been able to threaten Guatemala by marching up troops in Soconusco. Such a venture became much less likely at a time when the Felicista rebellion held its ground in the Mexican southeast.

The enmity between Carranza and Estrada Cabrera suggests a continuity of policy from the Díaz to the Carranza regime. For lack of adequate sources, it is impossible to ascertain exactly how and why the hostile relations between the two rulers began. It seems likely, however, that Carranza shared Díaz's and Mariscal's assessment of Estrada Cabrera as an implacable enemy and a friend of the Yankees. Indeed, rumors circulated that Estrada Cabrera had sent agents to Mexico to assassinate Carranza, Obregón, and Foreign Secretary Cándido Aguilar.[57] Estrada Cabrera, on the other hand, resented the chaos in Mexico and might have feared that the unrest would spread into his own country—there is no evidence that he disliked the Carranza regime for ideological reasons.

Mexican trouble with Guatemala illustrates to what extent the turmoil during the Revolution had forced a defensive orientation upon the country's foreign policy. As in the period of the 1860s and 1870s, Mexico once again needed to defend its southeastern boundary. Estrada Cabrera never launched an attempt to wrest Soconusco or all of Chiapas from Mexico. Nevertheless, Carranza's posture in Central America—at least initially—was a defensive one, since the Felicistas posed a peril to Constitutionalist supremacy in Chiapas.

Carranza's primary goals in the isthmus were thus limited and pragmatic. As war still raged throughout much of the country, Carranza did not have much diplomatic clout. Relations with the Central American republics had been interrupted since Huerta's presidency. But on the other hand, Carranza could only hope to free the Mexican prisoners and assert his control in Chiapas with Estrada Cabrera's help.[58] Therefore, by late 1916, he felt compelled to come to terms with Estrada Cabrera.

The reestablishment of diplomatic relations—more likely now that the Wilson administration had awarded de facto recognition—appeared a necessary prerequisite to both ends. Therefore, Carranza sent one of his most trusted aides, the poet Salvador Martínez Alomía, on a mission to all of the Central American capitals. As the main purpose of the mission, he instructed his envoy to procure the recognition of the Constitutionalist government and reestablishment of diplomatic relations. Much less significantly, Carranza also wished to gauge the possibilities for Mexican cooperation with the isthmian countries.

Upon arrival in Guatemala, Martínez Alomía encountered instant success, finding Estrada Cabrera amenable to his mission. "Estrada Cabrera is neither in favor of nor against any Mexican government," he wrote to Aguilar. "If he does not feel threatened, he can get along with any government."[59] Estrada Cabrera agreed to free all political prisoners, recognize the Carranza government, and exchange ministers with Mexico.[60] Then, on September 9, 1916, the Mexican envoy and Guatemalan representatives signed a protocol promising to stop violations of the border on both sides.[61] Martínez Alomía well understood the merely symbolic character of the convention, reporting that Estrada Cabrera would not cease to meddle in the Mexican conflict.[62] Nevertheless, the mission had gotten off to an auspicious beginning. Both sides had grown tired of the protracted controversy. The Estrada Cabrera regime, facing a deepening economic slump,[63] simply could not afford to commit increasing military resources to Guatemala's western border.

In San Salvador, the envoy's luck continued, as President Carlos Meléndez received the Mexican mission with great enthusiasm. While in that capital city, Martínez Alomía purchased a vast amount of military supplies from the Salvadoran government.[64] For his part, the Mexican envoy presented a wireless station to the Salvadorans, and reportedly reached a "secret understanding" with Meléndez that contained a defensive alliance against Guatemala.[65] As had been the case during the 1885–1903 period, El Salvador once again emerged as Mexico's principal base of support in Central America.

It is not certain, however, that Meléndez dealt entirely honestly with the Carranza regime. As late as April 1914, his foreign minister had shown himself an enemy of Carranza, declaring to the Mexican [Huertista] consul that "even if Don Venustiano Carranza came here in person, he would leave with empty hands in whatever he tried to accomplish, and even if his revolution were triumphant . . . the government of El Salvador would be one of the last to recognize him."[66] One explanation for Meléndez's change of heart could be his dire financial situation, which prompted him to offer one million cartridges for sale to the Mexican government.

Martínez Alomía's upcoming visit to Managua was of particular significance. Because the Bryan-Chamorro Treaty tied the U.S. government to further intervention, Nicaragua appeared to present a potential problem for Mexico.[67] Yet there seemed to be an opportunity for action: at that very moment the old Zelayista Julián Irías was planning an insurrection against the Conservative government. Martínez Alomía's aide Samuel Sediles, for one, favored supporting the revolt: "For Mexico, the issue is of vital importance. If we do not proceed actively, Mexico will end up completely isolated . . . with Yankee borders in all four directions."[68] But Irías obviously could not overcome a Nicaraguan army trained and armed by U.S. officers. Therefore, the plea fell on deaf ears in Mexico.[69]

Aware of Mexico's limited options, Martínez Alomía tried the opposite route—showing support for a beleaguered government. At a time when the leaders of Guatemala, El Salvador, and Costa Rica denounced the treaty as a work of U.S. imperialism,[70] Nicaragua would do well to establish cordial relations with Mexico. Thus, discarding political principle, Martínez Alomía worked for an understanding with Emiliano Chamorro, whom he regarded as less of a U.S. lackey than had been his predecessor Adolfo Díaz.[71] Prodded by his envoy, even Carranza decided to play ball with the existing authorities: upon request by the financially strapped Chamorro, Carranza advanced a small sum of money to the Nicaraguan government through his agent in New York.[72]

The Carrancistas gained materially from this rapprochement. Nicaragua presented a great opportunity to obtain arms and cartridges at a time when the purchase of these items in the United States had become difficult. During his stay in San Salvador, Martínez Alomía learned that the Chamorro government possessed an excess amount of U.S. cartridges. As the envoy soon found out, Chamorro sold the supplies to the highest bidder. Fearing that the Felicistas might snag the ammunition, Martínez Alomía, with the help of Meléndez, concluded a deal with the Nicaraguan strongman in the spring of 1917 and purchased several million cartridges at prices slightly above the world market level.[73]

These episodes went a long way to improving the conflictive relationship with Nicaragua. In June 1917, after a brief stay in Tegucigalpa,

Martínez Alomía rendered Chamorro a friendly visit. After almost a year in Central America, he then sailed home, but not without having reestablished relations with Nicaragua in an atmosphere of cordiality.[74] Two years later, Mexico and Nicaragua even signed a treaty of amity, commerce, and navigation, which unnecessarily alarmed the U.S. legation in Managua as an "implementation of the Carranza Doctrine."[75]

As these gestures show, Carranza's diplomacy hardly acted to promote the "goals of the Mexican Revolution" throughout the hemisphere. Rather, the Martínez Alomía mission had proven the value of hard-nosed political pragmatism. At this critical juncture in Mexico's history, Carranza could not play a power game in Central America. The Carranza Doctrine would have become a hollow statement indeed, had Mexican diplomacy attempted to subvert the sovereignty of other states. The prime goal of Mexican diplomacy, at this point, was the international protection of the fragile revolutionary government. Viewed from this vantage point, Martínez Alomía's mission had been a success. Very soon, however, the effects of a world war and new Guatemalan support for the Felicistas would undo a great part of the envoy's achievements.[76]

Mexico, Central America, and a Colossus at War, 1917–1918

The U.S. entry into the war in April 1917 scuttled Carranza's newfound activism in foreign relations. The global crisis kept the United States out of Mexican internal politics: preoccupied with the global conflict, the U.S. government extended de jure recognition to Carranza and withdrew the punitive expedition.[77] But the war enhanced U.S. fears about German influence in Latin America, as well as apprehension about Mexican policies in the hemisphere. U.S. participation in World War One therefore further reduced Mexico's limited scope of action in Central America by boosting aggressive U.S. policies.

Wilson's decision to go to war with Germany heightened U.S. fears about the strategic vulnerability of Central America. Concern about the canal route ensured the ratification of the Bryan-Chamorro Treaty. If the U.S. Senate earlier might have balked at a treaty committing the United States to an "entangling alliance" in an area chronically beset by instability, the prospect of German meddling swayed many lawmakers.

In 1916, the Senate reluctantly ratified the treaty. The Wilson administration then proceeded to destroy the Central American arbitration framework created in the 1907 Washington Conventions. When the Court of Central American Justice rejected the Bryan-Chamorro Treaty, called to action by El Salvador and Costa Rica's complaints that the treaty violated their territorial rights, U.S. diplomats advised Nicaragua to withdraw from the 1907 agreement. With this step, Wilson, who had started his work with the pretense of putting an end to the "big stick" and dollar diplomacy, had made Roosevelt's and Taft's policy look tame by comparison. Wilson's aggressive diplomacy alienated the governments of El Salvador, Costa Rica, and even that of Guatemala. By late 1917, the isthmus was awash in anti-Yankee sentiments.[78]

But Carranza could not take advantage of this seemingly favorable climate. His government still wielded little authority in Mexico, and the Central American elites loathed the continuing instability. The United States was sure to oppose any effort to exploit the backlash against U.S. intervention, particularly one undertaken by an unstable "revolutionary" regime.[79] Moreover, the effects of the war on the direction of U.S. foreign policy exacerbated existing problems between Carranza and Wilson and therefore made a Central American policy much more difficult.

Most significantly, the war helped fuel a U.S. effort to fight the economic nationalism of the 1917 Constitution. Even though the U.S. State Department could not force Carranza to scrap Article 27, it was clear that the two governments would eventually clash over oil—a "strategic commodity" particularly crucial in times of war. Eager to guarantee continued access to this commodity, the State Department awarded special diplomatic protection to U.S. oil companies operating in Mexico. While Wilson had long railed against special economic interest groups, the oilmen now received a firm—albeit thus far theoretical—commitment to protect their holdings from possible nationalization. Wartime considerations therefore dovetailed with the views of many U.S. businessmen in Mexico, even if Secretary of State Robert Lansing hesitated to demand an outright repeal of the nationalist provisions.[80]

While the war thus gave the hawks in Washington ammunition to demand an inflexible policy toward the Carranza government, German activities in Mexico further accentuated U.S. apprehensions. The uncovering of the "Zimmermann note" (a German proposal for an alliance with Mexico in case the United States joined the Allies) contributed to Wilson's decision to declare war. Even though Carranza immediately rejected the proposal, the Zimmermann note became the source of much undue U.S. paranoia about the Constitutionalist government. Ambassador Fletcher even labeled the 1917 Constitution the work of secret agents of the Kaiser, disregarding the fact that Article 27 imperiled German economic interests as much as it did those of the United States.[81] The anti-Carranza voices in Washington became even shriller when the Mexican leader refused to limit German activities in his country, let alone declare war on Germany or Austria.

This stance, however, should not have surprised anyone. The United States had brought Huerta to power, occupied Veracruz, and sent the punitive expedition into Mexico. Great Britain, the informal ally of the United States, had supported Huerta and the Felicista forces. By contrast, Germany had never violated Mexican sovereignty. Therefore, Carranza stayed on good terms with Germany throughout the war.[82] Since Germans living in Mexico expressed loyalty to his regime, he also successfully resisted U.S. pressure to remove them from positions of economic power.[83] To the wrath of Lansing, Carranza would not consider being drawn into a war on the side of "los Yanquis," a move that would almost certainly have ended his tenure as president of Mexico.[84] But Carranza did not wish to antagonize the Wilson administration over the issue, and he made sure that his friendship with Germany remained low in profile.[85] He did not permit German ships to use Mexican ports and insisted that Germany, like other nations, respect Mexico's neutrality.[86]

The issue of participation in the war provided a further impediment to Mexican initiatives in Central America, as Nicaragua, Guatemala, and Honduras followed the path of the United States. The Nicaraguan government was the first to declare war on Germany, but it did not harm the German citizens in Nicaragua. Estrada Cabrera hesitated much longer, but ultimately found it convenient to join the United States in a state of belligerency—mainly for economic reasons. The price of coffee, one of the country's main sources of income, had collapsed during the war. Guatemala needed help to mitigate the consequences of this decline in revenues, and as a neutral it could not expect U.S. assistance.[87]

Therefore, three weeks after Wilson had declared war, Estrada Cabrera broke off relations with Germany and declared that Guatemala assumed the same attitude with regard to the world war as the United States. He also granted U.S. forces the use of Guatemalan ports and railways.[88] To end tensions caused by German agents in the coffee region, Estrada Cabrera imposed a state of siege on the departments affected and expropriated some German-owned coffee fincas.[89] In addition, he appointed a U.S. resident of Guatemala trustee of a German-owned electric company.[90] In March 1918, he finally declared war on Germany, stopping short, however, of the wholesale confiscation of German property that the U.S. government had desired.[91]

Mexico's and Guatemala's different positions in the war led to yet further deterioration in relations between the two countries. For one thing, Estrada Cabrera repeatedly attempted to exploit his pro-Allied stance to Mexico's disadvantage. In August 1917, for example, his minister to the United States approached one of Lansing's aides with a request for protection against the "bitter [Mexican] enemies of Guatemala" and made reference to Guatemala's supportive attitude toward the U.S. war effort. The aide, however, would not buy into the scheme, stating that his government "would give Guatemala every support in the present conflict with Germany provided that . . . Estrada Cabrera had placed his services at the disposal of the United States."[92]

Desperate to find some sort of political success somewhere, Estrada Cabrera renewed support for the Felicistas and Chiapanecan separatists under the leadership of Tirso Castañón. From bases in the region of Los Altos, the rebels helped spark a sustained renaissance of the counterrevolution in southeastern Mexico in late 1917.[93] Minister of War Alvaro Obregón responded by sending more troops to Chiapas. His forces needed two years, however, to snuff out the embers of the rebellion.

Mexico once again appeared to become ensnared in a web of hostile governments—always Porfirio Díaz's nightmare. The country bordered two nations allied in their war effort against imperial Germany. The fact that El Salvador had joined Mexico among the ranks of the neutral powers mattered little. Despite the bad rapport between Estrada Cabrera and the State Department, the fear existed that a new U.S.-Guatemalan entente, like the one between James Blaine and Justo Rufino Barrios in the early 1880s, might create problems for Mexico.

The effects of the war had thus undone many of Martínez Alomía's achievements. Guatemala looked like a perennial adversary unwilling ever to give up support for Carranza's rivals; the U.S. government was watching Mexico's every move in the region; the war had enhanced U.S. status in the hemisphere; and Mexican neutrality contrasted with the pro-Allied stance of most of Central America. In sum, Mexico and the Central American countries had drifted farther apart. Other than the leadership of tiny El Salvador, Carranza had no friends in the isthmus. At this juncture, the fostering of a Central American union under Salvadoran leadership emerged as the only way for Mexico to break out of its international isolation.

Carranza and Another Effort at Central American Unification

The task of establishing a Central American union, however, seemed an even taller order in 1917 than ever before. As we have seen, the five states had long bred strong, independent camarillas unwilling to give up part of their power to a larger federation. Further, Central American leaders could not agree on the form of government of the new union, much less consent to a capital city.[94] In the words of Tomás Guardia, the former president of Costa Rica, the idea of union would always be held hostage to rivaling personal ambitions: "one republic, one president; five republics, five presidents."[95]

But the idea of Central American unification never died; indeed, it experienced periodic revivals. In 1917, one of these attempts at revival originated from Francisco Bertrand, the president of Honduras. Riding a groundswell of unionist sentiment, Bertrand embraced the cause in the hope that the Honduran congress might amend a constitutional provision preventing his reelection. Being the least prosperous and least populated of the Central American countries, Honduras had much to gain from an association with El Salvador, its smaller but densely populated neighbor. Therefore, Bertrand first won Meléndez's cooperation and then invited all five republics to attend a conference to be held in Tegucigalpa. He also invited Mexico and the United States to attend as possible guarantors of the union.[96] In fact, for a short time, Mexico City was itself considered as the conference site.[97]

As in the last years of the Díaz regime, Mexican diplomacy was sympathetic to those plans for union that did not originate in Guatemala. In fact, the young Carrancista military officers who made up the bulk of Mexico's new diplomatic corps displayed an almost naïve excitement about the possibility of a Central American union. "If two or three countries like . . . Argentina, Chile and Mexico could . . . give moral and material aid to . . . this truly patriotic idea . . . while the United States is at war," one of them wrote, "confederation would become possible."[98]

Foreign Secretary Aguilar, however, took a more realistic position and decided to wait in the wings to assess the attitude of the State Department and that of the other Central American states. There was another reason for Mexico's reticence: even though Bertrand had first approached El Salvador with his unionist plan, the possibility existed that he had acted on Estrada Cabrera's orders. After 1910, the Honduran government had fallen under strong Guatemalan influence, and Carranza had no intention of abetting an Estrada Cabrera scheme to dominate the isthmus.

Mexico's stance was well chosen, as Bertrand's plan soon fell apart. The Costa Rican government under Federico Tinoco was not internationally recognized, and Chamorro refused to participate. Estrada Cabrera, for his part, caused further complications. Nervous about the Honduran-Salvadoran association, he made plans to have himself elected provisional president of the remaining federation.[99] Afraid of Guatemalan dominance, Bertrand and Meléndez then signed a bilateral agreement creating the República de Morazán, named after the foremost leader of the old United Provinces of the Center of America—apparently with prodding from Carranza.[100] The projected union of five countries had become much more modest, embracing only two of the republics of Central America.

Whereas Mexico had not aided the larger unionist project for fear that Guatemala would dominate it, the Republic of Morazán appeared to Carranza as an opportunity to weaken Estrada Cabrera. Because of its larger population, friendly El Salvador was the senior partner in the union with Honduras. Therefore, Carranza responded positively to the repeated pleas of Salvadoran agents to help the new state, and agreed to a swap of two Mexican planes for two million cartridges left in San Salvador by an ex-Carrancista general. Officials in El Salvador responded enthusiastically to the prospect of future cooperation with the

Carranza regime and sold Mexico an additional two million cartridges.[101] In return, the Mexican leader provided financial assistance for the victims of a 1917 earthquake in San Salvador and reportedly offered to send Meléndez fifty thousand troops in case of Guatemalan aggression.[102] Carranza also pledged his assistance to the Republic of Morazán.[103]

Soon thereafter, however, Mexico had to withdraw from the scene. Concerned about the cordial relationship between Mexico and El Salvador, Estrada Cabrera pleaded with U.S. officials to assist Guatemala in repelling what he viewed a military threat. When that effort failed, he pressed Bertrand not to accept any assistance from Mexico for the union project. Playing out his influence over the Honduran government, Estrada Cabrera soon succeeded. Bertrand told the U.S. minister that he would seek only U.S.—and not Mexican—assistance, and he even offered a naval base in the Gulf of Fonseca in exchange for support for the union.[104]

Bertrand's about-face was not surprising. In principle friendly to Mexico,[105] he faced formidable opponents at home and owed his position to Guatemalan goodwill. He could not appear to be in league with Carranza. But even without Bertrand's change of heart, U.S. opposition to the project would have doomed it. Viewing Central America as a potential base for "anti-American" sentiments, Wilson was "unalterably opposed" to the unification of the isthmus.[106] The State Department also expressed skepticism about the idea; one of Lansing's aides viewed the union as reflecting personal ambitions and Mexican and German influence rather than a carefully thought-out plan.[107]

Ultimately, the Republic of Morazán proved an elusive dream. When Meléndez pressured Bertrand to allow him to become the first president of the new entity and to cede a strip of the Honduran Atlantic coast to El Salvador, the Honduran president terminated all negotiations. Seeing that none of the Central American nations was any more willing now to accept a Salvadoran-led union than it had been to acquiesce in a Guatemalan-led scheme in 1885, Meléndez finally gave up his pretensions to becoming the leader of the isthmus. Frustrated, Carranza also lost interest in the union, stating that the matter was "one for the two countries to decide."[108]

The idea of union, however, was by no means dead. Neither Meléndez nor Bertrand had given up hope that their plan would ultimately succeed, and Meléndez waited for the overthrow or death of the ailing Estrada Cabrera. As we shall see, when that old dictator finally lost power in April 1920, Mexico would once again welcome an attempt to merge the republics of Central America into one larger unit. It would not again, however, become involved in promoting what seemed a purposeless exercise.

Nor would Mexico—at least between 1918 and 1924—risk antagonizing the United States in Central America at a time when U.S.–Mexican relations went through their most serious crisis since 1847. This crisis, which had long festered, only to erupt at the end of the world war, would require an even more cautious approach to the isthmus.

Another Retreat in the Face of U.S. Pressure, 1918–1920

By 1920, Carranza had finally achieved a consolidation of his rule. Apart from some small pockets of resistance, the Constitutionalists controlled all of Mexico. In 1919, Zapata was assassinated on government orders, and Villa retired to a large hacienda. Carranza might have thought that a long period of difficulties was finally approaching its conclusion.

Events, however, soon proved otherwise. Free to act after the end of World War One in November 1918, the hawks in the State Department launched their long-awaited offensive to prevent implementation of the controversial articles of the 1917 Constitution. As a result, the 1918–20 period witnessed a clash over U.S. property rights in Mexico that poisoned U.S.–Mexican relations until 1942. Over that same period, this clash would limit Mexican policies in Central America.

While Ambassador Fletcher had long been the lone crusader to ensure the compatibility of the Revolution with U.S. property interests, he now received help from his superiors. Stung by press criticism of his failure to reverse revolutionary legislation, Lansing joined Fletcher in urging Wilson to apply pressure on Carranza. When a "Red Scare" swept the United States in the summer of 1919, President Wilson's Democrats became even more vulnerable to the charges of "losing Mexico." The hawks in Washington received a final boost from Wilson's personal misfortune: in the fall of 1919, the U.S. president went down with a stroke that seriously impaired his ability to direct U.S. foreign policy. With Wilson incapacitated, Fletcher and Senator Albert B.

Fall—an interventionist par excellence—enjoyed free rein to clamp down on Mexico. As a result, by late 1919, the idea that the allegedly "anti-American" Mexican Revolution should not be countenanced by U.S. diplomacy had attained a virtually axiomatic character in Washington.

The fact that Carranza remained true *in practice* to his own ideas helped little. The Mexican government only expropriated a token number of acres under the provisions of Article 27, it made little headway on the labor reform stipulated by Article 123, and Carranza, an avowed Catholic, did not even consider implementing Article 3.[109] The State Department, however, was not satisfied with this show of restraint. Instead, Lansing demanded the lifting of a new tax on subsoil products as well as requiring an unequivocal declaration that Carranza would not apply Article 27 retroactively to U.S. property in Mexico. Vulnerable to domestic criticism, the Mexican government rejected these demands.

Not surprisingly, the Carranza government soon needed to muster all its strength to tackle its bilateral problems with the United States. Even if another intervention in Mexico was never a real possibility, U.S. actions in Nicaragua, Cuba, Haiti, and the Dominican Republic served as a vivid warning to audacious Latin American regimes. Thus, by late 1918, the Carranza administration retreated from almost all activity in Central America in order to avoid further conflicts with the State Department. It confined itself to dealing with border problems with Guatemala that did not involve the United States, while neglecting the strategically sensitive countries (e.g., Nicaragua and Costa Rica) close to the Panama Canal.

Mexican inaction became especially apparent in the Central American efforts to mediate between the Wilson government and the Costa Rican regime of Federico Tinoco, which had come to power through a coup d'état. True to Wilsonian ideas, the U.S. government refused to recognize Tinoco, citing a provision in the 1907 Washington Conventions that forbade the recognition of "unconstitutional" governments.[110] With the withholding of recognition, Wilson and Lansing effectively cut off all U.S. government loans to Costa Rica and dealt its economy a serious blow. Fearing that the United States might one day put the practice of nonrecognition to more general use in Central America, Salvadoran president Carlos Meléndez invited Mexico, Honduras, Guatemala, and Nicaragua to join in the effort. But mindful of current U.S. involvement in the region (and perhaps of the fact that Carranza himself had come to power fighting a de facto regime), Aguilar stayed out of the fray. In the words of one of his aides, "the chancelleries of Costa Rica's neighbors are in a better position to . . . solve these problems."[111]

Mexican diplomacy did display some activism in attempting to scuttle a U.S. initiative that Carranza deemed injurious to Mexican sovereignty. On the occasion of the approval of the League of Nations Charter at the 1919 Peace Conference in Versailles, U.S. diplomats had motioned to establish the Monroe Doctrine as a principle of international law.[112] Interviewed on the subject by a U.S. journalist, Carranza reiterated Díaz's position of 1896 in infinitely harsher terms: "[The Monroe Doctrine] constitutes an arbitrary protectorate imposed on peoples who have neither asked for it nor needed it; it contains no reciprocity and thus is unjust if applied only to the American republics. [The Doctrine] should be applied to the entire world; otherwise it constitutes a tutelage over Latin America."[113] To Carranza's delight, El Salvador immediately adopted Mexico's stance. Aguilar then sent a circular to all Latin American chancelleries enjoining them to adopt the same position.[114] No other countries followed suit, however, and the matter died when the U.S. Senate did not ratify the League of Nations treaty. Once again, Carranza had assumed an internationally prestigious but potentially hazardous stand.

All in all, however, the years 1918–20 constituted another hiatus in Mexican activism in Central America. With the Felicistas crushed and the southeastern border secured, Carranza did not need to worry about Guatemala. No easy opportunity for Mexican involvement presented itself in Central America. In a period of deteriorating U.S.–Mexican relations, the time hardly seemed propitious to push more ambitious objectives: the support for nationalist movements and the prevention of U.S. intervention.

The Carranza regime had blended Porfirian strategies with revolutionary rhetoric to achieve realistic and narrowly defined objectives.[115] Indeed, Carranza's Central America policy was necessarily modest, cautious, and conservative, much more so than that of Díaz. In the 1910s, Mexico could not pursue ambitious goals in Central America.

Therefore, Mexican foreign policy had not played a role in many of the most important Central American political issues of the time: U.S. intervention in Nicaragua, the Bryan-Chamorro Treaty, the question of participation in the world war, the end of the Washington Conventions, and U.S.–Costa Rican relations in the era of Tinoco. Mexico was, in other words, a "nonpower" that could not assert its traditional objectives in the region.

Nevertheless, Carranza had enjoyed some success in his Guatemala policy. He had contained Estrada Cabrera's efforts to weaken his authority in the border region. Like the Liberals of the nineteenth century, Carranza had found that the nonexistence of state authority left Chiapas vulnerable. If his regime looked relatively conservative in its approach to Guatemala, its policies bore notable resemblance to Juárez's and Díaz's efforts to secure Mexico's southeastern border. Carranza could boast other achievements as well. He had renewed diplomatic relations with all of the Central American countries. With his Salvadoran connection, Mexico could once again count on a sympathetic regime to help oppose U.S. hegemony and Guatemalan attempts at regional dominance. By aiding the cause of Central American union, Carranza had gained many admirers on the isthmus, such as Meléndez and the Nicaraguan Julián Irías. In sum, Carranza had attempted to further Mexican aims in Central America during a difficult period— Mexico had never completely "turned in on itself."[116]

Carranza's track record in Central America suggests that his regime was fundamentally pragmatic in orientation. His Constitutionalists had pursued one main goal in the Revolution: the reestablishment of a state strong enough to withstand internal turmoil and independent enough to resist outside interference. To achieve these objectives, the Carrancistas wrote a constitution that appealed to many different sectors of the Mexican population, and they defended Mexico's right to make its own laws vis-à-vis foreign pressure. Many a nationalist provision embodied in the 1917 Constitution, however, remained a dead letter during his rule. Thus, Carranza's role in the Mexican Revolution, and his foreign policy in particular, resembled the careful negotiating of a dangerous river rather than a surging ride on a nationalist floodtide.[117]

During the 1910s, Central America had been a threat to Mexico but hardly an opportunity. Carranza had acquitted himself well in countering this threat. It was left for another regime to renew the Porfirian challenge to the United States in Central America. The story of this renewed challenge would tell to what extent Mexico—and the world around it—had changed between the 1900s and the 1920s.

6   Alvaro Obregón's Hands-Off Policy, 1920–1924

> Mexico is marching on the canal with music, banners, and flowers. We are marching with machine guns, dollars, and Marines.
>
> U.S. journalist Carleton Beals, 1926

Alvaro Obregón eschewed power politics in Central America in favor of an approach geared to making gains over the long haul. He passed up a number of opportunities to expand Mexican political influence in the region. But his government did lay the groundwork for future opportunities: it worked to enhance cultural, social, and economic ties between the Mexican and Central American peoples.

U.S. policies provided much of the reason for Obregón's caution. While he maintained better relations with the U.S. State Department than did Carranza, the new Mexican president spent almost three years chasing U.S. diplomatic recognition. U.S. policies toward Central America continued to make Mexican initiatives even more difficult. The administrations of Warren G. Harding and Calvin Coolidge desired to disengage U.S. forces from the ongoing Nicaraguan imbroglio, but they shared Taft's and Wilson's opposition to Mexican influence in the isthmus. The fact that many conservative U.S. businessmen, journalists, and politicians compared Mexico's Revolution to the Bolshevik one in Russia did not help matters.

But U.S. policies were not Obregón's only problem in Central America. Scared by popular unrest in the 1918–21 period, the isthmian elites feared the influence of a society that was just emerging from a decade of social revolution and civil war. At the same time, the Mexican president had to satisfy the radical wing of his own faction, which clamored for a show of Pan–Latin American fraternity in the face of Yankee aggression.

Torn between these exigencies, Obregón pursued a balancing act. With the help of a policy oriented toward long-term gains in the social, economic, and cultural spheres, he hoped to assuage his domestic constituency yet avoid antagonizing U.S. and Central American leaders.[1]

Obregón Tames the Revolution and the United States

In May 1920, an uprising led by three generals from the northern Mexican state of Sonora—Obregón, Adolfo de la Huerta and Plutarco Elías Calles—seized power in a bloody coup that took Carranza's life. Known as the "Sonoran dynasty," the new rulers represented a new political breed. Describing themselves as Mexico's Californians, the Sonorans introduced the values, practices, and politics of the rugged northwestern frontier into the rest of Mexico.[2] Brashly secular, capitalist, and pragmatic, Obregón and his allies represented the petite bourgeoisie of the Mexican Revolution: those who had forced Carranza to include the anti-clerical, nationalist, and pro-labor provisions in the new constitution. But even while they represented the more radical wing of the victorious Constitutionalists, the Sonorans were less interested in ideology than in staying in power and reconstructing effective state control.[3] To achieve these goals, the Sonorans ruled through compromise and accommodation; a strategy they applied to their foreign policy as well.

Obregón, who controlled the Sonoran faction due to his command of the army, illustrated well this combination of coercion and compromise. After he had succeeded interim president de la Huerta as Mexico's ruler, he successfully portrayed himself as the foremost caudillo of the Revolution, an image that rested both on his image as a military leader and on his shrewd maneuvering in the Carrancista coalition. No one could doubt Obregón's military prowess, which he had demonstrated in his campaign against Pancho Villa's numerically superior army, and which he showed off yet again in crushing a series of rebellions against his regime. These exploits had gained him national prominence, and the fact that he had lost an arm in battle only served to underscore Obregón's image as a hero.[4] Like Díaz, who had been a successful general in the war against the French, Obregón could also point to his military feats. Obregón's reputation, added to a good measure of political savvy, helped him attract formerly hostile factions to form a diverse coalition which sustained him in office. Never "embarrassed by considerations of doctrine,"[5] the Sonoran had aligned himself with the majority "Jacobins" during the Constitutional Convention of 1917, yet had kept Carranza's confidence up to the day that he began his revolt. Throughout this period, Obregón carefully cultivated the (partially manufactured) image of a humble chickpea farmer who had risen to the top by hard work, personal sacrifice, and concern for his country. Once in power, Obregón used this image in order to shrug off any remaining association with the unpopular Carranza.[6]

As president, Obregón—the "great compromiser of Mexico's time of troubles"[7]—proved a moderate social reformer. During his reign from 1920 to 1924, he gave a little to everybody: a little land to the peasants, educational reform to the middle class, official support to urban labor, influence in the government to his generals, and an hacienda to send Villa into retirement. As a result, the Sonorans could broaden their power base beyond the army to include peasants, urban labor, formal political parties, and the middle classes.[8] By the time he stepped down in 1924, Obregón had created the nucleus of a populist regime, and he had reduced the army's role in politics.[9]

The appropriation of an emergent revolutionary political culture in the service of an "official cultural nationalism" played a crucial role in Obregón's attempt at state building. Manipulating "radical" art, music, literature, and political thought as elements of an official mythology of the Mexican Revolution, Obregón succeeded in portraying his faction as the standard-bearer for the ideals of all of the groups fighting in the military struggle of the 1910s. Despite the bitter divisions among the factions, this mythology wove them all together in a "revolutionary family."[10] Situating the Sonoran dynasty atop such a historical construct as a "revolutionary family" only a few years after the end of the fighting was no easy task. The matter was complicated by Obregón's role in the assassinations of Carranza and—in 1923—Villa.[11] Nevertheless, by the mid-1920s, the Sonorans had synthesized a "myth of the Revolution" by manipulating the public image of Madero, Carranza, Villa, and Zapata. They glorified Villa's and Zapata's contributions, extolled Madero as a virtuous fighter for democracy, and lauded Carranza for his work for the Constitution.[12] Just as Díaz had done in his deification of Juárez, the Sonorans had thus stocked up the pantheon of national heroes to fit their political needs.

How did Obregón and his allies disseminate their message in a country just emerging from a long period of upheaval? First and foremost, they spread the mystification of the Revolution by means of school reform. The Obregón regime brought elementary schooling to many remote areas of the country. In these new rural schools, a renovated curriculum acquainted many Mexicans who had identified themselves primarily in terms of their region with the notion of a Mexican nationality. The man in charge of the reform, Education Secretary José Vasconcelos, also propounded a complementary racial ideology: Mexico, he claimed, was the cradle of a "cosmic race," a blend of peoples from Europe, America, Africa, and Asia that combined the best of the qualities of their ancestors. The Revolution, Vasconcelos went on, redeemed this cosmic race, and specifically the Indian element in it, from European domination. Thus, the Sonorans had advanced an ideology that tied a vindication of Mexico's mestizo and indigenous majority to the Revolution, of which the Sonoran dynasty claimed to be the faithful heirs.[13]

In his attempt to promote this ideology further, Obregón hired the services of Mexico's foremost revolutionary artists, the *muralistas*. In the early 1920s, the Mexican government commissioned Diego Rivera and other radical muralists to put their interpretation of Mexican history on the walls of many public buildings. The result was a view of the Revolution more critical of the Sonoran-led government than Obregón would have liked. The Marxist Rivera in particular depicted Mexican history as a class struggle. His paintings emphasized the native Mexicans' ongoing sufferings under the alliance of the Mexican upper class and foreign investors, and they foretold the ultimate salvation of the country by a proletarian, indigenous Revolution. Nevertheless, the mural art brought Mexico international praise, and it helped placate Mexicans dissatisfied with Obregón's compromises to the old order and with the slow pace of reform.[14]

As Obregón's promotion of the muralists showed, the revolutionary experience in general had broadened Mexican nationalism both in social and in cultural terms. The common fight against Díaz and Huerta had amounted to a baptism by fire. For all its destructiveness, the Revolution had brought a new sense of dignity both to those who fought in it and to those who joined in the rebuilding effort. The upheaval uprooted many from their *patrias chicas,* propelling them through a variety of regions hitherto unknown to them. Now that the country was settling down after a decade of military struggle, many more Mexicans could conceive of it as a nation. In addition, new technologies helped spread nationalism in Mexico. A host of newspapers, the telegraph, and the radio spread notice of national and international events into all areas of the country, and thus made it easier for the Sonorans to distribute their message. Even as U.S. culture made its influence ever more strongly felt on Mexico, Mexican official nationalism had attained a strong cultural component.[15] To a large extent, then, Obregón and his Sonoran allies had won control of the Mexican Revolution by responding to an emergent revolutionary political culture.

Obregón's approach to domestic problems set the tone for his policy toward the United States: faced with tremendous political obstacles, he combined flexibility in diplomatic matters with an attempt to promote international awareness and understanding for Mexican culture. The official promotion of Mexican culture abroad strengthened the nationalist image of Obregón's government at home. At the same time, in the United States, this "vogue of things Mexican" helped mobilize public opinion in its favor.[16]

Problems with the United States made Obregón's foreign policy exceedingly difficult at the outset. Wary about "revolutionary change," whether from Soviet Russia or from Mexico,[17] U.S. President Woodrow Wilson refused to recognize both de la Huerta and his successor, Obregón, in the hopes of extracting significant guarantees for U.S. property owners. This lack of diplomatic ties was dangerous: without recognition, the Mexican government could not borrow money abroad, and U.S. neutrality laws did not apply to hinder activities of rebel groups in the United States. With the notoriously interventionist senator Albert B. Fall at the apex of his congressional career, the next U.S. president, Warren G. Harding, continued this hard-line policy.

U.S. claims, Mexican debts, and a protracted oil controversy underlay these difficulties. After the end of the military phase of the Revolution, many U.S. citizens and companies pressed claims for damages incurred during the fighting. Destructive uprisings continued into the 1920s and added to the high dollar amounts these interests sought to extract from the Mexican government as compensation. Following the advice of Fall, the State Department pushed vigorously for the resolution of such claims. Efforts on the part of U.S. banks to recover overdue loans, on the other hand, worked to counteract the influence of U.S. claimants: the Obregón regime soon threatened to default on these loans. Since the Mexican government owed the majority of these funds to U.S. banks, financial circles close to the Harding administration pressed for a conciliatory policy. U.S. creditors, these bankers argued, only stood to lose from a policy of nonrecognition. But if the influences of claimants and bankers offset each other, the oil controversy tipped the scale in favor of a hawkish policy. Oil production had soared despite the revolutionary turmoil. By 1921, Mexico had become the world's largest exporter of crude. The ongoing debate around the nationalizing Article 27 alarmed the oil companies. Not surprisingly, the predominantly U.S.- and British-owned oil industry threw its weight behind the hard-liners in Washington and insisted on full advance guarantees that their property rights would not be impinged upon.[18]

What was Obregón to do? He was under pressure to implement the nationalist provisions of the Constitution. As he well knew, reform as stipulated by the Constitution would please many different groups: workers, peasants, the middle sectors, and idealistic members of the elite.[19] Moreover, the establishment of nominal national control over the oil fields promised considerable fiscal benefit: so far, the oil companies had been drilling under the laissez-faire petroleum code of 1884, which allowed them to extract oil at low rates of taxation. At the same time, Obregón, who had decried Carranza's "anti-American" policies, had ample reason to proceed with a "minimum of reform."[20] U.S. recognition was crucial to the survival of his government. Moreover, implementation of the Constitution threatened to alienate two powerful groups other than foreign businessmen: landowners, who feared the expropriation of their holdings, and the Church, as the target of the secularization schemes in Article 3.

As a result, "radicals" and "moderates" fought over the direction of Mexican foreign policy. Led by Vasconcelos and Francisco Múgica, the radicals followed the lead of the 1917 Jacobins. Supported mainly by university students, labor, and members of the urban bourgeoisie, the radicals demanded substantial moves to Mexicanize the economy. Seeking international solidarity, the radicals, in the vein of the Porfirian Reyistas, also advocated an active Latin America policy.[21] The moderates, led by Foreign Secretary Alberto Pani, advocated a more cautious approach and warned about the dangers of openly antagonizing Mexican capitalists and the U.S. government. The leaders of this group, many of whom had gained experience with U.S. diplomacy as Carrancista agents to the Wilson administration, argued in favor of making temporary concessions in order to obtain U.S. recognition. In the vein of the Porfirian científicos, the moderates saw little value in fostering open antagonism with the United States and advocated a gradualist policy. Predictably, Obregón—himself no radical in any way—sided with the moderates. While he kept the radicals satisfied by rebuffing calls to amend the Constitution, he held talks with U.S. government and business interests. Recognizing the divisions within these interests, Obregón targeted the dovish banking sector and soon encountered success: by 1921, U.S. bankers lobbied Harding for recognition.[22]

With this strategy, Obregón showed a keen sense of political expediency: in 1923, his patience was rewarded with the Bucareli treaties that resulted in the awarding of U.S. diplomatic recognition. Obregón, for his part, promised not to apply Article 27 retroactively and to settle U.S. claims. Much like Díaz in 1876, he had purchased the recognition of his government with guarantees for U.S. investments. But nevertheless, the Bucareli accords amounted to a Mexican victory. The agreements had no internationally binding character, since they were never submitted for ratification by either the Mexican or the U.S. legislature. Thus, they would not tie his hands forever.[23]

A Rapprochement with Guatemala

Mexico's Central America policy in the early 1920s must be seen in the context of these parallel developments in Obregón's reconstruction efforts and his relations with the United States. In both spheres, Obregón understood the enormous difficulties facing his government and thus adopted a conciliatory approach. The complications with the United States in particular restricted Mexico's options in Central America. Not only did the lack of diplomatic recognition constitute a grave enough problem, but the revolutionary upheavals, ably exploited by U.S. diplomats in the area, had scared the conservative Central American elites. Mexico, as a prominent Carrancista editorialized in June 1921, was alone in its conflict with the United States and could not count on its old friends in Central America.[24] Therefore, Obregón's Central America policy was even more cautious and pragmatic than his approach toward the United States.

The touchstone of this cautious policy was a long overdue rapprochement with Guatemala—a rapprochement that seemed difficult as long as Estrada Cabrera remained in office. During his long rule, Estrada Cabrera had frequently cast Mexico as his prime international adversary. As we have seen, he had often truckled to the United States in Central American conflicts, his *jefes políticos* had jailed thousands of Mexican residents of Guatemala, and he had sheltered and aided Carranza's enemies. Neither Porfirio Díaz's hostility nor Carranza's rhetoric had made a dent in this pattern.

But in April 1920, the unthinkable happened. Following an uprising by the "Unionist Party," the Guatemalan congress declared Estrada Cabrera insane and removed him from office.[25] Under the leadership of Carlos Herrera, a coffee planter who favored political reform and Central American union but no great transformations in Guatemalan society, the Unionist Party then assumed power to the acclaim of most Guatemalans. An alliance of dissident students, workers, and opposition Conservatives, the Unionist Party resembled Madero's anti-Díaz coalition: it lacked internal cohesion, but it did agree on the old dictator's ouster.[26]

Provisional president Herrera had strong incentives to seek better relations with Mexico. Knowing that he owed his position to the Unionist Party, he desired the unification of Central America by peaceful means, and he saw a chance to link his party's "revolution" to the Mexican experience. The Unionist Party had chapters in all of the Central American countries, and the party's grassroots constituency demanded the swift convocation of an isthmian congress to pave the way for unification.[27] Herrera did not delude himself that Mexico could provide active help. Rather, he approached the Mexican government to achieve support in his negotiations with the other Central American countries, especially El Salvador. Since Carranza had found the Salvadoran regime the most congenial one in his Central American diplomacy, Herrera intended to exploit this connection.[28] Hoping to receive at least a symbolic endorsement of his provisional government, which would position him to become president of the proposed federation, he sent a special mission to Mexico in June 1920.

The Sonorans gladly took the opportunity to furnish such a symbolic endorsement of the Unionist coup. Both de la Huerta and Obregón warmly received the Guatemalan delegation. In August, Obregón, still in his capacity as informal leader of the Sonorans, visited a Guatemalan delegation at the Mexican-Guatemalan border and offered cautious praise of the new order in Guatemala. The Guatemalan foreign minister reciprocated, declaring that "in the future, the two peoples will travel . . . arm in arm." Guatemala, the envoy added, had carried out a "revolution in . . . government" whose ideas drew on the Mexican experience.[29]

While Obregón had manifested his elation at the political change in Guatemala, he refused to endorse the idea of Central American union. For one thing, the disparate base of the unionist movement foreboded both future political instability and potential trouble with the United States. For another, the well-intended but hyperbolic words of the Guatemalan foreign minister made a Mexican role in the unification effort even more dangerous. Indeed, any comparison between the Mexican Revolution and progressive movements in Central America might only seem to substantiate former U.S. Ambassador Henry P. Fletcher's charge that Mexico sought to "export" its revolution to Latin America.[30] But most important, at this early date, the stance of the U.S. government seemed uncertain. As we have seen, lame-duck President Wilson had been opposed to the abortive project of union in 1917–18.[31] Therefore, when delegates from all five isthmian countries signed a Pact of Union in San José in December 1920, the Mexican government made no official comment.[32]

Obregón's reticence proved a matter of prudence. Upon the withdrawal of Nicaragua owing to uncertainties regarding the application of the Bryan-Chamorro Treaty to the new, federated structure,[33] only Guatemala, El Salvador, and Honduras signed the federal constitution in September 1921. To make matters worse, U.S. policies did not help the fledgling union. The State Department, warming slowly to the project as a way to secure peace in the area, refused to award diplomatic recognition to the new federal government. Without two states, and without U.S. support, the union had no chance: on December 6, 1921, a group of Estrada Cabrera supporters overthrew Herrera. Soon afterwards, the new Guatemalan government denounced the Pact of Union.[34]

Mexican participation in the venture surely would not have made a difference, and might even have backfired. According to the Mexican minister to Guatemala, Juan de Dios Bojórquez, Herrera had merely used the unionist movement as a vehicle for his personal ambitions.[35] The Guatemalan president, another Mexican diplomat surmised, had engineered an *autogolpe,* or self-coup: Herrera, he thought, had betrayed the *unionistas* to the Estrada Cabrera faction and had arranged for his own ouster before the official merger of the three countries took effect on January 1, 1923.[36] This allegation, however, proved groundless.

The coup appeared to nip in the bud the beginning of a rapprochement. The backers of the new president, José María Orellana, included the notoriously anti-Mexican Jorge Ubico, "Estrada Cabrera's servant up to the last minute," as well as other prominent members of the old dictator's inner circle. As one Mexican diplomat feared, Orellana would now play into the hands of the United States by alleging Mexican revolutionary propaganda in Central America and appealing for help against such subversive activities.[37] These fears that the U.S. government backed Orellana appeared to have some substance. Reversing Wilson's policy of not recognizing governments that had come to power through violence (a policy that had been applied to Costa Rica's Federico Tinoco and Mexico's de la Huerta and Obregón), Harding's Secretary of State Charles Evans Hughes warned all other Central American nations against interference in Guatemala and awarded recognition to Orellana.[38] Disgusted at this manifestation of a U.S. double standard, Obregón withheld recognition from the Orellana government for almost a year.

This policy of nonrecognition, however, was ill-advised and inconsistent with Mexico's own international position. As one of the moderates close to Obregón pointed out, it was disingenuous of the Mexican government to demand recognition by the Harding administration at a time when Obregón refused to recognize the new regime in Guatemala. Obregón's posture, the aide added, only strengthened U.S. hegemony in Guatemala. Neither Obregón nor Orellana had come to power by constitutional means, but both leaders exerted control over their respective countries, and (at least in 1922) neither faced a serious challenge to his rule.[39]

Moreover, it soon became obvious that the new government in Guatemala City would not resume Estrada Cabrera's anti-Mexican policies. In view of Mexico's apparent inability to resume its Porfirian stature in Central America, Orellana found no cause to make the Mexican government his enemy. Unlike Estrada Cabrera, Orellana never played the old, broken, irredentist record of the country's Chiapas claims.[40] Much of this shift probably owed to the influence of Orellana's first foreign minister, Adrián Recinos. In the words of Bojórquez, Recinos, who spent his spare time studying the pre-Columbian past which his country shared with Mexico, "was one of the Guatemalan officials who most loved our country."[41] Recinos indeed seems to have been active in neutralizing the influence of the anti-Mexican Ubico faction in the Guatemalan government. At one point, he even assisted Bojórquez in expatriating a Guatemalan worker who had sought refuge in the Mexican legation in order to escape persecution by Ubico's military police.[42]

Recinos' efforts set the stage for "unusually cordial"[43] relations between Mexico and Guatemala. The Obregón administration now was able to make Guatemala the keystone of its relations with the rest of Central America. Even though Orellana remained reluctant to challenge U.S. political and economic hegemony along Mexican lines, Mexican diplomacy found the Guatemalan president a partner for a modest attempt to increase ties with the Central American republics.[44] As an indication of this new relationship—albeit a symbolic one—the two governments upgraded their legations to embassies in 1924. This move gave the Mexican representative, at least for a brief while, the diplomatic deanship in Guatemala, and it "flattered" the Guatemalan government.[45]

To sum up, Mexican-Guatemalan relations improved drastically in the early 1920s, but it had been the Guatemalan government that had taken the initiative, not Obregón. Much in keeping with his strategies toward the Harding administration, Obregón did not move actively to assert Mexican interests, but seized upon low-risk opportunities to advance them. His tenure was a difficult period for Mexican action in Central America; yet Obregón's caution had served Mexico well. A more aggressive diplomacy might have alienated the traditionally anti-Mexican elites in Guatemala, and it is quite conceivable that Mexican hesitation helped officials like Recinos prevail over Ubico's men.

Compared to Díaz's active diplomacy and Carranza's great rhetorical emphasis on relations among the Latin American countries, then, Obregón's Central America policy was modest by necessity. Many Mexican diplomats, however, desired a more active Mexican role in the isthmus. In the years following Estrada Cabrera's fall, these officials inundated the Foreign Ministry with pleas for assistance to progressive ideas and factions in Central America. A look at these diplomats and their political views yields important insights into the nature of the Sonoran coalition and the formulation of its foreign policy.

The Debate over Mexico's Central America Policy, 1921–1923

In nominating the most important officials in the Mexican Foreign Ministry, Obregón essentially followed the practices of his Porfirian predecessors. Indeed, the structure of the Foreign Ministry returned to Porfirian patterns after the brief interlude of Carranza's military-dominated diplomatic staff. Most significantly, the four key parties involved in the formulation of Mexico's Central America policy resumed the alignment they had known under Díaz: the president, the foreign secretary, the Mexican ambassador to the United States, and the diplomats accredited to the Central American countries.

As in Díaz's days, the president himself made most of the important decisions in Mexican foreign policy in consultation with the foreign secretary. Needless to say, relations with the United States took up most of the time during these almost daily meetings. Policy toward Central America, an important subject in the conversations between Díaz and Mariscal, assumed a lesser role in the turbulent 1920s. Obregón desired a Mexican presence in Central America; but he was only too well aware of the increased political risks.

The choice of the Mexican ambassador to the United States reflected this measure of caution. Like Díaz and Carranza, the Sonorans sent only their most "acceptable" diplomats to Washington. In most cases, as with Matías Romero, Enrique Creel, and Carranza's appointee Ygnacio Bonillas, these officials advocated a moderate approach toward the United States that would not unduly jeopardize U.S.–Mexican relations for the benefit of an activist foreign policy. All too often, their wariness exceeded that of their superiors in Mexico City. As to Obregón's Central America policy, his envoys to Washington often played the role that Creel had assumed in the Nicaraguan crisis of 1909–10: aware of U.S. hostility toward Mexican activism in Central America, they advocated a hands-off policy.

By contrast, revolutionary Mexico's diplomats in Central America often represented the more radical faction. Just as Díaz had, Obregón frequently filled the posts in the legations in Central America with progressive intellectuals, several of whom were noted men of letters dissatisfied with the slow pace of reform in Mexico. If the Porfiriato had sent its Gamboas to Central America, the Sonorans countered with the Floresmagonista Alfonso Cravioto,[46] Juan de Dios Bojórquez, and, later, the Yucatecan poet Antonio Mediz Bolio. Whether these men were sent off to Central America to keep them from stirring up trouble in Mexico or as an advertisement of Mexico's rich cultural contributions, they had one thing in common. Like many of Díaz's appointees, many of them advocated a Central America policy antagonistic to the United States even at the expense of a deterioration in U.S.–Mexican relations. For some of them, life and work in the isthmus seemed too slow; as Bojórquez wrote in 1924, "in Central America one walks like a crab."[47]

The relationship between these radical diplomats and President Obregón was first tested during the days of the short-lived Central American Federation. Quite in contrast to the opinions of Obregón and Foreign Secretary Alberto Pani, many Mexican diplomats in the isthmus regarded the federation as a great opportunity to expand their country's influence there at the expense of the United States.[48] In the view of the Mexican minister to El Salvador, Salvador Martínez de Alva, Mexico now could mold the political future of the isthmus by forging economic ties: "it is natural," he stated, "that we will participate actively in [Central America's] economic situation to model its politics to our liking."[49] In another letter, Martínez, in paternalistic fashion, advocated a dose of heavy-handed "peso diplomacy" to gain influence in Central America: "Mexico . . . should take advantage of the good intentions and the lack of experience of the future officials [of the Federation]. This moment of . . . uncertainties is the propitious moment for Mexico to assert itself . . . in its role as older brother with the establishment of economic hegemony over Central America. . . . If Mexico does not do this, the United States will." Central America, he claimed, was "thirsty for foreign manufactured goods," which Mexico could supply in exchange for raw materials.[50] Understandably, moderates Obregón and Pani did not react to these initiatives. These dispatches, however, revealed profound policy differences between the Obregón regime and its radical diplomats in Central America.

When the Herrera regime fell in Guatemala, one Mexican diplomat once again lobbied Obregón for intervention. The Mexican legation, former minister to Guatemala Luis Caballero stated, should attempt to rally the unionists and parts of the army around a new candidate to oppose Orellana. Obregón refused, pointing out that that country's internal affairs "should be resolved solely and exclusively by the sons of Guatemala."[51]

It was Obregón's nephew, Eduardo Ruiz, Mexican minister to Costa Rica, who launched the most eloquent challenge to his uncle's diplomacy. In a long letter to Obregón, Ruiz vigorously attacked Mexico's Central America policy as a cowardly surrender in the face of the Yankees: "We . . . are playing a sad role here; while the Yankee overtly . . . makes propaganda in his favor, we cannot countervail in any way for lack of instructions. . . . We have talked to [the Latin American leaders] in verse and lyricisms, and they have answered us accordingly."[52] In another letter to the Foreign Ministry, Ruiz laid out his vision of a different Mexican policy, which in many ways resembled Gamboa's and other Porfirian diplomats' ideas. In his opinion, Mexico needed to win over the peoples rather than the governments of the Latin American countries, "strengthening in them the ideals of race and inculcating in them our principles of renovation." With the peoples of Latin America, Ruiz maintained, Mexico had a "virgin territory . . . to sow the seeds."[53] On another occasion, he even proposed to procure the liberation of Nicaragua by "patriotic" exile forces.[54]

The Mexican government, however, would not be swayed by Ruiz's own lyricisms. In the view of one of Obregón's aides, Mexico had no enemies in Central America and did not need such rash action. Insinuating that a more assertive policy in the area would have alienated the Orellana government, he cited the Estrada Cabrera dictatorship as the only example in which a Central American regime had portrayed Mexico as its "natural enemy."[55]

The debate between the Obregón regime and its diplomats in Central America reflected the continuing schism between the moderate center of diplomatic decision making in Mexico City and the radical periphery in Central America. Mexican diplomats in the isthmus desired to revive their country's old political role. In contrast, Obregón and Pani favored an official hands-off approach so as not to give the U.S. government a pretext for intervention either in Central America or in Mexico itself.

The two groups found common ground in the form of Mexican cultural policy toward Central America. Following initiatives begun in the last phase of the Carranza regime, the Mexican government presented wireless stations to Guatemala, El Salvador, Honduras, and Costa Rica, which subsequently broadcast programs from Mexico's ARIEL news agency. To promote mutual understanding further, it commissioned the founding of Mexican libraries in some of the Central American cities.[56] Obregón also gave a number of scholarships to Central American students who desired to attend a Mexican university.[57] While these modest steps failed to yield immediate results, the intent of these measures was clear: although Mexico was unable to act assertively at the moment, the enhancement of ties among the Central American and Mexican peoples might bring opportunities for the future.

Toward a More Assertive Policy

As long as his regime lacked U.S. diplomatic recognition, Obregón took a low-key stance as far as U.S. interests in Central America were concerned. But toward the end of his rule, with U.S. recognition secured and diplomatic relations improving, he became somewhat more daring—a trend that would carry over into the Calles administration. This pattern became obvious in Obregón's policies toward the 1922–23 Washington Conference and in his very different approach toward a 1924 change of government in Nicaragua.

The second Washington Conference resulted from the ongoing strife on the isthmus. The end of the attempt at union spawned a new era of Central American warfare, with the Liberal governments of Guatemala and Honduras facing off against Conservative regimes in El Salvador and Nicaragua. Such conflicts invariably attracted U.S. intercession— and indeed, border trouble between Nicaragua and Honduras in early 1922 prompted just such a response. In August 1922, the U.S. government summoned delegates from Honduras, El Salvador, and Nicaragua aboard the warship *Tacoma* to put an end to the unrest. As a result of the *Tacoma* conference, the participants promised to abstain from further intervention in the affairs of their neighbors, and they agreed to refrain from awarding diplomatic recognition to any regime that had come to power through a coup d'état.[58]

In October 1922, U.S. Secretary of State Hughes decided to take matters into his own hands. Discarding the existing framework of 1907, he summoned representatives from all of the Central American republics to the U.S. capital. In contrast to the 1907 meeting, the second Washington Conference, which began work in December 1922, was a dictate rather than an agreement. It was Hughes, not the Central American delegates, who drew up a series of tough accords. Diplomatic recognition was to be withheld from governments that came to power through a coup d'état, a Central American Tribunal replaced the Court of Justice, and the principle of mandatory arbitration was rescinded. With this set of treaties, Hughes had shrewdly reconciled U.S. and Central American policy goals. Since the nonrecognition clause gave an insurance policy to the incumbent governments, the Central American delegates gladly signed the accords and then negotiated a number of additional treaties without U.S. participation.[59] The subject of union, discouraged by Hughes, was never discussed. Significantly, the United States became the sole guarantor of the new framework: in the absence of diplomatic ties with Mexico, Hughes had not solicited Obregón's participation.[60]

The reaction of the Mexican press and government to this conference graphically illustrates the widespread frustration with Mexico's extremely limited policy options in the isthmus during the early 1920s. Calling the conference the "reaffirmation of tutelage," *El Universal* wrote that Mexico "would have nothing to do there, unless it were to authorize through its presence the humiliation of five brother nations."[61] A few days later, that same newspaper lamented in almost wistful terms the passing of an era in which the United States and Mexico had both assumed responsibility for Central America: "The Central American Conferences will be in December, but how different! . . . [They will not have the] characteristics of a convention of peace and love, under the aegis of a friendly nation, as the United States is said to be, nor of a sister nation like Mexico; no, these are different times, and now, those men [of the 1907 conference] . . . have gone."[62]

The Obregón regime shared the assessment that this was a party that Mexico truly could afford to miss. When the Mexican Congress considered a resolution of protest against the exclusion of Mexico from the Washington Conference, Pani induced the legislature to reject the motion, reasoning that Mexico "was not really an interested party."[63]

Strikingly, the Mexican government assumed a similar attitude toward the Fifth Inter-American Conference in Santiago de Chile. Absent again for lack of U.S. recognition, the Mexican government did not protest against its exclusion. Instead, the Mexican legation in Santiago served as a meeting ground for Latin American delegates dissatisfied with heavy-handed U.S. policies, where these delegates—often with Mexican advice—freely plotted strategies to thwart U.S. goals.[64]

As long as Obregón's regime lacked U.S. diplomatic recognition, then, it refused to antagonize the U.S. government either on bilateral affairs or on issues affecting the rest of Latin America. Instead, as shown in the Santiago meeting, it often played a more indirect role. After the Bucareli agreements, however, Mexican policy gradually began to change. This change first became visible in Mexican attitudes toward a more favorable political climate in Nicaragua.

With the sponsorship of the new Washington Conventions, U.S. government officials believed they had done enough to ensure political stability on the isthmus. In most of Central America, the calm persisted. Ruled by relatively weak leaders, the isthmus seemed pacified, outside threats eliminated, and no Central American ruler even contemplated pursuing anti-Yankee, nationalist policies. But in the spring of 1923, a civil war in Honduras revealed that the U.S. effort at pacification of Central America had again failed. Backed by rivaling U.S. fruit companies, the Honduran Conservatives and Liberals waged a bitter war for more than a year. In the end, only the threat of direct U.S. intervention led these forces to compromise and call for fair elections for late 1924. This experience gave U.S. diplomats a new idea: U.S. election supervision might be more effective in preventing unrest than either a Central American legal framework or U.S. intervention.[65]

In this context, Hughes and his successor, Frank B. Kellogg, proceeded to extricate the United States from what had become an irritant to both U.S. public opinion and the Central American elites:[66] the presence of a U.S. legation guard in Nicaragua. The timing looked propitious for a pullout. By 1923, two Conservative presidents had continued Emiliano Chamorro's pro-U.S. policies, and the Liberal opposition seemed incapable of mounting a serious challenge. A State Department expert had drawn up a new electoral code for the country, and elections were scheduled for mid-1924. As a result, the Zelayistas had lost control of the Liberal party to a group of moderates who hoped to curry favor with the U.S. legation in Managua in order to win the 1924 vote. In short, circumstances no longer warranted a U.S. military role in Nicaragua, and a supervised election offered the United States a way out without allowing the anti-Yankee Zelayistas back in.[67]

Just as the U.S. contemplated loosening its grip, the Nicaraguan political scene awakened from its long dormant state. Interestingly, it was not the Liberals who provided the initial spark but a group of disenchanted Conservatives under the direction of interim president Bartolomé Martínez. This faction resented the United States for its imposition of the Washington Conventions, which forbade Martínez's reelection. Initially, Martínez openly defied the conventions and announced his intention to run again for president, foreclosing Chamorro's path back to power. Moreover, he invited Nicaraguan bidders to buy out U.S.-owned shares of the Nicaraguan railroad company.[68]

These gestures precipitated the final collapse of the Chamorrista political edifice. Pressured by the U.S. chargé in Managua, Martínez agreed to give up his candidacy and thus any hope of keeping the Conservative party alive as a unified entity. Subsequent to the U.S. démarche, the Conservatives split into two factions: Chamorro's *genuinos,* and the "Republican Conservatives" under the leadership of the Martínez protégé Carlos Solórzano.[69] Impressed by the president's moves to nationalize the railroad, and by the apparent viability of a democratic road to power,[70] a majority of Liberals broke ranks with their party and allied themselves with the Republican Conservatives. Assured of a sizable political base, Solórzano and his Liberal running mate Juan B. Sacasa defeated Chamorro and the Zelayista candidate, Luis Corea, in the 1924 elections.[71] Content with the establishment in Nicaragua of a freely elected regime that did not jeopardize U.S. property interests, Kellogg then announced that the United States would withdraw its Marines in August 1925, thirteen years after the first military contingent had entered Managua.[72]

Once in power, the coalition government appeared to move toward emulating some of the revolutionary reforms in Mexico. For the first time ever, a fledgling labor movement emerged in Nicaragua with the help of the American Federation of Labor.[73] Conscious of his fragile political position, Solórzano also attempted, albeit unsuccessfully, to lay the foundations of a multiclass alliance based on this sponsorship of the interests of urban labor. The Mexican legation in Nicaragua was not only immensely pleased with this turn of events; it actively helped in the transformation of Nicaraguan society.[74] Indeed, officials of a prominent Mexican labor union worked hand in hand with the AFL representatives in the incipient unionization of the Nicaraguan urban work force.[75] But as long as Obregón was in power, the Mexican government limited itself to such "unofficial" influence in Nicaragua and refused to show ostensible support for what still appeared to be a shaky experiment in reform.

Mexican sympathy with the coalition government in Managua may have been less pronounced than Díaz's aid to Zelaya, but it stemmed from the same motivations. The establishment of a moderately nationalist regime in Nicaragua vindicated Obregón's own gradualist notions of reform. Moreover, the rise of Solórzano amidst the U.S. pullout provided Mexican diplomacy with a chance to bring Nicaragua into play again as a counterweight to U.S. influence in Mexico and Central America. While Obregón himself never reaped the fruits of his labor, his successor, Plutarco Elías Calles, would once again be able to make Mexican influence felt in Nicaragua.

Even though Obregón was unable and unwilling to play an assertive political role in Central America, Mexico's position in the isthmus had improved during his reign. Comparable to his approach to the United States—an approach emphasizing negotiation and the enhancement of cultural ties over confrontation—his hands-off policy had succeeded in gaining Mexico the friendship of Guatemala and a promising new opportunity in Nicaragua. At least part of Obregón's relative success was based on luck: the disappearance of Estrada Cabrera and the decision of the U.S. government to withdraw its forces from Nicaragua had helped greatly in furthering Mexican policy objectives. But Obregón's low-key approach to foreign relations proved appropriate. By refusing to move more assertively at a historically inopportune moment, the Mexican government alarmed neither the U.S. State Department nor the Guatemalan governing elite—a group that, as we have seen, included more than just a few leaders hostile to Mexican influence. Ultimately, Obregón's diplomacy had led to an improved climate that promised to lead Mexico out of the virtual "nonpower" status in which it had languished since 1911.

Obregón's modest cultural initiatives were a promising sign of a reorientation in Mexican foreign policy, but they attained few practical

results. The Mexican government did not have the means for a wholesale cultural campaign in Central America, and Central American interest in the matter proved lacking. As a result, the promotion and ma-
nipulation of Mexican culture, a keystone both in Obregón's domestic
policy and in his approach toward the United States, did not meet with
the success for which some of the Mexican policy makers had hoped.
Nevertheless, these cultural initiatives and the role of Mexican labor in
Nicaragua were significant, signaling a change in the old pattern of
pursuing merely political objectives in Central America.

Obregón's foreign policy thus had been limited by external constraints. Unlike Díaz and to some extent Carranza, the Sonorans had so
far not taken any risks in Central America. But as the radical challenge
to Obregón within his own government illustrates, there were voices in
his coalition that called for a different stance, one that applied to Central America the strategies the Sonorans had used for the benefit of
their rule at home.

7 Another Quest for "Nicaragua Libre," 1924–1930

> Mexico should abstain from expressing its fraternal feelings toward Central America, since no one here believes in Mexican altruism.
>
> Mexican minister to Nicaragua Gustavo Madero, 1926

Obregón's closest confidant, Plutarco Elías Calles, ended fourteen years of relative caution in Central American affairs. Assured of U.S. diplomatic recognition, Calles once again asserted a strong Mexican political role in Central America. This effort heavily concentrated on Nicaragua. Calles's policies were reminiscent of Porfirio Díaz's efforts on behalf of Zelaya: in 1924–25, his diplomats offered help to a Nicaraguan government that attempted to lessen the pervasive U.S. political and economic influence in that country. In 1926, he gave financial, military, and political assistance to Nicaraguan Liberal leader Juan B. Sacasa in a civil war with the pro-U.S. Conservatives. And in 1929–30, Calles's handpicked successor, Emilio Portes Gil, offered asylum to Augusto C. Sandino, a rebel who had made his fame eluding and fighting a new U.S. occupation force in Nicaragua.

Calles's time in power can be divided into two different periods: an activist phase from 1924 to early 1927, and a stabilizing phase from 1927 to 1934. During the activist phase, Calles made bold moves in his foreign policy, including antagonizing the United States over oil and Central America. During the stabilizing phase—a period in which he ruled directly for two years and as *jefe máximo* (supreme boss) behind the scenes for another six years—he turned his attention to internal affairs, including the entrenchment of his faction's rule. It is the activist phase that deserves most attention: during this time, Calles launched the most significant challenge to U.S. influence in Central America between the Porfiriato and the late 1970s.

Foreign Policy in the Activist Phase, 1924–1927

Regarded as more progressive than Obregón, Calles initially had many incentives to move the Mexican government to the left. Popular discontent with the slow pace of agrarian reform had become evident in a series of revolts, and Calles felt the need to deliver on some of Obregón's promises. The new president also entered office weak in political stature. Unlike Obregón, a bona fide hero of the campaigns against Díaz, Huerta, and Villa, he had no military victories or political achievements to call his own, and he owed his office to his mentor's backing. To escape the shadow of his predecessor—an effort in which he did not fully succeed until Obregón's assassination in 1928—Calles cultivated ties with leaders who enjoyed no close personal ties with Obregón. With most army and peasant leaders firmly behind the former president, he cast his lot with Luis N. Morones, the head of the moderate labor organization CROM (Confederación Regional Obrera Mexicana, or Regional Mexican Workers' Federation). As a price for Morones' support, Calles helped the CROM to national dominance over the other, more radical unions. With Morones as his Secretary of Labor, he stood primed to increase the power of the revolutionary state by alliances with mass organizations. By early 1925, Calles had proclaimed himself a champion of urban labor causes, and he moved to put the nationalist and anti-clerical provisions of the 1917 Constitution into effect.[1]

Like Carranza and Obregón, Calles hardly fit the mold of a radical, as his initiatives were similarly guided by pragmatism rather than an idealistic commitment to the "ideas of the Mexican Revolution." Even as Calles's measures elicited U.S. opposition and alienated powerful sectors of Mexican society, they primarily sought to combine a claim to the revolutionary heritage with the goal of creating a strong, centralist state. Significantly, the reforms mainly targeted groups that stood in the way of such a state: the Church, oilmen, and landowners. A strong believer in a capitalist economy owned and controlled by Mexicans, Calles had no desire to create trouble. Like Obregón, he envisioned a Revolution driven into orderly channels and controlled by his government. As his well-documented subsequent turnarounds on most of his early reform measures indicate, Calles found political principle as expedient as did his two predecessors.[2]

Plutarco Elías Calles as *jefe máximo*, 1930 (Courtesy of the Fideicomiso
Archivos Plutarco Elías Calles y Fernando Torreblanca, Mexico City)

But prodded by Morones, Calles did show from the beginning that he intended to tackle some of the unfinished business of the Constitution. Shortly after coming to power, he signed a series of decrees aimed at enforcing its anti-clerical provisions, and he also refused to endorse the Bucareli agreements. In 1925, when oil production had fallen precipitously for the fourth straight year, Calles took on the powerful oil industry. Accusing the oilmen of deliberately cutting back production (and thus, their tax payments) in order to force his government to abrogate Article 27, he rushed a new Petroleum Law through the Mexican Congress. This new oil code required foreign oil companies operating in Mexico to apply for confirmatory concessions and threatened them with nationalization should they fail to comply.[3]

These measures led to new problems with the United States. The new U.S. ambassador, James R. Sheffield, who enjoyed close personal ties to the oil interests, protested against the new laws and demanded for foreign property owners guarantees exceeding those given in the Bucareli agreements. But the racist Sheffield, who deemed Mexicans a primitive and backward people,[4] was hardly the only voice for an aggressive policy. The oil companies and Catholic groups also pressured Secretary of State Frank B. Kellogg to put a stop to the Petroleum Law and the decrees directed against the church. Even the interventionist yellow press of William R. Hearst got in on the act, running a series of articles that depicted Mexico as a "Bolshevik" country in the mold of the Soviet Union. The hard-liners quickly carried the day in Washington: on June 12, 1925, Kellogg declared Mexico to be "on trial before the world."[5]

Initially, Kellogg's antics proved beneficial to Calles. The declaration gave his regime nationalist credentials and thus helped him to consolidate his control. Much in the mold of Santa Anna, Juárez, Díaz, and Carranza, who had often pointed to their valiant leadership in wars against foreign invaders, Calles could sell himself to the Mexican public as a patriot who would not back down in the face of outside intervention. Thus, he portrayed himself as a vigorous defender of Mexican sovereignty vis-à-vis the "Yankee threat," which looked more serious through Sheffield's words than it was in reality.[6]

But by the summer of 1926, the conflict had escalated into a major crisis. Sheffield played up the activities of a few small Marxist organizations in order to show that Mexico was becoming "Sovietized." He also labeled the strongly anti-Communist Morones a "Bolshevist" [sic] and even accused the recently established Soviet legation of steering Mexico toward Bolshevism.[7] Sheffield's anti-Communist paranoia never found many converts in the State Department, as Kellogg and his aides did not give much credit to his dispatches. An internal memorandum circulating in the State Department admitted that "there is little tangible evidence . . . that the Mexican Government is itself a bolshevist [sic] government." In fact, the memorandum went on, "the word 'bolshevist' has become an epithet rather than a useful definition."[8] But Sheffield's reports played into Kellogg's hands in helping him to justify a hard-line policy toward Mexico. Knowing that a well-formulated analogy between Mexico and the Soviet Union could arouse U.S. public opinion against the Calles government, Kellogg expediently leaked the dispatches to the Hearst press. Therefore, the Secretary of State used the issue of "Bolshevism" to put pressure on Calles to repeal the reforms.

By the end of the year, Calles was concerned enough about the growing crisis to attempt to stave off further confrontation. Facing an imminent fiscal crisis and the Cristero rebellion, he quietly backed away from many of his reforms while blaming others for these reversals. For instance, he induced the Mexican Supreme Court to hand down a ruling that affirmed the nonretroactive nature of the Constitution. This strategy was successful in containing potential political damage to the Mexican president—the courts, not Calles himself, had stalled the drive toward the implementation of Article 27. Calles also used existing anti-interventionist sentiments in the United States against Kellogg. His New York consul ran a press-management campaign that helped a coalition of opposition Democrats, Democrat-leaning newspapers, liberal intellectuals, and progressive Republican senators to pressure Kellogg toward a more moderate stance.[9]

To the chagrin of the oil companies, the Coolidge administration backed away from the unpopular confrontation. In mid-1927, Kellogg recalled Ambassador Sheffield from his post. His successor, Dwight Morrow, received instructions to tone down the conflict. Taking a conciliatory approach and avoiding the offensive talk of his predecessor, Morrow accomplished his mission. Helped by Calles's and Foreign Secretary Aarón Sáenz's desire to improve relations, the Mexican government and the U.S. diplomat resolved many of the pending issues over the next three years.[10]

The coming and going of Calles's reform activism and the concomitant crisis in U.S.–Mexican relations found a close parallel in his Central America policy. While he still pursued Obregón's approach of social and cultural diplomacy, Calles once again played power politics in the region during the activist period of his rule. But when domestic issues and U.S. pressures forced him to retreat vis-à-vis both the domestic opposition and the U.S. State Department, he withdrew from the Central American scene. In no instance did this fact become more evident than in Calles's banner initiative in Central America: assistance to the Liberal faction of Juan B. Sacasa.

Déjà Vu: Support for Nicaraguan Liberalism

As we saw in the previous chapter, the Mexican government welcomed the political change that had come about in Nicaragua as a result of the split in the Conservative party and the 1924 U.S.-supervised elections. As the date of the U.S. military pullout from Managua neared, opportunities for Mexican action increased. To monitor these exciting events, Calles appointed a new diplomat to the post of Mexican minister to Costa Rica and Nicaragua and ordered him to reside in Managua: the Yucatecan poet Antonio Mediz Bolio, a member of the radical faction within the Sonoran coalition.

From the outset of his tenure, Mediz Bolio praised the new regime for its defense of national sovereignty. In Mediz Bolio's view, the Conservative-Liberal coalition headed by Carlos Solórzano represented "the sanest and strongest elements in public opinion." He particularly lauded Solórzano for moves toward nationalizing the Nicaraguan railroads, his succor for urban labor, and his ostensible support for the withdrawal of the U.S. Marines, scheduled for August 1925. Mexico, the poet emphasized, could count on the sympathy of the government as well as of the Nicaraguan public.[11]

Had the Mexican minister known Solórzano's true feelings about the withdrawal of the Yankees, he would have been more cautious in his approving remarks. Former President Emiliano Chamorro, still steaming over his electoral defeat, only waited for the U.S. departure to overthrow the newly elected government. Therefore, Solórzano petitioned Kellogg not to withdraw the U.S. constabulary force. Eager to end its direct military involvement, however, the State Department rejected Solórzano's request and informed him that the Marines would be withdrawn in August 1925.[12] Nicaragua entered a new phase of uncertainty: the days of the U.S. Marines were numbered, but could the Solórzano regime remain in power without outside help against the well-organized Chamorrista faction? Aware of this problem, yet desiring to speed up the departure of the Marines, Mediz Bolio told Solórzano that his government greatly wished to "be useful to Nicaragua" within the limits of its obligations.[13]

As soon as the U.S. forces had left Managua, Solórzano's worries became reality. A few weeks after the U.S. disengagement, the Chamorristas used a pretext to occupy the fortress of La Loma, thus controlling the Nicaraguan capital from this vantage point above Managua.[14] Backed by a large armed faction, the Conservative strongman pressured the president into the exclusion of key Liberals from the cabinet. In November 1925, he packed the Nicaraguan congress with his supporters by forcing the resignation of most of its Liberal members. Chamorro then drove Vice President Sacasa into exile and induced the new congress to strip him of his post. Solórzano remained president only by Chamorro's grace.[15]

As in 1909, Mexican diplomacy once again faced off with Chamorrismo in Nicaragua. The chances of success appeared good: in view of its commitment to the 1923 Washington treaties forbidding the recognition of coup d'état regimes, the U.S. government could not approve of Chamorro's rebellion.[16] Therefore, U.S. chargé Charles L. Eberhardt cooperated with Mediz Bolio in trying to find a negotiated solution that would be compatible with the Washington Conventions.[17] The Chamorro coup thus amounted to a golden opportunity. If Calles attempted to save the coalition government in Nicaragua, public opinion at home and abroad would view this effort as a valiant attempt to make elected governments respected in Central America. In that event, Calles would be regarded as the champion of constitutional government and as a friend of democratic forces throughout the region.

As in 1906–7, then, Mexico and the United States favored the same goals in Central America, but for different reasons. Both Coolidge and Calles worked for constitutional rule in Nicaragua. Coolidge did so to keep the country stable and minimize U.S. involvement; Calles helped Solórzano in order to save an experiment in progressive reform and to reassert Mexican influence.[18]

In view of this opportunity, Mediz Bolio wasted no time trying to prop up Solórzano. In a striking parallel with Díaz's efforts on behalf of Zelaya, he repeatedly offered the Nicaraguan president the services of a Mexican gunboat to take him into exile. As a U.S. official in Managua reported, Mediz Bolio even offered Mexican military aid if Solórzano decided to stay and fight for his position. Resigned to his fate and unwilling to risk an open association with Mexico, however, Solórzano refused both suggestions.[19]

With the Chamorristas growing stronger by the day, Solórzano, now under house arrest, could no longer remain in power. Even as Eberhardt and Mediz Bolio continued their efforts to prevent an overthrow of the "legitimate" government of Nicaragua, Chamorro, by alternately coaxing and threatening the president, tried to force Solórzano to relinquish his post in Chamorro's favor. Finally, on January 14, 1926, Solórzano caved in, notwithstanding Mediz Bolio's last-minute plea to resist. After some maneuvering in the Nicaraguan congress, Emiliano Chamorro again became president.[20]

Whereas Mexico had kept a low profile during earlier coups against Central American governments during the 1920s, this time the Calles regime openly displayed its opposition to Chamorro's maneuvers. Immediately after Solórzano's resignation, Sáenz ordered the closure of the Mexican legation in Managua, stating that Mexico would not countenance the overthrow of the constitutional order in Nicaragua.[21] Again, U.S. policies helped Mexico. Because of Kellogg's commitment to the Washington treaties, Calles's move to close the legation met with no reaction in Washington, and Calles had scored a small but cheap propaganda victory amidst Chamorro's cries of Mexican "Bolshevism" spreading into Central America.[22]

Soon afterwards, the Nicaraguan Liberals rallied around the figure of former Vice President Sacasa to mount a new challenge to Chamorrista rule. This time, however, it seemed that Calles would not get a chance to assert Mexican influence in Nicaragua. Living in exile in Guatemala City, Sacasa knew that the fortunes of his faction depended on the attitude of the U.S. State Department. He also knew that Kellogg would never sanction Chamorro's return to power, as too much of the State Department's prestige at home and abroad hinged on making the Washington Conventions respected in Central America. But would Kellogg support Sacasa's claim that he had been stripped illegally of his vice presidential post, and thus was Solórzano's rightful successor to the presidency? As Sacasa and other Liberal leaders scattered throughout Central America deliberated their options, U.S. assistance for either the reinstatement of the Solórzano regime or a military movement with Sacasa at its head appeared the best possible solution. Help from Mexico was a distant second choice in this scenario.[23]

But when Sacasa arrived in Washington in January 1926, the State Department sorely disappointed him. Kellogg refused to receive the Nicaraguan Liberal in person, and his aides hardly proved any more forthcoming. Over the course of several meetings with a member of Kellogg's staff, Sacasa got an unequivocal message: the U.S. government would not recognize the Chamorro regime, but it also refused to support any positive steps to achieve its overthrow. Kellogg, the aide informed Sacasa, counted on the success of his policy of "moral suasion."[24] The U.S. government was more than reluctant to meddle once again in the Nicaraguan imbroglio—as events seventeen years before had revealed, any such intervention would inevitably have led to more intervention and another military role for the United States in Central America.

Therefore, Sacasa was forced to turn to his second option: covert aid from Mexico for a Liberal insurgency in Nicaragua. Throughout his weeks of frustration in the State Department, he repeatedly visited the Mexican embassy in Washington, where Ambassador Manuel C. Téllez gave him a warm reception. Mexican commercial ships, Sacasa hoped, could help the Liberals slip weapons into Nicaragua for an uprising planned for May 1926. If done surreptitiously, this assistance would not be detected by U.S. intelligence. As early as late January 1926, Sáenz gave his preliminary approval to this plan, conditional upon Sacasa's visiting Mexico City.[25]

Sacasa's smooth ride with the Mexicans soon ended, however, as Téllez's initial enthusiasm gave way to a well-founded skepticism. Politically an unknown quantity, Sacasa could not be trusted as a Mexican ally in Central America. Since he was still trying to convince the U.S. government to come to his aid, he constantly wavered on whether he should antagonize Kellogg by visiting Mexico City to negotiate with Calles. In his meetings with Téllez, he seemed nervous and timid, and not sure whether he desired Mexican support.[26] Therefore, Téllez, true to his role as the most "cautionary" element in Mexican foreign-policy making, sent an unfavorable recommendation to Sáenz.[27]

Sacasa's waffling cost his movement precious time and momentum. In fact, his delays probably doomed the Liberal uprising, which began without outside assistance on Nicaragua's Atlantic coast in May 1926. Seeing his rebellion quickly crushed by the well-equipped Chamorro forces, Sacasa now decided to take the risk he had earlier eschewed: in June, he traveled to Mexico City and negotiated a treaty of assistance with Calles and Sáenz.[28]

Even though Mexican and U.S. archives contain no conclusive evidence about the precise terms of this agreement, Sacasa's conferences in Mexico City yielded the desired results for both sides. Apparently, Calles committed himself to aiding a new Liberal insurgency in return for a pledge of cooperation with Mexican foreign policy in Central America. According to letters intercepted by a U.S. double agent in Guatemala City, Sacasa and Calles also promised to act together against U.S. interests on a broad front, including the abrogation of the Bryan-Chamorro treaty.[29] Whatever the exact nature of the understanding, by August 1926 a new uprising was under way in Nicaragua, galvanized by Sacasa's confidant José M. Moncada and the old Zelayista Julián Irías, and bolstered by Mexican arms and ammunition.[30] Throughout the fall of 1926, Mexico helped the Sacasa faction financially, politically, and militarily.

In financial terms, the strapped Mexican treasury managed to free up several hundred thousand dollars to fund Sacasa's effort. Paid through the medium of Mexico's ambassador to Guatemala, Alfonso Cravioto, these funds helped the Liberals purchase weapons throughout Central America. The money also helped Sacasa lobby for support in the other Central American countries, whose leaders remained divided on the subject of recognizing the Chamorro regime.[31]

On the political front, Mexican diplomacy attempted with limited success to forge a regional coalition against Chamorro. Prodded by Cravioto, the government of Guatemala proved a reliable if reluctant partner in this effort, as president Orellana allowed the Liberals to make the country their principal base of operations.[32] El Salvador leaned toward a "benevolent neutrality" in favor of the rebellion, but was correctly perceived as unreliable by the Mexican diplomats in the area.[33] Conservative-ruled Honduras, by contrast, proved a loyal supporter of Chamorro and awarded diplomatic recognition to his government. Finally, Costa Rica pursued its traditional policy of complete neutrality in isthmian disputes. Thus, the two countries that shared land borders with Nicaragua were of no help to Mexico and Sacasa, and the help of distant Guatemala remained of little value. Nevertheless, for the first time since Díaz's era, Mexico had assembled a modest coalition of forces that worked together to achieve a common goal.

Calles's most significant contribution, however, was his military aid to the Liberal insurgency. Beginning in August 1926, at least seven different Mexican commercial ships brought rifles, ammunition, and other weaponry to Nicaragua. Departing from Puerto México (today Coatzacoalcos) on the Atlantic coast, and from Salina Cruz on Mexico's Pacific coast, these vessels also carried Mexican volunteers and Nicaraguan exiles to boost the insurrection.[34] In some cases, the boats made several voyages to Nicaragua within two or three months. It was hardly surprising that the second Liberal uprising, thanks to better organization and Mexican aid, proved much stronger than the first and soon threatened to put an end to Chamorrista rule.

Calles and Sáenz had calculated correctly. By early October 1926, the Sacasa forces had seized control of much of both Nicaraguan coasts and stood poised to move into the mountainous heartland. The U.S. government so far had remained inactive, unwilling to come to the rescue of a strongman who had gained power in defiance of the Washington Conventions. Mexico had emerged as a major force behind the Liberal rebellion, and the imminent Sacasa victory was bound to increase Mexico's prestige and influence in the area. By September 1926, in sum, it seemed that revolutionary Mexico finally had found a loophole to engage in an assertive isthmian diplomacy. The Sonoran leadership had waited patiently to seize upon just such an opportunity to help a friendly Central American faction without running into the opposition of the United States.

The Mexican government was not motivated by "revolutionary nationalism" in its decision to aid the Nicaraguan Liberals.[35] The fact that a Liberal government in Nicaragua might emulate the reforms of the Mexican revolutionary governments played only a minor role in the formulation of Mexico's Nicaragua policy, even though the country's radical diplomats like Mediz Bolio liked to see it that way. At a time when the moderate Aarón Sáenz led Mexico's Foreign Ministry, and when Calles was already seeking face-saving ways out of an impending conflict with the United States, surely no one in the Mexican government seriously considered "exporting" revolutionary ideas to Central America.

Rather, Calles came to Sacasa's aid because of more modest and "realistic" considerations.[36] Most significantly, the Mexican leadership hoped to expand its own influence in Central America. With Guatemala already a congenial partner (see chapter 6), Sacasa's victory in Nicaragua would have given Mexico an unprecedented degree of influence in Central America. Calles also might have hoped that a Liberal government in Nicaragua would resume Zelaya's independent posture vis-à-vis the United States. In addition, the matter held in reserve a potential propaganda dividend for the Calles government. If Kellogg forced Calles to retreat on the oil issue, as indeed happened in 1927, a Mexican-sponsored ouster of the pro-U.S. Chamorro regime surely would ease the sting of such a defeat.

All of these considerations would become moot, however, if the U.S. government gave up its neutral position toward the conflict in Nicaragua. As we have seen, Calles had not taken up the fight for Sacasa primarily to stave off U.S. influence. But when Kellogg made it clear that he *perceived* Calles's actions as a menace to U.S. goals in Nicaragua, the Mexican adventure on behalf of the Sacasa faction became suffused with the larger, conflictive context of U.S.–Mexican relations.

U.S. Intervention Forces Mexico Out Again

By the fall of 1926, the U.S. State Department was in a difficult situation. Outright recognition of the Chamorro regime was out of the question, but a Sacasa presidency hardly seemed a palatable alternative. Hated by Conservatives and despised by many in his own party, Sacasa promised to be at best a weak interim leader, one who would require outside assistance to stay in power. Moreover, intelligence reports had already implicated the Mexican government in the Liberal rebellion, and Kellogg did not want to concede "Bolshevik Mexico" a political victory in Central America. Seen from this vantage point, Kellogg had precious few possibilities: withhold recognition from both Chamorro and Sacasa and stay out of the trouble, or end the conflict by sponsoring a negotiated settlement.

In view of the potential damage a protracted civil war might inflict on U.S. property in Nicaragua and on political stability close to the

Panama Canal, the second option looked better than the first. During a process of negotiation, Kellogg hoped, Chamorro and Sacasa could be persuaded to step aside in favor of a third, and presumably Conservative, candidate. This candidate would then stand a good chance of stabilizing Nicaragua without the help of the U.S. Marines. Therefore, in early October, U.S. chargé Lawrence Dennis summoned delegates from both of the feuding camps aboard the U.S.S. *Denver*. Hopes for a settlement initially ran high, as the Conservatives indicated that Chamorro would step aside in favor of another Conservative.[37]

Despite U.S. pressure to come to a solution, however, the week-long talks failed due to the intransigence of both sides. With justification, the Liberals complained about Dennis's overt favoring of the Conservatives and left the meeting when it had become clear that the U.S. government only wanted a smoke screen for yet another Conservative government in Nicaragua. Frustrated about their predicament, the Liberals finally blundered and openly implicated Mexico in the affair. During the closing session of the talks, one of Sacasa's delegates admitted that his faction had been receiving military aid from Mexico.[38] Thinking no doubt about the warning of Calles's chief of staff that aid to Sacasa would be cut off if the Liberals compromised,[39] the delegate further stated that accepting a Conservative as president of Nicaragua would amount to a breach of faith with Sacasa's Mexican allies. Kellogg had a perfect excuse for backing the Conservatives: the Sacasa faction was supported by a foreign government, and a supposedly "Bolshevik" one at that.[40]

In building a case for supporting yet another intervention in Nicaragua, Kellogg did not need to look far for additional evidence of Mexican meddling. Throughout the fall, a stream of military intelligence reports reached the State Department confirming that the Calles government was engaging in substantial gunrunning. Moreover, the rulers of Honduras and Costa Rica had privately expressed concern about Mexican meddling.[41] The misfortunes of a Mexican vessel, with weapons for Sacasa on board, further helped Kellogg with his argument: stopping for supplies in the port of La Unión, El Salvador, the *Tropical* was detained by local authorities. The Salvadoran government then let the ship sail only upon the intercession of the Mexican minister, and upon securing the promise of its captain to return to Mexican waters.[42]

It helped little that Foreign Secretary Sáenz and the Mexican press denied Mexican military involvement in Nicaragua.[43]

Kellogg then attempted to use Calles's intervention in Nicaragua for the larger goal of suppressing Mexican reform legislation. Following Sheffield's earlier dispatches, he began to leak information to the press to the effect that the Soviets worked hand in hand with the Mexicans in Nicaragua.[44] This supposed Soviet-Mexican-Nicaraguan connection was a classic smoke screen for U.S. intervention. No one in Washington truly believed the charges of Mexican Bolshevism. Mexico's aid to the Nicaraguan Liberals concerned Kellogg, but the State Department had known about it for months without making an issue out of it. Rather, the hard-liners in the State Department saw an opportunity to achieve several goals at once. A campaign to convince the U.S. public of a connection between Soviet Bolsheviks, the Mexican government, and the Nicaraguan Liberals could make Calles retreat on both the oil and Nicaraguan fronts. Moreover, at a time when Kellogg's State Department stood alone in its harsh Mexico policy against Herbert Hoover's Department of Commerce and an anti-interventionist U.S. Senate, a Red Scare in Mexico and Central America could only help the hard-liners. Thus, Kellogg's linkage of Mexican "Bolshevism" to the unrest in Nicaragua was the best way to convince a recalcitrant U.S. Congress and public that the U.S. government needed to take assertive action.[45]

It was in the Nicaraguan arena that Kellogg moved first. Since recognition of Chamorro still seemed out of the question, the U.S. chargé in Managua took up the Conservatives on their previous offer and persuaded them to nominate former president Adolfo Díaz as Chamorro's successor. Once that matter was settled, the Conservatives removed from the Nicaraguan congress those *genuinos* who had usurped seats after the coup and replaced them with Díaz allies or, in some cases, the original incumbents. With the possibility of another Liberal-Conservative coalition foreclosed, Díaz handily won the congress's endorsement as interim president. With these semilegal maneuvers, Díaz theoretically satisfied the Washington Conventions' requirements for recognition. Accordingly, the United States recognized the Díaz regime on December 24, 1926.[46]

Neither the Sacasa faction nor Calles acquiesced easily, however. Sacasa, still in residence in Guatemala City, had finally decided to give the Liberal insurgency the figurehead it badly needed. On December 2, he had returned to set up a "provisional government" in the port town of Puerto Cabezas on Nicaragua's Atlantic coast. This move achieved its desired effect: by the end of December, Liberal General José M. Moncada controlled more than half of the coast and stood poised to thrust inland.[47] The Sacasa government had also received international stature when the Calles regime, in accordance with the June agreements, had recognized it as the legitimate authority of Nicaragua on December 7, 1926.[48] In addition, even after the U.S. recognition of Díaz, which allowed the Conservatives to purchase arms legally in the United States, the Calles government continued to ship weapons to the Nicaraguan Liberals.[49]

Beleaguered, the Nicaraguan Conservatives finally made a pitch for direct U.S. military assistance.[50] In a letter to Dennis written on the day that Calles recognized the Sacasa government, Díaz blamed Mexico for the success of the uprising against his regime and called for decisive action to defend the sovereignty of Nicaragua.[51] Only a week later, he elaborated that "Mexican aid, if not checked, would inevitably overthrow . . . [his] government."[52] The U.S. response to Díaz's plea was not long in coming. Alerted to the Mexican shipments, U.S. warships patrolled the Nicaraguan Atlantic coast: as early as mid-December 1926, one Mexican gunrunning mission found it impossible to disembark its shipment.[53] On December 24, 1926, U.S. Marines seized Puerto Cabezas and other important port towns held by the Liberals. Invoking the threat posed by the fighting to U.S. lives and property, the U.S. military commanders declared all Liberal strongholds along the Atlantic coast "neutral zones." The commanders then ordered Sacasa's military units in the area to lay down their arms, and threatened to disarm forcibly those who did not comply. Throughout the next two months, the U.S. troops enlarged the "neutral zones." As a result, the insurgency failed to win new ground, even though the overt U.S. intervention gave the Liberals a measure of popular support.[54]

Nevertheless, Moncada and his forces hung tough through the spring of 1927. By then, however, the Liberals could no longer count on Mexican military assistance. The documentary evidence for this phase of Mexican involvement is skimpy, but we have reason to believe that Calles discontinued the arms shipments soon after the establishment of the "neutral zones."[55]

Certainly, the U.S. naval blockade of both coasts played a role in Calles's decision to end his material assistance. Warships in the area made access difficult if not impossible for Mexican gunrunners. The presence of U.S. forces also applied indirect pressure on the Calles government to keep out of Nicaragua—as Sheffield wrote to former President Taft, "those marines in Nicaragua are better than all the diplomatic notes that could be written to the Mexican Government. They understand and respect only force."[56] Calles, for his part, was just as unwilling as Porfirio Díaz had been to oppose the U.S. government overtly over a conflict in Central America at a time when U.S. intervention made the victory of Mexico's favorite faction unlikely. Moreover, the Mexican government experienced a fiscal crisis and a decline in oil revenues at the end of 1926, which further explains Calles's reluctance to commit more resources to the Nicaraguan Liberals.[57] Finally, by early 1927, Calles had a major domestic crisis on his hands with the onset of the Cristero rebellion in north-central Mexico. For all these reasons, the Mexican government could no longer send weapons and ammunition to the Sacasa forces. Calles did persist, though, in his diplomatic support of the Sacasa government: he never recognized the Adolfo Díaz regime.

Despite this retrenchment, the Nicaraguan issue contributed to heightening the existing tensions between Mexico and the United States. On January 10, 1927, Coolidge railed against Mexican intervention in a message to Congress.[58] In a meeting with the Senate Foreign Relations Committee on January 12, Kellogg accused the Calles government of spreading Bolshevism to Latin America and announced that the U.S. government would not countenance an export of radical ideologies.[59] After the meeting, U.S. and Mexican newspapers editorialized about the possibility of war between the two countries.[60] For all the excited rhetoric, however, direct U.S. intervention in Mexico was never a real possibility.[61]

The U.S. propaganda against Mexico found receptive ears in Central America. As we have seen, the Salvadoran government had already cooperated with the U.S. State Department, detaining a Mexican vessel loaded with weapons for Sacasa. In addition, Conservative-ruled Honduras had always supported Chamorro and Díaz and opposed Mexican efforts. By early 1927, another Central American government joined the fray: concerned about the growth of Mexican influence, the Costa Rican government secretly asked Kellogg to take action against Mexico.[62] Only Guatemala, now under the leadership of Lázaro Chacón, straddled the fence. Even though Chacón had refused Ambassador Cravioto's efforts to persuade him to recognize Sacasa through the medium of a pro-Mexican newspaper, he likewise spurned intense U.S. pressure to award immediate recognition to Díaz.[63]

Kellogg's latest attacks prompted a response from Calles in which he ably asserted his own political stature. In a press release prepared by a former Costa Rican justice with the Court of Central American Justice and a sympathetic U.S. journalist, Calles launched a valiant defense of his government's Nicaragua policies. In response to the charges of Bolshevism, he declared that Mexico had "no use for such exotic doctrines." Furthermore, he asserted that two Nicaraguan governments existed, "one founded on violence, and one on legality." He then denied that Mexico had awarded anything other than diplomatic recognition to Sacasa's provisional government but asserted that Mexico had the same right to support a friendly government as had the United States.[64] Mexico, Sáenz stated a few days later, had no interests in Nicaragua of an economic, political, or territorial nature. The Mexico City press chimed in with a barrage of attacks on Kellogg's policies.[65] In the course of the next several months, Calles received much praise both at home and abroad for his "principled" Nicaragua policy. While he had yielded on matters of substance in Nicaragua, he had scored a significant propaganda victory in standing up against the U.S. imposition of an illegitimate government.

The crisis was not completely over, however. In October 1927, the Hearst press, purporting to reveal a giant international conspiracy involving the Soviet Union, Mexico, and the Nicaraguan Liberals, published apocryphal documents about Mexico's aid to Sacasa. Once again, Calles used the services of his cousin and New York consul Arturo Elías to quell the emerging uproar in the United States. With U.S. public opinion firmly secured on the side of peaceful relations with Mexico, the incident blew over quickly. In fact, the sensationalist reporting of the Hearst press helped Calles more than it hurt him: it gave the Mexican government an exquisite chance to expound once again on the values of its foreign policy.[66] In addition, the shoddily produced forgeries, which were riddled with grammatical and other errors,[67] helped discredit the anti-Calles forces in the United States as a coalition of special interest groups that would stop at nothing to harm the Mexican government.[68]

Once again, Mexico had unsuccessfully challenged the United States in Nicaragua. As in 1909–10, the Mexican government had gone to great lengths in assisting a Liberal faction including imperiling to a certain extent its relations with the United States. In 1926 as in 1909, the Mexican government encountered a U.S. State Department committed to a unilateral imposition of its solutions in Central America. Even the advantages extracted from the affair were similar in nature: though Calles had not had his way in Nicaragua, he—just like Díaz—had scored a propagandistic victory from his near showdown with the United States.

As instructive as these similarities are, important differences highlight the evolution of Mexican foreign policy. Díaz's involvement in Nicaragua manifested Mexico's decades-old status in Central American disputes as a participant and mediator recognized and respected by the U.S. government. But by 1926, the United States held virtually unlimited sway over the area and guarded it jealously against all forms of foreign influence. The Mexico of the Sonoran dynasty, perceived by Kellogg as the pariah country of the western hemisphere rather than the model Latin American republic that Díaz had governed, was the last country that the United States wanted as a competitor in Central America. As a result, Calles's intervention in Nicaragua was necessarily more sporadic, less successful, and more short-lived than Díaz's longstanding efforts on behalf of the Zelaya regime.

Nicaragua, for its part, once again was pressured by direct U.S. intervention. In May 1927, U.S. special envoy Henry L. Stimson, threatening the Liberals with an even more active U.S. military role, brokered an armistice that held out the possibility of a Liberal victory at the polls in 1928 in exchange for an end to the rebellion.[69] Moncada and most of his generals complied with the agreement and surrendered their arms to the U.S. forces. The Liberals finally were allowed to return to power, as Moncada won election to the presidency in 1928 and Sacasa in 1932.[70]

Many of the rebels, however, resented Stimson's intervention. The most daring of these, one of Moncada's youngest generals by the name of Augusto C. Sandino, labeled the agreement "treason" on the part of the Liberals and decided to take the insurrection into his own hands. During the next six years, a growing U.S. military force chased Sandino's troops, whose numbers only increased because of the U.S. action.

Another Quest for "Nicaragua Libre" 177

Mexico and Sandino, 1927–1930

When Sandino declared war on the U.S. occupation troops in Nicaragua in May 1927, he hoped for support from Mexico.[71] After all, more than any other Central American leader, he had been influenced by events in Mexico: as a mine worker in the area of Cerro Azul, Veracruz, in 1926, Sandino had received first-hand experience with the growth of radical labor unions. Upon the outbreak of the Liberal rebellion, he had returned to Nicaragua to fight on the side of Moncada and Sacasa. From his perspective, the Calles government was a logical contributor to his cause.

Indeed, Sandino had his advocates in the Mexican government. In many ways, he was the darling of those radical Mexican diplomats who had vainly enjoined Obregón to take action on behalf of progressive factions in the Central America of the early 1920s. Unlike Herrera, Orellana, Sacasa, and Moncada, Sandino was a true outsider in the conservative Central American political system. Anarchist, communist, socialist, anti-imperialist, nationalist, "precursor of Fidel Castro"[72]— these are some of the attributes that have been used to describe Sandino and his ideology. Moreover, he represented a road not taken in the Mexican Revolution: the radical anarcho-syndicalism of the Flores Magón brothers,[73] which was popular with Cravioto and other Mexican diplomats in Central America. Support for his cause offered Calles a chance to reaffirm his commitment to bringing radicals into the fold, as well as an opportunity to camouflage his swing toward more conservative policies.

But at the time of the stabilizing phase, the Mexican government stayed out of the fray. As Calles knew only too well, any move in favor of Sandino, even diplomatic recognition, would once again fan the glowing embers of the recent crisis between the United States and Mexico. Even as a private Mexican expedition shipped weapons to the Sandino forces,[74] he rejected all calls for assistance. Threatened by the Cristeros and other rebels, his regime would not endanger the nascent rapprochement with the United States—strengthened by the arrival of the conciliatory U.S. Ambassador Dwight Morrow—by embarking on an adventure in Central America. As a sole sign of protest against the status quo, the Mexican government announced that it would not recognize any Nicaraguan regime as long as Yankee soldiers remained on the country's soil. Thus, Emilio Portes Gil, who nominally succeeded Calles in the fall of 1928, denied recognition to Moncada.

This modest symbolic action became an irritant in U.S.–Mexican relations, as the U.S. government desired a universal diplomatic acceptance of Moncada in order to isolate Sandino and withdraw its forces. In January 1929, one of Morrow's aides asked Foreign Secretary Genaro Estrada to reconsider Mexico's position on diplomatic recognition. Pointing out that all other countries had recognized the Moncada government, the aide asked Estrada to award recognition as well. But the Mexican government would not be swayed. Estrada stated that Mexico could never recognize a regime whose sovereignty was limited by the presence of foreign troops. One month later, he reiterated this position in a conversation with Morrow.[75] When the ambassador finally took up the subject of Moncada's recognition with the president himself, he was rebuffed once again: Mexico, Portes Gil stated, could never change its stance toward Nicaragua as long as U.S. troops remained on that country's soil. "I'd like you to suppose for a moment," Portes Gil said, "that ... instead of Nicaragua, the United States were the invaded country. What would you think, Mr. Morrow?"[76]

By that time, Sandino had appealed again to the Mexican government for help. In a letter to Portes Gil, he asked to visit Mexico to discuss some "highly important projects" with the president.[77] Unwilling to risk a crisis with the United States over such an invitation, Portes Gil asked Morrow for his opinion. Surprisingly, neither Morrow nor Kellogg objected to the idea. Kellogg, however, qualified his approval by tacking three conditions onto the visit: Sandino could not continue the war effort from Mexico, he could not enter Mexico City, and he had to take up residence in a "remote state."[78] The U.S. government would "much prefer to have Sandino in Mexico under surveillance," Kellogg added, "than in Costa Rica, Guatemala, or Honduras, where he might otherwise go."[79]

Portes Gil realized that the upcoming Sandino visit afforded him a great opportunity to address conjointly the two related problems of the permanence of U.S. forces in Nicaragua and his recognition of the Moncada government. He thus instructed the Mexican minister in San José, Antonio Mediz Bolio, to offer Moncada a quid pro quo: if he agreed to a U.S. withdrawal of troops from Nicaragua, Portes Gil would make sure that Sandino could do no harm from Mexican soil. Upon departure of the Marines, Portes Gil proposed, Mexico would recognize Moncada.[80] But aware of his precarious political position, Moncada rejected the proposal. "The North American troops are necessary here to maintain order," Moncada told Mediz Bolio's agent; "when the last Yankee Marine leaves, my government will have no way to maintain itself in power."[81] Obviously, Moncada feared going the way of Solórzano, who was ousted by the Chamorristas as soon as the U.S. government withdrew its occupation forces in August 1925.

With his grand plan in shambles, Portes Gil had now exhausted his options. As long as U.S. forces remained in Nicaragua, Mexico could not recognize the Moncada regime, and Sandino would continue his fight against the U.S. Marines. Conversely, as long as the Chamorristas remained a factor and Sandino operated in the Nicaraguan mountains, Moncada would ask the U.S. forces to stay. At this point, Mexico could not make a constructive contribution to solving the Nicaraguan conundrum.

If Moncada's rejection ended Mexican mediation of the Nicaraguan conflict, the issue of Sandino's upcoming visit still preoccupied the Mexican government. As Porfirio Díaz had in granting asylum to Zelaya and José Madriz, Portes Gil could score a small propaganda victory by accepting Sandino into Mexican exile. Morrow's three qualifiers, however, complicated the situation. As Portes Gil well knew, Sandino was not coming to Mexico to retire to a humble peasant life in a "remote state," but to request help from his government. In his reply to Sandino, the Mexican president decided to sidestep the issue: in sympathy with his struggle against the United States, he wrote, Mexico would gladly offer asylum to Sandino and even pay his expenses. Moreover, Portes Gil added, Sandino was free to leave the country at any time.[82]

Sandino obviously misunderstood this offer of asylum as a proposition for Mexican political and military aid.[83] When the Nicaraguan rebel and his entourage arrived in the Mexican port city of Veracruz full of hopes,[84] they received an unpleasant surprise. Rather than escorting the group to Mexico City, an army official made Sandino an honorary general but then ushered him and his aides onto a boat to Progreso, Yucatán, whence they traveled to Mérida.[85] There, the Mexican government paid the group a miserable living stipend and made sure that Sandino could not direct the military campaign in Nicaragua, much less leave the Mérida area. For six months, Sandino waited impatiently, still hoping for support for his cause.[86] When Portes Gil finally granted an interview to the Nicaraguan leader in January 1930, it was in his last week in office as a lame-duck president, with his successor already elected.[87] Nothing substantial came out of the meeting, and Sandino now knew that the Mexican government held him prisoner.[88] Thus, his only interview with Portes Gil proved a good-bye visit. Three months later, Sandino and several of his aides eluded Mexican surveillance and escaped to Nicaragua, after having pretended that they intended to settle down as farmers on an hacienda near Mérida.[89]

While the Mexican government had not helped the Nicaraguan rebel, however, that fact did not stop Portes Gil from exploiting Sandino's asylum for his own political benefit. In public, he often paid lip service to Sandino's cause and praised the Nicaraguan as a patriot who defended his homeland against the Yankee invader. The following interview with U.S. journalist Waldo Frank is indicative of Portes Gil's desire to make his views on Sandino public:

> W.F.: What do you think about Sandino?
> E.P.G.: He is a patriot.
> W.F.: Can I publish your answer?
> E.P.G.: You are authorized to do that.[90]

As much as Portes Gil felt bound to comply with the wishes of the United States when it came to Sandino's internment in Yucatán, the Nicaraguan served a powerful symbolic purpose. He represented the realization of the ongoing, frustrated aspirations of the Mexican people to stand up to the "Yankee oppressor." Moreover, in Yucatán itself, where the Revolution had taken a more radical course than elsewhere, Sandino had become a veritable folk hero.[91]

Had the Mexican government played a cynical double game with Sandino, and had it departed from a fifty-year-old strategy of "cautious competition" with the United States in Central America? Portes Gil had acted true to his promise to Morrow, and he had played into the hands of the United States. His plan to tuck Sandino away in a remote corner of the country hardly meshed with his professed sympathy for the rebel's cause. Portes Gil had made the offer of asylum as part of a larger scheme, the primary goal of which had been an understanding with the United States over the Nicaraguan question, and not aid for Sandino's cause. Seen from this vantage point, the Sandino incident marked the end of a long period of at least tacit Mexican solidarity with anti-U.S. movements in Central America.

This interpretation, however, is much too simplistic. Portes Gil had no reason to become Kellogg's and Morrow's handmaiden in this matter, and in fact, he had many reasons not to do so. More likely, Portes Gil had not given up on his plan to achieve the removal of U.S. soldiers from Nicaragua. To be sure, the Mexican government did "betray" Sandino in pawning off his liberty in exchange for Morrow's goodwill. But Portes Gil's abortive plan for the withdrawal of the marines from Nicaragua suggests that the true motive for his involvement lay in the removal of U.S. troops rather than in improving relations with the U.S. government.

A glimpse at the Sandino faction gives this second interpretation even more credence. In contrast to the "moderate," bourgeois Zelaya and Sacasa, Sandino and his followers represented the frustrated aspirations of the lower classes in the Mexican Revolution: with reason, the contemporary historian and novelist Paco Ignacio Taibo II has compared him to Emiliano Zapata.[92] The earlier Nicaraguan rebel factions had proven ideologically compatible with the men in power in Mexico City: just as Zelaya often appeared a "progressive" Porfirista, Sacasa, at least in rhetoric, claimed allegiance to the middle-class ideology of the Sonorans. Sandino, on the other hand, if given free reign in Mexico, potentially loomed as a dangerous political adversary for Portes Gil's regime, particularly given his grass-roots ideology and support. In Sandino's request for assistance, Calles and Portes Gil therefore might have seen a great opportunity to achieve several goals at once: reaping propagandistic benefit, increasing the likelihood of a U.S. withdrawal from Nicaragua, and preventing the Mexican opposition from appropriating the strong, radical political symbolism of Sandinismo.

Thus, Mexican policy toward the Sandino movement must be understood in terms of Mexico's desire to lessen U.S. influence in Central America rather than of Portes Gil's attitude toward the Sandino rebellion. The Mexican government did not invite Sandino to show support for his cause, nor did it intern him in Yucatán because it did not like his movement. Rather, Portes Gil mistakenly assumed that Sandino's removal from the Nicaraguan scene might result in the liberation of Central America from U.S. military forces. Whether Ambassador Morrow ever gave the Mexican government hope for such a turn of events is subject to speculation.[93] Put succinctly, Portes Gil had regarded Sandino as a convenient tool to achieve the withdrawal of the U.S. Marines *and* the continuation of the thaw in U.S.–Mexican relations.

The fact that both Portes Gil and Sandino attempted each in his own way to bring about the removal of the Marines adds an ironic twist to the story. While the two men agreed on the desirability of an end to U.S. military intervention in Central America, they had precious little else in common as regards their political ideologies. The Mexican government, under the leadership of Calles and Portes Gil, had begun to negotiate a new social and political arrangement that ultimately disappointed the Mexican left in its authoritarian and elitist nature. Sandino, on the other hand, envisioned a revolution *desde abajo,* from below, one that would fundamentally restructure Nicaraguan society. What Portes Gil really thought about Sandino and his political ideology remains an interesting subject for future scholarship, as is the issue of Sandino's considerable appeal to the Mexican popular classes. Most probably, however, the Mexican president—himself no more ideologically driven than Calles—never really understood Sandino as anybody but a "patriot."

When Sandino was assassinated at the hands of the Nicaraguan National Guard in 1934, many Mexicans—including President Abelardo Rodríguez—mourned him.[94] But while the Mexican government decried the loss of a great patriot who had stood up to foreign intervention, other Mexicans must have perceived this loss differently: as the death of a popular hero. This hero had struggled for the liberation of the Latin American peoples from both U.S. intervention and the unjust social, economic, and political structures existing within each of the Latin American societies.[95] Calles and Portes Gil either never understood the radical implications of Sandino's ideology, or they chose to ignore and suppress them.

Retrospect: The Sonoran Dynasty and Central America

The Sandino affair marked the last instance of Mexican activism in Latin America for a long time. Already at the Sixth Inter-American Conference in Havana in 1928, the Mexican delegation had kept a low profile, following the order not to display "an attitude of systematic opposition" toward the United States.[96] From now on, the Mexican leadership dedicated itself to other foreign-policy priorities. Sandino's departure from Yucatán pushed Central America further down the agenda of the Mexican government. Mexico no longer had an opportunity for action in the isthmus, but the ongoing détente with Guatemala had also removed a pressing problem from Mexico's southern border. For the remainder of Calles's time as *jefe máximo*, foreign policy in general did not figure as a response to domestic threats.

In sum, Mexico had confronted a dilemma in Central America during the 1920s. The function of a nationalist Mexican foreign policy as a mode of state building and the end of the old antagonism with Guatemala constituted strong incentives for an active policy in the isthmus. On the other hand, Mexico's conflictive relationship with the United States, and the tightly woven web of U.S. hegemony in Central America, appeared as virtually forbidding obstacles to assertive foreign-policy initiatives during the rule of the Sonorans.

Under these circumstances, it is not surprising that the Mexican government faced difficulties in the Central America of the 1920s. Therefore, its renewed challenge to the United States was a sporadic one, one that sought out small windows of opportunity within which it could operate. The Díaz regime, which had been able to act in Central America as an arbiter between Guatemala and its neighbors, and between pro-U.S., pro-European, and nationalist factions, generally enjoyed U.S. respect for its influence in the isthmus. Obregón and Calles, by contrast, needed to fight for a Mexican role, even if the role they sought strongly resembled the Porfirian one.

If the Sonorans had faced an uphill struggle in Central America, they had acquitted themselves well in taking advantage of their few possibilities. The rapprochement with Guatemala, helped by the fact that Chiapas became ever more integrated into the national state, offered the Mexican government the chance to look at Central America as an opportunity rather than a problem. Calles had lost his confrontation with the United States in Nicaragua, but his principled rhetoric and diplomacy had earned him international and domestic respect. In addition, by aiding Sacasa, he had shown the progressive forces in the isthmus that the United States had to expend major resources to keep them from winning, and he probably encouraged Sandino to start his rebellion in the first place. Portes Gil had given a peculiar sort of asylum to a Nicaraguan patriot without risking a break with the United States. In a decade when an open challenge to the U.S. government was costly, the Sonorans had reclaimed much ground that had been lost in the decade of violent struggle.

Mexican policies in the Sonoran era had been motivated more by domestic and bilateral concerns than by fear of the United States. With the exception of the assistance to Sacasa (a policy choice made in part because of a misjudgment of U.S. policies), the desire to lessen U.S. policies played a secondary role. But the reason for this renewed assertion of bilateral rather than great-power driven strategies lay in the very strength of the dominant power in the area: Obregón and Calles knew only too well that they could not oppose the United States over Central America.

8 Epilogue

Mexico's Central America Policy Since 1930

Mexico: So Close to the United States, So Far from Latin America.

Jorge Chabat, 1993

Sandino's departure from Yucatán in March 1930 marked the end of an era of strong Mexican interest in Central America. For the next three decades, the Mexican government lacked both the desire and the opportunity to play an active role in the isthmus. Other issues dominated: a deepening rapprochement with the U.S. government in the wake of the Great Depression, the oil expropriation of 1938, World War Two, and the country's involvement in a newly created Pan-American system. The Central American elites had grown increasingly indifferent and even hostile to Mexico. U.S. influence in the isthmus had assumed hegemonic proportions, with few possibilities for forces inside and outside the area to challenge that influence. Finally, U.S. intervention, the fear of which had helped drive Mexican diplomacy toward activism in the region, no longer loomed as a great threat in the era of the "good neighbor policy."

After a period of relative inaction lasting almost thirty years, Mexico slowly crept back to an assertive Central America policy in the 1960s and 1970s. By 1982, the Mexican government had emerged as an important and vocal supporter of the revolutionary Sandinista government. In addition, the administration of José López Portillo had issued a joint declaration with French President François Mitterrand, recognizing the Marxist rebels of El Salvador as a legitimate political force. Indeed, the López Portillo regime became recognized as one of the key elements in a Latin American effort to stem another tide of U.S. interventionism in Central America. Mexico, at least for a period of about three years, had resumed its position as an important player in Central America.[1]

Years of Inaction, 1930–1944

Throughout the 1876–1930 period, a succession of Mexican governments had pursued their own goals and blunted to a degree U.S. influence in Central America. After 1930, the timing superficially appeared auspicious for further Mexican action in the region: Lázaro Cárdenas and his successors consummated Calles's state-building project, and the U.S. government renounced the use of military force in Latin America by means of what came to be known as the good neighbor policy. But an increasing neglect of Central America in favor of other priorities, the rise of anti-Mexican military dictatorships in the isthmus, and the advent of World War Two thwarted any such possibility over the next fifteen years.

Of these trends, the shift in foreign-policy priorities beginning in Calles's stabilizing period was the earliest and perhaps the most significant. As we have seen, the late 1920s witnessed both the resolution of a number of contentious issues in U.S.–Mexican relations and the creation of a powerful ruling party in Mexico. During his time as *jefe máximo*, in which he ruled from behind the scenes, Calles built upon these foundations: he used his good rapport with Ambassador Dwight Morrow and Morrow's successor, Josephus Daniels, to strengthen his own political base.[2] With the most pressing difficulties with the United States resolved, Calles dedicated himself to furthering the Sonoran project of constructing the modern Mexican corporatist state. By 1934, after ruling directly for four years and with the help of presidents loyal to him for another six years, he had created a political party, the PNR (National Revolutionary Party), which has to this day never lost a presidential election. Calles had also aided in the forging of peasant and labor movements loyal to the government.[3] He was loath to endanger this project with an aggressive Central America policy that might have brought to an end his vital cooperation with the U.S. ambassador.

With the onset of the Great Depression, cooperation with the United States and a dedication to domestic issues became even more imperative for Mexico. Throughout the 1930s, the worldwide economic crisis and especially the punitive Smoot-Hawley tariff of 1931 exacted a heavy toll on the Mexican export sector. Thus, after Sandino's departure in 1930, Calles and his successors increasingly assumed a posture of benign neglect toward the isthmus while working out a number of bilateral U.S.–Mexican problems.[4]

While the *jefe máximo*, Calles, had abandoned his interest in the isthmus, the onset of Cardenismo made action in Central America even less likely. After ridding himself of Calles's tutelage in 1935, new president Lázaro Cárdenas, backed by widespread popular support, initiated a "genuinely radical movement" that revitalized the promise of the 1917 Constitution. Cárdenas undertook the most ambitious land reform in Mexican history, mobilized workers and peasants in mass organizations, and pushed forward substantial educational reform. In order to ensure the success of his agenda, Cárdenas at least initially sought to assure himself of U.S. goodwill. In Ambassador Daniels, he found an ally sympathetic to his reform efforts.[5] In a sense, Mexico and the United States pursued "broadly parallel social agendas,"[6] with U.S. President Franklin D. Roosevelt's New Deal juxtaposed to Cardenismo. Roosevelt's good neighbor policy, which pledged nonintervention and a cooperative approach to Latin America, thus was put to work in Mexico. To avoid alienating hawks critical of Daniels such as U.S. Secretary of State Cordell Hull, however, Cárdenas needed to step lightly in Central America. At a time when geopolitical thinking once again helped shape U.S. foreign policy making due to the advances of the Axis powers, Mexican activism in Central America could have disrupted the rapport between Cardenistas and Rooseveltian Democrats.[7]

But even if the strongly nationalist Cárdenas might have wished to turn toward Central America, further obstacles stood in the way. A number of entrenched dictatorships, helped to power in part by the collapse of the region's export economies after the Great Depression, made the idea of pursuing traditional Mexican strategies unfeasible. Since 1931, Guatemala once again was under the boot of an anti-Mexican strongman, the notorious but initially popular Jorge Ubico.[8] An ally of former president Manuel Estrada Cabrera, Ubico, as *jefe político* of the border department of Retalhuleu, had made life miserable for Mexican sojourners in Guatemala. Like the Salvadoran Maximiliano Hernández Martínez and the Nicaraguan Anastasio Somoza García,[9] Ubico represented a new breed of Central American tyrant. Helped by a few modest infrastructure projects and U.S. reciprocal trade agreements, all three dictators modernized their societies.[10] Each enforced his rule with a well-trained, brutally repressive professional militia—witness, for example, the Nicaraguan Guardia Nacional.[11] These militias (in Nicaragua's case trained with the help of U.S. advisers) proved far more effective in maintaining order than had the sporadic U.S. interventions of yesteryear.[12]

The existence of these stable dictatorships not only obviated armed U.S. intervention and precluded Mexican action; they put Mexico on the defensive. Ubico, of course, constituted Cárdenas's greatest problem in Central America. Taking a cue from his former mentor Estrada Cabrera, Ubico claimed that "very little good has ever come to Guatemala from its northern neighbor"[13] and pleaded with the United States for protection from Mexican press agitation against his government.[14] He also accused the Mexican ambassador to Guatemala, Eduardo Hay, of using the embassy as an outpost to spread "Bolshevik" revolutionary propaganda in Central America.[15] These charges lacked any basis in fact, but they sufficed to undermine the tentative understanding that had existed between the two countries in the 1920s. As this understanding unraveled, Mexico lost much of its remaining leverage in the isthmus. Nicaragua's Anastasio Somoza García, the head of the Guardia Nacional who assumed formal power via coup d'état in 1936, proved equally unhelpful to any Mexican initiatives. Owing his position largely to the consequences of U.S. influence, the nominally Liberal Somoza was certainly no Zelaya who would welcome Mexican influence.

Nevertheless, Mexico might have played a role in the isthmus during the 1930s had it thrown its weight behind Ubico's and Somoza's regional rival, El Salvador's Hernández Martínez.[16] However, with that dictator's hand bloodied by the 1932 slaying of thousands of peasant insurgents in the so-called Matanza, such a move was politically unpalatable for Cárdenas. In fact, the Mexican president showed little interest in Central America, which looked to him like a backward region ruled by neo-Porfirian despots. Apart from periodic rebuttals to Ubico's charges and half-hearted efforts to increase economic ties with the Central American republics,[17] Cárdenas did not show much interest in the isthmus.

Instead, he found other outlets for a display of his assertive, nationalist policies—both in Spain and in the Mexican subsoil. From 1936 to 1939, Mexico was the only country to provide active diplomatic and military help to Spain's Popular Front government in its fight against Francisco Franco's Falangista forces. Cárdenas—who abhorred European totalitarianism—thus came to oppose indirectly Franco's international supporters, principally Nazi Germany and Fascist Italy. This aid to the Popular Front and the concomitant opposition to the spread of rightist totalitarianism in Europe enjoyed the backing of many Mexicans. Helping the anti-Franco forces also proved politically expedient abroad, as the Roosevelt administration, while officially neutral, privately sympathized with the Popular Front. In addition, Mexico benefited from the influx of thousands of well-educated and often wealthy partisans.[18]

Then, in March 1938, Cárdenas moved on another front: he nationalized the petroleum industry. To the acclaim of his radical supporters, Cárdenas for years had backed the oil workers in a protracted labor dispute with their foreign-owned companies. When the sixteen largest companies, which produced 97 percent of Mexican crude, refused to budge and even disobeyed a court order to give in to the workers' demands, Cárdenas seized the opportunity to expropriate their holdings.[19] The decree soon proved one of the most popular measures ever taken by a Mexican government. "Nuestro petróleo"—our oil—had become a symbol of Mexican nationalism.

Seizure of the Mexican oil industry dealt a blow, albeit not a definitive one, to U.S.–Mexican relations. Whereas Cárdenas' Spanish policy had not damaged relations with the United States, the oil expropriation put them at grave risk. Immediately after the signing of the nationalization decree, the British Foreign Office called for joint intervention with the U.S. government on behalf of the industry.[20] For their part, the oil companies, owners of most of the vessels that transported Mexican crude, refused to ship oil from the expropriated fields until Cárdenas agreed to award restitution or compensation. The controversy also resurrected long dormant allegations of Mexican "Bolshevism" in the U.S. Congress and parts of the U.S. press.

As subsequent events showed, however, Cárdenas had calculated correctly that the crisis would pass. In the age of the good neighbor policy, Roosevelt and Daniels would not allow the oil controversy to interfere with their goal of establishing an inter-American system to defend against potential Nazi and Japanese threats to the hemisphere. To add to these concerns, Mexico, deprived of markets, had begun to sell crude to Germany and Italy.[21] Therefore, the doves around Daniels prevailed over the hawks around Hull, and the companies ultimately had to settle for modest compensation payments.

The oil controversy further limited Mexico's radius of action in Central America. With U.S.–Mexican relations strained, Cárdenas needed to assure himself of good relations with the Central American countries. Therefore, he grudgingly suppressed anti-Guatemalan articles in the Mexican press in order to appease the Ubico regime.[22] This amounted to an unprecedented step to please a Guatemalan leader—both Díaz and Carranza had always steadfastly refused to restrain anti-Guatemalan commentary in the press. In this case, however, Cárdenas could not afford a distraction on Mexico's southern border. The affair illustrated to what extent the country's Central America policy had become subsidiary to other considerations.

World War Two and U.S. diplomatic efforts to unite the American countries in the face of extrahemispheric threats constituted additional obstacles to Mexican initiatives. In May 1942, German submarines sank a Mexican vessel off the coast of Florida, and Mexico soon joined the war against the Axis powers on the side of the United States. The war effort, which was also joined by all of the Central American countries, forbade an assertive Mexican diplomacy in the area, at least for the 1941–45 period. Another consequence of the war proved even more significant: the United States used the occasion of global conflict to promote the creation of an "inter–American system." Formed during a series of Pan-American meetings and culminating in the foundation of the Organization of American States in 1948, this treaty system outlawed U.S. intervention but practically codified U.S. hegemony over the Americas. The treaty system worked to forge a united front against the Axis powers, and later, the Soviet Union.[23] Moreover, the new Pan–American institutions would later permit the United States to contain Latin American reform movements that threatened U.S. property interests. Initially welcomed by Mexico as the implementation of the country's long–standing desire for a multilateral Pan–American forum for the adjudication of international disputes,[24] the OAS ultimately became a U.S. vehicle for new interventionist policies in the Cold War, thus further constraining Mexican policies and initiatives.[25]

Mexico, the Cold War, and Guatemala's "Ten Years of Spring"

Soon, however, an experiment in social and economic reform in Guatemala seized Mexican attention. With great suddenness (and the overwhelming approval of the Mexican government) a student revolt ended the Ubico regime in October 1944. Ubico's repressive political machine had antagonized the Guatemalan middle class; Guatemala was beset by a host of economic problems; U.S. diplomats had grown increasingly critical of Ubico; and blatant corruption among government officials had alienated much of the oligarchy that had hitherto supported his regime. Although Mexico had taken no part in the student revolt, its ambassador publicly expressed his "sympathy—and that of his government—for the Guatemalan people and the triumph of democracy in . . . [that] country."[26]

The Mexican government had even more reason to be excited when Juan José Arévalo became Guatemala's new president in 1945. Arévalo launched the most ambitious attempt to date to forge a more inclusionary political and economic system. An admirer of the Mexican revolutionary model, the former university professor advocated bourgeois social reform, a modest land redistribution program, and political democracy. Labeled "spiritual socialism," Arévalo's program probably contained more rhetoric than substance; nevertheless, his commitment to a more democratic Guatemala appeared genuine.[27] At any other period in time, Arévalo undoubtedly would have been the darling of Mexican foreign policy and the focus of an effort to expand ties with the Central American countries. With Arévalo, middle-class rule—the essence of Mexico's own corporatist arrangement—had arrived in Guatemala.

A changed environment of Mexican foreign policy, however, thwarted any hopes for cooperation between the two neighbors. At the same time that Guatemala took a decisive turn toward policies more independent of the United States, Mexico moved in the opposite direction. President Manuel Avila Camacho, who governed Mexico from 1940 to 1946, cooperated fully with the Allied effort in World War Two.[28] He also acted quickly to resolve such outstanding disputes as compensation for the expropriated oil companies and the question of the Mexican debt. His successors, Miguel Alemán Valdés and Adolfo

Ruiz Cortines, continued on the same track, encouraging the lifting of fetters on foreign investments in Mexico. In part as a result of these policies, the rapid U.S. economic expansion of the 1940s dragged Mexico out of its economic doldrums. Convinced that political stability and guarantees for foreign capital rested secure with Avila Camacho, U.S. investors, awash in cash from the wartime boom, once again poured funds into Mexico. This new boom in investments, encouraged by the Mexican government, ushered in an age of cooperation between the two countries that far surpassed the Porfirian program of limited friendship with the United States. At this juncture, an activist Central American policy might have endangered the beneficial economic links to the United States.

This turn toward the United States was accompanied by a shift to the right within Mexico's leadership—a shift that was due both to changed dynamics in the ruling party and to Mexico's entry into a closer economic relationship with the United States. Avila Camacho eliminated the influence of the ruling party's left wing led by Francisco Múgica. He also slowed down the process of land redistribution and did not pursue policies of economic nationalism.[29] By 1952, a "developmentalist" faction among the governing elite steered the Mexican state—a faction that would have resembled the Porfirian científicos but for its pro-Yankee orientation. Avila Camacho (and, to an even greater extent, his successors) followed the old maxim of "order and progress" made possible by the shrewd corporatist engineering of mass movements begun by the Cardenistas in the last days of their rule. "Order" could be achieved by government mediation among the various interest groups within Mexican society, and the suppression of small but vociferous socialist and communist opposition groups. Anticommunism now became official policy, as Alemán, following U.S. President Harry S Truman's "Containment" speech, proclaimed communism incompatible with "Mexicanness."[30] "Progress," on the other hand (and, once again, U.S. support) beckoned with an ambitious program of import-substitution industrialization helped by the wartime economic expansion.[31]

In this scheme, there was no room for an assertive Mexican foreign policy, except insofar as it could provide a sop to the disenchanted Mexican left. Even that motive for an active involvement in foreign affairs, however, faded fast: during the 1945–60 period, rapid if uneven economic growth and the suppression of leftist dissent ensured a relatively weak opposition. Thus, as Washington assumed leadership over the pan-American institutions it had created, and as Mexico focused on its industrial development, Mexican support for Arévalo remained limited to words of cordiality and a contract for a small-scale sale of war materiel.[32] Former president Cárdenas, by contrast, in unofficial opposition to the government, praised the Arévalo government as an "example for oppressed people" and affirmed his support of Arévalo in "these times of armed aggression of the big interests opposed to progress."[33] Avila Camacho's and Alemán's attitude toward Arévalo's Guatemala can therefore be characterized as friendly but indifferent.

But a change of leadership in Guatemala drove the two countries further apart. While Arévalo had been the "Carranza" of Guatemala, who sought political democracy and some degree of economic change, his elected successor, Jacobo Arbenz, would have allied himself with Múgica, on Cárdenas's left, on most counts. To be sure, Arbenz was not the pro-Soviet Bolshevik that the U.S. Central Intelligence Agency made him out to be. His actions could hardly be labeled radical: as his most controversial act, Arbenz redistributed fallow land owned by the United Fruit Company and other large-scale proprietors. By all accounts, this agrarian reform was more modest than Cárdenas' expropriations of the 1930s.[34]

The Mexican government soon backed away from its rhetorical support of the Guatemalan experiment in reform. We can only speculate on the reasons for this shift. While Avila Camacho had sympathized with Arévalo's efforts at political democracy, the more conservative Ruiz Cortines could hardly approve of Arbenz's more sweeping reforms, which looked too much like those of Cardenismo. He reminded Mexicans of a cherished, not-too-remote past in which many of the promises of the Revolution had been taken more seriously than under Avila Camacho, Alemán, and Ruiz Cortines. Mexico's increased economic dependence on the United States, a product of the world war, further reduced the likelihood of an anti-U.S. stance.

This time, unlike in the Zelaya episode, growing U.S. opposition to the Arbenz government did not prompt Mexico to act. The Truman administration had paid little attention to events in Guatemala, regarding Arévalo as a "starry-eyed reformer" who would do little harm to U.S. strategic and economic interests.[35] Thus, Truman's concept of containment applied to an extrahemispheric aggression by a communist nation but not to the threat of "subversion"—a word that would become a key term in U.S. foreign policies in the following three decades.[36] But with the victory of Dwight D. Eisenhower in the U.S. presidential elections of 1952, this scenario changed. As much as his government demonstrated restraint in relations with the Soviet Union, it pursued an aggressively anticommunist foreign policy in Latin America. Whether to safeguard U.S. economic interests or to thwart perceived acts of Soviet subversion, U.S. Secretary of State John F. Dulles acted decisively against a number of social reformist governments in the Third World.[37] In Dulles's global crusade to link movements of national liberation and social reform to Soviet subversion—a crusade that responded to overblown perceptions and manifest economic interests rather than actual evidence of "communism"—Arbenz and the Mossadegh regime in Iran became its most prominent victims. Therefore, when the Eisenhower administration branded Arbenz's modest land reform as "communist," Mexico could not lend any direct diplomatic assistance to the Guatemalan government without risking also being tarred with the communist label.

The existence of the inter-American system, however, at least gave Mexico a chance to voice its objections. Instead of proceeding unilaterally against Guatemala, Secretary of State Dulles attempted to rally Latin American opposition to "communist" influence in the Americas. To achieve this goal, Dulles presented at the Tenth Inter-American Conference held in Caracas in March 1954 a resolution invoking the hemispheric defense system created during the 1940s against "communist subversion."[38] Since it was a thinly veiled attack on the Arbenz government, many Latin Americans lamented that passage of the motion would essentially give the United States a free hand to mount an intervention in Guatemala.

The Mexican government had to make a decision as to its vote on the motion at the Caracas conference. While the resolution seemed a particularly insidious tactic to advance the State Department's rabid anticommunism, it also forced the Ruiz Cortines government to make its stance publicly known. Either way, the Mexican delegation appeared headed for problems. If it approved the resolution, it tarnished the Mexican government's self-styled image of revolutionary nationalism. On the other hand, if Mexico opposed the United States over the measure, it opened itself up to the charge of favoring communism in the

Americas, and risked antagonizing the Eisenhower administration over a matter of limited significance. Mexican public opinion was split on the subject.[39]

Attempting to strike a middle ground, Ruiz Cortines instructed his government's delegation to assert Mexico's time-honored principles of nonintervention and national self-determination. At the conference, the Mexican delegate, Roberto Córdoba, argued passionately against the resolution and presented various amendments that affirmed each country's inalienable right to choose its own form of government and institutions. Unable to influence the other Latin American countries or sway U.S. opinion on the matter, Córdoba hoped to extract at least propagandistic benefit from the affair.[40] In the end, though, he faced up to the realities of the Cold War and did not vote against the motion. The U.S.-led majority neutralized all amendments that attempted to weaken the measure, and the assembly overwhelmingly approved the resolution. Only Mexico, Costa Rica, and Argentina abstained, and Guatemala cast the lone dissenting vote.[41]

Córdoba's abstention at Caracas revealed the tightrope which Mexico was walking in its Cold War–era foreign policy. Within Mexico, many inside and outside the government disagreed with Ruiz Cortines's cautious stand. Many Mexicans—including labor leaders, intellectuals, and peasant representatives—demanded an assertive stand against what appeared to be an impending intervention. For example, when pressure began to mount on Arbenz, former president Cárdenas sent a cable to the Guatemalan foreign minister, expressing his "personal friendship and sympathy" with a country which saw "its sovereignty threatened."[42] Even an old Carrancista voiced his dissatisfaction with Mexican inaction. Carefully couching his criticism in words of praise for the Ruiz Cortines regime, Isidro Fabela characterized the abstention, in his words an "act of mere courtesy" toward the United States, as a "diplomatic formula of not saying no."[43] On the other hand, many conservative groups in Mexico opposed any diplomatic maneuvers that would help what they viewed as "communist infiltration" of the hemisphere.[44]

Only a few months after the conclusion of the Caracas conference, the U.S. government rendered moot this entire discussion. A shipment of weapons of Czech origin to Guatemala served as a pretext for the U.S. government to overthrow the Arbenz regime. On June 17, 1954, the

CIA-assisted invasion of Colonel Carlos Castillo Armas and several thousand mercenaries put an end to Guatemala's "Ten Years of Spring." Arbenz fled, Castillo Armas became president, and the United Fruit Company gained back the property lost under Arbenz's land reform. Exploiting internal Guatemalan opposition to Arbenz, U.S. intervention had helped end Central America's first experiment in representative democracy and social reform.[45]

If his delegation had uttered some beautiful words at Caracas, Ruiz Cortines decided to forsake the principles espoused there. Even as Cárdenas enjoined the Mexican president to mediate between the United States and Guatemala to forestall this "aggression by business,"[46] Ruiz Cortines refused to comment on the subject of Arbenz's overthrow.[47] Over the course of the next several weeks, no comment on the issue could be extracted either from Ruiz Cortines or from any other top-level official in Mexico City. With one exception, even the mass organizations associated with the government did not protest this blatant act of U.S. intervention,[48] even though many of their leaders privately decried the invasion. At the height of the Cold War, the Mexican authorities had no choice but to concede Central America to unilateral U.S. action. But the government's refusal to comment and to permit anti-interventionist demonstrations reflected the changed political climate within Mexico. Mexico, under Ruiz Cortines, had become less anti-Yankee than even under Juárez.

The late 1950s constituted another low point of Mexican influence in Central America. Following Arbenz's overthrow, Mexican-Guatemalan relations soured once again, a situation highlighted by a fishing dispute in 1959 during which Guatemalan warplanes sank a Mexican fishing vessel off the Pacific coast.[49] Apart from this confrontation, Mexico and Central America went separate ways. It would take both a shift within the Mexican political arena and a challenge to U.S. hegemony from within Central America for Mexico to look once more to the isthmus as an area of international opportunity.

The Long Climb Back to Activism, 1960–1978

By means of a series of cultural, economic, and trade initiatives, President Adolfo López Mateos after 1960 began sending a clear message: Central America mattered to Mexico.[50] In the late 1960s, many of

these tentative measures—except for the trade program—were abandoned during the administration of Gustavo Díaz Ordaz, only to be re-
vived under President Luis Echeverría, who proclaimed Mexico the
champion of the Third World. By 1976, the Mexican government—still
reluctant to challenge the United States in Central America—was once
again poised to play a role in the isthmus.

The change in U.S. policies certainly facilitated a Mexican resumption of international initiatives. Starting in the second half of the
Eisenhower administration, the U.S. government shifted its approach
to Latin America from the hawkish interventionism of the early 1950s
to the "Alliance for Progress," formally launched under President
John F. Kennedy. To be sure, the United States still intervened in Latin
America—witness the 1965 episode in the Dominican Republic. Nevertheless, the Alliance for Progress, which advocated as its stated goal the
fostering of democratic forces and economic development throughout
Latin America, gave Mexico more room to operate, since Kennedy actively sought the cooperation of the larger Latin American countries in
order to implement the program.

Within Mexico, a new leadership complemented these changes in the
international arena. The passing of the torch from Ruiz Cortines to
López Mateos signaled the end of a neo-científico era and the beginning of a period of social and economic reform from above. During his
six-year term that lasted from 1958 to 1964, López Mateos parceled out
thirty million acres of land. He also instituted women's suffrage, and
his administration bought controlling shares in a number of foreign-
owned electrical companies. In many ways a kindred spirit to Kennedy,
López Mateos appeared committed to revitalizing the promises of "the
Mexican Revolution"—a term that by now had become a cliché.[51]

An assertive foreign policy appeared a natural complement to López
Mateos's agenda in an age when radio, newspapers, and television
reached an increasing number of Mexicans. Now more than ever before,
international initiatives might serve as an effective rallying point for
promoting a reform program against recalcitrant factions within the
PRI (Institutional Revolutionary Party; the former PNR). Therefore,
López Mateos made foreign policy one of the cornerstones of his administration.

Such an assertive international agenda, unfortunately, proved harder to implement than to conceive. Mexico's response to the triumph of Fidel Castro's revolution in Cuba is a good case in point. The victory of Castro—who had often referred to the Mexican Revolution as his guide during the period of military struggle against the regime of Fulgencio Batista—struck a chord with many Mexicans. Numerous Mexican intellectuals felt that their country was no longer alone as a "revolutionary society," and should reach out to help the new regime in Havana. López Mateos recognized the power of this political symbolism when he declared in June 1960: "We, who have gone through similar stages, understand and value the Cuban effort at transformation. . . . We hope that the Cuban Revolution might be, like ours has been, another step toward the greatness of America."[52]

These beautiful protestations of solidarity, however, quickly vanished under the weight of U.S. hostility toward the Cuban Revolution. Even though López Mateos again praised Castro's Revolution when the Eisenhower administration cut the Cuban sugar quota,[53] mounting U.S. pressure soon forced Mexico to take a different tack. In April 1961, CIA-trained Cuban exile forces landed at the Bay of Pigs in southern Cuba. Castro's troops quickly crushed the invasion, but the incident, officially ignored by the Mexican government, highlighted continuing U.S. efforts to topple "communist" regimes in the hemisphere.

López Mateos soon realized that any evidence of Mexican sympathy with Castro might seriously endanger U.S.–Mexican relations. Thus, he shifted his posture from defending the Cuban Revolution to defending its time-honored "international principles." When the United States moved to expel Cuba from the OAS in 1962, Mexican diplomats steadfastly, if vainly, asserted each country's right to national sovereignty. As a symbolic demonstration of an independent stance, the López Mateos administration, unlike all other Latin American governments, refused to break diplomatic relations with Cuba. At the same time, however, Mexican diplomats consciously avoided contact with the Cuban government. As had happened so often during the Porfiriato and the revolutionary era, Mexico had shrewdly changed its diplomacy in the face of U.S. pressure.[54]

While López Mateos had presided over a relatively serene period of Mexican history, the terms of Gustavo Díaz Ordaz (1964–70) and Luis Echeverría (1970–76) witnessed a deepening crisis within Mexican society which called forth a more audacious diplomacy. Díaz Ordaz, by many accounts Mexico's most conservative leader since the Revolution,[55] eroded López Mateos's reform program and strengthened the PRI's stranglehold on the political process. In addition, Mexico entered an economic downturn that hit the growing middle class especially hard, resulting in widespread unemployment and declining real wages. Therefore, when Díaz Ordaz became the first Mexican president to visit all of the Central American countries in January 1966, the trip and the rhetoric that accompanied it primarily served as a sop to a groundswell of popular and middle-class protest.

By 1968, Díaz Ordaz faced an increasingly vocal opposition, especially among university students, demanding a more participatory political system, a genuine commitment to the goals of the Mexican Revolution, and, generally, a more equitable society. In a year when the world's eyes were fixed upon Mexico as the host nation for the upcoming Olympic Games, popular discontent erupted with an intensity not seen since the days of the Revolution. Vowing to keep Mexico quiet during the event, Díaz Ordaz ordered the police to crack down on the mounting protests to prevent "social dissolution." On October 2, 1968, Interior Secretary Echeverría's actions revealed the authoritarian character of the Mexican government: during a peaceful protest at the Plaza de las Tres Culturas in Tlatelolco, Mexico City, government troops gunned down hundreds of protesters.

When Echeverría became the PRI's official candidate for president in 1970, then, he started with the tough task of regaining the confidence of a group whose loved ones he had helped murder at Tlatelolco. By 1970, no Mexican president could merely rule through a small camarilla or even through extensive clientelist networks. Rather, in an age of mass communications, Mexican governments would have to assure themselves of a significant level of middle-class and popular support. Echeverría thus faced a choice: he either had to make substantial concessions to the proponents of reform, many of whom desired more radical change in Mexican society than he was prepared to offer, or he had to attempt some sort of window dressing to placate the more moderate malcontents.

Echeverría embraced the second option and undertook ambitious foreign-policy initiatives to help fashion the propaganda punch he sorely required. Accordingly, he launched a campaign to negotiate a new economic world order, emerging as an exponent of an aggressive Tercermundismo, or "Third-Worldism." In the process, he also became one of the leaders of the "nonaligned movement" within the United Nations, and in a clear snub of the United States, he maintained a dialogue with Cuba's Fidel Castro.

Echeverría truly desired to play an active role as a world leader, but he used his international posturing primarily to cover up the political bankruptcy of the PRI. Inside Mexico, he ruthlessly crushed dissent, which had gone underground after the Tlatelolco massacre. He also presided over an administration rife with unprecedented venality. While Echeverría showed off his solidarity with movements of national liberation during photo sessions with the likes of Palestinian leader Yasser Arafat, he muzzled Mexico's own opposition.

Aided by a gradual economic recovery, Echeverría's policies encountered at least partial support among the Mexican intelligentsia. Many eminent social scientists in Mexico—scholars who otherwise might well have stood at the forefront of opposition to his government—lauded Echeverría's "new foreign policy," which "opened the country to the outside world."[56] In the view of one of these scholars, Mexico now departed from "a passive international attitude . . . based on principles of a clearly negative character"[57] to embrace a more active role in the solution of global problems.

Echeverría's international posturing, however, did not entail an active diplomacy toward Central America. During his tenure, rebel movements rocked Nicaragua and Guatemala, yet the Mexican president remained on good terms with the Nicaraguan dictator Anastasio Somoza Debayle, the son of the aforementioned elder Somoza. Ultimately, Echeverría's foreign policy, just like that of Carranza and López Mateos, was founded on rhetoric (important for internal cohesion) rather than action (to achieve international goals). In an age when the CIA had undermined and aided the overthrow of the socialist government of Salvador Allende in Chile, such restraint probably reflected Echeverría's ultimate pragmatism.[58] By 1978, the Mexican government once again desired to wield influence in Central America, but it would take a change of administrations in Washington and a social revolution in Nicaragua to activate this potential.

The Latest Challenge: Mexico and the Sandinistas

In May 1979, the Mexican government headed by José López Portillo amazed many observers when it became the first government to break relations with the Somoza dictatorship in Nicaragua. No problems between Nicaragua and Mexico had preceded the rupture of relations. The Sandinista rebels, who had fought Somoza first from the countryside, then in the towns and cities since 1963, still appeared a year away from victory. Given the historical context of Mexico's Central America policy analyzed in this study, however, no one should have been surprised at López Portillo's bold step. By 1979, the Mexican government encountered favorable conditions for an active Central American diplomacy for the first time since the 1920s.

At home, the discovery of new oil deposits fueled optimism in government circles about Mexico's future as an economic power; at the same time, the political crisis that had commenced ten years earlier continued to fester. Corruption remained rampant, dissatisfaction with López Portillo ran high, and criticism against Mexico's one-party system and the PRI's stranglehold on the political process even resonated in the government-sponsored newspapers. Like Echeverría, López Portillo attempted to use an active foreign policy to cover up the domestic shortcomings of his regime. And like Porfirio Díaz, López Portillo, convinced of the virtual omnipotence of the new gushing oil wells, attempted to translate newfound economic riches and diplomatic successes into political capital.

Unlike Echeverría, however, López Portillo found Central America available as an outlet for assertive international initiatives. The Sandinistas' rise to national prominence had given Mexico the chance to deal with a friendly political force in Central America for the first time since the days of Arévalo and Arbenz. In its fight against Somoza, the Sandinista Front, as diverse a coalition as Madero's alliance of 1910–11 but more organized and ideologically focused, often invoked the Mexican Revolution as a model and inspiration for their struggle. For its part, the U.S. government, led by President Jimmy Carter, publicly criticized the dismal human-rights record of the Somoza regime and thus appeared to oppose the status quo in Nicaragua. In many respects, the situation resembled the one of January 1926: Mexico and the United States both disliked the regime in power in Managua, and Mexico, mistakenly confident of U.S. sympathy for its actions, took the initiative to help change this undesirable state of affairs.

Upon Somoza's ouster in July 1979, Mexican influence in Nicaragua arrived with the Sandinista revolutionary junta, which was flown into Managua aboard a Mexican jet. In the first years of the revolution, as Carter extended economic assistance to the Sandinistas, López Portillo generously lavished favors on the "new Nicaragua." Not only did the Mexican government award thirty-nine million dollars in cash and goods to the Sandinistas; it also extended loans worth almost twice that amount and allowed Nicaragua to buy Mexican oil on favorable terms.[59] Then, when the Sandinistas clashed for the first time with Carter's successor, Ronald Reagan, López Portillo also helped Nicaragua on the diplomatic front. While Reagan's State Department depicted the Nicaraguan revolution as the work of "Cuban-Soviet" subversion and cut off U.S. economic aid, López Portillo sponsored a U.S.-Nicaraguan dialogue in the Mexican port town of Manzanillo. He also took up the subject of Nicaragua in the course of two meetings with Reagan in January and June 1981.[60] Even if he failed to persuade the U.S. president to assume a more conciliatory posture toward the Sandinistas, he had put his personal prestige—and in some ways, that of his country—on the line for a risky foreign-policy initiative.[61]

Beginning in 1981, López Portillo also got involved in attempts at ending a protracted civil war between a government controlled by right-wing death squads in El Salvador and two left-wing opposition groups. In August 1981, López Portillo issued the now famous joint communiqué with French President François Mitterrand, recognizing both opposition groups as "political forces representative of the Salvadoran people."[62] Mexico, however, never provided actual aid to the Salvadoran rebels, as their chances for success appeared too slim. Quite possibly, López Portillo also regarded the main Salvadoran guerrilla group, the Marxist-oriented FMLN (Frente Farabundo Martí de Liberación Nacional), as too radical.

While Mexico supported the Sandinistas and attempted to award a degree of political legitimacy to the Salvadoran rebels, Mexico cooperated with the repressive government of Guatemala against the peasant-based revolt of the Guerrilla Army of the Poor (EPG) and other rebel groups. Based on the patterns identified in this study, however, this seemingly paradoxical attitude followed historical precedents. In this case, Mexico's own security appeared threatened by the existence of large guerrilla bases along the Mexican-Guatemalan border. In addition, the ongoing warfare—and the scorched-earth policies of the Guatemalan military—swelled the ranks of Guatemalan refugees in Mexico. The Mexican government, then, saw little choice but to cooperate with the Guatemalan military, easily the most ruthless and repressive in the Central America of the 1980s.[63]

Mexico's new activism in Central America yielded considerable payoff at home and abroad. Even as the López Portillo administration came under increasing criticism for its domestic policies, its stand in Central America earned it a great degree of support in Mexico. Whereas Echeverría's Tercermundismo had appeared pointless to many, squandering its attention among a multiplicity of global issues without any apparent regard for Mexico's slim possibilities of assuming such a global role, López Portillo's Central American initiatives seemed practical. Even though the Reagan administration resented Mexican support for the Sandinistas, it too accorded López Portillo a grudging respect and often negotiated Central American issues bilaterally with the Mexican government—something that had last occurred in 1909.

Once again, Mexico was able to pursue an active policy. This active Mexican role in Central America, however, depended in great part on the personal interest of the Mexican president, the economic and political stability of Mexico, and restraint in U.S. policies toward the isthmus. After 1982, all of these conditions disappeared: in short order, the United States decided to step up its pressure on the Sandinista government at a time when declining oil prices sent the Mexican economy into a tailspin.

Citing "Soviet influence" in the Sandinista junta and alleging Nicaraguan aid to the rebels in El Salvador, the Reagan government put its foot down on the Sandinistas, training and arming a large force of Nicaraguan exiles in bases in Florida and Honduras.[64] Known as the "Contras" because they proudly referred to themselves as counterrevolutionaries, the rebels then launched forays into Nicaragua, wreaking havoc on both the countryside and towns of northwestern Nicaragua. By the time the U.S. Navy mined Nicaraguan harbors in 1984, Reagan was waging an undeclared war on the Sandinista government. Throughout the 1980s, this war became more and more one of attrition, in which the U.S. government, acting through its Contra agents, attempted to grind down the Sandinista revolution. Faced with U.S. intervention, Mexico had to back off from assertive action.[65]

At the same time, Mexican domestic factors also conspired to push policy toward caution in Central America. The new Mexican president, Miguel de la Madrid, did not share López Portillo's admiration for the Sandinistas. Moreover, beginning in 1982 Mexico entered a severe economic crisis due to the collapse in oil prices, mounting foreign debt, and the endemic corruption during the López Portillo regime.[66] By the end of 1982, an acute debt problem and a plummeting peso had increased Mexico's dependency on U.S. goodwill—and support for the Sandinistas was not too likely to bring about the goodwill of the Reagan administration.

In the words of two scholars, Mexico now began "its return march to the traditional limits of its foreign policy."[67] In August 1983, the Mexican government suspended oil shipments to Nicaragua. At the same time, Mexico shifted from lending direct assistance to the Sandinistas to accomplishing more general goals: defending Nicaragua's right to self-determination, and contributing to a political solution to the multiple crises in Central America. With the destabilization of regimes in the isthmus by social revolutions and U.S. intervention, the Mexican government—in a striking parallel to Porfirian policies in the years 1898–1908—perceived a need to mediate in the growing crises to help avert threats to its own security.[68] Just as Porfirio Díaz had done successfully around the turn of the century, Mexico undertook this effort through a variety of international mechanisms. Along with Venezuela, Colombia, and Panama, Mexico formed the Contadora group, which attempted mediation between the United States and the Sandinista government. In addition, the country's representatives voted against the Reagan administration on a number of U.N. resolutions concerning Central America.

As the conflict deepened, de la Madrid retreated ever further from Mexico's erstwhile activist position. Even though it showed its verbal support for the venture, the Mexican government did not help in the successful efforts spearheaded by Costa Rica to find a Central American solution to the problem. When Violeta Chamorro and her coalition defeated the Sandinistas at the ballot box in February 1990, the Mexican government remained notably silent. U.S. President George H. W. Bush's promises of financial aid and an end to the U.S. intervention in case of a Chamorro victory had registered a great impact on the Nicaraguan electorate; nevertheless, the Mexican government could ill denigrate the outcome of a democratic election.

The beginning of the economic liberalization project under de la Madrid and his successor, Carlos Salinas de Gortari, has ushered in a new phase in Mexico's status in Central America. By both necessity and choice, Mexico has cast its lot with North America to a greater extent than ever before. With the arrival of the North American Free Trade Agreement, a Mexican challenge to the United States in Central America seems unlikely.

Internal Mexican politics have further militated against activism in Central America. The Salinas administration embraced Porfirian solutions for Mexico's problems, but not Díaz's rejection of U.S. political influence. It even abandoned much of the revolutionary nationalist discourse, as the dismantling of the 1917 Constitution and efforts to rewrite the Porfirian sections of the primary history textbook for Mexican public schools well attest.[69] The current Mexican president, Ernesto Zedillo Ponce de León, has had his hands full with a rebellion in Chiapas, a severe economic crisis, and the aftermath of several politically motivated assassinations of high-ranking officials. Understood as an effort to rein in the great power, then, Mexico's position as a middle power in Central America has become most difficult.[70]

The new age of economic globalization, however, may have transformed rather than ended Mexican interest in Central America. Compared to de la Madrid, Salinas de Gortari dramatically stepped up the Mexican diplomatic presence in Latin America. The negotiation of a free trade agreement with Chile and bilateral treaties making Mexico an intermediary between the Central American countries and the new, unified North American market might mark the beginning of a new, "economic" presence in Latin America. It remains to be seen whether the North American Free Trade Agreement will bring about a novel, economic middle-power status for Mexico. While overall trade between Mexico and Central America has remained relatively insignificant, Mexican items of mass culture such as *telenovelas* have been swamping Central America for more than a decade. If a stronger economic and political role complemented this cultural presence, Mexico's relations with Central America might one day flourish.

The political stability of Central America constitutes another area of continuing Mexican concern. Since recent efforts to end the civil wars in the region (and in particular, those in Guatemala) have only encountered limited success, Mexico might one day find itself involved in another effort at peacekeeping in order to forestall serious complications at its southeastern border. An unlikely U.S. military intervention in Guatemala or Nicaragua would be a political nightmare for Zedillo; right now, it is the direct effects of these wars—and, most notably, a flood of refugees in Chiapas—that preoccupy Mexican policy makers.

Zedillo's June 1995 trip to Guatemala illustrates this last point well. The visit was the Mexican president's first travel abroad since taking office, and his second sojourn in Guatemala since being elected. The fact that President Zedillo went to Guatemala before visiting the United States is significant enough proof of Mexican interest in its southeastern neighbor. Yet the present Mexican-Guatemalan entente, begun in the 1980s, extends beyond amity and commerce. The two issues on top of the agenda at the meeting—Guatemalan migration into Mexico and peasant rebellions on both sides of the border—show that both governments share common security interests.[71] Irrespective of U.S. policies, then, contemporary Mexico cannot afford to ignore Central America for economic and security reasons.

Since the reign of Porfirio Díaz, Mexico has played a substantial role in Central America. In doing so, the Mexican government has sought to prevent armed U.S. intervention; it has addressed bilateral problems with Guatemala; and it has attempted to assert its own leadership in Central America. In addition, throughout the 1876–1930 period and for some of the time since, a succession of Mexican leaders have projected an assertive, independent foreign policy as one important means to forge a Mexican nation, an ever more strongly "imagined community," out of the "many Mexicos" that have persisted from pre-Columbian times to our days.

The exact strategy to pursue in Central America has often been the subject of considerable debate within Mexico's governing elite. Clearly, Central American issues often pitted radicals advocating assertive Mexican action against moderates who counseled a cautious approach and científicos who looked upon the isthmus as a backward region with which Mexico need not bother. Mexico's Central America policy has therefore been neither consistent nor monolithic.

Border disputes with Guatemala, not the influence of the United States, motivated the regime of Porfirio Díaz to become an active player in the isthmus. Until 1898, Díaz made alliances with El Salvador, Costa Rica, and Nicaragua the cornerstone of an effort to forestall the emergence of Guatemala as the dominant regional power. The United States played a secondary role in this endeavor, even though it often served as arbiter in the border disputes and during frequent international crises in Central America. When Mexico had emerged from its destructive wars of the early and mid-1800s, it primarily pursued bilateral middle-power policies geared toward asserting the country's own goals.

By the 1890s, however, the U.S. presence in Central America (and not just the implications of that presence for Mexican-Guatemalan relations) had evolved as a major source of concern. Between 1898 and 1930, Mexican foreign policy often sought to stave off U.S. intervention in Central America and to assure itself of Central American friendship—a behavior typical of great power-driven middle-power policies. Nevertheless, bilateral problems with Guatemala flared up frequently and remained an important concern. Central American policies also figured prominently in government efforts to appropriate nationalist sentiments. Witness, for instance, the asylum granted to Zelaya or Calles's stump speech following his termination of assistance to the Sacasa faction. With advances in mass communication and the transformation of nationalism in the 1876–1930 period—first through Porfirian patriotism, then through economic nationalism, and finally through revolutionary cultural nationalism, this domestic function of Mexican foreign policy grew in importance.

Mexico has pursued its goals in the region through a variety of means. It has attempted to counter U.S. influence by forging strong ties with friendly factions within Central American elite politics. It has also used international forums to limit U.S. and Guatemalan ambitions in Central America, and it has occasionally even resorted to political and military intervention of its own. In these efforts, the years 1885, 1906–10, and 1925–27 stand out as high points. But Mexico's persistent, low-key presence in isthmian affairs has been equally if not more effective in advancing Mexican aims and has therefore received equal attention in this study. To import James Scott's conceptualization of peasant resistance into the realm of foreign policy, Mexico's Central America policy has been a good example of "the weapons of the weak," characterized more by foot-dragging and other "everyday forms of resistance" than by a violent and vocal assertion of the country's position.

Mexico has encountered increasing obstacles to asserting its own position. Over the course of the past century, the United States has vastly increased its influence in Latin America. While Díaz, at least until the last year of his rule, still had considerable leverage to carry out a successful policy, the era of the Mexican Revolution witnessed a weakening of the country's role in Central America. Unable to act unilaterally, the U.S. government had allowed Díaz to play a relatively strong role in the isthmus. During the decade of violent struggle, however, Mexico's regional status vanished completely as a result of an increased U.S. presence. More confident about its own power in Central America and preoccupied with the revolutionary reforms in Mexico, the U.S. State Department did not countenance any renewed Mexican influence in the 1920s. At the same time, the revolutionary governments could not pay as much attention to Central America as Díaz had done. Carranza and the Sonorans attended to the immediate tasks of rebuilding functioning national authority and confronting a menacing U.S. government over the issue of reform legislation. The reconstruction of Mexico's regional status under the Sonorans thus remained incomplete, and a long period of relative dormancy in Mexico's Central America policy ensued. Only recently—when Mexican resources, the personal interest of the Mexican president, and U.S. policies permitted—did Mexico once again assert its goals in Central America.[72]

Since 1930, U.S. influence has remained one of the strongest constraints on Mexico's Central America policy; as powerful a constraint as the country's lack of resources to carry out an assertive foreign policy. And yet, contemporary Mexico still pursues its own goals in Central America for its own reasons. It is the mark of a middle power like Mexico that the presence of the great power is a vital but not an all-encompassing concern. Even as the shadow of the giant grows ever larger, Mexico will always play a role in Central America.

Notes

PREFACE

In the United States, the term *American* denotes something or someone pertaining to the United States of America. Other cultures in this hemisphere have taken offense at this exclusive usage, since America is a continent rather than a country. Because of the cultural sensitivity surrounding this term, it will only be used in quotes, unless it denotes the continent. The term *North American,* widely used, constitutes no great improvement. Therefore, the term *United States* or its abbreviation is used consistently throughout this text.

1. The term *Central America* is here used in a historical rather than a geographical sense. Therefore, it includes present-day Guatemala, Honduras, El Salvador, Nicaragua, and Costa Rica but not Belize, Panama, and Mexico east of the Isthmus of Tehuantepec.

2. Among the most influential studies, see Mario Ojeda, ed., *Las relaciones de México con los países de América Central* (Mexico: El Colegio de México, 1985); Bruce M. Bagley, "Mexico in Central America: The Limits of Regional Power," in *Political Change in Central America: Internal and External Dimensions,* ed. Wolf Grabendorff, Heinrich-W. Krumwiede, and Jörg Todt (Boulder, Co.: Westview Press, 1984), 261–84; idem, "Mexican Foreign Policy: The Decline of a Regional Power?" *Current History* 82 (Dec. 1983), 406–9, 437; Wolf Grabendorff, "The Role of Regional Powers in Central America: Mexico, Venezuela, Cuba, and Colombia," in *Latin American Nations in World Politics,* ed. Heraldo Muñoz and Joseph S. Tulchin (Boulder, Co.: Westview Press, 1984), 83–100; René Herrera Zúñiga and Mario Ojeda, "La política de México en la región de Centroamérica," *Foro Internacional* 23:4 (Apr. 1983), 423–40; Olga Pellicer de Brody, "Mexico in Central America: The Difficult Exercise of Regional Power," Mario Ojeda, "Mexican Policy toward Central America in the Context of U.S.–Mexico Relations," and Adolfo Aguilar Zinser, "Mexico and the Guatemalan Crisis," in *The Future of Central America: Policy Choices for the United States and Mexico,* ed. Richard R. Fagen and Olga Pellicer de Brody (Stanford, Calif.: Stanford University Press, 1983), 119–33, 135–60, and 161–86, respectively. To conserve space, instead of using the full, correct names of Ciudad de México, or México, D.F., or Mexico City, and Ciudad de Guatemala, or Guatemala City, these capitals will be referred to as Mexico and Guatemala, respectively, when referring to a place of publication or the place of origin of a

document. Likewise, Washington, D.C., will be referenced as Washington in the notes.

3. Daniel Cosío Villegas, *Historia moderna de México* (Mexico: Editorial Hermes, 1960), vol. 5:1 (hereafter cited as *HMM*). Volume 5:1 is devoted entirely to Mexico's relations with Central America, but its main value lies in the analysis of the 1870s and 1880s. Due to Mexican and European restrictions on archival access, Cosío Villegas could not review many of the most important documents on the 1890–1910 period.

4. This problem is even more acute for Central Americanists than for Mexicanists. For an attempt to correct this imbalance with regard to Central America, see Thomas M. Leonard, "Central America and the United States: Overlooked Foreign-Policy Objectives," *The Americas* 50:1 (July 1993), 1–30.

5. We will assume that the negotiation of power in Mexico has always been a dialectic process between the elite and the governed, rather than the result of an "elite program." For a volume providing rich analyses of this point for the revolutionary era, consult Gilbert M. Joseph and Daniel Nugent, eds., *Everyday Forms of State Formation: Revolution and the Negotiation of Rule in Modern Mexico* (Durham, N.C.: Duke University Press, 1994).

6. The term *governing elite* denotes that circle of persons formulating policy at the national level. Until the creation of a ruling party in the 1930s, the Mexican governing elite was always a very small group, never numbering more than one hundred people. Only rarely were women included in this circle, even though the wives and mistresses of many policy makers came to play important roles.

7. For a study that makes this point for Argentine foreign policy, see Carlos Escudé, *Education, Political Culture, and Foreign Policy: The Case of Argentina* (Durham and Chapel Hill, N.C.: Duke-UNC Program in Latin American Studies Occasional Paper Series no. 3, 1992).

8. For an alternate, "structurally realist" view that suggests that the international states system plays the greatest role in determining Mexico's Central America policy, see David Mares, "Mexico's Foreign Policy as a Middle Power: The Nicaragua Connection, 1884–1986," *LARR* 18:1 (Fall 1988), 81–107.

9. Thus, nationalism by far predates the Revolution. For an older, opposite view, see Frederick C. Turner, *The Dynamic of Mexican Nationalism* (Chapel Hill: University of North Carolina Press, 1968).

10. Carsten Holbraad, *Middle Powers in International Politics* (New York: St. Martin's Press, 1984), 4.

11. Lynn D. Bender, "Contained Nationalism: The Mexican Foreign-Policy Example," *Review/Revista Interamericana* 5:1 (Spring 1975), 3; and Ojeda, *Las relaciones de México*, 11.

12. In my emphasis on multiarchival work and the congruence of interna-

tional and domestic variables, I am indebted to Friedrich Katz, *The Secret War in Mexico: Europe, the United States, and the Mexican Revolution* (Chicago: University of Chicago Press, 1981); Gilbert M. Joseph, *Revolution from Without: Yucatán, Mexico, and the United States, 1880–1924*, 2nd ed. (Durham, N.C.: Duke University Press, 1988); and Michael H. Hunt, "The Long Crisis in Diplomatic History: Coming to Closure," *Diplomatic History* 16:1 (Feb. 1992), 115–40.

CHAPTER 1. PROLOGUE:
MEXICO BETWEEN THE UNITED STATES
AND CENTRAL AMERICA, 1823–1876

1. David Bushnell and Neill Macaulay, *The Emergence of Latin America in the Nineteenth Century* (New York and Oxford: Oxford University Press, 1988), 55.

2. Gran Colombia fell apart into the states of Colombia, Venezuela, and Ecuador. Present-day Panama later seceded from Colombia.

3. In fact, Foreign Secretary Lucas Alamán did not try to prevent Central America's secession. In his view, Mexico should "not assume the role that Spain has played in this hemisphere . . . in opposing movements of independence." José C. Valadés, *Lucas Alamán: estadista e historiador* (Mexico: Editorial Porrúa, 1938), 170.

4. American-born whites of Spanish descent.

5. In Chiapas and Guatemala, this term denotes mestizos.

6. Thomas Benjamin, *A Rich Land, A Poor People: Politics and Society in Modern Chiapas* (Albuquerque: University of New Mexico Press, 1989), 7.

7. Ibid., 8.

8. Ibid., 8–9.

9. Luis G. Zorrilla, *Relaciones de México con la República de Centro América y con Guatemala* (Mexico: Editorial Porrúa, 1984), 148–67. Zorrilla defends the Mexican position.

10. Zorrilla, *Relaciones con Centro América*, 158.

11. *HMM* 5:1, xxi–xxii.

12. Ralph L. Woodward, *Rafael Carrera and the Emergence of the Republic of Guatemala, 1821–1871* (Athens: University of Georgia Press, 1993), 154–55.

13. Benjamin, *A Rich Land*, 11. The statement is Luis Echeverría's.

14. Guatemala had no more right to incorporate Chiapas than to annex any of the other provinces of Central America.

15. Nelson Reed, *The Caste War of Yucatan* (Stanford, Calif.: Stanford University Press, 1964), passim and 85.

16. For the foreign-policy debate of this period, see Nettie Lee Benson, "Territorial Integrity in Mexican Politics, 1821–1833," in *The Independence of Mexico and the Creation of the New Nation*, ed. Jaime E. Rodríguez O. (Los Angeles: University of California, Los Angeles, Latin American Center, 1989), 275–307.

17. There is an enormous literature on the loss of Texas and the "Mexican War." For a balanced account, see Michael C. Meyer and William L. Sherman, *The Course of Mexican History*, 5th ed. (New York and Oxford: Oxford University Press, 1995), 335–53. Three good studies are Gene M. Brack, *Mexico Views Manifest Destiny, 1821–1846: An Essay on the Origins of the Mexican War* (Albuquerque: University of New Mexico Press, 1975); David M. Pletcher, *The Diplomacy of Annexation: Texas, Oregon and the Mexican War* (Columbia: University of Missouri Press, 1969); and Luis Zorrilla, *Historia de las relaciones entre México y los Estados Unidos de América, 1800–1958*, vol. 1 (Mexico: Editorial Porrúa, 1965).

18. Thomas M. Leonard, *Central America and the United States* (Athens: University of Georgia Press, 1989), 7–8.

19. Jan Bazant, "Mexico from Independence to 1867," in Leslie Bethell, ed., *Cambridge History of Latin America* (Cambridge: Cambridge University Press, 1985), 3:449. This series will hereafter be cited as *CHLA*.

20. Charles A. Hale, *Mexican Liberalism in the Age of Mora, 1821–1853* (New Haven, Conn.: Yale University Press, 1968), 16–19.

21. Ibid.

22. Brian Hamnett, *Juárez* (London and New York: Longman, 1994), 52.

23. Donathon C. Olliff, *Reforma Mexico and the United States: A Search for Alternatives to Annexation, 1854–1861* (University: University of Alabama Press, 1981), 4.

24. Hale, *Mexican Liberalism*, 79.

25. Alan Knight, "El liberalismo mexicano desde la Reforma hasta la Revolución (una interpretación)," *Historia Mexicana* 35:1 (July 1985), 73.

26. Olliff, *Reforma Mexico and the United States*, 6.

27. Valadés, *Lucas Alamán*, 175.

28. Bolívar's supranationalist ideas are discussed in Simon Collier, "Nationality, Nationalism, and Supranationalism in the Writings of Simón Bolívar," *HAHR* 63:1 (Feb. 1983), 48–56.

29. For instance, peasants from the state of Guerrero had figured among the most important backers of Juan Alvarez, the Liberal caudillo who headed the movement that overthrew the Conservatives. For Liberal caudillos with peasant support, see Leticia Reina, *Las rebeliones campesinas en México, 1819–1906* (Mexico: Siglo XXI Editores, 1980), esp. 127 and 235–36.

30. Olliff, *Reforma Mexico and the United States*, passim.

31. Ibid., 4–6.

32. Colin M. MacLachlan and William H. Beezley, *El Gran Pueblo: A History of Greater Mexico* (Englewood Cliffs, N.J.: Prentice Hall, 1994), 55–56.

33. Walter V. Scholes, *Mexican Politics During the Juárez Regime, 1855–1872* (Columbia: University of Missouri Press, 1957), 36–37.

34. Bazant, "Mexico from Independence to 1867," 469.

35. Laurens B. Perry, *Juárez and Díaz: Machine Politics in Mexico* (DeKalb: Northern Illinois University Press, 1978).

36. Charles A. Hale, *The Transformation of Liberalism in Late Nineteenth-Century Mexico* (Princeton, N.J.: Princeton University Press, 1989), 20.

37. The científicos were not officially known as such until the 1890s.

38. Bismarck's words "blood and iron" are usually only used to describe the German unification.

39. There has been some debate as to whether the label "puros" is still applicable to this Liberal faction after 1867. The programmatic and personal continuities in this group up to the 1890s, however, justify the use of this label.

40. At least that was the case for Juárez himself. Hamnett, *Juárez*, 8 and passim.

41. For a discussion of these ideas, see Hale, *The Transformation of Liberalism*, 251.

42. Moisés González Navarro, "Las ideas raciales de los científicos," *Historia Mexicana* 37:4 (Apr. 1988), 565–84, and Kennett Cott, "Mexican Diplomacy and the Chinese Issue, 1876–1910," *HAHR* 67:1 (Feb. 1987), 63–85.

43. The coalition was known thus in Mexico, not in Europe.

44. See Thomas D. Schoonover, *Dollars Over Dominion: The Triumph of Liberalism in Mexican–United States Relations* (Baton Rouge: Louisiana State University Press), 1978.

45. *HMM* 5:2, xx. See also Robert J. Deger, Jr., "Porfirian Foreign Policy and Mexican Nationalism: A Study of Cooperation and Conflict in Mexican-American Relations, 1884–1904," Ph.D. diss., Indiana University, 1979, 18–20.

46. In *HMM* 5:2, xxiii, Cosío Villegas finds "the highest utility" in Juárez's position.

47. Hamnett, *Juárez*, 53.

48. Olliff, *Reforma Mexico and the United States*, 7.

49. There has been a long argument about the nature of U.S. foreign policy after the Civil War. For the case of the primacy of economic interests, see Walter LaFeber, *The New Empire: An Interpretation of American Expansion, 1860–1898* (Ithaca, N.Y.: Cornell University Press, 1963). For a critique of this view, see Robert L. Beisner, *From the Old Diplomacy to the New* (New York: Harlan Davidson, 1986), 11–19. For a new case for the primacy of strategic considerations, see Lester G. Langley, *America and the Americas: The*

United States in the Western Hemisphere (Athens: University of Georgia Press, 1989), chap. 3.

50. Indeed, to Juárez, few options other than lobbying for U.S. investment presented themselves. Old World colonialism in Africa and Asia had removed many European banks as viable future creditors for Latin America.

51. Ralph L. Woodward, *Central America: A Nation Divided*, 2nd ed. (Oxford and New York: Oxford University Press, 1985), 119.

52. Daniela Spenser, "Los inicios del cultivo de café en Soconusco y la inmigración extranjera," in *Los empresarios alemanes, el Tercer Reich y la oposición de derecha a Cárdenas*, ed. Brígida von Mentz, Verena Radkau, Daniela Spenser et al. (Mexico: Colección Miguel Othón de Mendizábal, 1988), 1:64.

53. John E. Dougherty, "Mexico and Guatemala, 1856–1872: A Case Study in Extra-Legal International Relations," Ph.D. diss., University of California, Los Angeles, 1969, especially chaps. 4 and 6.

54. Ralph L. Woodward, "Central America from Independence to *c.* 1870," *CHLA* 3:505.

55. Distant Costa Rica, however, usually remained aloof from its neighbors' struggles and again forms the exception here.

56. Thomas L. Karnes, *The Failure of Union: Central America, 1824–1960* (Chapel Hill: University of North Carolina Press, 1964), chap. 1.

57. Ibid., 12–147.

58. Woodward, *Rafael Carrera*, 467 and 461.

59. Idem, *Central America*, 170.

60. Idem, *Rafael Carrera*, 347; Wayne M. Clegern, *The Origins of Liberal Dictatorship in Central America: Guatemala, 1865–1873* (Boulder: University Press of Colorado, 1993), 150; Dougherty, "Mexico and Guatemala," 151–53.

61. In Nicaragua, where the Liberals had been discredited by their association with William Walker, the Conservatives remained in power until 1893 but embarked on Liberal economic reforms.

Chapter 2. The Beginnings of the Fatal
Triangle, 1876–1898

1. Friedrich Katz, "Mexico: Restored Republic and Porfiriato," *CHLA* 5:19.

2. The political life of the Restored Republic was dominated by civilians.

3. For discussion of factionalism in the Restored Republic, see chap. 1.

4. For a "structuralist" analysis of the Porfiriato, see W. Dirk Raat, *Mexico*

and the United States: Ambivalent Vistas (Athens: University of Georgia Press, 1992), 82–101.

5. Katz, "Restored Republic and Porfiriato," 20–21.

6. As recent research has shown, González was by no means a mere "puppet" of Díaz. Don M. Coerver, *The Porfirian Interregnum: The Presidency of Manuel Gonzalez of Mexico, 1880–1884* (Fort Worth: Texas Christian University Press, 1979).

7. Katz, "Restored Republic and Porfiriato," 22.

8. William E. Gibbs, "Díaz's Executive Agents and United States Foreign Policy," *JIAS* 20:2 (May 1978), 165–90.

9. John M. Hart, *Revolutionary Mexico: The Coming and Process of the Mexican Revolution* (Berkeley: University of California Press, 1987), 103–31.

10. For a good account of the episode, consult Daniel Cosío Villegas, *The United States versus Porfirio Díaz,* trans. Nettie Lee Benson (Austin: University of Texas Press, 1964).

11. Katz, "Restored Republic and Porfiriato," 25.

12. Alan Knight, "Peasants into Patriots: Thoughts on the Making of the Mexican Nation," *Mexican Studies/Estudios Mexicanos* 10:1 (Winter 1994), 135–61.

13. Luis González, "The Dictatorship of Porfirio Díaz," in Hugh M. Hamill, ed., *Caudillos: Dictators in Spanish America* (Norman: University of Oklahoma Press, 1992), 176.

14. Katz, "Restored Republic and Porfiriato," 56–59.

15. For the Porfirian promotion of the "Juárez myth," see Charles Weeks, *The Juárez Myth in Mexico* (Tuscaloosa: University of Alabama Press, 1987), 29–53.

16. Ibid.

17. See Benedict Anderson, *Imagined Communities: Reflections on the Origins and Spread of Nationalism* (London: Verso, 1983), especially chap. 4.

18. Deger, "Porfirian Foreign Policy," 60.

19. *HMM* 5:1, 395.

20. In 1890, Mexico and the United States upgraded their legations to embassies. The one in Washington remained Mexico's only embassy until 1924.

21. The pro-U.S. character of many Mexican emissaries, such as Matías Romero, Manuel Azpíroz, Joaquín Casasús, and Enrique Creel, is one reason why researchers who have relied on U.S. archives only have exaggerated Díaz's friendship with the United States.

22. See chaps. 6 and 7.

23. See the epigraph to chap. 1 as a good example.

24. See, especially, *El Imparcial,* June 10 and 12, 1907.

25. Daniela Spenser, "Los inicios del cultivo de café," 1:63.

26. For an analysis of the economic and political incorporation of Chiapas and the area's modernization in the 1880–1910 period, see Benjamin, *A Rich Land*, chaps. 1 and 2.

27. This term is taken from the caption next to Barrios's portrait on the current five-quetzal banknotes.

28. Matías Romero, "Mr. Blaine and the Boundary Question between Mexico and Guatemala," *Bulletin of the American Geographical Society*, 29 (1897), 280–98.

29. Coerver, *Porfirian Interregnum*, 150–51.

30. Ubico to Blaine, Washington, June 15, 1881, and Blaine to Ubico, Washington, June 16, 1881, *Foreign Relations of the United States*, 1881 (Washington: Government Printing Office, 1882), 598–99. This yearly publication will hereafter be cited as *FRUS*.

31. Blaine was not alone with his assessment. His predecessor, Hamilton Fish, had already instructed the U.S. minister to Central America to work for the realization of the union. Leonard, *Central America and the United States*, 36.

32. Stephen Palmer, "Central American Union or Guatemalan Republic? The National Question in Liberal Guatemala, 1871–1885," *The Americas* 49:4 (Apr. 1993), 513–50.

33. John E. Findling, *Close Neighbors, Distant Friends: United States–Central American Relations* (Westport, Conn.: Greenwood Press, 1987), 37.

34. Blaine to U.S. minister in Guatemala, Washington, May 7, 1881, National Archives, Washington, Record Group 59, Diplomatic Instructions, Central America. All U.S. State Department records will hereafter be cited as NADS. Instructions to the U.S. ministers in Central America will be referred to as DICA. Likewise, instructions to the U.S. representative in Mexico City will be referenced as DIM. Dispatches from the U.S. representatives in Central America and Mexico will be cited as DDCAG, DDCACR, and DDM, respectively; the mail from the minister to Guatemala and Honduras was filed separately from that of his counterpart accredited in Costa Rica, El Salvador, and Nicaragua.

35. Coerver, *Porfirian Interregnum*, 153.

36. Morgan to Blaine, Mexico, July 12 and 19, 1881, *FRUS*, 1881, 773–78.

37. Blaine to U.S. minister in Guatemala, Nov. 28, 1881, NADS, DICA.

38. *HMM* 5:1, 395; J. B. Caamaño to Díaz, Mexico, Jan. 5, 1882, Díaz to Caamaño, Oaxaca, no date, and Antonio R. Flores to Díaz, undated memorandum, Acervos Históricos, Universidad Ibero-Americana, Mexico City, Colección General Porfirio Díaz (hereafter cited as CPD), series 7, box 1, leaves 68–69, 70, and 94–111, respectively. Subsequent citation is by (series number):(box number)/(leaf numbers).

39. Karnes, *The Failure of Union*, 155.

40. Matías Romero, "The Settlement of the Mexico-Guatemalan Boundary Question, 1882," *Bulletin of the American Geographical Society*, 29 (1897), 130–32.

41. Findling, *Close Neighbors, Distant Friends*, 50.

42. For a recent condemnation of Barrios on that score, see Héctor Gaitán A., *Los Presidentes de Guatemala: Historia y Anécdotas* (Guatemala: Librería Artemis-Edinter, 1992), 50.

43. For analyses of the various attempts at union in Central America, see Karnes, *The Failure of Union*, and Vincent Peloso, "The Politics of Federation: Central America, 1885–1921," Ph.D. diss., University of Arizona, 1969.

44. Palmer, "Central American Union," 519–20.

45. At least the U.S. minister to Central America thought so. See Whitehouse to Secretary, Guatemala, Mar. 6, 1885, *FRUS*, 1885, 73.

46. Díaz Mimiaga to Secretary, Guatemala, Mar. 6, 1885, Archivo Histórico de la Secretaría de Relaciones Exteriores, Mexico City (hereafter cited as AHSRE), L-E-2201. Unless otherwise noted, all references are to files in the "Serie Gaveta." The abbreviation L-E denotes the bound documents available in the "Serie L-E."

47. Barrios to Díaz, Guatemala, Mar. 7, 1885, Secretaría de Relaciones Exteriores, *Correspondencia diplomática cambiada entre el gobierno de los Estados Unidos Mexicanos y los de varias potencias extranjeras desde el 30 de junio de 1881 al 30 de junio de 1886* (Mexico: Imprenta del Gobierno, 1887), 4:1010. This volume is henceforth cited as *Correspondencia*.

48. Karnes, *The Failure of Union*, 157.

49. Zaldívar to Díaz, San Salvador, Mar. 9, 1885; Castellón to Mariscal, Managua, Mar. 9, 1885; and Fernández to Díaz, San José, Mar. 10, 1885, *Correspondencia*, 1010–11 and 1013.

50. *HMM* 5:1, 404–13.

51. Díaz to Barrios, Mexico, Mar. 10, 1885, *Correspondencia*, 1011–12.

52. Mariscal to Cruz, Mexico, Mar. 10, 1885, ibid., 1016–18.

53. Ibid.

54. Zaldívar to Díaz, San Salvador, Mar. 11, 1885, and Castellón to Mariscal, Panama, Mar. 12, 1885, ibid., 1019–20.

55. In Romero's view, only the U.S. government had the power to ask Barrios to back off.

56. Bayard to Hall, Washington, Mar. 10, 1885, *FRUS*, 1885, 81.

57. Hall to Secretary, Guatemala, Mar. 14 and 16, 1885, *FRUS*, 1885, 83–84 and 87.

58. *HMM* 5:1, 414.

59. Mariscal to Díaz Mimiaga, Mexico, Mar. 14, 1885, AHSRE, L-E-2201, 247.

60. Romero to Secretary, Washington, Mar. 18, 1885, AHSRE, L-E-2204, 121–28.

61. Mariscal to Romero, Mexico, Mar. 21, 1885, ibid., 67–68.

62. Same to same, Mexico, Mar. 25, 1885, AHSRE, L-E-2201, 326.

63. Romero to Secretary, Washington, Apr. 8, 1885, AHSRE, L-E-2205, 47–52.

64. Díaz Mimiaga to Secretary, San Salvador, Apr. 3, 1885, AHSRE, 7-21-91.

65. *HMM* 5:1, 444–68.

66. Coerver, *Porfirian Interregnum,* 160.

67. Langley, *America and the Americas,* 95–96; Deger, "Porfirian Foreign Policy," 221–23.

68. As early as April, 1885, Díaz had been concerned enough about U.S. canal plans to inquire what the British government thought of the situation. Carden to Granville, Mexico, Apr. 3, 1885, Public Records Office, Richmond, Surrey, Great Britain: Foreign Office Files (hereafter cited as PRO FO) 881/5329/36.

69. *HMM* 5:1, 561–79.

70. Leonard, *Central America and the United States,* 45–47.

71. Deger, "Porfirian Foreign Policy," 224.

72. Díaz to Romero, Oct. 18, 1894, Banco de México, Archivo Histórico, Archivo Particular de Matías Romero, Box 108.

73. *FRUS,* 1895, 1:562. For a discussion of the Olney corollary, see Dexter Perkins, *A History of the Monroe Doctrine,* 2nd ed. (Boston: Little, Brown, 1955), 181–90.

74. In some cases, however, such support was lukewarm at best. In October 1895, the Brazilian minister approached Romero with a proposal to make Chile, Argentina, Brazil, Mexico, and the United States the regional policemen of the hemisphere. Brazil, however, accepted the Monroe Doctrine because of its own border with the Guyanas and its large unassimilated German population in the south. Romero to Secretary, Washington, Oct. 19, 1895, AHSRE, L-E-1845, 154–58.

75. Romero to Mariscal, Washington, Dec. 21, 1895, AHSRE, L-E-1845, 200–4.

76. Porfirio Díaz, message to Congress, Mexico, Apr. 1, 1896; text found in Luis González y González, ed. *Los Presidentes de México ante la nación,* vol. 2 (Mexico: Cámara de Diputados, 1966), 462–63.

77. Díaz to Lancaster Jones, Mexico, Jan. 31, 1896, CPD 41:8, vol. 18, 397–99. Bound volumes in box; hence citation is different.

78. This shift was accentuated by Romero's death in 1898. See Harry Bernstein, *Matías Romero, 1837–1898* (Mexico: Fondo de Cultura Económica, 1973), 300–1.

79. Romero to Secretary, Washington, May 21, 1895, AHSRE, L-E-1845, 286–90.

80. See the clippings reprinted in the *Mexican Herald,* Apr. 7, 1896.

81. For a different interpretation that sees continuities in U.S. nineteenth-

century policy, see Walter LaFeber, *Inevitable Revolutions: The United States in Central America,* 2nd ed. (New York: W. W. Norton, 1993), 28–34.

82. For a recent synthesis, see Louis A. Pérez, *Cuba and the United States: Ties of Singular Intimacy* (Athens: University of Georgia Press, 1990), chap. 4.

83. Deger, "Porfirian Foreign Policy," 235–52; Paolo Riguzzi, "México, Estados Unidos y Gran Bretaña: una difícil relación triangular," *Historia Mexicana* 41:3 (Jan. 1992), 414.

84. *HMM* 5:2, 313.

85. Hale, *The Transformation of Liberalism,* 248–49.

86. Olliff, *Reforma Mexico and the United States,* 7.

87. Lorenzo Meyer, *Mexico and the United States in the Oil Controversy, 1917–1942* (Austin: University of Texas Press, 1972), 28.

88. Alan Knight, *The Mexican Revolution* (Cambridge: Cambridge University Press, 1986), 1:22–23; and William B. Schell, Jr., "American Investment in Tropical Mexico: Rubber Plantations, Fraud, and Dollar Diplomacy, 1897–1913," *Business History Review* 64 (Spring 1990), 220.

89. For Sierra's nationalism, see Juan Gómez Quiñones, *Porfirio Díaz, los intelectuales y la Revolución* (Mexico City: Ediciones El Caballito, 1981), 85–100. For his views on Cuba, see *El Diario del Hogar,* Jan. 7, 1898.

90. In 1903, for example, Díaz granted British entrepreneur Weetman Pearson the largest oil drilling rights to date. Lorenzo Meyer, *Su majestad británica contra la Revolución mexicana, 1900–1950: El fin de un imperio informal* (Mexico: El Colegio de México, 1991), 81–91. For the hypothesis that Díaz attracted British funds as a balance to U.S. investment only after 1900, see Cathryn Thorup, "La competencia económica británica y norteamericana en México (1887–1910): El caso de Weetman Pearson," *Historia Mexicana* 31:4 (Apr. 1982), 639–40.

 Díaz also attempted to "Mexicanize" parts of the mining sector. Gerald Theisen, "La mexicanización de la industria en la época de Porfirio Díaz," *Foro Internacional* 12:4 (Apr. 1972), 497–506.

91. See José Y. Limantour, *Apuntes de mi vida pública* (Mexico: Editorial Porrúa, 1965), 195–99 and passim.

92. For the origin of these labels and evidence of nationalist rhetoric, see Wangenheim to Bülow, Mexico, May 15, 1907, Politisches Archiv, Auswärtiges Amt, Bonn (subsequently AAB), IA, R 18695.

93. For this transformation of nationalism, consult Juan Gómez Quiñones, "Social Change and Intellectual Discontent: The Growth of Mexican Nationalism, 1890–1911," Ph.D. diss., University of California, Los Angeles, 1972.

94. See José Emilio Pacheco, ed., *Diario de Federico Gamboa, 1892–1939* (Mexico: Siglo Veintiuno Editores, 1977); and Gómez Quiñones, *Porfirio*

Díaz, los intelectuales y la Revolución, 79–81. Gamboa was an eminent Mexican literary figure.

95.   Bernstein, *Romero,* 299.

CHAPTER 3. DON PORFIRIO AND UNCLE SAM BRING THE
"PORFIRITOS" INTO LINE, 1898–1907

1.   Elihu Root, who served as Secretary of State from 1905 to 1909, recognized this fact. See Philip C. Jessup, *Elihu Root* (New York: Dodd, Mead and Co., 1938), 1:501.

2.   This analysis contests the prevailing judgment that Porfirian policy toward Central America served merely as an exercise in diplomatic grandstanding and ultimately provided a convenient justification for U.S. intervention. See Zorrilla, *Relaciones con Centro América,* 531–57, and Josefina Z. Vázquez and Lorenzo Meyer, *The United States and Mexico* (Chicago: University of Chicago Press, 1985).

3.   Díaz had reacted with skepticism to this attempt at union. *HMM* 5:1, 591. See also John E. Findling, "The United States and Zelaya: A Study in the Diplomacy of Expediency," Ph.D. diss., University of Texas, Austin, 1971, 68–69.

4.   *HMM* 5:1, xxi.

5.   Paul J. Dosal, *Doing Business with the Dictators: A Political History of United Fruit in Guatemala, 1899–1944* (Wilmington, Del.: Scholarly Resources, 1993), 39–71, passim.

6.   For a lucid Guatemalan work of fiction that highlights this aspect of Estrada Cabrera's rule, see Miguel Angel Asturias, *El señor presidente* (New York: Atheneum, 1964).

7.   Gamboa to Secretary, San José, Jan. 22, 1900, AHSRE, 6-13-107.

8.   David H. Dinwoodie, "Expedient Diplomacy: The United States and Guatemala, 1898–1920," Ph.D. diss., University of Colorado, 1966, 7–11.

9.   *HMM* 5:1, ill. facing p. 608. Combs had connections to the Stahl banking house, which operated a large part of the Guatemalan debt.

10.   Combs' successor, William F. Sands, was a notable exception to this rule. Sands attacked U.S. diplomacy in Guatemala for perpetuating tyrannical governments and proposed a more critical position instead. See Sands, *Our Jungle Diplomacy* (Chapel Hill: University of North Carolina Press, 1944), 85–114.

11.   *HMM* 5:1, 610.

12.   Mariscal to Gamboa, Mexico, Nov. 18, 1899, AHSRE, 6-13-107.

13.   Gamboa to Secretary, San José, Jan. 20, 1900, ibid.; Gamboa, *Diario de*

Federico Gamboa, 1892–1939, 132. Gamboa, who hailed from cool, highland Mexico City, despised the tropical climate.

14. Gamboa to Secretary, San José, Jan. 20, 1900, AHSRE, 6-13-107.

15. Gamboa to Secretary, Managua, Feb. 19, 1900, and Guatemala, Feb. 24, 1900, ibid.

16. Mariscal to Gamboa, Mexico, Mar. 28, 1900, ibid.

17. In 1901, Díaz even shipped Regalado guns and ammunition. Flöckner to Bülow, Mexico, Feb. 10, 1903, AAB, IA, R 16347.

18. Leonard, *Central America and the United States,* 58, claims that Zelaya convened the Corinto conference in response to his failure to procure the canal concession. But that same month, the U.S. House debated a bill that would have awarded the concession to Nicaragua.

19. Findling, "The United States and Zelaya," 135.

20. Merry to Secretary, San José, Jan. 21, 25, and 26; Feb. 9; and Mar. 1, 1902, NADS, DDCACR.

21. Woodward, *Central America: A Nation Divided,* 191.

22. Mexico had opposed mandatory U.S. arbitration, because it would "extend and consolidate the hegemony of the Anglo-Saxon race in all parts of Latin America." Memorandum of a meeting of the Mexican delegates to the conference by Genaro Raigosa, Mexico, July 1, 1901, AHSRE, L-E-145-A, 19–21.

23. Leonard, *Central America and the United States,* 51.

24. Thomas D. Schoonover, *The United States in Central America: Episodes of Social Imperialism and Imperial Rivalry in the World System, 1850–1910* (Durham, N.C.: Duke University Press, 1991), 152.

25. Merry to Hay, San José, Oct. 2 and 25, 1903, NADS, DDCACR; Findling, "The United States and Zelaya," 134.

26. Zelaya to Díaz, Managua, May 7, 1903, CPD 28:24/9370.

27. Schoonover, *The United States in Central America,* 136.

28. Findling, "The United States and Zelaya," 191.

29. The fairest assessment of Zelaya is Charles L. Stansifer, "José Santos Zelaya: A New Look at Nicaragua's 'Liberal' Dictator," *Review/Revista Interamericana* 7:3 (Fall 1977), 468–85.

30. Leonard, *Central America and the United States,* 54.

31. Zorrilla, *México y los Estados Unidos,* 2:190.

32. Díaz to Rafael Reyes, Mexico, Nov. 9, 1903, AHSRE, 15-11-23.

33. Mariscal to Manuel Azpíroz, Mexico, Jan. 4, 1904, AHSRE, 15-11-24. Many of the South American governments saw advantages to the canal; Argentina and Chile in particular no longer needed to worry about U.S. warships at their shores.

34.   See Root to Adee, Freeport, N.Y., n.d. (probably July 1907), NADS, Numeri-
      cal File (hereafter cited as NF) 6775/82 2/11; and Chivot to Pichon, Mexico,
      Sep. 10, 1907, Arvice du Ministère des Affaires Étrangères (hereafter cited
      as AMAE), Paris, Nouvelle Série (hereafter cited as NS), Mexique, Poli-
      tique Etrangère, Dossier 1, vol. 18, 104.

35.   Dana G. Munro, *Intervention and Dollar Diplomacy in the Caribbean, 1900–
      1921* (Princeton, N.J.: Princeton University Press, 1964), 143.

36.   See Ragnhild Fiebig-von Hase, *Lateinamerika als Konfliktherd der deutsch-
      amerikanischen Beziehungen, 1890–1903: Vom Beginn der Panamerikapolitik
      bis zur Venezuelakrise von 1902/03* (Göttingen: Vandenhoeck und Ruprecht,
      1986), 2:984–1083.

37.   For the text of the corollary, see James D. Richardson, ed., *A Compilation
      of the Messages and Papers of the Presidents* (New York: Bureau of National
      Literature, 1918), 15:6894–930.

38.   Quoted in Emily S. Rosenberg, *Spreading the American Dream: American
      Economic and Cultural Expansion, 1890–1945* (New York: Hill and Wang,
      1982), 41.

39.   This doctrine of Argentine origin postulated that force could not be used
      to collect outstanding debts. For Mexico's support of the Drago doctrine,
      see Joaquín Casasús, "Proyecto de un acuerdo acerca de los límites de la
      responsabilidad de los gobiernos," n.d., AHSRE, L-E-145-B, 23–25.

40.   For the fiscal problems of Guatemala, see David H. Dinwoodie, "Dollar
      Diplomacy in the Light of the Guatemalan Loan Project, 1909–1913," *The
      Americas* 26:3 (Jan. 1970), 241–45.

41.   Zelaya to Díaz, Managua, Mar. 15, 1904, CPD 29:14/5290–91.

42.   Azpíroz to Secretary, Washington, Dec. 24, 1904, AHSRE, L-E-1845, 315–17.
      No evidence of this conversation can be found in either the Theodore
      Roosevelt Papers or the State Department files, but we nevertheless have lit-
      tle reason to doubt the ambassador's report. It is obvious from the dispatch
      that Roosevelt was speaking off the record. No other U.S. official ever ap-
      proached a Mexican diplomatic representative with a similar offer: it is
      likely that the creation of a "Great Mexico" was Roosevelt's own idea.

43.   Casasús to Secretary, Washington, Nov. 16, 1905, and Godoy to Secretary,
      Washington, Oct. 5, 1905, AHSRE, L-E-1846, 58–62 and 33–36; Greville to
      Foreign Office, Mexico, June 2, 1905, PRO FO 50/541.

44.   Fiebig-von Hase, *Lateinamerika*, 193; for this issue, see also Gerhard Brunn,
      Deutschland und Brasilien, 1889–1914 (Cologne: Böhlau, 1971).

45.   Casasús to Secretary, Washington, Nov. 16, 1905, AHSRE, L-E-1846, 60–62.

46.   Joaquín Casasús to Secretary, memorandum of conversations with the
      Chilean minister and Theodore Roosevelt, Washington, Feb. 14, 1906,

AHSRE, Archivo de la Embajada de México en Washington (subsequently cited as AEMW), vol. 190, 2–7. The quote is translated from the Spanish original.

47. Ibid.

48. Casasús to Secretary, Washington, Mar. 2, 1906, ibid., 56–61.

49. Karnes, *The Failure of Union,* 184–85.

50. Combs to Secretary, Guatemala, May 26, 1906, NADS, DDCAG; Root to Combs, Washington, May 31, 1906, NADS, DICA; and Root to Thompson, Washington, May 26, 1906, NADS, DIM.

51. Dinwoodie, "Expedient Diplomacy," 22.

52. Blondel to Bourgeois, Mexico, June 6, 1906, AMAE, NS, Mexique, Politique Etrangère, Dossier 1, vol. 18, 69–71.

53. Müller to Foreign Office, Mexico, Mar. 31, 1906, PRO FO 371/89. Díaz's worries ultimately proved unfounded.

54. Thompson to Secretary, Mexico, June 5, 7, and 8, 1906, NADS, DDM; Munro, *Dollar Diplomacy,* 145.

55. Mariscal to Gamboa, Mexico, May 30, 1906, AHSRE, L-E-1390, 14–15; Díaz to Escalón, June 6 and 15, 1906, CPD, 65:3/1126 and 1209; Combs to Secretary, Guatemala, May 29, 1906, NADS, DDCA, vol. 53; Acting Secretary Robert Bacon to Combs, Washington, June 26 and 27, 1906, NADS, DICA; *El Imparcial,* May 30, 1906; Bacon to Thompson, Washington, July 16, 1906, NADS, DIM; Thompson to Secretary, Mexico, July 17, 1906, NADS, DDM.

56. Karnes, *The Failure of Union,* 185–86.

57. This pattern still holds true today, as U.S. President William J. Clinton's Haiti policy well demonstrates.

58. Bacon to Thompson, Washington, July 11, 1906, *FRUS,* 1906, 1:836; Thompson to Secretary, Mexico, July 12, 1906, NADS, DDM; Thompson to Secretary, July 16, 1906; Bacon to Thompson, Washington, July 17, 1906; and Thompson to Díaz, Mexico, July 17, 1906, CPD 31:21/8328–29 and 8332–33. Here, as often, Thompson, who maintained excellent relations with Díaz, shared confidential correspondence with the Mexican president.

59. Dinwoodie, "Expedient Diplomacy," 27.

60. AHSRE, L-E-1390, 227–43; Bacon to Merry, Washington, July 18, 1906, NADS, DICA.

61. Bacon to Combs and Merry, Washington, July 17, 1906, NADS, DICA.

62. Combs to Secretary, Guatemala, July 24, 1906, NADS, DICA.

63. Gamboa, *Diario de Federico Gamboa,* 155.

64. Before the meeting, Escalón had touched base with Díaz to discuss the "basis of settlement to be exacted by Salvador." Thompson to Secretary,

Mexico, July 19, 1906, *FRUS,* 1906, 1:846; and Escalón to Díaz, San Salvador, July 18, 1906, AHSRE, L-E-1390, 251–59.

65. Gamboa to Secretary, Guatemala, July 24, 1906, AHSRE, L-E-1391, 64.

66. Gamboa, *Diario de Federico Gamboa,* 137. Gamboa quotes Combs in English.

67. The State Department earlier had received notice of the differences between Merry and Combs, yet declined to intercede. See Adee, memorandum, Aug. 14, 1906, Merry to Bacon, July 22, 1906, and Merry to Root, Apr. 17, 1906, NADS, DDCA.

68. Gamboa to Secretary, Guatemala, July 27, 1906, AHSRE, L-E-1391, 64.

69. Combs to Secretary, Guatemala, July 24, 1906, NADS, DDCAG. For the text of the protocol, see *FRUS,* 1906, 1:851.

70. Findling, "The United States and Zelaya," 137.

71. See, for instance, the *New York Herald,* July 19 and 20, 1906.

72. As shown here, Roosevelt's ministers to Mexico and Central America often placed their business connections above the policy goals of the State Department. Those interests frequently demanded a greater degree of accommodation of the host government than the Secretary of State desired.

73. Karnes, *The Failure of Union,* 187.

74. Leonard, *Central America and the United States,* 58.

75. Ordoñez to Zelaya, Zelaya to Ordoñez, Jan. 5, 1907, Bonilla to Zelaya, Zelaya to Bonilla, Jan. 9, 1907, *FRUS,* 1907, 1:609–12.

76. Zelaya to Roosevelt, Managua, Feb. 12–13, 1907, Library of Congress, Manuscript Division, Theodore Roosevelt Papers. Documents housed in the Library of Congress are hereafter referenced as LCMSS with the name of the collection. For the Nicaraguan view of the crisis, see Ministerio de Relaciones Exteriores Nicaragua, *Documentos oficiales referentes á la guerra entre Nicaragua y Honduras y a la participación de El Salvador como aliado de la última* (Managua, n.p., 1907).

77. Creel, memorandum, Washington, Feb. 6, 1907, AHSRE, AEMW, vol. 190, 383–84; Root to Thompson, Washington, Feb. 2, 1907, NADS, NF 3691/25A; Thompson to Secretary, Mexico, Feb. 12, 1907, NADS, NF 3691/unnumbered; Díaz to Mariscal, Mexico, Feb. 7, 1907, CPD 32:4/1301–2. Since the Zelaya regime was a signatory to the Corinto but not to the San José agreements, only the former treaty applied in this situation.

78. Thompson to Roosevelt, Mexico, Mar. 7, 1907, LCMSS, Theodore Roosevelt Papers. In Roosevelt's reply, he reiterated his "regional policemen" idea. Roosevelt to Thompson, Washington, Mar. 12, 1907, CPD 32:8/3179.

79. Juan Barrios to foreign ministers of El Salvador and Costa Rica, Guatemala, Feb. 13, 1907, and Barrios to Mariscal, Guatemala, Feb. 14,

Archivo General de Centroamérica, Ramo Ministro de Relaciones Exteriores, Guatemala City (hereafter cited as AGCA), signatura B-99-7-2-1, legajo 4685, expediente 93695, 322–23 and 326. Barrios responds to a note from Mariscal that can no longer be found in AHSRE.

80. *FRUS*, 1907, 1:616.

81. Thompson to Roosevelt, Mexico, Mar. 7, 1907, LCMSS, Theodore Roosevelt Papers.

82. Ibid., 619–22; Zelaya to Estrada Cabrera, Managua, Feb. 16, 1907, NADS, NF 3691/69.

83. Schoonover, *The United States in Central America,* 152.

84. Fenton McCreery to Secretary, Mexico, Feb. 13, 1907, NADS, NF 3691/51; Zelaya to Díaz, Managua, Mar. 7 and 9, 1907, and Díaz to Zelaya, Mexico, Mar. 9, AHSRE, L-E-1392-II, 3–9.

85. Memorandum of conversation between Root and Creel, Mar. 28, 1907, and memorandum by Adee, Mar. 27, 1907, NADS, NF 3691/256 and 295. Adee had military action in mind.

86. Gamboa to Secretary, Guatemala, Apr. 1, 1907, AHSRE, Archivo de la Embajada de México en Guatemala (hereafter cited as AEMG), box 7, folder 3.

87. *El Tiempo,* Apr. 13, 1907.

88. International practice stipulated that any official communication with an unrecognized government constituted an implicit recognition of that government. Díaz to Dávila, Mexico, Apr. 24, 1907, AHSRE, L-E-1380 (3), 1.

89. *FRUS*, 1907, 1:629–35.

90. These matters included the application of U.S. neutrality laws to Mexican dissidents in the United States.

91. *El Imparcial,* Apr. 9, 1907; David E. Thompson to Secretary, Mexico City, Apr. 8 and 9, 1907, NADS, NF 5717/1 and 2. For Barillas' schemes against Estrada Cabrera, see Lazo Arriaga to Díaz, New York, Sep. 1, 1906, and Díaz to Lazo Arriaga, Mexico, Sep. 12, 1906, CPD 31:29/11952–56.

92. Thompson to Root, Mexico, Apr. 6, 1907, CPD 32:13/4859–66.

93. Wangenheim to Auswärtiges Amt, Mexico, May 8, 1907, AAB, IA, R 16895; Francisco Bulnes, *El verdadero Díaz y la Revolución* (Mexico: Gómez de la Puente, 1920), 282. Bulnes was a científico ally of Díaz's and always quick to condemn the Reyistas.

94. Tower to Grey, Mexico, May 14, 1907, PRO FO 371/278.

95. Thompson to Secretary, Mexico, Apr. 26, 1907, NADS, NF 5717/9; Wangenheim to Bülow, Mexico, Apr. 26, AAB, IA, R 16895.

96. Root to Thompson, Washington, May 8, 1907, NADS, NF 5717/16; Juan

Barrios to Root, May 10, 1907, NADS, NF 5717/24; Wangenheim to Auswärtiges Amt, Mexico, May 8, 1907, AAB, IA, R 16895; Mariscal to Creel, Mexico, May 3, 1907, Creel to Mariscal, May 8, 1907, AHSRE, AEMW, vol. 190, 441–47.

97. Wangenheim to Bülow, Mexico, Apr. 22, 1907, AAB, IA, R 16895.

98. At least that is what the Mexican ambassador told officials of the State Department years later. Huntington Wilson to Adee, Washington, Nov. 26, 1909, NADS, NF 6369/334.

99. Albert de Baer to Secretary, Mexico, June 6, 1907, NADS, NF 5717/48; Wangenheim to Bülow, Mexico, May 15, 1907, AAB, IA, R 16895.

100. Wangenheim to Bülow, Mexico, May 21, AAB, IA, R 16348; Thompson to Secretary, Mexico, May 9, 1907, NADS, NF 5717/20; Secretaría de Relaciones Exteriores, Boletín (Mexico: Secretaría de Relaciones Exteriores, 1907).

101. Quoted in Wangenheim to Bülow, Mexico, May 15, 1907, AAB, IA, R 16895. Justo Sierra was secretary of education and one of the leading científicos.

102. Díaz to Creel, Mexico, May 29, 1907, CPD 32:16/6098; El Imparcial, June 10, 1907. Proponents of the "Black Legend" have portrayed this incident as a particularly good example of the vanity of the Díaz government. See Zorrilla, Relaciones con Centro América, 685.

103. Barrios to Gamboa, Apr. 29, 1907, NADS, NF 5717/41.

104. Gamboa to Barrios, Apr. 30, 1907, NADS, NF 5717/42.

105. Brown to Secretary, Guatemala, May 7, 1907, NADS, NF 5717/17. Guatemalan Foreign Minister Juan Barrios was furious about the move of the legation. Barrios to Mariscal, Guatemala, May 14, 1907, AHSRE, L-E-2047, 121–22.

106. Thompson to Secretary, Mexico, June 12, 1907, NADS, NF 5717/62.

107. Creel to Secretary, Washington, May 7 and 8, 1907, and Mariscal to Mexican Ambassador, Mexico, May 12, 1907, ibid., 54 and 66–70.

108. Creel to Secretary, Washington, May 2, 1907, AHSRE, AEMW, vol. 190, 429–33; Creel to Díaz, Washington, May 3, 1907, and Díaz to Creel, Mexico, May 11, 1907, CPD 32:16/6019–20.

109. Creel to Secretary, Washington, June 13, 1907, AHSRE, AEMW, 459–60.

110. NADS, NF 5316, passim; El Imparcial, June 12, 1907.

111. El Tiempo, May 14, 1907.

112. Munro, Dollar Diplomacy, 149.

113. Zelaya dispatched an agent to Mexico with the hope of receiving Díaz's formal assurances of support at a moment when Mexico appeared in need of friends in Central America. Díaz replied affirmatively, promising to "help with the Central American Union, [but only] within the limits of discretion and on the basis of the will of the people . . . clearly and perfectly ex-

pressed." Zelaya to Díaz, Managua, May 25, 1907, Díaz to Zelaya, Mexico, July 12, 1907, CPD 32:20/7822–23.

114.   Creel to Secretary, Washington, June 10, 1907, AHSRE, AEMW, vol. 190, 457–58; Merry to Root, San José, July 20, 1907, NADS, NF 6775/42.

115.   Root to Adee, Freeport, N.Y., July 1, 1907, NADS, NF 6775/82 $^2/_{11}$.

116.   Adee memorandum, July 27, 1907, NADS, NF 7805/1.

117.   Díaz to Roosevelt, Mexico, Aug. 26, 1907, LCMSS, Theodore Roosevelt Papers. Díaz used this opportunity to try to patch up relations with Estrada Cabrera. In contrast to Gamboa and Mariscal, he approached the Guatemalan with some degree of pragmatism. In July, Díaz sent a confidential agent to Guatemala. Estrada Cabrera sent an emissary in return, and both leaders exchanged promises to work together more fruitfully in the future. Estrada Cabrera to Díaz, Guatemala, Aug. 10, 1907, CPD 32:28/10961–63.

118.   Díaz to Roosevelt, Mexico, Sep. 1, 1907, NADS, NF 6775/83.

119.   Godoy to Secretary, Washington, Aug. 30 and 31 and Sep. 3, 1907, AHSRE, AEMW, vol. 190, 563–65, 569–73, 576–80. Root to Adee, Clinton, N.Y., Aug. 29, 1907, NADS, NF 6775/74.

120.   See the documents in NADS, NF 6775/82a, and Figueroa to Roosevelt, San Salvador, Sep. 1, 1907, NADS, NF 6775/84.

121.   Bryce to Grey, Washington, Nov. 15, 1907, PRO FO 881/9219/40.

122.   Adee, memorandum, Washington, Oct. 1907, NADS, NF 6775–.

123.   Chivot to Pichon, Mexico, Oct. 9, 1907, AMAE, NS, Mexique, Politique Etrangère, Dossier 1, vol. 18, 111–13.

124.   Undersecretary José Algara to Godoy, Mexico, Oct. 22, 1907, AHSRE, L-E-1393.

125.   Same to same, Mexico, Oct. 30, 1907, ibid., 372–76.

126.   Richard V. Salisbury, *Anti-Imperialism and International Competition in Central America, 1920–1929* (Wilmington, Del.: Scholarly Resources, 1989), 20 n. 14.

127.   For the text of the treaties and the diplomatic correspondence preceding the conference, see *FRUS,* 1907, 636–727, and William I. Buchanan, *Report of the Central American Peace Conference Held at Washington, D.C, in 1907* (Washington: Government Printing Office, 1908).

128.   Creel, however, believed that the State Department favored the proposal; Mariscal replied that Mexico would second any general sentiment in favor of union. Creel to Mariscal, Washington, Nov. 20, 1907, and Mariscal to Creel, Mexico, Nov. 21, 1907, AHSRE, L-E-1394, 134–36.

129.   Creel to Díaz, Washington, Dec. 7, 1907, CPD 32:39/15319.

130.   Creel to Díaz, Washington, Dec. 17, 1907, CPD 32:39/15383.

Chapter 4. Díaz Confronts U.S. Intervention in Nicaragua, 1908–1910

1. The U.S. journalist not only interviewed Díaz, he also drew upon statements made by other members of the Mexican government and U.S. investors. Consequently, historian William B. Schell has speculated that much of the article was in fact written by Americans close to the Díaz administration. See "Integral Outsiders, Mexico City's American Colony, 1876–1911: Society and Political Economy in Porfirian Mexico," Ph.D. diss., University of North Carolina at Chapel Hill, 1992, 484–92.

    The Porfirio Díaz archive, however, contains evidence that Creelman mailed Díaz a copy of his projected article more than three weeks in advance of the publication, and that Díaz approved its content. See Creelman to Díaz, New York, Feb. 14, 1908, and Díaz to Creelman, Mexico, Feb. 22, 1908, CPD 33:7/2625 and 2627.

2. *Pearson's Magazine*, Mar. 8, 1908.

3. Katz, "The Liberal Republic and the Porfiriato," *CHLA* 5:115.

4. For the argument that pre-Revolutionary economic nationalism was mainly an elite phenomenon, see Alan Knight, *U.S.–Mexican Relations, 1910–1940: An Interpretation* (San Diego: Center for U.S.-Mexican Studies, University of California, San Diego, 1987), 55. For an opposing view, see Hart, *Revolutionary Mexico*.

5. While the Drago doctrine remained narrow in scope in its prohibition of armed force for debt collection, the Calvo doctrine covered one of the key arguments of nineteenth-century economic nationalists. Foreign-owned businesses, the Argentine diplomat Carlos Calvo had maintained in 1865, ought not to count on the protection of their embassies, since such a company was a juridical citizen of the country in which it operated. The U.S. government opposed both doctrines.

6. Cevallos to Díaz, San Salvador, Jan. 2, 1908, CPD 33:3/1209–10; Creel to Secretary, Washington, Dec. 28, 1907, Mariscal to Creel, Mexico, Jan. 3, 1908, AHSRE, 15-18-10.

7. Díaz to Figueroa, Mexico, Feb. 11, 1908, CPD 33:7/2490.

8. Leonard, *Central America and the United States*, 60.

9. Karl Bermann, *Under the Big Stick: Nicaragua and the United States Since 1848* (Boston: South End Press, 1986), 140.

10. Schoonover, *The United States in Central America*, 143; Merry to Secretary, San José, Jan. 21, 1908, May 7 and 28, 1909, NADS, NF 6775/664 and 670.

11. *New York Times*, Feb. 14, 1908.

12. See, for instance, the *Mexican Herald*, Feb. 15 and 22, 1908. For the effect on

Central American public opinion, see Radowitz to Bülow, Guatemala, Feb. 26, 1908, AAB, IA, R 16349.

13. *Mexican Herald,* Mar. 6, 1908.

14. To be sure, the State Department usually cooperated with Mexican demands for protection of the border. In fact, Root often was solicitous to help Díaz with extradition requests.

    Often incapable of understanding U.S. political procedures, Mariscal perceived the issue differently, however. He frequently could not understand why officers of the executive branch needed to go through official channels to achieve their objectives. Therefore, he was often exasperated with the time taken up by legal proceedings in the United States.

15. Root to Thompson, Washington, Mar. 18 and 20, 1908, NADS, NF 6775/362.

16. Creel to Secretary, Washington, Mar. 21, 1908, AHSRE, AEMW, vol. 191.

17. Thompson to Secretary, Mexico, Mar. 23, 1908, NADS, NF 6775/365.

18. *El Diario del Hogar,* Mar. 25, 1908.

19. Thompson to Secretary, Mexico, Mar. 20 and 27, Apr. 8 and 16, 1908, NADS, NF 6775/367, 369, 402 and 408; Creel to Díaz, Chihuahua, Apr. 9, 1908, CPD 33:14/5292. Both the Mexican and the U.S. governments increased the number of legations in Central America from three to five, respectively.

20. See *El Diario del Hogar,* Apr. 23, 1908, *Daily Record,* enclosed without date in Thompson to Root, Mexico, Apr. 24, 1908, NADS, NF 6775/447.

21. Creel to Díaz, Chihuahua, Apr. 21, 1908, CPD 33:14/5319; see correspondence in NADS, NF 6775/433–42 and Creel to Root, Chihuahua, Apr. 23, 1908, NADS, NF 6775/446.

22. Creel to Díaz, Washington, July 28, 1908, CPD 33:27/10462–63.

23. García Granados to Secretary, San Salvador, Mar. 18, 1908, AHSRE, AEMG, box 8, file 2.

24. For the quote, see Creel to Secretary, Washington, Dec. 25, 1909, AHSRE, L-E-1015, 84–87.

25. Richardson, *Messages and Papers of the Presidents,* 17:7770–71.

26. See chap. 2, last section.

27. Dinwoodie, "Dollar Diplomacy in the Light of the Guatemalan Loan Project," 241–53.

28. Schmidthals to Bülow, Guatemala, Feb. 21, 1908; and Schwerin to Bülow, Guatemala, Apr. 30, 1908, AAB, IA, R 16349.

29. Frederick Ryder to Assistant Secretary, San Juan del Norte, Nicaragua, Jan. 25, 1908, NADS, NF 6775/304.

30. John G. Coolidge to Secretary, Managua, Nov. 19, 1908, NADS, NF 6369/41.

31.   Leonard, *Central America and the United States,* 61.

32.   Findling, "The United States and Zelaya," 189–91.

33.   For the controversy surrounding the Emery claim, see ibid., 182–87, and NADS, NF 924.

34.   Bermann, *Under the Big Stick,* 143.

35.   Knox, memoranda, Mar. 12 and 13, 1909, Heimké to Secretary, Guatemala, Mar. 17, 1909, NADS, NF 18432/22, 23, and 61.

36.   Huntington Wilson, memorandum, Mar. 14, 1909, NADS, NF 18432/24. There is no Mexican archival evidence of this conversation. Therefore, we have no way of knowing how the ambassador's remarks were intended.

37.   De la Barra to Secretary, Washington, Mar. 26, 1909; Knox to de la Barra, Washington, Mar. 26, 1909, AHSRE, AEMW, vol. 191, 680–84.

38.   Macleay to Foreign Office, Mexico, Mar. 20, 1909, PRO FO 371/609, p. 260.

39.   De la Barra to Secretary, Washington, Mar. 20, 1909, AHSRE, AEMW, vol. 191, 680–81; Thompson to Secretary, Mexico, Apr. 26, 1909, NADS, NF 18432/24.

40.   *El Imparcial,* Apr. 1, 1909.

41.   Mariscal to de la Barra, Mexico, de la Barra to Secretary, Washington, Apr. 2 and 12, 1909, AHSRE, AEMW, vol. 191, 703, 710–14.

42.   Knox, memorandum, Apr. 17, 1909, LCMSS, Knox Papers, box 27, fol. 7.

43.   Moore to Secretary of the Navy, Amapala, Honduras, Apr. 24, 1909; Thompson to Mariscal, Mexico, May 2, 1909, NADS, NF 18432/127 and 129.

44.   Thompson to Knox, Mexico, Apr. 15, 1909, LCMSS, Knox Papers, box 7, fol. 27.

45.   Mariscal to de Alvarez, Mexico, Apr. 21, 1909, AHSRE, AEMW, vol. 191, 753–54.

46.   Memorandum, July 26, 1909, LCMSS, Knox Papers, vol. 7, 1125–27.

47.   Walter V. and Marie V. Scholes, *The Foreign Policies of the Taft Administration* (Columbia: University of Missouri Press, 1966), 16.

48.   Carbajal to Díaz, San José, July 10, 1909, CPD 34:28/13767; W. S. Benson to Secretary of the Navy, U.S.S. *Albany,* Corinto, June 21, 1909, NADS, NF 6369/128.

49.   Zelaya to Díaz, Managua, June 28, 1909, CPD 34:25/12353–54.

50.   Díaz to Zelaya, Mexico, Mar. 31 and June 11, 1909, CPD 34:22/10650 and 34:42/20815.

51.   Merry, who had cooperated with Gamboa during the 1906 *Marblehead* conference, now wrote that "our Government cannot rely upon Mexico in Central American affairs." Merry to Heimké, San José, Aug. 25, 1909, NADS, NF 6775/691.

52.   German diplomats, ever nervous about the growing ties between the United States and Latin America, shared this assessment. See Bünz to

Bethmann-Hollweg, Mexico, Oct. 1, 1909, AAB, IA, R 16359. Creel, by contrast, characterized the meeting as a "triumphant walk." Creel to Rafael Chousal, Oct. 21, 1909, Centro de Estudios sobre la Universidad, Universidad Nacional Autónoma de México, Mexico City, Archivo Rafael Chousal, box 32, exp. 315.

53.   Ronald Macleay, "Mexico: Annual Report 1909," Mexico, Jan. 9, 1910, PRO FO 371/926.

54.   Henry B. Oakman to Root, New York, Oct. 26, 1909, NADS, NF 6369/251.

55.   Findling, "The United States and Zelaya," 208. Guatemala also helped with the rebellion: Emiliano Chamorro, a key rebel general, had spent the past two years as an official in Estrada Cabrera's government. José Mariano Orechos to Guatemalan Foreign Ministry, no date, AHSRE, L-E-1011, vol. 2, 49 and 53.

56.   Memorandum by Huntington Wilson, Oct. 21, 1909, and Adee to Wilson, Washington, Oct. 30, 1909, NADS, NF 6369/226 and 241.

57.   See the correspondence in NADS, NF 22372.

58.   For Zelaya's own account of the executions and the U.S. role in the rebellion, see José Santos Zelaya, *La Revolución de Nicaragua y los Estados Unidos* (Madrid: Imprenta de Bernardo Rodríguez, 1910).

59.   Knox to Rodríguez, Washington, Nov. 18, 1909, NADS, NF 22372/1.

60.   Scholes and Scholes, *The Foreign Policies of the Taft Administration,* 53; Findling, "The United States and Zelaya," 214–15.

61.   Chaparro to Díaz, Managua, Nov. 22, 1909, AHSRE, L-E-1013, 24; Zelaya to Díaz, Managua, Nov. 22, 1909, printed in Zelaya, *La Revolución de Nicaragua,* 109–10; Mariscal to de la Barra, Mexico, Nov. 24, 1909, AHSRE, AEMW, vol. 193, 143–46.

62.   Accord of Díaz cabinet, Mexico, Nov. 1909; Díaz to Chaparro, Nov. 25, 1909, AHSRE, L-E-1013, 54 and 89.

63.   Mariscal to Carbajal, Mexico, Dec. 6, 1909, Carbajal to Secretary, Managua, Dec. 7, 1909, AHSRE, L-E-1013, 106, 109, and 127.

64.   Chaparro to Secretary, Managua, Nov. 23, 1909, AHSRE, L-E-1013, 30; and Carbajal to Secretary, Managua, Dec. 22, 1909, L-E-1015, 111–29.

65.   Díaz to Taft, Mexico, Nov. 24, 25, 1909, Taft to Díaz, Washington, Nov. 29, 1909, memorandum by the Mexican chargé, Nov. 29, 1909, NADS, NF 6369/323, 320, and 326; Dávalos to Secretary, Washington, Nov. 25, 1909, AHSRE, AEMW, vol. 193, 143–46.

66.   Díaz to Creel, Mexico, Nov. 25, 1909, AHSRE, AEMW, vol. 193, 57.

67.   Taft to Díaz, Washington, Nov. 29, 1909, AHSRE, L-E-1013, 67–68.

68.   Huntington Wilson to Adee, Washington, Nov. 26, 1909, NADS,

NF 6369/334. Draft of note to the Mexican chargé, Doyle, n.d., NADS, NF 6369/359a.

69. Knox to Rodríguez, Washington, Dec. 1, 1909, NADS, NF 6369/346. Even before the note, the Mexican chargé in Washington had reported growing uneasiness among the Central American ministers regarding Knox's unusual and discourteous tone. Dávalos to Secretary, Washington, Nov. 24, 1909, AHSRE, L-E-1014, 66–68.

70. *El Tiempo,* Dec. 3, 1909; Macleay to Grey, Mexico, Dec. 4, 1909, PRO FO 371/610, p. 392.

71. For that eventuality, Mariscal instructed Creel to suspend the negotiations in Washington and to state publicly that the United States now acted alone in the isthmus. Mariscal to Creel, Mexico, Dec. 17, 1909, AHSRE, L-E-1014, 55.

72. *Mexican Herald,* Dec. 3, 1909. Mariscal was deeply offended about Knox's unilateral step. Richthofen to Bethmann-Hollweg, Mexico, Dec. 9, 1909, AAB, IA, R 16928.

73. Merry to Secretary, San José, Nov. 27, 1909, and Moffat to Secretary, Bluefields, Dec. 12, 1909, NADS, NF 6369/378 and 411.

74. *Mexican Herald,* Nov. 14, 23, and 30 and Dec. 18, 1909; *El Diario del Hogar,* Dec. 3 and 14, 1909; *El Tiempo,* Dec. 14 and 16, 1909.

75. Knox, Memoranda, Dec. 14, 1909, and no date, NADS, NF 6369/400 $^2/_9$.

76. Creel to Secretary, Washington, Dec. 16, 1909, AHSRE, L-E-1015, 181–84.

77. Greigueil to Pichon, Mexico, Dec. 8, 1909, AMAE, NS, Nicaragua, politique étrangère, vol. 2, 33.

78. Creel to Secretary, Washington, Dec. 14, 1909, AHSRE, L-E-1015, 162–69; Knox, memorandum, Dec. 15, 1909, LCMSS, Knox Papers, box 28, folder 2; Adee to H. Wilson, Dec. 12 and 15, 1909, Adee, memorandum, no date, NADS, NF 6369/400 $^2/_9$.

79. Creel to Root, Washington, Dec. 20, 1909, LCMSS, Elihu Root Papers, box 59; Creel to Secretary, Washington, Dec. 17, 1909, AHSRE, L-E-1015, 187–89; Doyle, memorandum of conversation between Taft and Creel, Dec. 17, 1909, NADS, NF 6369/480.

80. Creel to Secretary, Washington, Dec. 23, 1909, AHSRE, L-E-1015, 10–12. Creel summarizes earlier telegrams.

81. Huntington Wilson, memorandum of conversation with Creel, Dec. 20, 1909, NADS, NF 6369/400 $^3/_9$.

82. Creel to Root, Washington, Dec. 20, 1909, LCMSS, Elihu Root Papers, box 59.

83. Creel correctly viewed Huntington Wilson as the main hard-liner in the Department of State; an official who disliked and distrusted Porfirian foreign policy. Creel to Secretary, Washington, Dec. 23, 1909, AHSRE, L-E-1015, 15–17.

84. *Washington Post,* Dec. 14 and 16, 1909.

85. Creel to Secretary, Washington, Dec. 24, 1909, AHSRE, L-E-1015, 28–29.

86. Bulnes, *El verdadero Díaz,* 282; Creel to Secretary, Washington, Dec. 18, 19, 20, 22, and 25, 1909, AHSRE, L-E-1014, 64, 77, and 83, L-E-1015, 1–7, 89–90, and 190–92; Creel to Díaz, Washington, Dec. 16, 17, 18, and 21, 1909, CPD 68:9/4423, 4431, 4434, and 4457. For Taft's initial position on asylum, see *HMM* 5:1, 722.

87. Díaz to Creel, Mexico, Dec. 21, 1909, CPD 68:9/4461.

88. Taft to Knox, Washington, Dec. 21, 1909, NADS, NF 6369/400 $^{5}/_{9}$.

89. Knox to Taft, Washington, Dec. 21, 1909, ibid.; Creel to Secretary, Washington, Jan. 12, 1910, AHSRE, L-E-1017, 24–39.

90. Taft to Knox, Washington, Dec. 22, 1909, LCMSS, William H. Taft Papers, series 5, case 1874. See also AHSRE file 15-14-60.

91. Zelaya to Díaz, Salina Cruz, Dec. 27, 1909, CPD 68:9/4499.

92. Bailey to Secretary, Mexico, Jan. 18, 1910, NADS, NF 6369/693.

93. Bailey to Secretary, Mexico, Jan. 31, 1910, NADS, NF 6269/712.

94. *El Diario del Hogar,* Dec. 28, 1909; *El País,* Dec. 29, 1909; *Mexican Herald,* Dec. 27, 1909.

95. French diplomats, always skeptical of Mexican moves against the United States, concurred with this assessment. See Jusserand to Pichon, Washington, Dec. 24, 1909 and Jan. 4, 1910, AMAE, NS, Mexique, politique étrangère, vol. 18, 148 and 150–51, and Lefaivre to Pichon, Mexico, Jan. 18, 1910, AMAE, NS, Nicaragua, politique étrangère, vol. 2, 44.

96. Lefaivre to Pichon, Mexico, Jan. 18, 1910, AMAE, NS, Nicaragua, politique étrangère, vol. 2, 41.

97. Pardo to Secretary, Guatemala, Dec. 30, 1909, AHSRE, AEMG, box 9, file 1.

98. The *New York Times* bluntly declared the mission a complete failure. *New York Times,* Dec. 30, 1909.

99. Huntington Wilson to Dawson, Jan. 29, 1910, NADS, NF 6369/748A.

100. See Creel's final report, Jan. 12, 1910, AHSRE, L-E-1017, 24–39.

101. Heriberto Barrón to Knox, New York, Dec. 13, 1909, LCMSS, Knox Papers, box 28, fol. 1; see also Barrón to Taft, New York, Jan. 22, 1910, NADS, NF 6369/710.

102. Huntington Wilson, memorandum, Washington, filed Apr. 23, 1910, NADS Decimal File (subsequently DF) 813.00/737. The decimal filing system replaced the Numerical Files in early 1910 and was maintained, with minor modifications, until 1963.

103. Creel, memorandum for the press, Dec. 30, 1909, AHSRE, L-E-1016, 58.

104. Carbajal to Secretary, Managua, Dec. 19 and 21, 1909, AHSRE, L-E-1014, 72 and 93.

105.   Creel to Secretary, Washington, Jan. 4, 1910, Carbajal to Secretary, Managua, Jan. 12, 1910, Mariscal to Carbajal, Mexico, Jan. 15, 1910, AHSRE, L-E-1017, 110–11 and 122–23; Merry to Secretary, San José, Jan. 19, 1910; Olivares to Secretary, Managua, Jan. 23, 1910; Moffat to Secretary, Bluefields, Dec. 19, 1909, NADS, NF 6369/466, 687, and 723; Merry to Secretary, San José, Feb. 12 and 19, 1910, NADS, DF 817.00/776 and 813.00/730; Bünz to Bethmann-Hollweg, Mexico, Feb. 24, 1910, AAB, IA, R 16928.

106.   Luis Corea, Memorandum for Huntington Wilson, Jan. 5, 1910, NADS, NF 6369/724; Scholes, *The Foreign Policies of the Taft Administration,* 57; Carbajal to Mariscal, Managua, Jan. 31, 1910, AHSRE, L-E-1019, 106–11.

107.   Carbajal to Secretary, Managua, Jan. 12, 1910, de la Barra to Secretary, Washington, Mar. 4, 1910, AHSRE, L-E-1016, 122, and L-E-1018, 6–7.

108.   Carbajal to Secretary, Managua, May 16, 1910, de la Barra to Secretary, Washington, May 12, 1910, AHSRE, L-E-1018, 208 and 228–29; Dávalos to Secretary, Washington, Jan. 14, 1910, AHSRE, AEMW, vol. 193, 203–4. On Britain's initiative to assure U.S. recognition of Madriz, see Reid to Secretary, London, June 16, 1910, NADS, DF 817.00/1037. On Costa Rica's position, see Domingo Nájera y de Pindter to Secretary, San José, Dec. 16, 1909, AHSRE, L-E-1016, 66. The German government even considered selling a gunboat to Madriz. See von Buch to Bethmann-Hollweg, Managua, Mar. 23, 1910, AAB, IA, R 16928.

109.   Carbajal to Creel, Managua, June 15, 1910; AHSRE, L-E-1020, 105.

110.   Díaz to Taft, Mexico, June 16, 1910, and Taft to Díaz, June 19, 1910, AHSRE, L-E-1020, 112–13 and 116–24.

111.   Huntington Wilson, memorandum, July 5, 1910; de la Barra, memorandum for Knox, June [should be July] 6, 1910, NADS, DF 817.00/1136 and 1140.

112.   For Creel's attempt at detente with Guatemala, see Memorandum, Dawson, May 3, 1910, Sands to Secretary, Guatemala, June 22, 1910, and Heimké to Secretary, San Salvador, Dec. 19, 1910, NADS, DF 712.14/64, 65, and 70.

113.   Madriz to Díaz, Managua, Aug. 10, 1910; Díaz to Madriz, Mexico, Aug. 13, 1910; Chaparro to Creel, Managua, Aug. 29, 1910; Creel to Nájera y de Pindter, Mexico, Aug. 25, 1910; AHSRE, L-E-1021, 25, 34–35, and 37–45; L-E-1022, 171.

114.   Henry Lane Wilson to Secretary, Mexico, Aug. 29, Sep. 2, and Nov. 16, 1910; NADS, DF 817.00/1383, 1388, and 812.00/447.

115.   *HMM* 5:1, 731–32.

116.   Salvador Castrillo, 1929, quoted in Bermann, *Under the Big Stick,* 150.

117.   Katz, *The Secret War in Mexico,* 38.

118.   The Chamizal was a strip of border territory near Ciudad Juárez claimed by the Díaz regime and awarded to Mexico in 1913.

119.   Panama excepted, of course.

CHAPTER 5. THE MEXICAN REVOLUTION AND
CENTRAL AMERICA, 1911–1920

1. Katz, *The Secret War in Mexico,* passim.

2. In El Salvador, President Manuel Enrique Araujo's nationalist policies created a different political climate from that found in the other Central American republics. For an analysis of Araujo's policies, see John C. Chasteen, "Manuel Enrique Araujo and the Failure of Reform in El Salvador, 1911–1913," *South Eastern Latin Americanist* 28:2 (Sept. 1984), 1–15.

3. Hart, *Revolutionary Mexico,* 327.

4. There is a vast body of literature about the various factions in the struggle. As an introduction to *Zapatismo,* consult John Womack, *Zapata and the Mexican Revolution* (New York: Knopf, 1968). The dynamics of *Villismo* are the subject of a forthcoming volume by Friedrich Katz. For Carranza's ideology, consult Douglas W. Richmond, *Venustiano Carranza's Nationalist Struggle, 1893–1920* (Lincoln: University of Nebraska Press, 1983). For the Sonoran middle-class revolutionaries, see Héctor Aguilar Camín, *La frontera nómada: Sonora y la revolución mexicana* (Mexico: Siglo Veintiuno Editores, 1977).

5. Quoted in Sands, *Our Jungle Diplomacy,* 104.

6. Meyer and Sherman, *Mexican History,* 530–31; and Michael C. Meyer, *Huerta: A Political Portrait* (Lincoln: University of Nebraska Press, 1971), passim. Meyer contends that the Huerta administration intended a gradual but profound departure from the Porfiriato.

7. Katz, *The Secret War in Mexico,* 17.

8. LaFeber, *Inevitable Revolutions,* 52–53.

9. Mark T. Gilderhus, *Diplomacy and Revolution: U.S.–Mexican Relations under Wilson and Carranza* (Tucson: University of Arizona Press, 1977), especially 8. Many U.S. and Latin American businessmen attended the fair at which Wilson gave his speech. The U.S. president's remarks were intended for both audiences.

10. Katz, *The Secret War in Mexico,* 162.

11. Hart, *Revolutionary Mexico.*

12. The quote appears in Ilene V. O'Malley, *The Myth of the Revolution: Hero Cults and the Institutionalization of the Mexican State, 1920–1940* (New York: Greenwood Press, 1979), 11.

13. Richmond, *Carranza's Nationalist Struggle,* passim. Carranza frequently referred to the "*re*-establishment" [emphasis added] of Mexico's dignity or national pride.

14. Of course, this characterization of the leaderships of the Revolutionary factions says little about the people doing the actual fighting. While

Zapata was commanding a peasant army, Villa's, Obregón's, and Carranza's armies were diverse in composition.

15. For U.S. diplomacy toward the Guatemalan loan problem, see Dinwoodie, "Dollar Diplomacy," 241–53.

16. Leonard, *Central America and the United States,* 64–68.

17. Ibid., 69–70.

18. Enrique Córdova to Secretary, San Salvador, Jan. 30, 1913, NADS, DF 813.00/802. All future reference to State Department correspondence, unless otherwise noted, is to the decimal file.

19. Carvajal to Secretary, AHSRE, L-E-1022.

20. He constantly offered his good offices for the "pacification of Mexico." See his address to the Guatemalan congress of Mar. 1, 1916, contained in NADS 814.032/6.

21. Knox to Wilson, Washington, Jan. 25, 1913; Wilson to Secretary, Mexico, Jan. 27, 1913; and Hill to Secretary, Jan. 28, 1913, NADS 814.00/198c, 199, and 200.

22. As demonstrations of this cordiality, see Pérez Verdía to Secretary, AEMG, box 5.

23. As discussed in chap. 3, Estrada Cabrera might have liked to lessen the influence of his country's European coffee planters. Before World War One, however, he was simply unable to do so, even with U.S. assistance.

24. Douglas W. Richmond, "Carranza: The Authoritarian Populist as Nationalist President," in *Essays on the Mexican Revolution: Revisionist Views of the Leaders,* ed. George Wolfskill and Douglas W. Richmond (Austin: University of Texas Press, 1979), 48–79.

25. For the alternate view, see Richmond, *Carranza's Nationalist Struggle,* chap. 9; Salisbury, *Anti-Imperialism,* 70–71; Edward H. Best, "Mexican Foreign Policy and Central America Since the Mexican Revolution," Ph.D. diss., Oxford University, 1988, 48–49; Floyd F. Ewing, Jr., "Carranza's Foreign Relations: An Experiment in Nationalism," Ph.D. diss., University of Texas, 1952; Christopher J. McMullen, "Calles and the Diplomacy of Revolution: Mexican-American Relations, 1924-1928," Ph.D. diss., Georgetown University, 1980, 5; Lorenzo Meyer, "México y las potencias anglosajonas: El fin de la confrontación y el inicio de la cooperación, 1924-1927," *Historia Mexicana* 34:2 (Oct. 1984), 300–52; and Benjamin T. Harrison, *Dollar Diplomat: Chandler Anderson and American Diplomacy in Mexico and Nicaragua, 1913–1928* (Pullman: Washington State University Press, 1988), 54–55.

26. For the first time since 1847, people had taken to the streets to protest U.S. intervention in Mexico, and mobs looted a number of U.S. businesses. Meyer and Sherman, *Mexican History,* 532.

27. For the U.S. government, on the other hand, the expedition served as

leverage for demanding the protection of U.S. lives and property. See Fletcher to Secretary, Mexico, June 28, 1916, LCMSS, Henry P. Fletcher Papers, box 4, file 8.

28. According to two estimates, the total worth of foreign-owned property either doubled or tripled between 1910 and 1920. For the first estimate, see John Womack, "The Mexican Economy During the Revolution, 1910–1920: Historiography and Analysis," *Marxist Perspectives* 1:4 (Winter 1978), 80–123. For the second, see George D. Beelen, "The Harding Administration and Mexico: Diplomacy by Economic Persuasion," *The Americas* 41:2 (Oct. 1984), 151.

29. Richmond, *Carranza's Nationalist Struggle,* 198–99.

30. Theisen, "La mexicanización de la industria," 497–506.

31. The argument for the elite nature of Mexican economic nationalism is discussed above in chap. 2, and in Knight, *U.S.-Mexican Relations,* 55–57.

32. L. S. Rowe to Fletcher, n.p., Dec. 26, 1916, LCMSS, Fletcher Papers, box 4, folder 6.

33. For the names of the factions, see Smith, *Revolutionary Nationalism,* 71–72.

34. For good accounts of factionalism during the Constitutional Convention, see Peter H. Smith, "La política dentro de la Revolución: El congreso constituyente de 1916–1917," *Historia Mexicana* 22:4 (Apr. 1973), 363–95, and E. Victor Niemeyer, Jr., *Revolution at Querétaro: The Mexican Constitutional Convention of 1916–1917* (Austin: University of Texas Press, 1974). A translated copy of the 1917 Constitution is found in *FRUS, 1917.*

35. Meyer and Sherman, *Mexican History,* 545.

36. Fletcher soon drummed up State Department opposition to the 1917 Constitution. Fletcher to Secretary, Mexico, Apr. 3, 1917, LCMSS, Fletcher Papers, box 5, file 6.

37. Venustiano Carranza, speech in Matamoros, Tamaulipas, Nov. 29, 1915, quoted in Raúl Mejía Zúñiga, *Venustiano Carranza en la Revolución Constitucionalista* (Mexico: Secretaría de Educación Pública, 1964), 107. This collection of Carranza's speeches reveals a shift to nationalist rhetoric after April 1914.

38. Speech in San Luis Potosí, Dec. 26, 1915, Centro de Estudios de la Historia de México, Archivo CONDUMEX, Mexico, Archivo Venustiano Carranza (hereafter cited as AVC), 7058.

39. Castillo to Carranza, Mexico, Sept. 23, 1916, AVC, 10902; Carranza to Aguilar, Mexico, Feb. 13, 1917, AVC, 12644; Prieto Laurens to Aguilar, n.d., n.p., AVC, 17119.

40. Luis Quintanilla, "La política internacional de la Revolución mexicana," *Foro Internacional* 5:1 (July 1964), 1.

41. Of course, Díaz had espoused the right to rebellion only as far as his own coup d'état of Tuxtepec—or other Latin American republics—were concerned.

42. González, *Los Presidentes de México,* 3:250.

43. Ibid.

44. See Isidro Fabela, "Memorándum sobre la Doctrina Carranza," enclosed in Fabela to Portes Gil, Mexico, Apr. 9, 1935, Archivo General de la Nación, (hereafter cited as AGN), Ramo Fondos Incorporados (hereafter cited as FI), Fondo Particular Emilio Portes Gil (hereafter cited as FI-EPG), box 141.

45. As previous chapters have illustrated, Díaz, like Carranza, had rejected foreign military intervention for debt collection and the use of diplomatic pressure to protect foreign investments in Mexico. Like Carranza, Díaz had believed in a system of collective hemispheric security as the best safeguard against foreign interference. And in striking similarity to Carranza's postulates, Díaz had viewed Mexico as an example to be followed in Latin America.

46. For an example of these more "radical" nationalists, see Antonio Manero, *México y la solidaridad americana: la Doctrina Carranza* (Madrid: Editorial América, 1918), 171–234.

47. As an example, see the *New York Times,* Mar. 9, 1917.

48. Gilderhus, *Diplomacy and Revolution,* 27–30.

49. Alban Young to Foreign Office, Guatemala, Aug. 23, 1915, PRO FO 371/2295.

50. Leavell to Secretary, Guatemala, Mar. 21, 1916, NADS 814.00/262.

51. Avrel to Minister of Foreign Affairs, Guatemala, Oct. 11, 1915, AMAE, Nouvelle Série, Guatemala, vol. 2: Politique Intérieure, 138; Lehmann to Bethmann-Hollweg, Guatemala, Oct. 3, 1915, AAB, IA, R 16896.

52. Robbins to Secretary of State, Guatemala, Nov. 1, 1915, Daniels to Secretary of the Navy, Washington, Nov. 15, 1915, NADS 814.00/245 and 247; Lehmann to Bethmann-Hollweg, Guatemala, Oct. 31, 1915, AAB, IA, R 16896.

53. See the cases compiled in AHSRE, AEMG, box 5, Alfonso León de Garay to Manuel Castro, Guatemala, May 2, 1916, AHSRE, L-E-798, part 16, 2–6; Robbins to Secretary, Guatemala, Dec. 1, 1915, NADS 814.00/251; and Toledo Herrarte to Aguilar, Guatemala, Feb. 3, 1916, AGCA, signatura B99-7-2-36, legajo 9381.

54. See Luis Cerda González, "¿Causas económicas de la Revolución mexicana?" (unpublished paper).

55. Frank L. Polk, memorandum, Mar. 20, 1916, Yale University Library, Frank L. Polk Papers, Series II, box 17.

56. Roberto Gayón to Guillermo Rosas, Guatemala, May 8, 1916, Centro de Estudios de la Historia de México, Archivo CONDUMEX, Mexico, Archivo Félix Díaz, doc. 103; Mexican consul to Luis Cabrera, New

Orleans, Mar. 11, 1916, AHSRE, 91-R-91; Villavicencios to Secretary, Dec. 24, 1916, AHSRE, 16-23-9; Antonio Hernández Ferrer to Secretary, Havana, Aug. 22, 1916, AHSRE, L-E-799, part 11, 2–3.

57. "Lista de los espías de Estrada Cabrera que traen consigna de matar al primer jefe . . . ," Mexico, May 17, 1916, Centro de Estudios Sobre la Universidad, Universidad Autónoma de México, Mexico, Archivo Juan Barragán, exp. 1567.2.

58. Armando Amador to Aguilar, Tapachula, Aug. 26, 1916, AHSRE, L-E-868, part 3, 118.

59. Martínez Alomía to Secretary, Guatemala, Aug. 21, 1916, AHSRE, 17-6-3. Indeed, Estrada Cabrera had earlier helped Villa.

60. Avrel to Minister of Foreign Affairs, Guatemala, Aug. 21, 1916, AMAE, Nouvelle Série, Guatemala, vol. 5: Politique Extérieure, 130.

61. A copy of the treaty can be found in AHSRE, 17-6-9.

62. Martínez Alomía to Secretary, Managua, Oct. 3, 1916, AHSRE, 18-1-167.

63. Leonard, *Central America and the United States,* 72.

64. Martínez Alomía to Secretary, San Salvador, Mar. 16, 1917, AHSRE, 17-8-231, 12; Pesqueira to Carranza, New Orleans, July 26, 1919, AVC, 15757.

65. Fletcher to Secretary, Mexico, June 14, 1917, Summerlin to Secretary, Mexico, Dec. 28, 1917, and Ryan to Secretary, San Salvador, Jan. 22, 1918, NADS 712.16/2, 3 and 6.

66. Ceballos to Secretary, San Salvador, Apr. 14, 1914, AHSRE, 17-8-231.

67. Foreign Secretary Cándido Aguilar saw it that way. Ricardo Corzo Ramírez, José G. González Sierra, and David A. Skerritt, *Nunca un desleal: Cándido Aguilar, 1889–1960* (Mexico: El Colegio de México, 1986), 168–69.

68. Sediles to Secretary, Managua, Jan. 20, 1917, AHSRE, 17-6-11.

69. There has been some speculation that Carranza heeded the advice of the Zelayista Nicaraguan Sediles. In 1917, Irías reportedly obtained Minister of War Obregón's support for the overthrow of Chamorro and the establishment of a Central American federation under his leadership. While in Managua, Martínez Alomía, according to the testimony of a U.S. secret agent in the U.S. House of Representatives, made good on Obregón's promise and helped Irías procure weapons for an insurrection (see Jefferson to Secretary, Managua, Feb. 16, 1917, NADS, 817.00/2565; and Salisbury, *Anti-Imperialism,* 70–71). The evidence for this purported assistance, however, remains inconclusive; no indication of any contact between Martínez Alomía and Irías exists in Mexican archives.

70. Leonard, *Central America and the United States,* 73.

71. Martínez Alomía to Secretary, Corinto, Jan. 31, 1917, AHSRE 17-8-161. As the envoy pointed out on another occasion, Díaz had been the only Latin

American leader to favor U.S. intervention in Mexico. Same to Medina, San Salvador, Feb. 20, 1916 [should be 1917], AHSRE 17-9-84.

72. Luis Cabrera to Carranza, New York, Dec. 6, 1916, AVC, 12030.

73. Martínez Alomía to Obregón, San Salvador, Mar. 24, 1917, same to Secretary, San Salvador, Mar. 28 and 31, 1917, Obregón to Martínez Alomía, Mexico, Apr. 4, 1917, AHSRE 17-8-231, pp. 19, 24–25, 31, 35–37.

74. Martínez Alomía to Secretary, San José, May 17, 1917, Garza Pérez to Martínez Alomía, Mexico, May 20, 1917, AHSRE, 17-6-13; Jefferson to Secretary, Managua, June 16, 1917, and July 2, 1917, NADS 712.16/1 and 712.17.

75. Phillips to Jefferson, Washington, Mar. 26, 1919, NADS 712.172/-.

76. The evidence of continued Guatemalan aid to the rebels in late 1916 and early 1917 is inconclusive. See, however, Martínez Alomía's correspondence in AHSRE, 18-1-167, which indicates ongoing low-level support.

77. Knight, *U.S.–Mexican Relations,* 15–17.

78. Leonard, *Central America and the United States,* 73.

79. For U.S. antirevolutionary attitudes toward the Mexican Revolution, see Michael H. Hunt, *Ideology and U.S. Foreign Policy* (New Haven, Conn.: Yale University Press, 1987), 108–10.

80. Joseph S. Tulchin, *The Aftermath of War: World War One and U.S. Policy towards Latin America* (New York: New York University Press, 1971); Lorenzo Meyer, *The United States and Mexico in the Oil Controversy,* 52–53, 57–59, and 69–74.

81. Fletcher to Secretary, Mexico, Apr. 3, 1918, NADS 711.12/77-1/2.

82. Fletcher to Secretary, Mexico, Mar. 13, 1917, LCMSS, Fletcher Papers, box 4, file 9, and Katz, *The Secret War in Mexico,* 387–459.

83. Notes on interview between Carranza and Howard E. Morton for the *Los Angeles Examiner,* Apr. 19, 1917, AVC, 12837.

84. In fact, shortly before Wilson declared war, Carranza had used the occasion audaciously to challenge the United States. Aguilar had sent a circular note to all neutral countries, in which Mexico offered to mediate the conflict and assailed those powers that used their neutral position for the prolongation of the war. See Aguilar to Nicaraguan Foreign Secretary, Querétaro, Feb. 12, 1917, enclosed in Jefferson to Secretary, Managua, Feb. 16, 1917, NADS 817.00/2565.

   In an obvious affront to the British, who depended on U.S. arms shipments, Aguilar had even enjoined all other neutrals to stop commerce with the belligerents. See undated, unsigned memorandum in AGN, Ramo Revolución, exp. "Estados Unidos Mexicanos." Once the United States entered the war, Carranza ended his crusade for neutrality.

85. Carranza repeatedly pledged neutrality in conversations with U.S.

diplomats and in interviews with the press. See *Excelsior,* Apr. 7, 1917, and *New York Times,* Sep. 2, 1917.

86. This declaration did not stop the German secret service, however, from infiltrating Mexico for use as a base of operations even after the end of the war. Katz, *The Secret War in Mexico,* 540–49.

87. Woodward, *Central America,* 210–19.

88. Joaquín Méndez to Lansing, Washington, Apr. 27, 1917, *FRUS 1917, Supplement I: The World War,* 271–72.

89. Bermúdez de Castro to Undersecretary Aarón Sáenz, Guatemala, Apr. 11, 1917, AHSRE, 16-24-126. Confiscation of German property in Guatemala started as early as Apr. 1917. See Martínez Alomía to Undersecretary, Belmopan, Belize, Apr. 16, 1917, AHSRE, 16-24-124.

90. Tulchin, *The Aftermath of War,* 47, and *New York Times,* Oct. 20, 1918.

91. Findling, *Close Neighbors, Distant Friends,* 74.

92. Stabler to Secretary, Washington, Aug. 20, 1917, NADS 712.14/73. For a similar episode later in the year, see Lansing to Wilson, Washington, Oct. 8, 1917, and Wilson to Lansing, Washington, Oct. 12, 1917, NADS 712.714/75 and 76.

93. Carothers to Secretary, Tuxtla Gutiérrez, Sep. 2, 1917, NADS 813.00/881. Estrada Cabrera denied his involvement with *Felicismo.* Leavell to Secretary, Guatemala, Feb. 12, 1917, NADS 813.00/846.

94. For an overview of these efforts, see Woodward, *Central America;* Vincent Peloso, "The Politics of Federation: Central America, 1885–1921," Ph.D. diss., University of Arizona, 1969; and Karnes, *The Failure of Union.*

95. Quoted in Merry to Secretary, San José, Feb. 19, 1910, NADS 813.00/730.

96. Belk to Long, Tegucigalpa, Aug. 29, 1917, NADS 813.00/875. The U.S. minister in Honduras, however, thought Estrada Cabrera was the instigator of the unionist movement. Carothers to Secretary, Sep. 13, 1917, NADS 813.00/881.

97. Hernández Ferrer to Secretary, San Salvador, Sep. 28, 1917, AHSRE 17-7-261.

98. J. G. León to Pérez Garza, San Salvador, Sep. 8, 1917, AHSRE 17-8-134.

99. Ibid.; and Hernández Ferrer to Secretary, Guatemala, Sep. 21, 1917, AHSRE 17-8-134.

100. Leavell to Secretary, Guatemala, Aug. 31, 1917, NADS 813.00/863.

101. Richmond, *Carranza's Nationalist Struggle,* 215.

102. Capt. R. E. Powell to Secretary of the Navy, n.p., Nov. 5, 1918, NADS 813.00/916. Given the continuing unrest in Mexico, however, it is hard to believe that Carranza made such an offer.

103. Pesqueira to Carranza, New Orleans, July 26, 1919, AVC, 15757; Arnold to

Secretary, San Salvador, Oct. 19, Jones to Secretary, Tegucigalpa, Oct. 31, 1918, NADS 813.00/907 and 910.

104. Ibid., Polk to Jones, Nov. 13, 1918, NADS 813.00/911. See also Hernández Ferrer to Secretary, San Salvador, Feb. 20, 1919, AHSRE 17-11-247.

105. Martínez Alomía to Secretary, San Salvador, Feb. 6, 1917, AHSRE, 6-14-41.

106. Kenneth J. Grieb, *The Latin American Policy of Warren G. Harding* (Fort Worth: Texas Christian University Press, 1976), 44.

107. Polk to Jones, Washington, Nov. 13, 1918, NADS 813.00/911.

108. Jones to Secretary, Tegucigalpa, Nov. 1 and 7, 1918, Fletcher to Secretary, Mexico, Nov. 7, 1918, NADS 813.00/912-14.

109. Meyer and Sherman, *Mexican History,* 545–46.

110. LaFeber, *Inevitable Revolutions,* 55. The U.S. argument was illogical. Having just destroyed the Court with the Bryan-Chamorro Treaty, Wilson now insisted that the Washington Conventions remained valid as far as Tinoco's recognition was concerned. Once again, the U.S. government had set a double standard regarding international treaties, at least in Central America. For the recognition problem and its consequences for U.S. policy toward Central America in the 1907–18 period, see Charles L. Stansifer, "Application of the Tobar Doctrine to Central America," *The Americas* 23:3 (Jan. 1967), 251–72.

111. Hernández Ferrer to Secretary, San Salvador, July 4 and Aug. 21, 1919, Salvador Fernández to Hernández Ferrer, Mexico, July 7, 1919, AHSRE 17-16-209.

112. Diego Fernández to Mexican Embassy in Washington and Legations in Latin America, Mexico, Apr. 21, 1919, AHSRE, L-E-1845, 59.

113. *Los Presidentes de México: Discursos políticos, 1910–1988* (Presidencia de la República y Colegio de México, 1988), 1:440.

114. Hernández Ferrer to Secretary, San Salvador, June 18, 1919, Aguilar, Circular to Latin American Chancelleries, Mar. 5, 1920, AHSRE, L-E-1849, 83 and L-E-1845, 82.

115. Riguzzi, "México, Estados Unidos y Gran Bretaña," 426, concurs. Riguzzi could not cite my unpublished paper "Cooperación, confrontación y nacionalismo: la política exterior mexicana, 1900–1910," 25, which was read at a conference August 1991, when his article was already in press. Riguzzi and I read papers at the same panel and realized that we had independently come to the same conclusions.

116. Lorenzo Meyer, "La Revolución mexicana y las potencias anglosajonas," 309.

117. Richmond, *Carranza's Nationalist Struggle,* passim. Richmond, who relied heavily on the Carranza archive for his study, apparently was taken in by the stridently nationalist comments of Carranza's supporters. As a docu-

ment from the archive showing such views, see Hernández Ferrer to
Carranza, San Salvador, July 2, 1919, AVC, 15528.

CHAPTER 6. ALVARO OBREGÓN'S HANDS-OFF POLICY, 1920–1924

1. For a study that makes a similar argument for Mexican-Soviet relations,
   see Daniela Spenser, "Encounter of the Mexican and Bolshevik Revolutions in the United States Sphere of Interests, 1917–1930," Ph.D. diss., University of North Carolina at Chapel Hill, 1994.

2. Jean Meyer, "Revolution and Reconstruction in the 1920s," *CHLA*, 5:201.
   See also Aguilar Camín, *La frontera nómada*, passim.

3. Smith, *Revolutionary Nationalism*, 71.

4. Linda B. Hall, *Alvaro Obregón: Power and Revolution in Mexico, 1911–1920*
   (College Station: Texas A&M University Press, 1981), particularly 249–50.

5. Jean Meyer, "Revolution and Reconstruction in the 1920s," *CHLA*, 5:201.

6. O'Malley, *The Myth of the Revolution*, 115.

7. David C. Bailey, "Obregón: Mexico's Accommodating President," in *Essays
   on the Mexican Revolution: Revisionist Views of the Leaders,* ed. George
   Wolfskill and Douglas W. Richmond (Austin: University of Texas Press,
   1979), 82.

8. Hall, *Obregón*, 252–57. To a great extent, Hall argues, it had been Obregón
   who had assured Carranza's success in the 1910s; now, the Sonorans reaped
   the rewards from a half-decade of successful political organization.

9. Córdova, *La ideología de la revolución mexicana*, chaps. 5 and 6.

10. Thomas Benjamin, " 'La Revolución es un bloque': The Origins of Official
    History of the Mexican Revolution," unpublished paper.

11. Zapata had been killed in 1919 on Carranza's orders.

12. O'Malley, *The Myth of the Revolution*, 119–32.

13. Benjamin, "La Revolución es un bloque." For the official "misappropria-
    tion" of *indigenismo,* see Alan Knight, "Racism, Revolution, and *Indi-
    genismo:* Mexico, 1910–1940," in *The Idea of Race in Latin America, 1870–
    1940,* ed. Richard Graham (Austin: University of Texas Press, 1990), 71–113.

14. O'Malley, *The Myth of the Revolution*, 122–23.

15. Helen Delpar, *The Enormous Vogue of Things Mexican: Cultural Relations
    between the United States and Mexico* (Tuscaloosa: The University of
    Alabama Press, 1992), 10–14.

16. Ibid., 52–53.

17. Michael L. Krenn, *U.S. Policy toward Economic Nationalism in Latin America, 1917–1929* (Wilmington, Del.: Scholarly Resources, 1990), 143–44.

18. For an analysis of these diverse U.S. economic interests and Carranza's and Obregón's approach toward them, see Linda B. Hall, *Oil, Banks, and Politics: The United States and Post-Revolutionary Mexico, 1917–1924* (Austin: University of Texas Press, 1995).

19. Indeed, even Pancho Villa had encountered the support of idealists such as Martín Luis Guzmán.

20. Smith, *Revolutionary Nationalism*, 144–45; Vázquez and Meyer, *The United States and Mexico*, 75.

21. At least in its approach to U.S. investments and foreign policy, the "radical" group bore resemblance to Lucas Alamán's Conservative faction and the Reyistas.

22. Hall, *Oil, Banks, and Politics.*

23. Vázquez and Meyer, *The United States and Mexico*, 130–32.

24. Isidro Fabela in *El Universal*, June 7, 1921.

25. For a Guatemalan account of Estrada Cabrera's fall, see Luis Beltranena Sinibaldi, *Como se produjo la caída de Estrada Cabrera* (Guatemala: n.p., 1970).

26. Wade Kit, "The Unionist Experiment in Guatemala, 1920–1921: Conciliation, Disintegration, and the Liberal Junta," *The Americas* 50:1 (July 1993), 33–35.

27. For the aims of the unionists, see Salomón de la Selva, "On the Proposed Union of Central America," *HAHR* 3:4 (Nov. 1920), 566–70.

28. For Herrera's attitude toward Mexico, see Luis Aguirre to Guatemalan chargé in Mexico, Guatemala, Dec. 8, 1920, AGCA, signatura B99-6-7, legajo 4523, expediente 93484, 828.

29. Newspaper clipping from *El Monitor Republicano*, Mexico, Aug. 31, 1920, enclosed in Summerlin to Secretary, Mexico, Sep. 1, 1920, NADS 712.14/80; Aguirre to Obregón, Mariscal, Chiapas, Aug. 29, 1920, Fideicomiso Archivos Plutarco Elías Calles y Fernando Torreblanca, Archivo Fernando Torreblanca (hereafter cited as APEC-FT), Series 30500, 19/676, "Guatemala," 6. This archive is still in the process of organization.

30. Fletcher to Secretary, Mexico, July 3, 1918, NADS 711.12/116 and enclosure.

31. Grieb, *The Latin American Policy of Warren G. Harding*, 44.

32. Obregón privately expressed his support, however. Obregón to José Azmitia, Mexico, Sep. 21, 1921, Archivo General de la Nación (hereafter cited as AGN), Ramo Presidentes, Fondo Obregón-Calles (hereafter cited as P-OC), 104-C-10.

33. Thurston to Secretary, San José, Jan. 16, 1921, NADS 813.00/1045.

34. Karnes, The Failure of Union, 219–22; Munro to Fletcher, Guatemala, Dec.

23, 1921; and Munro, memoranda, Guatemala, Nov. 22 and Dec. 15, 1921, NADS, 813.00/1166, 1187 and 1218.

35. Bojórquez to Secretary, Guatemala, Aug. 9, 1922, AHSRE, 39-8-75.

36. Caballero to Obregón, Guatemala, Dec. 21, 1921, AGN, P-OC, 104-G-10.

37. Alfonso Herrera Salcedo to Secretary, Guatemala, Apr. 6, 1922, AHSRE, 39-8-75.

38. Karnes, *The Failure of Union*, 220.

39. Memorandum, Carlos Díaz, n.p., July 14, 1922, AGN, P-OC, 104-G-10.

40. To this date, there is no comprehensive study of the Orellana administration and politics in the Guatemala of the 1920s. See, however, Juan de Dios Aguilar de León, *José María Orellana: Presidente de Guatemala, 1922–1926* (Guatemala: n.p., 1986); and Joseph A. Pitti, "Jorge Ubico and Guatemalan Politics in the 1920s," Ph.D. diss., University of New Mexico, 1975, 62–190.

41. Juan de Dios Bojórquez, *Hombres y aspectos de México en la tercera etapa de la Revolución* (Mexico: Biblioteca del Instituto Nacional de Estudios Históricos de la Revolución Mexicana, 1963), 133. Bojórquez's chargé José Benítez concurred with this assessment and added that the Guatemalan Liberal Party had "two faces: Recinos and Ubico." Benítez to Secretary, Guatemala, Apr. 22, 1922, AHSRE, 39-8-75.

42. Bojórquez, *Hombres y aspectos de México,* 134. In the Orellana administration, Ubico held the post of minister of war.

43. Aguilar de León, *Orellana,* 251.

44. Cravioto to Secretary, Guatemala, Mar. 4, and May 14, 1925, AHSRE, 39-8-78.

45. Kuhlemann to Auswärtiges Amt, Guatemala, Feb. 5, 1926, AAB, III, R 79456. No other country maintained an embassy in Guatemala at that point in time.

46. Juan de Dios Bojórquez, *Forjadores de la Revolución mexicana* (Mexico: Biblioteca del Instituto Nacional de Estudios Históricos de la Revolución Mexicana, 1960), 83.

47. Bojórquez to Calles, Guatemala, June 1, 1924, Fideicomiso Archivos Plutarco Elías Calles y Fernando Torreblanca, Archivo Plutarco Elías Calles (hereafter cited as APEC-PEC), 8/109.

48. Bojórquez to Fernando Torreblanca, Tegucigalpa, Sep. 14, 1921, AGN, P-OC, 104-C-10, 5.

49. Salvador Martínez de Alva to Foreign Ministry, San Salvador, Dec. 14, 1921, AHSRE, 10-4-1.

50. Idem, memorandum, San Salvador, Oct. 21, 1921, ibid.

51. Caballero to Obregón, Guatemala, Dec. 21, 1921; Obregón to Caballero, Mexico, Jan. 10, 1922, AGN, P-OC, 104-G-10. The original word for "sons" in the Spanish text is *hijos,* which can mean either "sons" or "children."

The former translation was chosen merely for its greater stylistic clarity in the context.

52.   Ruiz to Obregón, Managua, Mar. 7, 1923, Archivo General de la Nación, *Boletín del Archivo General de la Nación,* vol. 11 (Mexico: Archivo General de la Nación, 1980), 5. Hereafter cited as AGN, *Boletín* vol. 11.

53.   Ruiz to Federico Jiménez O'Farril, Managua, Mar. 14, 1923, ibid., 6–7.

54.   Idem to Obregón, San José, Aug. 2, 1922, AGN, P-OC, 429-S-4.

55.   Jiménez O'Farril to Ruiz, Mexico, Apr. 20, 1923, ibid., 7–9.

56.   Ruiz to Federico Jiménez O'Farril, Managua, Mar. 14, 1923, ibid., 6–7.

57.   *Excelsior* (Guatemala), Aug. 31, 1921. The place of publication is henceforth given to distinguish this publication from its Mexican counterpart of the same name.

58.   Findling, *Close Neighbors, Distant Friends,* 75.

59.   Thomas M. Leonard, *U.S. Policy and Arms Limitation in Central America: The Washington Conference of 1923* (Los Angeles: Center for the Study of Armament and Disarmament, California State University, Los Angeles, 1992). It is significant to note, however, that some of the agreements that Hughes considered most essential were not ratified by the Salvadoran legislature.

60.   Karnes, *The Failure of Union,* 223–27.

61.   *El Universal,* Oct. 27, 1922.

62.   *El Universal,* Oct. 30, 1922.

63.   Summerlin to Secretary, Mexico, Dec. 15, 1922, NADS 813.00/Washington/157.

64.   Langley, *America and the Americas,* 128.

65.   Leonard, *Central America and the United States,* 84–85.

66.   Except, of course, the Nicaraguan Conservative government itself.

67.   William A. Kamman, *A Search for Stability: United States Policy towards Nicaragua, 1925–1933* (Notre Dame, Ind.: University of Notre Dame Press, 1968), chap. 1; and Thomas J. Dodd, *Managing Democracy in Central America: A Case Study, U.S. Election Supervision in Nicaragua, 1927– 1933* (New Brunswick, N.J.: Transaction Publishers, 1992).

68.   Joaquín Meza to Secretary, Managua, July 31, 1923; Fernández de la Regata to Secretary, Managua, July 31 and Aug. 1, 1924, AHSRE, 39-9-8 and 39-9-9. Surprisingly, the State Department remained indifferent to this nationalization scheme.

69.   In fact, the Conservatives had never been unified as a party since the beginning of their rule. As early as 1911, the Cuadra Pasos clan and others had resented the supremacy of the Chamorros. See Kamman, *A Search for Stability,* 12–13. Such divisions reflected the *personalista* fractiousness within Central American political parties.

70.   Virginia L. Greer, "State Department Policy in Regard to the Nicaraguan Election of 1924," *HAHR* 34:4 (Nov. 1954), 448.

71.   There have been some doubts about the fairness of the election. See Tulchin, *The Aftermath of War*, 248. Chamorro loudly protested against what he viewed as a rigged contest. See Emiliano Chamorro, *El último caudillo: Autobiografía* (Managua: Ediciones del Partido Conservador Demócrata, 1983), 311.

72.   Kamman, *A Search for Stability*, 32.

73.   On the participation of the A.F. of L., see White to Secretary, Managua, Dec. 8, 1925, NADS 817.00/3244.

74.   Salisbury, *Anti-Imperialism*, 73.

75.   On the role of the CROM (Confederación Regional Obrera Mexicana, or Regional Mexican Workers' Federation), see Fernández de Regata to Secretary, Managua, Oct. 2, 1924, AHSRE, 39-9-9.

CHAPTER 7. ANOTHER QUEST FOR
"NICARAGUA LIBRE," 1924–1930

1.   Lorenzo Meyer, *Mexico and the United States in the Oil Controversy*, 107.

2.   To date, there is no good biography of Calles. For a lucid survey of Calles' term in office, see Jean Meyer, Enrique Krauze, and Cayetano Reyes, *Historia de la Revolución Mexicana, 1924–1928: Estado y sociedad con Calles* (Mexico: Colegio de México, 1977).

3.   Lorenzo Meyer, *Mexico and the United States in the Oil Controversy*, 107–14. In fact, oil production declined because some of the existing deposits were being exhausted.

4.   At one point, Sheffield had declared that "the United States . . . with its well orderly [sic] civilization owes to Mexico . . . all the help it can render to uplift . . . this backward people." Sheffield to Wadsworth, Mexico, Mar. 4, 1924, Yale University Library, James R. Sheffield Papers, Series I, box 5, folder 49.

5.   Lorenzo Meyer, *Mexico and the United States in the Oil Controversy*, 113.

6.   Ibid., 114. For Calles's response to Kellogg's speech, see n.a., *Mexico "On Trial Before the World": Guilty?* (Mexico: Imprenta del Gobierno, 1925).

7.   James J. Horn, "El embajador Sheffield contra el presidente Calles," *Historia Mexicana* 20:2 (Oct. 1970), 265–84; and idem, "U.S. Diplomacy and the 'Specter of Bolshevism' in Mexico (1924–1927)," *The Americas* 32:1 (July 1975), 32–33.

8.   "Confidential Memorandum," unsigned, initialed REO [authored either by

Robert E. Olds or by Arthur B. Lane for Olds], 1926 (no exact date), Yale University Library, Arthur Bliss Lane Papers, box 56a, folder 986.

9. Most important among these individuals were the journalists Carleton Beals, Frank Tannenbaum, and Ernest Gruening, and the U.S. senators William Borah and Burton Wheeler. The press effort was led by the Democratic *New York World.*

10. For a balanced account of Morrow's role in U.S.–Mexican relations and the Mexican Revolution itself, see Richard A. Melzer, "Dwight Morrow's Role in the Mexican Revolution: Good Neighbor or Meddling Yankee?" Ph.D. diss., University of New Mexico, 1979.

11. Mediz Bolio to Secretary, Managua, Aug. 4, 1925, AHSRE, 39-9-18.

12. Kamman, *A Search for Stability,* 32.

13. Mediz Bolio to Secretary, Managua, Aug. 4, 1925, AHSRE, 39-9-18.

14. Eberhardt to Secretary, Managua, Sep. 5, 1925, NADS 817.00/3318.

15. Kamman, *A Search for Stability,* 44–47.

16. Kellogg to U.S. Legation in Managua, Washington, Dec. 9, 1925, NADS 817.00/3354; Joseph C. Grew, *Turbulent Era: A Diplomatic Record of Forty Years, 1904–1945* (Boston: Houghton Mifflin, 1952), 1:665–66.

17. Mediz Bolio to Secretary, San José, Jan. 27, 1926, AHSRE, 20-2-15 (I), 52.

18. For the U.S. goal of constitutional rule, see Leonard, *Central America and the United States,* 79–84 and passim.

19. Ibid., 53; undated, unsigned memorandum by the U.S. legation in Nicaragua, APEC-PEC (Anexo Soledad González), box 30, file 600, 8–9.

20. Mediz Bolio to Secretary, San José, Jan. 27, 1926, AHSRE, 20-2-15 (I), 46–74.

21. Sáenz to Mediz Bolio, Mexico, Jan. 20, 1926, AHSRE, 20-2-15 (I).

22. Here, Chamorro and his lobbyist Chandler P. Anderson sought to play U.S. Ambassador Sheffield's tune in Washington. See Anderson to William Borah, Washington, Feb. 13, 1926, LCMSS, Chandler P. Anderson Papers, box 53, folder 1.

23. Bermann, *Under the Big Stick,* 185.

24. Stokeley Morgan, memoranda of conversations with Juan B. Sacasa, Washington, Mar. 2 and 16, Apr. 2, 1926, NADS 817.00/3490, 3506, and 3532.

25. Sáenz to Téllez, Mexico, Jan. 30, 1926, AHSRE, 20-2-15 (I), 139.

26. Téllez to Secretary, Washington, Feb. 16, 1926, AHSRE, 20-2-15 (I), 146. One writer has confirmed Téllez's impression of Sacasa as a nervous, bland leader who lacked personality and stature. See Gregorio Selser, *El pequeño ejército loco: Operación México-Nicaragua,* 2nd ed. (Mexico: Bruguera Mexicana de Ediciones, 1980), 18.

27.   Téllez to Secretary, Washington, Feb. 16 and Mar. 17, 1926, AHSRE, 20-2-15 (I), 146–49, and 165–66.

28.   Mediz Bolio to Secretary, San José, May 17 and 26, 1926, ibid., 86 and 91.

29.   See Stanley Hawks to Secretary, Guatemala, Oct. 27, 1927, NADS 817.00/5130, and Salisbury, *Anti-Imperialism*, 77–78. Considering that Sacasa was reluctant to seek Mexican help for his cause, the documents sent by the U.S. agent that suggest the existence of such a treaty are probably apocryphal.

30.   Humberto Osorno Fonseca, *La Revolución Liberal Constitucionalista de 1926* (Managua: Editorial Atlántida, 1926), 25–33.

31.   See, for instance, Cravioto to Secretary, Guatemala, Oct. 5, 1926, and Estrada to Arturo Elías, Mexico, Nov. 3, 1926, AHSRE, 20-2-15 (II), 452 and 490.

32.   Orellana even offered money to the *Sacasistas*. See Cravioto to Secretary, Guatemala, Aug. 22 and Sep. 13, 1926, AHSRE, 20-2-15 (II), 390 and 408. After Orellana's death, however, new president Lázaro Chacón, who reappointed Estrada Cabrera's last foreign minister Toledo Herrarte to his old post, moved away from cooperation with Mexico.

33.   Engert to Secretary, San Salvador, May 7, 1926, NADS 817.00/3552; Cravioto to Secretary, Guatemala, July 23, 1926, AHSRE, 20-2-15 (II), 368.

34.   For an analysis of these shipments, see my essay *Calles y el movimiento liberal en Nicaragua*, Boletín 9 (Mexico: Fideicomiso Archivos Plutarco Elías Calles y Fernando Torreblanca, 1992), 10–12.

35.   For the opposite view, see McMullen, "Calles and the Diplomacy of Revolution," 122–50.

36.   Ernest LaGarde to Briand, Mexico, Aug. 28, 1926, AMAE, Amérique, 1918–1940, Mexique, Correspondance générale politique, vol. 11, 83.

37.   Kamman, *A Search for Stability*, 64.

38.   Dennis to Secretary, Corinto, Oct. 19, 1926, *FRUS*, 1926, 2:796–97.

39.   Schoenfeld to Secretary, Mexico, Oct. 23, 1926, APEC-PEC (Anexo Soledad González), "Informe México-Nicaragua," box 30, file 601, 53.

40.   Dennis to Secretary, Corinto, Oct. 19, 1926, *FRUS*, 1926, 2:796–97.

41.   Caffery to Secretary, San Salvador, Aug. 26, 1926, and Sep. 24, 1926, NADS 817.00/3796 and 3936; Davis to Secretary, San José, Sep. 13 and 15, and Oct. 29, 1926, NADS 817.00/3787 and 3800, and 712.13/2.

42.   See the correspondence between Mexican minister Julio Madero and the Foreign Ministry in AHSRE, 20-2-15 (I), 194–225. Madero to Secretary, San Salvador, Dec. 3, 1927, AHSRE, 32-21-10. The weaponry from the *Tropical* was then transferred onto another boat in Puerto México. See Cravioto to Estrada, Guatemala, Oct. 5, 1926; and Estrada to Cravioto, Mexico, Oct. 6,

1926, AHSRE, 20-2-15 (II), 458–59. See also Calvin B. Carter, "The Kentucky Feud in Nicaragua: Why Civil War Has Become Her National Sport," *World's Work* 54:3 (July 1927), 321.

43. Schoenfeld to Secretary, Mexico, Nov. 19, 1926, NADS 817.00/4127; *Excelsior,* Nov. 18, 1926.

44. *New York Times,* Dec. 9, 1926.

45. Bermann, *Under the Big Stick,* 188.

46. Kamman, *A Search for Stability,* 77–84.

47. Bermann, *Under the Big Stick,* 194.

48. Sheffield to Secretary, Mexico, Dec. 8, 1926, *FRUS,* 1926, 2:810.

49. Eberhardt to Secretary, Managua, Dec. 19, 1926, NADS 817.00/4275.

50. "Statement of President Díaz," Managua, Jan. 2, 1927, found in LCMSS, Chandler P. Anderson Papers, box 53, file 4.

51. Dennis to Secretary, Managua, Dec. 8, 1926, NADS 817.00/4197.

52. Eberhardt to Secretary, Managua, Dec. 15, 1926, NADS 817.00/4257. See also *New York Times,* Dec. 24, 1926.

53. Hiram Toledo to Luis Beltrán Sandoval, aboard the steamship *Superior,* Man of War Cay, Nicaragua, Dec. 9, 1926, APEC-PEC, "Toledo, Hiram," 54/48, 4–5.

54. George Black, *Triumph of the People: The Sandinista Revolution in Nicaragua* (London: Zed Press, 1982), 18.

55. For this dating of the cancelation of Mexican military assistance at the end of December 1926, see Henry L. Stimson, *American Policy in Nicaragua* (New York: Scribner and Sons, 1927), and Ovey to Foreign Office, Mexico, Jan. 10, 1927, PRO FO 371/11969, p. 58. There is no documentary evidence of Mexican aid past late December.

56. Sheffield to Taft, Mexico, Mar. 5, 1927, Yale University Library, Sheffield Papers, Series I, box 5, folder 52.

57. Richard Tardanico, "State Dependency and Nationalism: Revolutionary Mexico, 1924–1928," *Comparative Studies in Society and History* 24:3 (July 1982), 416–17.

58. Calvin Coolidge, *Conditions in Nicaragua: Message from the President of the United States Transmitting to the Congress of the United States the Conditions and the Action of the Government in the Present Disturbances in Nicaragua* (Washington: Government Printing Office, 1927).

59. Kellogg, "Bolshevik Aims and Policies in Mexico and Latin America," LCMSS, Frank B. Kellogg Papers (microfilmed), reel 24, frames 141–59.

60. *New York Times,* Jan. 13, 1927; *Excelsior,* Jan. 15, 1927.

61. James J. Horn, "Did the United States Plan an Invasion of Mexico in 1927?"

JIAS 15:4 (Nov. 1973), 454–71. As Horn relates, Calles and many of his advisers were indeed concerned about such a possibility.

62. Leonard, *Central America and the United States,* 86.

63. *Excelsior* (Guatemala) Dec. 3, 1926; Clark Kerr to Foreign Office, Guatemala, Dec. 14, 1926, PRO FO 371/11969, p. 7–8.

64. *Excelsior* (Mexico) Jan. 9, 1927. A copy of this statement and the story of its origins can be found in Arturo M. Elías to Soledad González, New York, Jan. 14, 1926, APEC-PEC, file "Elías, Arturo M.," 21/54, 45–47. For a statement along the same lines, see the interview between Calles and Hubert C. Herring contained in Sheffield to Secretary, Mexico, Jan. 10, 1927, NADS 711.12/869.

65. *Excelsior,* Jan. 12, 13, 14, and 15, 1927; *Universal,* Jan. 13 and 15, 1927.

66. See the press clippings and correspondence contained in APEC-PEC, Fondo Reservado, folder Asuntos México-Nicaragua.

67. *Boston Herald,* Nov. 15, 1927, found in AGN, P-OC, 104-N-18, 115.

68. Among these interest groups, the oilmen and the Knights of Columbus, a Catholic organization, were most important.

69. To win over the Liberals, Stimson offered Moncada, among other things, the appointment of six Liberal *jefes políticos.* These local and regional strongmen were in charge of overseeing the vote tally in their respective districts. Stimson to Moncada, Tipitapa, Nicaragua, May 11, 1927, Yale University Library, Henry L. Stimson Papers, reel 71.

70. Dodds, *Managing Democracy in Central America,* passim.

71. There is no discussion of decision making within the Mexican government in this section. Despite a thorough search, I could not find a single document in the Archivo Histórico de la Secretaría de Relaciones Exteriores that shed more light on the issue. These documents have been destroyed, lost, or classified. Therefore, this section relies heavily on Portes Gil's memoirs, his private archive, and U.S. sources.

72. Neill Macaulay, *The Sandino Affair* (Chicago: Quadrangle Books, 1967), cover.

73. Donald C. Hodges, *Intellectual Foundations of the Nicaraguan Revolution* (Austin: University of Texas Press, 1986), 24–29.

74. Francisco Navarro, "Informe de la misión confidencial desempeñada por el suscrito ante el gobierno del presidente Moncada, de Nicaragua, en 1929," Oslo, Oct. 31, 1939, AGN, FI-EPG, box 28, file 4/2. This document will hereafter be cited as "Navarro memorandum."

Portes Gil, in *Quince años de política mexicana,* 2nd ed., (Mexico: Ediciones Botas, 1941), 346–49, reproduced Navarro's letter but deleted the reference to this military mission. In fact, Portes Gil underlined the relevant passage in the original document and wrote the word "NO" in the margin. This is a clear case of historical revisionism. Portes Gil obviously did not want to admit that a Mexican gunboat had carried arms to Sandino's forces.

75. Schoenfeld to Secretary, Mexico, Jan. 31, 1929, and Morrow to Secretary, Mexico, Feb. 21, 1929, *FRUS*, 1929, 3:580–82.

76. Portes Gil, *Quince años*, 343.

77. Macaulay, *The Sandino Rebellion*, 146.

78. Morrow to Secretary, Mexico, Feb. 21, 1929, NADS 711.12/1160.

79. Kellogg to Morrow, Washington, Feb. 25, 1929, *FRUS*, 1929, 3:583–84.

80. "Navarro memorandum"; Portes Gil, *Quince años*, 344–45. Portes Gil claims here that he discussed this plan with Morrow as well. Morrow, however, makes no mention of such a conversation in his dispatches to the Department of State. According to Morrow, Portes Gil merely told him that he had sent an agent to Managua, without stating the purpose of that visit. Morrow to Secretary, Mexico, Feb. 21, 1929, *FRUS*, 1929, 3:581–82. Given that Portes Gil, in an account that served an obvious political purpose, deleted references to Mexican military aid to Sandino in the "Navarro memorandum" (see note 139), there is little reason why we should trust his account entirely here.

81. "Navarro memorandum."

82. Portes Gil, *Quince años*, 351.

83. Melzer, "Dwight Morrow," 436.

84. Sandino to Portes Gil, Veracruz, June 30, 1929, AGN, FI-EPG, box 28, file 4/2.

85. Portes Gil, *Quince años*, 353; Portes Gil to J. J. Méndez, Mexico, June 25, 1929, AGN, FI-EPG, box 28, file 4/2.

86. Sandino to Portes Gil, Aug. 1, 1929, in Carlos Villanueva, *Sandino en Yucatán, 1929–1930* (Mexico: Secretaría de Educación Pública, 1988), 84–87.

87. Portes Gil, *Quince años*, 361.

88. Gustavo Alemán Bolaños, *¡Sandino! Estudio completo del héroe de las Segovias* (Mexico and Buenos Aires: Imprenta de la República, 1932), 4; Sandino to Zepeda, Mérida, Jan. 25, 1930, AGN, *Boletín*, vol. 11, 46–49.

89. Alvaro Torre Díaz to Portes Gil, Mérida, Aug. 23, 1929; and Obregón to Torre Díaz, Mexico, Sep. 2, 1929, AGN, Ramo Presidentes, Fondo Emilio Portes Gil; Macaulay, *The Sandino Affair*, 159–60.

90. Portes Gil proudly published this exchange in *Quince años*, 356.

91. See the Yucatecan press coverage of Sandino's stay printed in Villanueva, *Sandino en Yucatán*. For the history of the Revolution in Yucatán, see Joseph, *Revolution from Without*.

92. Paco Ignacio Taibo II, *Sombra de la sombra* (Mexico City: Fascículos Planeta, 1986).

93. Apart from Portes Gil's memoirs, a few State Department documents, and the correspondence in the AGN, no evidence has been found to date that might illuminate Morrow's opinion of this matter. In this regard, the Dwight Morrow papers in Amherst, Mass., are of little help, as are the files of the Mexican Foreign Ministry.

94. See the documents contained in Archivo General de la Nación, Mexico City, Ramo Archivos Incorporados, Fondo Emilio Portes Gil, box 28, folder 3.

95. Hodges, *Intellectual Foundations of the Nicaraguan Revolution*, chap. 1.

96. N.a. [probably Salvador Urbina], "Preliminar sobre la actitud de la delegación mexicana en la conferencia," n.d., AHSRE, L-E-202, 168.

CHAPTER 8. EPILOGUE: MEXICO'S CENTRAL AMERICA
POLICY SINCE 1930

1. The reader must be cautioned that subsequent archival research, especially on the 1965–92 period, may substantially revise our view of the more recent Mexican policies toward Central America.

2. In particular, Calles involved the U.S. embassy as a point of leverage with the U.S. government in efforts to quell a series of rebellions. See Melzer, "Dwight Morrow," passim.

3. Nora Hamilton, *The Limits of State Autonomy: Post-Revolutionary Mexico* (Princeton, N.J.: Princeton University Press, 1982), chap. 3.

4. Vázquez and Meyer, *The United States and Mexico*, 140–45.

5. Alan Knight, "Cardenismo: Juggernaut or Jalopy," *JLAS* 26:1 (Spring 1994), 73–107.

6. Knight, *U.S.–Mexican Relations*, 8.

7. Aside from Daniels, most State Department officials, including Hull, were critical of Cárdenas's reforms and espoused a more "hawkish" interpretation of the "Good Neighbor Policy." For a study of various debates within the State Department about its Mexican policy, see Bryce Wood, *The Making of the Good Neighbor Policy* (New York: Columbia University Press, 1961), 203–33.

8. For Ubico's career and the widespread support that helped sweep him into office, see Pitti, "Ubico," especially ix.

9. On the Hernández Martínez regime in El Salvador, see Carmelo F. Astilla, "The Martinez Era: Salvadoran-American Relations, 1931–1944," Ph.D. diss., Louisiana State University, 1976; and Thomas P. Anderson, *Matanza: El Salvador's Communist Revolt of 1932* (Lincoln: University of Nebraska Press, 1971). On Nicaragua, consult Knut Walter, *The Regime of Anastasio*

Somoza García and State Formation in Nicaragua, 1936–1956 (Chapel Hill: University of North Carolina Press, 1992).

10.   Leonard, *Central America and the United States,* 102–8.

11.   Woodward, *Central America,* 215–20.

12.   Richard Millett, *Guardians of the Dynasty: The Nicaraguan National Guard* (Maryknoll, N.Y.: Orbis Books, 1977).

13.   Kenneth Grieb, *Guatemalan Caudillo: The Regime of Jorge Ubico* (Athens: Ohio University Press, 1983), 207.

14.   Best, "Mexican Foreign Policy," 137.

15.   Relations with Guatemala deteriorated after Hay became Cárdenas's Foreign Secretary beginning in 1934. Grieb, *Guatemalan Caudillo,* 209. Ubico's rhetoric, while effective in Guatemala, fell on deaf ears in Washington, as the "specter of Bolshevism" had long ceased to be useful.

16.   Indeed, Hernández Martínez had his admirers among Mexican diplomats, one of whom praised his "adherence to order, his honesty in the management of public funds, and his effort to harmonize capitalism with the interests of the worker." See Huerta to Secretary, San Salvador, Feb. 5, 1933, AHSRE, 34-2-22.

17.   Best, "Mexican Foreign Policy," 115–24.

18.   Thomas G. Powell, *Mexico and the Spanish Civil War* (Albuquerque: University of New Mexico Press, 1980).

19.   International conditions were also favorable at this time, as the world's attention was drawn toward Germany's recent annexation of Austria.

20.   Lorenzo Meyer, *Su majestad británica,* 475–76.

21.   See the files contained in NADS, 812.6363/W. R. Davis for information about these oil shipments.

22.   Grieb, *Guatemalan Caudillo,* 217–18.

23.   This united front never really became reality, as Argentina entered the war against Germany only at the eleventh hour. In fact, Brazil was the only major Latin American country entirely supportive of U.S. policies in the 1930s and 1940s.

24.   Olga Pellicer de Brody and Esteban L. Mancilla, *Historia de la Revolución Mexicana, 1952–1960: El entendimiento con los Estados Unidos y la gestación del desarrollo estabilizador* (Mexico: El Colegio de México, 1978), 97.

25.   Blanca Torres Ramírez, *Historia de la Revolución Mexicana, 1940–1952: Hacia la utopía industrial* (Mexico: El Colegio de México, 1984), 282–300.

26.   Piero Gleijeses, *Shattered Hope: The Guatemalan Revolution and the United States* (Princeton, N.J.: Princeton University Press, 1991), 26.

27.   Ibid., 29. Another study argues, however, that Arévalo was a genuine idealist who advocated all those steps later undertaken by Arbenz. See Richard

H. Immerman, *The CIA in Guatemala: The Foreign Policy of Intervention* (Austin: University of Texas Press, 1982), 48.

28.   In an unprecedented step, Mexico agreed to a number of joint defense schemes for the protection of Baja California and the Pacific coast. Blanca Torres Ramírez, *Historia de la Revolución Mexicana, 1940–1952: México en la segunda guerra mundial* (Mexico: El Colegio de México, 1979), 113–21.

29.   Meyer and Sherman, *Mexican History,* 627–28. Rafael Segovia, "El nacionalismo mexicano: los programas políticos revolucionarios, 1929–1964," *Foro Internacional* 8:4 (Apr. 1968), 356–59.

30.   Luis Medina, *Historia de la Revolución Mexicana, 1940–1952: Civilismo y modernización del autoritarismo* (Mexico: El Colegio de México, 1979), 176–80.

31.   On Mexico's import-substitution industrialization program, see Raymond Vernon, *The Dilemma of Mexico's Development: The Roles of the Private and Public Sectors* (Cambridge: Harvard University Press, 1963).

32.   Best, "Mexican Foreign Policy," 168.

33.   Cárdenas to Arévalo, Pátzcuaro, Michoacán, October 20, 1945, and Morelia, Michoacán, Apr. 6, 1949, AGN, Archivo Personal Lázaro Cárdenas (microfilmed copy of the archive in Apatzingán, Michoacán), 5:2.

34.   Immerman, *The CIA in Guatemala,* 65.

35.   Ibid., 48.

36.   Leonard, *Central America and the United States,* 121–23.

37.   Stephen G. Rabe, *Eisenhower and Latin America: The Foreign Policy of Anticommunism* (Chapel Hill: University of North Carolina Press, 1988).

38.   Leonard, *Central America and the United States,* 139.

39.   Best, "Mexican Foreign Policy," 174.

40.   Pellicer de Brody and Mancilla, *Historia,* 101–2.

41.   Gleijeses, *Shattered Hope,* 277, 274–75.

42.   Pellicer de Brody and Mancilla, *Historia,* 104.

43.   Isidro Fabela, "La conferencia de Caracas y la actitud anticomunista de México," *Cuadernos Americanos,* 75:3 (May–June 1954), 16.

44.   Best, "Mexican Foreign Policy," 174.

45.   For a good account of the invasion and its ramifications, see Immerman, *The CIA in Guatemala,* especially 133–86.

46.   Cárdenas to Ruiz Cortines, Apatzingán, Michoacán, June 21, 1954, AGN, Fondos Incorporados, Archivo Personal Lázaro Cárdenas, 5:2.

47.   As the intervention approached, the Mexican government even softened its stand displayed at Caracas. When the U.S. government suggested convening a "Consultative Meeting" of the OAS foreign ministers in June 1954, on

the issue of the arms imported from Czechoslovakia, Mexico offered to vote with the United States on a projected, harshly worded resolution. Best, "Mexican Foreign Policy," 175.

48. Pellicer de Brody and Mancilla, *Historia,* 102–3.

49. Thomas Wolff, "Mexican-Guatemalan Imbroglio: Fishery Rights and National Honor," *The Americas* 38:2 (Oct. 1981), 235–48.

50. Donald F. Mayer, "Mexican Policy toward Central America and Panama, 1958–1971," Ph.D. diss., American University, 1974, chap. 2; and Ramón Medina Luna, "Proyección de México sobre Centroamérica," in *México y América Latina: La nueva política exterior,* ed. Centro de Estudios Internacionales (Mexico: El Colegio de México, 1976), 11–45.

51. Meyer and Sherman, *Mexican History,* 651–52.

52. Pellicer de Brody and Mancilla, *Historia,* 111.

53. Ibid., 111–12.

54. For detailed analysis of Mexican policy toward Castro's Cuba in the 1960s, see Olga Pellicer de Brody, *México y la revolución cubana* (Mexico: El Colegio de México, 1972).

55. Meyer and Sherman, *Mexican History,* 664.

56. Rosario Green, "México: La política exterior del nuevo régimen," in *Continuidad y cambio en la política exterior de México: 1977,* ed. Centro de Estudios Internacionales (Mexico: El Colegio de México, 1977), 3–4.

57. Mario Ojeda, *Alcances y límites de la política exterior de México* (Mexico: El Colegio de México, 1976), 100–1. Too many researchers have bought into this ahistorical perspective, which disregards Mexican foreign policy prior to 1930.

58. In another striking parallel to earlier Mexican actions in Latin America, Echeverría awarded asylum to Hortensia Allende, the widow of the slain Chilean president.

59. Hugh G. Campbell, "Mexico and Central America: The Continuity of Policy," in *Central America: Historical Perspectives on the Contemporary Crises,* ed. Ralph L. Woodward (New York: Greenwood Press, 1988), 220–21.

60. This had not happened since the Díaz-Taft meeting of 1910.

61. As a small victory, López Portillo did secure Reagan's attendance at a North-South meeting at Cancún in October 1981. Campbell, "Mexico and Central America," 221.

62. H. Rodrigo Jauberth, Gilbertp Castañeda, Jesús Hernández et al., *The Difficult Triangle: Mexico, Central America, and the United States* (Boulder, Co.: Westview Press, 1992), 33.

63. Aguilar Zinser, "Mexico and the Guatemalan Crisis," 161–63 and passim.

64. These exile forces constituted a motley crew of malcontents, even though

ex-National Guardsmen initially constituted the most important recruiting base.

65.   Bagley, "Mexican Foreign Policy," 406–9, 437.

66.   Campbell, "Mexico and Central America," 222.

67.   René Herrera Zúñiga and Manuel Chavarría, "México en Contadora: Una búsqueda de límites a su compromiso en Centroamérica," *Foro Internacional*, 24:4 (Apr. 1984), 458. The quote applies to the 1930–79 period.

68.   See chap. 3 for a discussion of these efforts.

69.   MacLachlan and Beezley, *El Gran Pueblo*, 444–45.

70.   Jauberth et al., *The Difficult Triangle*, 7.

71.   *Excelsior*, June 9 and 10, 1995.

72.   Of course, López Portillo—quite in contrast to Díaz—found himself able to help Nicaragua economically.

Bibliography

Primary Sources

Archives and Manuscript Collections

Mexico

Archivo General de la Nación, Mexico City:
  Ramo Presidentes:
    Emilio Portes Gil
    Obregón-Calles
    Revolución
  Ramo Archivos Incorporados:
    Emilio Portes Gil
    Francisco Bulnes
    Lázaro Cárdenas (on microfilm)
Archivo de la Secretaría de Relaciones Exteriores, Mexico City:
    Archivo de la Embajada de México en Guatemala
    Archivo de la Embajada de México en Honduras
    Archivo de la Embajada de México en Washington
    Serie Gaveta (General Archive)
    Serie L-E (General Archive)
Centro de Estudios de la Historia de México, Archivo CONDUMEX, Mexico
        City:
    Archivo Félix Díaz
    Archivo Venustiano Carranza
Centro de Estudios Sobre la Universidad, Universidad Nacional Autónoma de
        México, Mexico City:
    Archivo Juan Barragán
    Archivo Rafael Chousal
Fideicomiso Archivos Plutarco Elías Calles y Fernando Torreblanca, Mexico
        City:
    Archivo Fernando Torreblanca
    Archivo Plutarco Elías Calles
    Colección Alvaro Obregón
    Fondo Soledad González
Universidad Ibero-Americana, Mexico City:
    Colección General Porfirio Díaz
Banco de México, Mexico City:
    Archivo Matías Romero

United States

National Archives, Washington, D.C.:
  Department of State, Record Group 59: Diplomatic Records (on microfilm)
Manuscript Division, Library of Congress, Washington D.C.:
  Papers of:
    Chandler P. Anderson
    Charles E. Hughes
    Henry P. Fletcher
    Frank B. Kellogg (on microfilm)
    Philander C. Knox
    Theodore Roosevelt
    Elihu Root
    William H. Taft
Sterling Library, Yale University, New Haven, Conn.:
  Papers of:
    Arthur B. Lane
    Frank L. Polk
    James R. Sheffield
    Henry L. Stimson

Central America

Archivo General de Centroamérica, Guatemala City:
  Ramo Ministro de Relaciones Exteriores

Europe

Politisches Archiv, Auswärtiges Amt, Bonn, Germany:
  Abteilung IA, 1871–1920
  Abteilung III, 1920–1945
Archive du Ministère des Affaires Étrangères, Paris:
  Nouvelle Série, 1896–1918
  Archive de l'Entre Deux Guerres, 1918–1940
Public Records Office Kew, Richmond, Surrey, England:
  Foreign Office Files

Newspapers

El Diario del Hogar, Mexico City
El Imparcial, Mexico City
El País, Mexico City
El Tiempo, Mexico City
El Universal, Mexico City
Excelsior, Guatemala City
Excelsior, Mexico City
Mexican Herald, Mexico City
New York Herald, New York
New York Times, New York
Washington Post, Washington, D.C.

Published Primary Sources

Alemán Bolaños, Gustavo. *¡Sandino! Estudio completo del héroe de las Segovias.* Mexico City and Buenos Aires: Imprenta de la República, 1932.

Archivo General de la Nación. *Boletín del Archivo de la Nación.* Mexico City: Archivo General de la Nación, 1977–.

Beals, Carleton. "Mexico Seeking Central American Leadership." *Current History* 24:6 (Sep. 1926), 839–44.

Bojórquez, Juan de Dios. *Forjadores de la Revolución Mexicana.* Mexico City: Biblioteca del Instituto Nacional de Estudios Históricos de la Revolución Mexicana, 1960.

————. *Hombres y aspectos de México en la tercera etapa de la Revolución.* Mexico City: Biblioteca del Instituto Nacional de Estudios Históricos de la Revolución Mexicana, 1963.

Buchanan, William I. *Report of the Central American Peace Conference Held at Washington, D.C., 1907.* Washington, D.C.: Government Printing Office, 1908.

Bulnes, Francisco. *El verdadero Díaz y la Revolución.* Mexico City: Gómez de la Puente, 1920.

Carter, Calvin B. "The Kentucky Feud in Nicaragua: Why Civil War Has Become Her National Sport." *World's Work* 54:3 (July 1927), 312–21.

Chamorro, Emiliano. *El último caudillo: Autobiografía.* Managua: Ediciones del Partido Conservador Demócrata, 1983.

Coolidge, Calvin. *Conditions in Nicaragua: Message from the President of the United States Transmitting to the Congress of the United States the Conditions and the Action of the Government in the Present Disturbances in Nicaragua.* Washington, D.C.: Government Printing Office, 1927.

De la Selva, Salomón. "On the Proposed Union of Central America." *HAHR* 3:4 (Nov. 1920), 566–70.

Gamboa, Federico. *Diario de Federico Gamboa, 1892–1939,* ed. José Emilio Pacheco. Mexico City: Siglo Veintiuno Editores, 1977.

González y González, Luis, ed. *Los Presidentes de México ante la nación.* 4 vols. Mexico City: Cámara de Diputados, 1966.

Grew, Joseph C. *Turbulent Era: A Diplomatic Record of Forty Years, 1904–1945.* 2 vols. Boston: Houghton Mifflin, 1952.

Limantour, José Y. *Apuntes de mi vida pública.* Mexico City: Editorial Porrúa, 1965.

Los Presidentes de México: Discursos políticos, 1910–1988. Mexico City: Presidencia de la República y Colegio de México, 1988.

Manero, Antonio. *México y la solidaridad americana: la Doctrina Carranza.* Madrid: Editorial América, 1918.

Mejía Zúñiga, Raúl. *Venustiano Carranza en la Revolución Constitucionalista.* Mexico City: Secretaría de Educación Pública, 1964.

Mexico "On Trial Before the World":—Guilty? Mexico City, Imprenta del Gobierno, 1925.

Ministerio de Relaciones Exteriores, Nicaragua. *Documentos oficiales referentes á la* guerra entre Nicaragua y Honduras y a la participación de El Salvador como aliado de la última. Managua: n.p., 1907.

Osorno Fonseca, Humberto. *La Revolución Liberal Constitucionalista de 1926*. Managua: Editorial Atlántida, 1926.

Portes Gil, Emilio. *Quince años de política mexicana*. 2nd ed. Mexico City: Ediciones Botas, 1941.

Richardson, James D., ed. *A Compilation of the Messages and Papers of the Presidents*. 20 vols. New York: Bureau of National Literature, 1918.

Romero, Matías. "Mr. Blaine and the Boundary Question between Mexico and Guatemala." *Bulletin of the American Geographical Society* 29 (1897), 280–98.

———. "The Settlement of the Mexico-Guatemalan Boundary Question, 1882." *Bulletin of the American Geographical Society* 29 (1897), 110–33.

Sands, William F. *Our Jungle Diplomacy*. Chapel Hill: University of North Carolina Press, 1944.

Secretaría de Relaciones Exteriores, Mexico. *Boletín*. Mexico City: Secretaría de Relaciones Exteriores, 1907.

———. *Correspondencia diplomática cambiada entre el gobierno de los Estados Unidos Mexicanos y los de varias potencias extranjeras desde el 30 de junio de 1881 al 30 de junio de 1886*. Mexico City: Imprenta del Gobierno, 1887.

Stimson, Henry L. *American Policy in Nicaragua*. New York, Scribner and Sons, 1927.

Turner, John K. *Barbarous Mexico*. Austin: University of Texas Press, 1985.

U.S. Department of State. *Foreign Relations of the United States*. Washington, D.C.: Government Printing Office, various publication dates.

Villanueva, Carlos. *Sandino en Yucatán, 1929–1930*. Mexico City: Secretaría de Educación Pública, 1988.

Zelaya, José Santos. *La Revolución de Nicaragua y los Estados Unidos*. Madrid: Imprenta de Bernardo Rodríguez, 1910.

Published Secondary Sources

Aguilar Camín, Héctor. *La frontera nómada: Sonora y la Revolución Mexicana*. Mexico City: Siglo Veintiuno Editores, 1977.

Aguilar de León, Juan de Dios. *José María Orellana: Presidente de Guatemala, 1922–1926*. Guatemala: n.p., 1986.

Aguilar Zinser, Adolfo. "Mexico and the Guatemalan Crisis." In *The Future of Central America: Policy Choices for the United States and Mexico,* ed. Richard R. Fagen and Olga Pellicer de Brody. Stanford, Calif.: Stanford University Press, 1983, 161–86.

Anderson, Benedict. *Imagined Communities: Reflections on the Spread of Nationalism*. London: Verso, 1983.

Anderson, Thomas P. *Matanza: El Salvador's Communist Revolt of 1932*. Lincoln: University of Nebraska Press, 1971.

Asturias, Miguel Angel. *El señor presidente*. New York: Atheneum, 1964.

Bagley, Bruce M. "Mexican Foreign Policy: The Decline of a Regional Power?" *Current History* 82 (Dec. 1983), 406–9, 437.

——. "Mexico in Central America: The Limits of Regional Power." In *Political Change in Central America: Internal and External Dimensions*, ed. Wolf Grabendorff, Heinrich-W. Krumwiede, and Jörg Todt. Boulder, Colo.: Westview Press, 1984, 261–84.

Bailey, David C. "Obregón: Mexico's Accommodating President." In *Essays on the Mexican Revolution: Revisionist Views of the Leaders*, ed. George Wolfskill and Douglas W. Richmond. Austin: University of Texas Press, 1979, 81–99.

Bazant, Jan, "Mexico from Independence to 1867." *CHLA* 3:423–70.

Beelen, George D. "The Harding Administration and Mexico: Diplomacy by Economic Persuasion." *The Americas* 41:2 (Oct. 1984), 177–89.

Beisner, Robert L. *From the Old Diplomacy to the New*. New York: Harlan Davidson, 1986.

Beltranena Sinibaldi, Luis. *Como se produjo la caída de Estrada Cabrera*. Guatemala: n.p., 1970.

Bender, Lynn D. "Contained Nationalism: The Mexican Foreign-Policy Example." *Revista/Review Interamericana* 5:1 (Spring 1975), 1–4.

Benjamin, Thomas. *A Rich Land, A Poor People: Politics and Society in Modern Chiapas*. Albuquerque: University of New Mexico Press, 1989.

Benson, Nettie Lee. "Territorial Integrity in Mexican Politics, 1821–1833," in *The Independence of Mexico and the Creation of the New Nation*, ed. Jaime E. Rodríguez O. Los Angeles: University of California, Los Angeles, Latin American Center, 1989 275–307.

Bermann, Karl. *Under the Big Stick: Nicaragua and the United States Since 1848*. Boston: South End Press, 1986.

Bernstein, Harry. *Matías Romero, 1837–1898*. Mexico City: Fondo de Cultura Económica, 1973.

Black, George. *Triumph of the People: The Sandinista Revolution in Nicaragua*. London: Zed Press, 1982.

Brack, Gene M. *Mexico Views Manifest Destiny, 1821–1846: An Essay on the Origins of the Mexican War*. Albuquerque: University of New Mexico Press, 1975.

Brading, David A. *Los orígenes del nacionalismo mexicano*. Mexico City: El Colegio de México, 1979.

Brunn, Gerhard. *Deutschland und Brasilien, 1889–1914*. Cologne: Böhlau, 1971.

Buchenau, Jürgen. *Calles y el movimiento liberal en Nicaragua*. Boletín 9. Mexico: Fideicomiso Archivos Plutarco Elías Calles y Fernando Torreblanca, 1992.

Bushnell, David, and Neill Macaulay. *The Emergence of Latin America in the Nineteenth Century*. New York and Oxford: Oxford University Press, 1988.

Campbell, Hugh G. "Mexico and Central America: The Continuity of Policy." In *Central America: Historical Perspectives on the Contemporary Crises*, ed. Ralph L. Woodward. New York: Greenwood Press, 1988, 219–40.

Chabat, Jorge. "Mexico: So Close to the United States, So Far from Latin America." *Current History* 92:568 (Feb. 1993), 55–58.

Chasteen, John C. "Manuel Enrique Araujo and the Failure of Reform in El Salvador, 1911–1913." *South Eastern Latin Americanist* 28:2 (Sep. 1984), 1–15.

Clegern, Wayne M. *The Origins of Liberal Dictatorship in Central America: Guatemala, 1865–1873*. Boulder: University Press of Colorado, 1993.

Coerver, Don M. *The Porfirian Interregnum: The Presidency of Manuel Gonzalez of Mexico, 1880–1884*. Fort Worth: Texas Christian University Press, 1979.

Collier, Simon. "Nationality, Nationalism, and Supranationalism in the Writings of Simón Bolívar." *HAHR* 63:1 (Feb. 1983), 37–64.

Córdova, Arnaldo. *La ideología de la revolución mexicana: La formación del nuevo régimen*. Mexico City: Era, 1973.

Corzo Ramírez, Ricardo, José G. González Sierra, and David A. Skerritt. *Nunca un desleal: Cándido Aguilar, 1889–1960*. Mexico City: El Colegio de México, 1986.

Cosío Villegas, Daniel. *The United States versus Porfirio Díaz*, trans. Nettie Lee Benson. Austin: University of Texas Press, 1964.

Cosío Villegas, Daniel, ed. *Historia moderna de México*. 9 vols. Mexico City: Editorial Hermes, 1956–1973.

Cott, Kennett. "Mexican Diplomacy and the Chinese Issue, 1876–1910." *HAHR* 67:1 (Feb. 1987), 63–85.

Delpar, Helen. *The Enormous Vogue of Things Mexican: Cultural Relations between the United States and Mexico*. Tuscaloosa: The University of Alabama Press, 1992.

Dinwoodie, David H. "Dollar Diplomacy in the Light of the Guatemalan Loan Project, 1909–1913." *The Americas* 26:3 (Jan. 1970), 241–53.

Dodd, Thomas J. *Managing Democracy in Central America: A Case Study, U.S. Election Supervision in Nicaragua, 1927–1933*. New Brunswick, N.J.: Transaction Publishers, 1992.

Dosal, Paul J. *Doing Business with the Dictators: A Political History of United Fruit in Guatemala, 1899–1944*. Wilmington, Del.: Scholarly Resources, 1993.

Escudé, Carlos. *Education, Political Culture, and Foreign Policy: The Case of Argentina*. Durham and Chapel Hill, N.C.: Duke–UNC Program in Latin American Studies Occasional Paper Series no. 3, 1992.

Fabela, Isidro. "La conferencia de Caracas y la actitud anticomunista de México." *Cuadernos Americanos* 75:3 (May 1954), 1–33.

Fiebig–von Hase, Ragnhild. *Lateinamerika als Konfliktherd der deutsch-amerikanischen Beziehungen, 1890–1903: Vom Beginn der Panamerikapolitik bis zur Venezuelakrise von 1902/03*. 2 vols. Göttingen: Vandenhoeck und Ruprecht, 1986.

Findling, John E. *Close Neighbors, Distant Friends: United States–Central American Relations*. Westport, Conn.: Greenwood Press, 1987.

Gaitán A., Héctor. *Los Presidentes de Guatemala: Historia y Anécdotas*. Guatemala: Librería Artemis–Edinter, 1992.

Gibbs, William F. "Díaz's Executive Agents and United States Foreign Policy." *JIAS* 20:2 (May 1978), 165–90.

Gilderhus, Mark T. *Diplomacy and Revolution: U.S.–Mexican Relations under Wilson and Carranza.* Tucson: University of Arizona Press, 1977.

Gleijeses, Piero. *Shattered Hope: The Guatemalan Revolution and the United States.* Princeton, N.J.: Princeton University Press, 1991.

Gómez Quiñones, Juan. *Porfirio Díaz, los intelectuales y la Revolución.* Mexico City: Ediciones El Caballito, 1981.

González Navarro, Moisés. "Las ideas raciales de los científicos." *Historia Mexicana* 37:4 (Apr. 1988), 565–84.

Grabendorff, Wolf. "The Role of Regional Powers in Central America: Mexico, Venezuela, Cuba, and Colombia." In *Latin American Nations in World Politics,* ed. Heraldo Muñoz and Joseph S. Tulchin. Boulder, Colo.: Westview Press, 1984, 83–100.

Green, Rosario. "México: La política exterior del nuevo régimen." In *Continuidad y cambio en la política exterior de México: 1977,* ed. Centro de Estudios Internacionales. Mexico: El Colegio de México, 1977, 3–18.

Greer, Virginia L. "State Department Policy in Regard to the Nicaraguan Election of 1924." *HAHR* 34:4 (Nov. 1954), 445–67.

Grieb, Kenneth J. *Guatemalan Caudillo: The Regime of Jorge Ubico.* Athens: Ohio University Press, 1983.

———. *The Latin American Policy of Warren G. Harding.* Fort Worth: Texas Christian University Press, 1976.

Guerra, François-Xavier. *Le Mexique de l'Ancien Régime a la Révolution.* Paris: Harmattan, 1985.

Hale, Charles A. *Mexican Liberalism in the Age of Mora, 1821–1853.* New Haven, Conn.: Yale University Press, 1968.

———. *The Transformation of Liberalism in Late Nineteenth-Century Mexico.* Princeton, N.J.: Princeton University Press, 1989.

Hall, Linda B. *Alvaro Obregón: Power and Revolution in Mexico, 1911–1920.* College Station: Texas A&M University Press, 1981.

———. *Oil, Banks, and Politics: The United States and Post-Revolutionary Mexico, 1917–1924.* Austin: University of Texas Press, 1995.

Hamill, Hugh M., ed. *Caudillos: Dictators in Spanish America.* Norman: University of Oklahoma Press, 1992.

Hamilton, Nora. *The Limits of State Autonomy: Post-Revolutionary Mexico.* Princeton, N.J.: Princeton University Press, 1982.

Hamnett, Brian. *Juárez.* London and New York: Longman, 1994.

Harrison, Benjamin T. *Dollar Diplomat: Chandler Anderson and American Diplomacy in Mexico and Nicaragua, 1913–1928.* Pullman: Washington State University Press, 1988.

Hart, John M. *Revolutionary Mexico: The Coming and Process of the Mexican Revolution.* Berkeley: University of California Press, 1987.

Herrera Zúñiga, René, and Manuel Chavarría. "México en Contadora: Una búsqueda de límites a su compromiso en Centroamérica." *Foro Internacional* 24:4 (Apr. 1984), 458–83.

Herrera Zúñiga, René, Manuel Chavarría, and Mario Ojeda. "La política de México en la región de Centroamérica." *Foro Internacional* 23:4 (Apr. 1983), 423–40.

Hodges, Donald C. *Intellectual Foundations of the Nicaraguan Revolution.* Austin: University of Texas Press, 1986.

Holbraad, Carsten. *Middle Powers in International Politics.* New York: St. Martin's Press, 1984.

Horn, James J. "Did the United States Plan an Invasion of Mexico in 1927?" *JIAS* 15:4 (Nov. 1973), 454–71.

———. "El embajador Sheffield contra el presidente Calles." *Historia Mexicana* 20:2 (Oct. 1970), 265–84.

———. "U.S. Diplomacy and the 'Specter of Bolshevism' in Mexico (1924–27)." *The Americas* 32:1 (July 1975), 31–45.

Hunt, Michael H. *Ideology and U.S. Foreign Policy.* New Haven, Conn: Yale University Press, 1987.

———. "The Long Crisis in Diplomatic History: Coming to Closure." *Diplomatic History* 16:1 (Feb. 1992), 115–40.

Immerman, Richard H. *The CIA in Guatemala: The Foreign Policy of Intervention.* Austin: University of Texas Press, 1982.

Jauberth, H. Rodrigo, Gilberto Castañeda, Jesús Hernández, et al. *The Difficult Triangle: Mexico, Central America, and the United States.* Boulder, Colo.: Westview Press, 1992.

Jessup, Philip C. *Elihu Root.* New York: Dodd, Mead and Co., 1938.

Joseph, Gilbert M. *Revolution from Without: Yucatán, Mexico, and the United States, 1880–1924.* 2nd ed. Durham, N.C.: Duke University Press, 1988.

Joseph, Gilbert M., and Daniel Nugent, eds. *Everyday Forms of State Formation: Revolution and the Negotiation of Rule in Modern Mexico.* Durham, N.C.: Duke University Press, 1994.

Kamman, William A. *A Search for Stability: United States Diplomacy towards Nicaragua, 1925–1933.* South Bend, Ind.: University of Notre Dame Press, 1968.

Karnes, Thomas L. *The Failure of Union: Central America, 1824–1960.* Chapel Hill: University of North Carolina Press, 1964.

Katz, Friedrich. "Mexico: Restored Republic and Porfiriato." *CHLA* 5:3–78.

———. *The Secret War in Mexico: Europe, the United States and the Mexican Revolution.* Chicago: University of Chicago Press, 1981.

Kit, Wade. "The Unionist Experiment in Guatemala, 1920–1921: Conciliation, Disintegration, and the Liberal Junta." *The Americas* 50:1 (July 1993), 31–65.

Knight, Alan. "Cardenismo: Juggernaut or Jalopy?" *JLAS* 26:1 (Spring 1994), 73–107.

———. "El liberalismo mexicano desde la Reforma hasta la Revolución (una interpretación)." *Historia Mexicana* 35:1 (July 1985), 59–91.

———. *The Mexican Revolution.* 2 vols. Cambridge: Cambridge University Press, 1986.

———. "Peasants into Patriots: Thoughts on the Making of the Mexican Nation." *Mexican Studies/Estudios Mexicanos* 10:1 (Winter 1994), 135–61.

———. "Racism, Revolution, and *Indigenismo:* Mexico, 1910–1940." In *The Idea of*

Race in Latin America, 1870–1940, ed. Richard Graham. Austin: University of Texas Press, 1990, 71–113.

———. U.S.–Mexican Relations, 1910–1940: An Interpretation. San Diego: Center for U.S.–Mexican Studies, University of California, San Diego, 1987.

Krenn, Michael L. U.S. Policy toward Economic Nationalism in Latin America, 1917–1929. Wilmington, Del.: Scholarly Resources, 1990.

LaFeber, Walter. Inevitable Revolutions: The United States in Central America. 2nd ed. New York: W. W. Norton, 1993.

———. The New Empire: An Interpretation of American Expansion, 1860–1898. Ithaca, N.Y.: Cornell University Press, 1963.

Langley, Lester G. America and the Americas: The United States in the Western Hemisphere. Athens: University of Georgia Press, 1989.

Leonard, Thomas M. Central America and the United States. Athens: University of Georgia Press, 1989.

———. "Central America and the United States: Overlooked Foreign–Policy Objectives." The Americas 50:1 (July 1993), 1–30.

———. U.S. Policy and Arms Limitation in Central America: The Washington Conference of 1923. Los Angeles: Center for the Study of Armament and Disarmament, California State University, Los Angeles, 1992.

Macaulay, Neill. The Sandino Affair. Chicago: Quadrangle Books, 1967.

MacLachlan, Colin M., and William H. Beezley. El Gran Pueblo: A History of Greater Mexico. Englewood Cliffs, N.J.: Prentice Hall, 1994.

Mares, David. "Mexico's Foreign Policy as a Middle Power: The Nicaragua Connection, 1884–1986." LARR 18:1 (Fall 1988), 81–107.

Medina, Luis. Historia de la Revolución Mexicana, 1940–1952: Civilismo y modernización del autoritarismo. Mexico City: El Colegio de México, 1979.

Medina Luna, Ramón, "Proyección de México sobre Centroamérica." In México y América Latina: La nueva política exterior, ed. Centro de Estudios Internacionales. Mexico: El Colegio de México, 1976, 11–45.

Meyer, Jean. La Révolution mexicaine. Paris: Harmattan, 1973.

———. "Revolution and Reconstruction in the 1920s." CHLA, 5:201.

Meyer, Jean, Enrique Krauze, and Cayetano Reyes. Historia de la Revolución Mexicana, 1924–1928: Estado y sociedad con Calles. Mexico City: El Colegio de México, 1977.

Meyer, Lorenzo. Mexico and the United States in the Oil Controversy, 1917–1942. Austin: University of Texas Press, 1972.

———. "México y las potencias anglosajonas: El fin de la confrontación y el inicio de la cooperación, 1924–1927." Historia Mexicana 34:2 (Oct. 1984), 300–52.

———. Su majestad británica contra la Revolución mexicana, 1900–1950: El fin de un imperio informal. Mexico City: El Colegio de México, 1991.

Meyer, Michael C. Huerta: A Political Portrait. Lincoln: University of Nebraska Press, 1971.

Meyer, Michael C., and William L. Sherman. The Course of Mexican History. 5th ed. New York and Oxford: Oxford University Press, 1995.

Millett, Richard. *Guardians of the Dynasty: The Nicaraguan National Guard.* Maryknoll, N.Y.: Orbis Books, 1977.

Munro, Dana G. *Intervention and Dollar Diplomacy in the Caribbean, 1900–1921.* Princeton, N.J.: Princeton University Press, 1964.

Niemeyer, E. Victor, Jr. *Revolution at Querétaro: The Mexican Constitutional Convention of 1916–1917.* Austin: University of Texas Press, 1974.

Ojeda, Mario, ed. *Las relaciones de México con los países de América Central.* Mexico City: El Colegio de México, 1985.

Ojeda, Mario. *Alcances y límites de la política exterior de México.* Mexico City: El Colegio de México, 1976.

———. "Mexican Policy toward Central America in the Context of U.S.–Mexico Relations." In *The Future of Central America: Policy Choices for the United States and Mexico,* ed. Richard R. Fagen and Olga Pellicer de Brody. Stanford, Calif.: Stanford University Press, 1983, 135–60.

Olliff, Donathon C. *Reforma Mexico and the United States: A Search for Alternatives to Annexation, 1854–1861.* University: University of Alabama Press, 1981.

O'Malley, Ilene V. *The Myth of the Revolution: Hero Cults and the Institutionalization of the Mexican State, 1920–1940.* New York: Greenwood Press, 1979.

Palmer, Stephen. "Central American Union or Guatemalan Republic? The National Question in Liberal Guatemala, 1871–1885." *The Americas* 49:4 (Apr. 1993), 513–50.

Pellicer de Brody, Olga. "Mexico in Central America: The Difficult Exercise of Regional Power." In *The Future of Central America: Policy Choices for the United States and Mexico,* ed. Richard R. Fagen and Olga Pellicer de Brody. Stanford, Calif.: Stanford University Press, 1983, 119–33.

———. *México y la revolución cubana.* Mexico City: El Colegio de México, 1972.

Pellicer de Brody, Olga, and Esteban L. Mancilla. *Historia de la Revolución Mexicana, 1952–1960: El entendimiento con los Estados Unidos y la gestación del desarrollo estabilizador.* Mexico City: El Colegio de México, 1978.

Pérez, Louis A. *Cuba and the United States: Ties of Singular Intimacy.* Athens: University of Georgia Press, 1990.

Perkins, Dexter. *A History of the Monroe Doctrine.* 2nd ed. Boston: Little, Brown, 1955.

Perry, Laurens B. *Juárez and Díaz: Machine Politics in Mexico.* DeKalb: Northern Illinois University Press, 1978.

Pletcher, David M. *The Diplomacy of Annexation: Texas, Oregon, and the Mexican War.* Columbia: University of Missouri Press, 1969.

Powell, Thomas G. *Mexico and the Spanish Civil War.* Albuquerque: University of New Mexico Press, 1980.

Quintanilla, Luis. "La política internacional de la Revolución mexicana." *Foro Internacional* 5:1 (July 1964), 1–26.

Raat, W. Dirk. *Mexico and the United States: Ambivalent Vistas.* Athens: University of Georgia Press, 1992.

Rabe, Stephen G. *Eisenhower and Latin America: The Foreign Policy of Anticommunism.* Chapel Hill: University of North Carolina Press, 1988.

Reed, Nelson. *The Caste War of Yucatan.* Stanford, Calif.: Stanford University Press, 1964.

Reina, Leticia. *Las rebeliones campesinas en México, 1819–1906.* Mexico City: Siglo Veintiuno Editores, 1980.

Richmond, Douglas W. "Carranza: The Authoritarian Populist as Nationalist President." In *Essays on the Mexican Revolution: Revisionist Views of the Leaders,* ed. George Wolfskill and Douglas W. Richmond. Austin: University of Texas Press, 1979, 48–79.

———. "Nationalism and Class Conflict in Mexico, 1910–1920." *The Americas* 43:3 (Jan. 1987), 279–303.

———. *Venustiano Carranza's Nationalist Struggle, 1893–1920.* Lincoln: University of Nebraska Press, 1983.

Riguzzi, Paolo. "México, Estados Unidos y Gran Bretaña: una difícil relación triangular." *Historia Mexicana* 41:3 (Jan. 1992), 365–436.

Rosenberg, Emily S. *Spreading the American Dream: American Economic and Cultural Expansion, 1890–1945.* New York: Hill and Wang, 1982.

Salisbury, Richard V. *Anti-Imperialism and International Competition in Central America, 1920–1929.* Wilmington, Del.: Scholarly Resources, 1989.

Schell, William Jr. "American Investment in Tropical Mexico: Rubber Plantations, Fraud, and Dollar Diplomacy, 1897–1913." *Business History Review* 64 (Spring 1990), 217–54.

Scholes, Walter V. *Mexican Politics During the Juárez Regime, 1855–1872.* Columbia: University of Missouri Press, 1957.

Scholes, Walter V., and Marie V. Scholes. *The Foreign Policies of the Taft Administration.* Columbia: University of Missouri Press, 1966.

Schoonover, Thomas D. *Dollars Over Dominion: The Triumph of Liberalism in Mexican–United States Relations.* Baton Rouge: Louisiana State University Press, 1978.

———. *The United States in Central America: Episodes of Social Imperialism and Imperial Rivalry in the World System, 1850–1910.* Durham, N.C.: Duke University Press, 1991.

Segovia, Rafael. "El nacionalismo mexicano: los programas políticos revolucionarios, 1929–1964." *Foro Internacional* 8:4 (Apr. 1968), 349–59.

Selser, Gregorio. *El pequeño ejército loco: operación México–Nicaragua.* Mexico City: Bruguera Mexicana de Ediciones, 1980.

Sinkin, Richard N. *The Mexican Reform, 1855–1876: A Study in Liberal Nation-Building.* Austin: University of Texas Press, 1979.

Smith, Peter H. "La política dentro de la Revolución: El congreso constituyente de 1916–1917." *Historia Mexicana* 22:4 (Apr. 1973), 363–95.

Smith, Robert F. *The United States and Revolutionary Nationalism in Mexico, 1916–1932.* Chicago: University of Chicago Press, 1972.

Spenser, Daniela. "Los inicios del cultivo de café en Soconusco y la inmigración extranjera." In *Los empresarios alemanes, el Tercer Reich y la oposición de derecha a Cárdenas,* ed. Brígida von Mentz, Verena Radkau, Daniela Spenser et al. Mexico City: Colección Miguel Othón de Mendizábal, 1988, 1:61–88.

Stansifer, Charles L. "Application of the Tobar Doctrine to Central America." *The Americas* 23:3 (Jan. 1967), 251–72.

———. "José Santos Zelaya: A New Look at Nicaragua's 'Liberal' Dictator." *Review/Revista Interamericana* 7:3 (Fall 1977), 468–85.

Taibo II, Paco Ignacio. *Sombra de la sombra.* Mexico City: Fascículos Planeta, 1986.

Tardanico, Richard. "State Dependency and Nationalism: Revolutionary Mexico, 1924–1928." *Comparative Studies in Society and History* 24:3 (July 1982), 400–423.

Theisen, Gerald. "La mexicanización de la industria en la época de Porfirio Díaz." *Foro Internacional* 12:4 (Apr. 1972), 497–506.

Thorup, Cathryn. "La competencia económica británica y norteamericana en México (1887–1910): El caso de Weetman Pearson." *Historia Mexicana* 31:4 (Apr. 1982), 599–641.

Torres Ramírez, Blanca. *Historia de la Revolución Mexicana, 1940–1952: Hacia la utopía industrial.* Mexico City: El Colegio de México, 1984.

———. *Historia de la Revolución Mexicana, 1940–1952: México en la segunda guerra mundial.* Mexico City: El Colegio de México, 1979.

Tulchin, Joseph S. *The Aftermath of War: World War One and U.S. Policy Towards Latin America.* New York: New York University Press, 1971.

Turner, Frederick C. *The Dynamic of Mexican Nationalism.* Chapel Hill: University of North Carolina Press, 1968.

Valadés, José C. *Lucas Alamán: estadista e historiador.* Mexico City: Editorial Porrúa, 1938.

Vázquez, Josefina Z., and Lorenzo Meyer. *The United States and Mexico.* Chicago: University of Chicago Press, 1985.

Vernon, Raymond. *The Dilemma of Mexico's Development: The Roles of the Private and Public Sectors.* Cambridge: Harvard University Press, 1963.

Walter, Knut. *The Regime of Anastasio Somoza García and State Formation in Nicaragua, 1936–1956.* Chapel Hill: University of North Carolina Press, 1992.

Weeks, Charles. *The Juárez Myth in Mexico.* Tuscaloosa: The University of Alabama Press, 1987.

Wolff, Thomas. "Mexican-Guatemalan Imbroglio: Fishery Rights and National Honor." *The Americas* 38:2 (Oct. 1981), 235–48.

Womack, John. "The Mexican Economy during the Revolution, 1910–1920: Historiography and Analysis." *Marxist Perspectives* 1:4 (Winter 1978), 80–123.

———. *Zapata and the Mexican Revolution.* New York: Knopf, 1968.

Wood, Bryce. *The Making of the Good Neighbor Policy.* New York: Columbia University Press, 1961.

Woodward, Ralph L. *Central America: A Nation Divided.* 2nd ed. New York: Oxford University Press, 1985.

———. "Central America from Independence to c. 1870." *CHLA* 3:471–506.

———. *Rafael Carrera and the Emergence of the Republic of Guatemala, 1821–1871.* Athens: University of Georgia Press, 1993.

Zorrilla, Luis G. *Historia de las relaciones entre México y los Estados Unidos de América, 1800–1958.* 2 vols. Mexico City: Editorial Porrúa, 1965.
——. *Relaciones de México con la República de Centro América y con Guatemala.* Mexico City: Editorial Porrúa, 1984.

Dissertations and Other Unpublished Material

Astilla, Carmelo F. "The Martinez Era: Salvadoran-American Relations, 1931–1944." Ph.D. diss., Louisiana State University, 1976.
Benjamin, Thomas. " 'La Revolución es un bloque': The Origins of the Official History on the Mexican Revolution." Unpublished paper.
Best, Edward H. "Mexican Foreign Policy and Central America Since the Mexican Revolution." Ph.D. diss., Oxford University, 1988.
Cerda González, Luis. "¿Causas económicas de la Revolución mexicana?" Unpublished paper.
Deger, Robert J., Jr. "Porfirian Foreign Policy and Mexican Nationalism: A Study of Cooperation and Conflict in Mexican-American Relations, 1884–1904." Ph.D. diss., Indiana University, 1979.
Dinwoodie, David H. "Expedient Diplomacy: The United States and Guatemala, 1898–1920." Ph.D. diss., University of Colorado, 1966.
Dougherty, John E. "Mexico and Guatemala, 1856–1872: A Case Study in Extra-Legal International Relations." Ph.D. diss., University of California, Los Angeles, 1969.
Eschbach, Cheryl L. "Dilemmas of Sovereignty: Mexican Policy toward Central America under Presidents López Portillo and De la Madrid." Ph.D. diss., Princeton University, 1989.
Ewing, Floyd F., Jr. "Carranza's Foreign Relations: An Experiment in Nationalism." Ph.D. diss., University of Texas, Austin, 1952.
Findling, John E. "The United States and Zelaya: A Study in the Diplomacy of Expediency." Ph.D. diss., University of Texas, Austin, 1971.
Gómez Quiñones, Juan. "Social Change and Intellectual Discontent: The Growth of Mexican Nationalism, 1890–1911." Ph.D. diss., University of California, Los Angeles, 1972.
Mayer, Donald F. "Mexican Policy toward Central America and Panama, 1958–1971." Ph.D. diss., American University, 1974.
McMullen, Christopher J. "Calles and the Diplomacy of Revolution: Mexican-American Relations, 1924–1928." Ph.D. diss., Georgetown University, 1980.
Melzer, Richard A. "Dwight Morrow's Role in the Mexican Revolution: Good Neighbor or Meddling Yankee?" Ph.D. diss., University of New Mexico, 1979.
Peloso, Vincent. "The Politics of Federation: Central America, 1885–1921." Ph.D. diss., University of Arizona, 1969.
Pitti, Joseph S. "Jorge Ubico and Guatemalan Politics in the 1920s." Ph.D. diss., University of New Mexico, 1975.

Schell, William B. "Integral Outsiders, Mexico City's American Colony, 1876–1911: Society and Political Economy in Porfirian Mexico." Ph.D. diss., University of North Carolina at Chapel Hill, 1992.

Spenser, Daniela. "Encounter of the Mexican and Bolshevik Revolutions in the United States Sphere of Interests." Ph.D. diss., University of North Carolina at Chapel Hill, 1994.

Index

anti-U.S. demonstrations, 102; and
Bryan-Chamorro Treaty, 127, 129; and
World War One, 131; adopts Mexican po-
sition on Monroe Doctrine, 137
El Tiempo, 45, 68, 73
El Universal, 155
Emery Company: claim against Nicaragua, 92
Escalón, Pedro J., 62–63
Estrada, Genaro, 179
Estrada, Juan, 96–97, 101, 104–6
Estrada Cabrera, Manuel: rise to power, 51–
52; quest for isthmian dominance, 51–52,
89, 115; relations with Mexico, 52–53, 61,
68–69, 71–73, 79, 102, 107, 109, 123–28, 131–
32, 138, 149, 153, 229 (n. 117); relations
with United States, 52–53, 91, 99, 107, 113;
rivalry with Regalado and Escalón, 53,
62–65; and peace negotiations, 53–55, 63–
65, 75–77; rivalry with Zelaya, 62, 66–69,
74–79, 85, 88, 96, 98; role in Barillas affair, 69, 71–73; meddles in Honduras, 74,
85, 88, 98; and Court of Central American Justice, 85; and Mexican Revolution,
115, 123–25; and Central American
unification, 133–34; fall from power, 135,
147, 158; his supporters after his fall, 148–
49, 188–89, 251 (n. 32)
Estradistas. *See* Estrada, Juan
Ethelburga syndicate, 92

Fabela, Isidro, 196
Falangistas, 190
Fall, Albert B., 135–36, 144
Fatal Triangle: Mexico, United States, and
Central America as a, 21–22
Felicista. *See* Díaz, Félix
Figueroa, Fernando, 65, 67, 73–76, 85, 89
Fletcher, Henry P., 121, 130, 135, 148
Flores Magón brothers, 82, 178. *See also*
Partido Liberal Mexicano
Floresmagonistas. *See* Partido Liberal
Mexicano
Florida: Contra bases in, 204
Foreign Ministry (Mexico), 17, 28, 86, 150;
archive, xii; reorganized, 28; debate
within, 151–54
Foreign policy conceptualized, x–xi
Foreign Relations Committee: of U.S.

House of Representatives, 86; of U.S.
Senate, 175
Forsyth, John, 11
France: interest in canal, 6, 56–57; interven-
tion in Mexico, 11–12, 14–15, 17, 23–24, 26;
relations with Mexico reestablished, 26;
colonial expansion, 40; and Mexican
Revolution, 109; and rebellion in El Sal-
vador, 186, 203. *See also* Pastry War
Franco, Francisco, 190
Frank, Waldo, 181
Frelinghuysen, Frederick, 33
French Intervention. *See* France, interven-
tion in Mexico; Intervention
Frente Farabundo Martí de Liberación Na-
cional (FMLN), 203
Fueros, 8, 10

Gamboa, Federico, 1, 20, 46, 49, 52–54, 57,
64–65, 67, 69, 72, 79, 152–53, 229 (n. 117)
García Granados, Miguel, 20
Genuinos, 157, 173. *See also* Chamorro,
Emiliano
Germany: unification admired in Mexico
and Guatemala, 13, 32; relations with
Mexico established, 26; role in Central
America, 53, 71, 114, 134; foreign policy of
imperial, 56, 58, 60; and Madriz, 104, 236
(n. 108); and Mexican Revolution, 109,
112; in World War One, 128–31; Nazi, 190–
91; in World War Two, 191. *See also* Axis
powers; Zimmermann note
Gilded Age, 24
González, Manuel, 13, 23–24, 28, 46, 217 (n.
6); border agreement with Guatemala,
30–33
González Víquez, Cleto, 92
Good Neighbor policy, 186
Goodwill Tour, U.S.-Mexican, 88–89
Granada (Nicaragua), 19
Gran Colombia, 2, 213 (n. 2)
Grant, Ulysses S., 25–26
Great Britain: interest in canal, 5–6, 56–57;
influence in Central America, 6, 18, 32,
39, 41, 52, 63, 113–14; in alliance against
Juárez, 11, 14–15; diplomatic relations
with Mexico reestablished, 26; colonial
expansion, 40; border conflicts with
Venezuela, 41–42, 58; loan to Nicaragua,

Marxism. *See* Communism

Matamoros: Carranza speech in, 121

Matanza, 189

Masonic lodges in Mexico, 7

Maximilian of Habsburg, 11–12, 20

Mediz Bolio, Antonio, 152, 165–67, 170, 179

Meléndez, Carlos, 126–27, 132–37

Mena, José, 106, 113–14

Mérida (Mexico), 180–81

Merry, William L., 64–65

Mexican Revolution: heritage, xi; causes, 81–84; outbreak of, 107–11; Central American perceptions of, 109, 129, 140, 146; impact on Central America policy, 109–10, 113–14, 146, 209; U.S. intervention in, 111–12, 116, 118; nationalism and foreign policy in, 116, 118–19, 121–23, 170–71; impact of World War One on, 128–30; end of hostilities in, 135; allegedly anti-U.S. nature, 136; and Sonoran dynasty, 141, 183; mythology, 142–44, 161; influence in Central America, 147–48; influence on Sandino, 178, 182; in Yucatán, 181; cliché of, 198, 200, 202

Mexico: relations with and attitudes toward United States, ix–x, 5–9, 13, 15–16, 24–26, 28–29, 39, 41–47, 49, 57–62, 72–73, 80, 84, 87, 103–5, 107–8, 111–12, 116, 118, 129–30, 132, 135–36, 140, 144–46, 160–61, 163–65, 171–88, 190–95, 197, 202–6, 231 (n. 14), 242 (n. 84); relations with Nicaragua, ix–xii, 53–54, 57, 95–107, 127–28, 151, 153–54, 156–58, 160, 165–83, 201–6, 208; Central America policy assessed, ix–xiii, 1, 7, 21–22, 40, 47–49, 55–56, 78–79, 107–10, 114–15, 125, 132, 137–41, 146, 150–54, 158–60, 165, 170–71, 177, 183–87, 197–201, 204, 206–9; U.S. role in Central America policy, ix–x, 21, 47–48, 55–56, 60–61, 80–81, 107–9, 114, 129, 140–41, 149, 151–53, 160, 171–86, 188, 194–99, 202–9; relations with Guatemala, x, 6, 17, 20–21, 24, 28–33, 38–39, 41, 52–53, 62–66, 68–69, 71–73, 77, 86–87, 105, 123–28, 131–32, 136–38, 146–54, 158, 169–70, 184, 189, 191–97, 203–4, 207–8, 229 (n. 117), 251 (n. 32); expansion of influence in Central America, x, 38, 46, 140, 150, 152, 154, 168–71, 220 (n. 74); influence of domestic politics and de-

bate on foreign policy, x–xi, 26–29, 45–47, 73, 84, 102, 116, 118–19, 121–23, 144–46, 150–54, 163, 187–89, 192–94, 196, 198, 200–1, 207–9; and peace negotiations in Central America, x–xi, 40–41, 49, 53–55, 61–69, 74–79, 85, 88, 154–55; conditions in, 1–3, 10–16, 23–29, 44–47, 81–84, 110–13, 135, 141–44, 160–61, 163, 192–94, 198, 200–2, 204–6; annexation of Chiapas, 3–4; and Central American unification, 35–38, 54, 59, 132–34, 148, 152, 222 (n. 3), 228–29 (n. 113), 229 (n. 128), 241 (n. 69); relations with El Salvador, 35–38, 53–54, 62–66, 109, 126–27, 132–34, 154, 169, 172, 175, 186, 203, 208, 256 (n. 16); relations with Costa Rica, 38, 53, 136–37, 154, 172, 175–76, 208; role in inter-American conferences, 39, 55, 63, 106, 154–56, 183, 195–97, 223 (n. 18); possible annexation of Central America, 41, 60, and Monroe Doctrine, 42–43, 55, 59–61, 63, 86, 137; co-mediation of isthmian disputes with United States, 49, 61–69, 73–81, 85–90, 93–96, 103–4, 107; relations with Honduras, 54, 154, 172 175; Díaz ends co-mediation of, with United States, 80–81, 85–90, 93–96, 103–4, 107; and World War One, 128–32; debate about Central America policy within government of, 150–54; government of, labeled Bolshevik, 163–64, 167, 171–73, 175–76; and Sandino rebellion, 178–83, 189–90; and World War Two, 186–87, 191–92; and Spanish Civil War, 189–90; and Cuban Revolution, 199, 201; relations with Chile, 206

Mexico City, xv, 2, 5, 23, 69, 82, 86–88, 132, 151, 168–69, 176, 179–80, 197; Inter-American Conference in, 55; discussed as site of peace conference, 75

Middle power: defined, xii; Mexico as a, xii, 21, 60, 208–9

Militarists, 13, 16, 23, 46; emergence and definition of group, 13; Mariscal leaning toward, 28. *See also* Reyes, Bernardo

Mobile (Alabama): Wilson speech in, 111, 237 (n. 9)

Modernization: in Mexico, 8, 10, 12, 22, 23–24, 27, 29, 82, 110; in Central America, 19–20, 106

Mossadegh, 195

Mining: in Mexico, 2, 15, 23, 221 (n. 90); in United States, 40; in Central America, 58, 74

Mitterrand, François, 186, 203

Moderados: emergence and definition of group, 8

Moffat, Thomas P., 96

Moncada, José M., 169, 174, 177–80

Monroe, James, 42

Monroe Doctrine, 40–43, 55, 58–59, 63, 86, 137, 220 (n. 74); Olney corollary, 42–43; Roosevelt corollary, 58–61, 90; Wilson corollary, 111–12

Montes-Forsyth Treaties, 11

Moore, C. B. J., 94

Morelos (Mexico), 83, 110

Morones, Luis N., 161, 163

Morrow, Dwight, 164, 178–82, 187

Mosquito Coast. *See* La Mosquitia

Múgica, Francisco, 145, 193–94

Muralistas, 143

Napoleon III, 11

National Guard (Nicaragua). *See* Guardia Nacional

National Guard (U.S.), 72

Nationalism in Guatemala, 17

Nationalism in Nicaragua, 57, 76, 97–99, 106

Nationalism in Mexico: role in politics and foreign policy, x–xi, 21–22, 26–27, 46–47, 81, 84, 116, 118–19, 121–23, 129, 138, 141–44, 188, 207; official, 22, 26–27; economic, 83, 116, 118–19, 121–22, 145, 208, 230 (n. 4); pragmatic, 116, 123; revolutionary, 123, 138–39, 170–71; cultural, 142–44, 208

Necesariato, 45

New Deal, 188

New Germany, 60

New international history, xii

New Liberals, 19–20. *See also* Conservative Liberalism; Positivism

New Orleans, 105

New Spain, Viceroyalty of, 1

New York, 127; Mexican consul in, 164, 176

Nicaragua: relations with Mexico, ix–xii, 53–54, 57, 95–107, 127–28, 151, 153–54, 156–58, 160, 165–83, 201–6, 208; relations with United States, ix, 5–6, 17, 21, 91–93, 75, 80, 90–93, 95–102, 104–7, 109, 113, 127, 136, 138, 154, 156–57, 165–68, 170–83, 202–6, 208; Sandinista Revolution in, ix, xi, 186, 201–5, origin of name, 1; conditions in, 5–6, 41, 92–93, 96–98, 102, 104–7, 113, 156–58; and attempts at Central American unification, 18, 34–35, 37, 51, 74, 77, 148, 241 (n. 69); relations with Honduras, 18–19, 62, 65–68, 74, 104, 154, 169, 175, 204; relations with Costa Rica, 19, 92, 104, 175–76; relations with El Salvador, 53–54, 65–68, 74, 78, 154, 169, 204; and Central American peace negotiations, 53–55, 65–66, 75–77, 154; relations with Guatemala, 66–67, 74, 78, 104, 115, 154, 169–70; and Court of Central American Justice, 85, 129; U.S. occupation of, 106–7, 109, 113, 136, 141; and World War One, 130

North American Free Trade Agreement, 206

Organization of American States (OAS), 191, 199

Oaxaca (Mexico), 23, 105

Obregón, Alvaro: role in Mexican Revolution, 110, 112–13, 119; portrait, 120; as Minister of War, 124–25, 131, 241 (n. 69); Central America policy in general, 140–41, 158–59; rise to power and government, 141–42; and Carranza, 141–42; and nationalism, 142–44; U.S. recognition of government, 144–46, 154; factions in government, 145–46; rapprochement with Guatemala, 146–54, 158, 184; his aides debate Central America policy, 151–55; and 1922–23 Washington Conference, 154–55; his foreign policy assessed, 158–59, 184–85; hands over power to Calles, 160–61; his assassination, 161

Oil: U.S.-Mexican controversy over, 129, 144–45, 160, 163–64, 171, 173, 186, 190–91; influences foreign policy, 202, 204–5

Olney, Richard, 42–43

Olney corollary. *See* Monroe Doctrine

Open Door, 39, 90–91

Orellana, José M., 149, 153, 169, 178

Romero Rubio, Carmen, 23
Romero, Matías, 14–15, 28, 30–31, 33, 35–37, 41, 44–45, 68, 151, 217 (n. 21), 220 (n. 74, 78)
Roosevelt, Franklin D., 188, 190
Roosevelt, Theodore, 57–62, 67–68, 74–75, 78, 84–85, 89–90, 103, 129, 224 (n. 42), 226 (n. 72). *See also* Big Stick
Roosevelt Corollary. *See* Monroe Doctrine
Root, Elihu, 63, 65–69, 72, 74–76, 86–92, 95, 103–4, 107, 222 (n. 1), 231 (n. 14)
Ruiz Cortines, Adolfo, 192–98
Ruiz, Eduardo, 153
Rurales, 12
Russia, 122, 140, 143. *See also* Soviet Union; Bolshevik Revolution

Sacasa, Juan B., 157, 160, 178, 182; Mexican assistance to rebellion of, 165–77, 208
Sáenz, Aarón, 164, 168–70, 172–73, 176
Salina Cruz (Mexico), 170
Salinas de Gortari, Carlos, 206
San Antonio (Texas), 2
San Cristóbal de las Casas, 3. *See also* Ciudad Real
Sandinistas, ix, xi, 186, 201–5
Sands, William F., 222 (n. 10)
Sandino, Augusto C., 160, 177, 184, 186, 188; Mexico and his rebellion against U.S. occupation forces, 178–83
San José (Costa Rica), 53, 65, 148, 179
San José Treaty, 64–66
San Juan del Norte (Nicaragua), 97
San Juan River, 34, 51, 97, 114
San Luis Potosí (Mexico): Carranza speech in, 121
San Salvador, 6, 19, 126–27; Mexican legation in, 37; Mexican aid after earthquake in, 134
Santa Anna, Antonio López de, 2, 5, 7, 9, 11, 163
Santa Fe (New Mexico), 2
Santiago (Chile): Inter-American Conference, 155–56
Santo Domingo, 18
Scientific Politics: doctrine of, 13
Scott, James, 208–9
Sediles, Samuel, 127, 241 (n. 69)
Senate, U.S., 56–57, 114, 128–29, 137, 173, 175

Seward, William H., 14
Sheffield, James R., 163–64, 173, 175, 249 (n. 4)
Sierra, Justo, 46, 71
Smoot-Hawley Tariff, 188
Soconusco: annexation by Mexico, 4, 36; controversy over, 17, 30, 33; Guatemalan rebels in, 63; Mexican troops in, 125. *See also* Border; Chiapas
Solórzano, Carlos, 157–58, 165–68, 180
Somoza Debayle, Anastasio, ix, xii, 201–3
Somoza García, Anastasio, 188–89, 201
Sonora (Mexico) 9, 11, 81, 141
Sonoran Dynasty, 141–43, 147, 151, 159, 170, 177, 182–85, 209
South Africa, 56
Soviet Mexico. *See* Bolshevik: government of Mexico labeled
Soviet Union, 164, 173, 191, 195, 203–4
Spain, 8–9, 13, 24; empire of, 1; attempted reconquest of Mexico, 5; in alliance against Juárez, 11, 14–15; legacy of rule in Central America, 18–19; diplomatic relations with Mexico reestablished, 26; war with United States, 43, 51, 56; Mexican role in Civil War, 189–90
State Department (U.S.), xiii, 28, 36–41, 52, 58, 63, 66–69, 71–74, 78, 84, 89–92, 95, 98–100, 102–3, 105–6, 113–15, 129, 131, 133–36, 144, 148, 156, 158, 164–65, 167–68, 171–73, 175, 177, 195, 203, 209
Stimson, Henry L., 177
Supreme Court, Mexican, 164

Tabasco (Mexico), 33
Tacoma Conference, 154
Taft, William H., 84, 90, 95, 98, 100–4, 108–9, 111, 113–15, 129, 175
Taibo II, Paco Ignacio, 182
Tampico (Mexico), 112
Tegucigalpa, 19, 67, 127, 132
Tehuantepec, Isthmus of: debate over U.S. transit rights in, 11
Telenovelas, 206
Téllez, Manuel C., 168
Ten Years of Spring: reform experiment in Guatemala, 192–97
Ten Years War. *See* Cuba
Tercermundismo, 201, 204

Wilson, Woodrow, 109, 111–16, 118, 122–23, 129–30, 134–36, 144–45, 148–49
World War One, 109, 135, 242 (n. 84); impact on Mexico and Central America, 128–32
World War Two, 186–87, 192, 194

Xenophobia, 80

Yellow Press, 43
Yucatán (Mexico): attempted secession, 5; Sandino in, 180–81, 184, 186

Zaldívar, Rafael, 35, 51, 105
Zapata, Emiliano, 83, 110–12, 118, 135, 142, 182
Zaragoza, Ignacio, 12
Zedillo Ponce de León, Ernesto, 206–7
Zelaya, José S., 41, 62, 105–8, 171, 194; attempts unification of Central America, 51, 55, 57, 74, 77, 228–29 (n. 113); and canal, 51, 53–54, 56, 223 (n. 18); desire for isthmian leadership, 51–52, 67; and peace negotiations, 53–55, 65–66, 75–77; nationalist policies of, 56–57; pro-Mexican attitude of, 57, 95, 182; rivalry with Estrada Cabrera, 62, 66–69, 74–79, 85, 88, 96, 98; meddles in Costa Rica, El Salvador, and Honduras, 66–68, 74, 77, 85, 92, 95; role in Barillas affair, 69, 71; U.S. opposition to, 75, 80, 90–93, 95; and Court of Central American Justice, 85; fall from power and Mexican assistance to, 96–102, 158, 160, 177; asylum in Mexico, 97, 101–2, 108, 208
Zelayistas, 80, 97, 156–57; fall from power, 105, 113; rebellions, 106, 127, 169. *See also* Irías, Julián
Zimmermann note, 129–30

About the Author

Jürgen Buchenau is Assistant Professor in the Department of History at Wingate University, North Carolina. He completed his undergraduate studies at the Universität zu Köln, Germany, and received his master's and doctorate degrees from the University of North Carolina at Chapel Hill.

/